WAR, JEWS, AND THE NEW EUROPE

Preface

SINCE the Second World War, the study of modern Jewish history has been dominated by the Nazi era and the genocidal thrust of the Holocaust. Attention has thus focused, if not on the Second World War itself, then on the origins and development of antisemitism.

While perhaps understandable, the attention given to the study of antisemitism has tended to obscure other aspects of recent Jewish history that are not only important in their own right but may also provide us with crucial answers to the nature of the trajectory towards that genocide. In particular, the First World War—the Great War, as it used to be known—of 1914–18 and the attempts in its immediate aftermath to find a durable settlement of the 'Jewish question' have until recently received much less attention than they deserve.

The Great War, as every schoolchild knows, was of course a major watershed in European and world history. Its repercussions and ramifications were immense, and are still with us today: the revolutions in Russia and the triumph of Bolshevism; the decisive entry of the United States on to the world stage; the termination of East European empires, and the emergence of a new territorial order based on the principle, if not the practice, of national self-determination; the defeat and humiliation of Germany; and so on.

Each of these events had a specific Jewish sub-text. On one level, because on the eastern front the war was largely fought over territory where the majority of world Jewry lived, it led to their physical dislocation, hardship, and violent death on a large scale. Hundreds of thousands of Jews were uprooted from their homes, in many cases because Jews became the targets for military retribution and attack. This process continued and intensified, with catastrophic effect, with the prolongation of war in the east into 1919 and 1920. On a more psychological level, that Jews increasingly came to be viewed by the warring parties as a collective entity which might be able to influence the war's outcome had momentous implications for the Jews themselves.

In the West, particularly in Britain, the assumption that a Jewish interest was in some collective sense pro-German threatened to negate a well-formed emancipatory political wisdom which had enabled Anglo-Jewry to view itself as both British and Jewish. The charge of dual allegiance was in fact taken so seriously by this community that its leadership feared that the community would go under in a wave of antisemitism. Paradoxically, however, non-Jewish notions of a collective Jewry actually squared with the self-perception of a growing Zionist tendency which in 1917 was able to wrest advantage from this situation, in the form of the Balfour Declaration.

It was inevitable, in the circumstances, that these two tendencies within Jewry would clash. Jewish assimilationists with an agenda for the future security and well-being of European Jewry found themselves pitted against Jewish nationalists whose vision was founded not only on an entirely different premiss but who actively sought to translocate European Jewry to a non-European homeland, in Palestine. The most famous element in this contest was the struggle for the Balfour Declaration, which Anglo-Jewish assimilationists opposed and lost. But in 1919 the contest was fought all over again in a much wider international arena, namely, the Paris peace conference. This time, the assimilationists won, but with one important proviso: the goal posts had changed. War itself, the demise of reactionary tsarism, and the possibility, if not probability, that the whole East and East-Central European imperial framework would be replaced by nation-states had crystallized concepts of Jewish autonomy. Across the East European Jewish political spectrum between 1917 and 1919, this broader but essentially non-territorial conception of Jewish nationalism received increasing popular support. When in Paris both Zionists and assimilationists thus presented formulas for the resolution of the Jewish question, they not only reflected the changed circumstances of Eastern Europe but borrowed heavily from the language of this diaspora national consciousness.

Since the Second World War, however, Zionist historiography has tended to focus only on the Zionist victory in this 1914–19 contest, a victory which when juxtaposed with the catastrophe of European Jewish existence in 1939 to 1945 implicitly carries a strong historical and possibly moral message. According to this view, the 'assimilationist' opponents of the Balfour Declaration, having failed to understand either the essential dynamics of European Jewish–non-Jewish relations or the fact that the course of modern Jewish history lay through Zionism, forfeited our sympathy and interest. Falling firmly into this category, our would-be hero, Lucien Wolf, has thus for decades been regarded as an assimilationist appendix to the corpus of Jewish history.

Except that there is one small problem of historical fact. Wolf, with his minimalist 1919 autonomy programme, as compared with the maximalist one offered by the Zionists, won round two of the contest. In his own historical context he was therefore not a loser. Indeed, contrary to the prevalent idea that it was primarily American Jews who helped shape the Minorities Treaties in Paris in 1919, it was primarily Wolf who did so.

The fact that the internationally endorsed framework for European Jewish existence in the inter-war years was founded on a formula largely propounded by Lucien Wolf surely suggests that the man and his policies do merit serious attention. Or put another way, the characterization of Wolf as 'that charlatan'—a comment made by a participant at a conference where I was about to deliver a paper on him some years ago—would now, I hope, be recognized as quite inappropriate.

The sort of re-examination which *War, Jews, and the New Europe* seeks to develop is consistent with the climate of Jewish historiographical scholarship in the 1980s and early 1990s. The emancipatory politics and behaviour of liberal and post-liberal European Jewish élites have come under fresh scrutiny in recent years, primarily (though not exclusively) from American historians. First premises have been questioned. The relationship of Jewish communities to the wider societies of which they formed part has been, and continues to be, reconsidered and re-evaluated. In this context, it was inevitable that sooner or later attention would once again focus on Lucien Wolf, the Anglo-Jewish historian, journalist, and diplomat. Eugene Black, for instance, devoted considerable attention to him in *The Social Politics of Anglo-Jewry, 1880–1920*, making it clear, as did Stuart Cohen in his *English Zionists and British Jews*, that Wolf and his Anglo-Jewish colleagues were not simply establishment toadies. However, the still-prevalent emphasis on the ideological struggle between Zionists and non-Zionists continues to obscure other critical factors which might help explain why and how they responded as they did.

This study, then, aims to refocus the analysis on certain key questions. What exactly, for instance, was the impact of war on Anglo-Jewry? To what extent did it handicap the pursuit of a traditional Anglo-Jewish foreign policy as carried out by Wolf's Conjoint Foreign Committee of British Jews, or force it to change its strategy? Did wartime developments such as the revolution in Russia or the re-emergence of Poland have a similar impact, or was Anglo-Jewry's foreign policy determined all along by ideological imperatives that

remained unchanged? In viewing the evolution of Anglo-Jewish foreign
affairs policy through the person of Lucien Wolf, this first full study of
his diplomacy certainly proposes to re-examine the contest with the
Zionists, but within the broader and not always ideologically determined framework of war, peace, and international diplomacy.

I was very fortunate when I began a doctoral dissertation on Lucien
Wolf in the late 1970s in that Chimen Abramsky recognized that here
was a subject which needed closer examination. I owe him many
thanks. Orientation came from many other helpful sources. Sefton
Temkin, Jeffrey Schneider, and Stuart Cohen all pointed me in useful
directions; Stuart Cohen also furnished me with copies of Wolf's
correspondence from the Zionist archives in Jerusalem. Zara Steiner
and Harry Shukman offered much appreciated critical insights on the
doctoral thesis from which this book later derived.

It would also be difficult to express how indispensable and critical
the enthusiasm and support of Steve Zipperstein, Robert Wistrich, and
David Sorkin have been in helping this work to see the light of day. My
thanks also go to Lionel Kochan, who throughout acted as a mentor
and guide. He, Chimen Abramsky, and Elizabeth Eppler kindly lent
me their own unpublished lecture papers on Lucien Wolf. In addition,
I owe particular gratitude to the late V. D. Lipman, who not only
laboured through a wordy first draft and offered a multitude of necessary, useful, and pertinent suggestions, but also went on to recommend
the manuscript to the Littman Library.

Neither can I forget the many institutions that made their facilities
available to me. I wish to express my particular appreciation of Marek
Web at YIVO, Barry Kosmin at the Board of Deputies, the staff at the
American Jewish Committee archives, and Mme Levyne at the
Alliance Israélite Universelle, who was so crucial in successfully ex-
pediting my rather short research visit to Paris. Mrs Trude Levi added
another important dimension to this study by recommending to me the
Gaster Papers at the Mocatta Library in London.

Other secrets were unlocked by special permission. Lady Stowhill
made available the Soskice Papers in the House of Lords, while
Professor Agnes Headlam-Morley not only did the same *vis-à-vis* the
papers of her father, Sir James Headlam-Morley, but also willingly
gave her time to discuss his relationship with Wolf at the Paris peace
conference. My sincere thanks to both her and Lady Stowhill.

Last but not least, I mention the people who at the end of the day
had to suffer a cut-and-paste manuscript, saved me from further

errors, or helped pull it all into some sort of shape. This work could not have reached completion without Annetta Bygott and Angela Fabricius, and above all Connie Wilsack. Nor, of course, without the forbearance, good humour, and understanding of my friend Jean.

Oxford M.L.
May 1991

Contents

List of Maps

Both maps are taken from Ezra Mendelsohn, *The Jews of East Central Europe between the Two World Wars* (Indiana University Press, 1983), and are reproduced with permission.

Abbreviations

AIU	(Archives of the) Alliance Israélite Universelle, Paris
AJA	Anglo-Jewish Association
AJC	American Jewish Committee, New York
BD	Board of Deputies of British Jews
BDAI	Board of Deputies of American Israelites, American Jewish Archives, Brandeis University, Boston, Mass.
BDOW	*British Documents on the Origins of the War, 1898–1914*, ed. G. P. Gooch and H. W. V. Temperley (London, 1932 et seq.)
CAB	Cabinet Papers, Public Record Office, Kew
C11	Series of Conjoint and Joint Foreign Committee files and Wolf correspondence held at Board of Deputies of British Jews, Woburn House, London
CHP	*Cambridge History of Poland*
CJC	Conjoint Foreign Committee
CZA	Central Zionist Archives, Jerusalem
DDF	*Documents diplomatiques français, 1871–1914*
EZF	English Zionist Federation
FO	Foreign Office Papers, Public Record Office, Kew
FRUS	*Papers relating to the Foreign Relations of the United States*, vol. v, Paris Peace Conference, 1919 (Washington, 1946)
HO	Home Office Papers, Public Record Office, Kew
ICA	Jewish Colonization Association
ITO	Jewish Territorial Association
JC	*Jewish Chronicle*
JFC	Joint Foreign Committee
JJS	*Jewish Journal of Sociology*
JSS	*Jewish Social Studies*
NUJR	National Union of Jewish Rights
MAE	Archives of the French Foreign Office, Paris
MWS	Mowschowitch Collection, YIVO Archives, New York
PAAJR	*Proceedings of the American Academy for Jewish Research*
PID	Political Intelligence Department, Foreign Office
PNC	Polish National Committee
RDJBE	*Report of the Delegation of Jews of the British Empire on the Peace Conference, 1919*
TJHSE	*Transactions of the Jewish Historical Society of England*
VJOD	Vereinigung Jüdischer Organisationen Deutschlands

A Note on Transliteration

SPELLINGS commonly used in England have been employed for Russian, Polish, and other foreign names. Thus, Mowschowitch, Sokolow, Tschenlow, but also Ianushkevich, Milyukov, Sazonov. This represents a departure from strict adherence to the transliteration system of the Library of Congress. However, it should make for immediate recognition for most English-speaking readers.

Introduction

THE British diplomat Harold Nicolson, writing a book on his profession and lost for a succinct introductory explanation, turned for assistance to the *Oxford English Dictionary*. Diplomacy, the dictionary informed him, 'is the management of international relations by negotiation, the method by which these relations are adjusted and managed by ambassadors and envoys, the business or art of the diplomatist'.[1]

The dictionary definition implies an important role for the diplomat. His professional abilities and skill may indeed determine the difference between success and failure. Underlying the human factor, however, is a more crucial assumption. The diplomat must bring to the negotiating table some bargaining counter with which to negotiate. And if we are speaking of international relations, that bargaining counter must be a rather substantial item. In all likelihood, it will be of economic, territorial, or military significance, perhaps an offer of territorial compensation, commercial preference, or military alliance, or obversely the threat of economic sanction or military force.

Diplomacy, in other words, is bound up with the possession and pursuit of power; as such, it would normally be considered the prerogative and function of sovereign states. This study therefore begins with an apparent paradox. Jewry in 1914 had no sovereign state, no specific Jewish territory, no national resources, no army, nor even, as in the case of the Catholic church, a single, all-powerful religious authority. Dispersed throughout the world and citizens or subjects of the states in which they lived, Jews were, as a collective entity, powerless. To speak therefore of Jewish diplomacy, or even, in our case, Anglo-Jewish diplomacy, seems on first inspection to be very much a contradiction in terms.

Yet this is a study of Anglo-Jewish diplomacy, as will be argued, and its key practitioner, Lucien Wolf. On one level it is a study of his abilities as a diplomat; on another, of the paradox which made that diplomacy possible. To understand that, however, we first must consider the specific framework within which Wolf was operating.

[1] Quoted in Harold Nicolson, *Diplomacy*, 3rd edn. (London, 1963), 15.

THE CONJOINT FOREIGN COMMITTEE OF BRITISH JEWS

The Conjoint Foreign Committee of British Jews, the body with which Wolf's name become almost synonymous in latter years, was founded in June 1878. Its purpose was to conduct an Anglo-Jewish foreign policy. Its formation, however, was the result of a dispute between two existing Anglo-Jewish organizations: the Board of Deputies of British Jews, and the Anglo-Jewish Association.

The Board of Deputies of British Jews was the acknowledged representative body of the community. Synagogally elected, it had been placing Jewish interests before governments of the day since 1760.[2] In foreign affairs it hardly had a track record. On the other hand, it did have the venerable Sir Moses Montefiore, and he, travelling under the protection of Her Majesty, and sometimes in Her Majesty's warships, had been acting as an old-style intercessionary or *shtadlan* on behalf of persecuted Jews everywhere, since before Queen Victoria's accession in 1837.[3]

The Anglo-Jewish Association was of more recent vintage (it was founded in 1871), and in the Board's eyes, it was thoroughly upstart.[4] In one sense this was surprising, as in social composition the two bodies were remarkably similar. The Association's chief protagonists, for instance—baronet Sir Francis Goldsmid, and his nephew Sir Julian Goldsmid—were from a leading scion of the Anglo-Jewish notability, otherwise known as the 'Cousinhood', to which Sir Moses Montefiore himself belonged.[5] Both organizations, moreover, were self-consciously élitist and oligarchic, albeit with the Association clearly having an edge over the theoretically representative Board through the imposition of an annual membership fee of not less than a guinea.[6]

The dispute between the two organizations, however, had less to do with power or status than with the direction of communal policy and

[2] On the Board of Deputies see Eugene Black, *The Social Politics of Anglo-Jewry*, 1880–1920 (Oxford, 1988), 38–43.

[3] For Moses Montefiore and his *shtadlan* pursuits see Sonia and V. D. Lipman, eds., *The Century of Moses Montefiore* (Oxford, 1985), Pt. ii, 'Foreign Affairs', 131–268. See also Chaim Bermant, *The Cousinhood* (London, 1971), 103–18.

[4] For the AJA's origins and development see David Mowschowitch MS, 'The Board of Deputies and the Anglo-Jewish Association', 7 Sept. 1943, MWS 23534–42; Black, *Social Politics*, 44–50. For pre-1879 BD complaints about the AJA see Mowschowitch MS, 'Board of Deputies Foreign Affairs', Sept. 1955, MWS 23512–28.

[5] See Black, *Social Politics*, 12–14; Bermant, *Cousinhood*, 77–9.

[6] See AJA Laws (1880), Mocatta Lib.

practice. The controversy dated back to the struggle for full Jewish civil and political rights in Britain in the 1830s and 1840s.[7] The majority of English Jews had played no part in this struggle; it was waged by a small, well-connected group of individuals—men such as Sir Francis Goldsmid—who had a major stake in the social and economic life of the country and objected to their restricted access to full participation in the 'political nation'. The implicit élitism of this small, emancipationist lobby certainly carried through into the Association's foreign policy thinking. In this respect, of course, there was no basic point of difference between it and the Board.

Nevertheless, the campaign Goldsmid and his associates fought represented, in a number of respects, a very radical departure from the traditionally low-profile methods of the Board. For one, it took place in the public arena, and since the process was continuously blocked by opponents both inside and outside parliament, it necessitated the enlistment of political allies, not to say public opinion, in its favour. This accorded well with the campaigners' presentation of their case not as a special group with sectarian interests but as Englishmen who happened to be members of the 'Mosaic persuasion'. A liberal polity demanded religious toleration. The passage of emancipation would in this respect be a triumph for Jews, but an even greater one for liberalism itself.[8]

In arguing their case in these wider political terms, Goldsmid and his associates were in effect challenging the community to accept a drastically altered ideological framework within which their Jewishness would be encompassed. Goldsmid had attempted to carry the point further in 1836 by leading a group of wealthy notables out of the confines of religious orthodoxy into a Reform Synagogue which in some respects attempted to mirror Anglican religious organization and practice. Sir Moses had responded by barring them access to the

[7] On this large subject see M. C. N. Salbstein, *The Emancipation of the Jews in Britain: The Question of the Admission of the Jews to Parliament 1828–1860* (Oxford, 1982), 91–4; Israel Finestein, 'Anglo-Jewish Opinion during the Struggle for Emancipation, 1828–1858', *TJHSE* 20 (1959–61), 113–43; U. R. Q. Henriques, 'The Jewish Emancipation Controversy in Nineteenth Century England', *Past and Present*, 40 (July 1968), 126–46; V. D. Lipman, 'The Age of Emancipation, 1815–1880', in V. D. Lipman, ed., *Three Centuries of Anglo-Jewish History* (London, 1961), 77–81.

[8] This did not mean, however, that emancipation was actually a victory for liberalism or the Liberal party, as the Whig interpretation of these events usually concludes. Geoffrey Alderman, *The Jewish Community in British Politics* (Oxford, 1983), esp. 26–46, thoroughly dismantles this thesis, but it was certainly perceived in this way at the time.

domestic politics of the Board.[9] Inadvertently thereby, Montefiore provided the rebels with a window of opportunity with which to make forays into the field of foreign affairs, forays which when ultimately consolidated in the form of the Anglo-Jewish Association served notice on Montefiore that his monopoly of this foreign domain was at an end.

Montefiore had, of course, won the first round of the domestic political battle in 1836. Few joined Goldsmid's Reform Synagogue. Even in this domestic arena, however, it was Goldsmid, not Montefiore, who most accurately reflected the new direction that mid-Victorian Anglo-Jewry was taking. Referred to by some historians as the 'Jewish liberal compromise',[10] this upheld the view that the English Jew should have the same status in society as the Congregationalist or Quaker. One's Jewishness was henceforth not a collective interest to be determined and safeguarded by a communal body, presumably with Montefiore at its head, but purely a matter of individual religious choice. Little more than a microcosm of the *laissez-faire* liberalism of the wider British political and social scene, this view argued that being Jewish in no way cut across one's identification with the British nation, nor could it be deemed to cut across one's loyalty to or ability to serve the British state.

As a model, it had two important consequences for the development and pursuit of an Anglo-Jewish foreign policy. Firstly, by placing the Jewish struggle for emancipation in a global context, it elevated Jewish civil and political rights, perhaps almost by default, to the status of a prerequisite for a tolerant, liberal world order.[11] Secondly, in perceiving the ministers and officials of the British state as an extension of the 'natural allies' who had supported emancipation, it posited the notion that there was a congruence of interests in the international arena between those of Britain and those of British Jews. This implied not only that the intercessionary activities of Montefiore were outworn and unnecessary but that they could be replaced by a 'special relationship' between the British Foreign Office and Anglo-Jewry's foreign arm.

[9] On Montefiore's communal politics, see Israel Finestein, 'The Uneasy Victorian: Montefiore as Communal Leader', in Sonia and V. D. Lipman, eds., *Century of Montefiore*, 45–70. Reform Jews were allowed to stand as delegates for the BD after Montefiore's death in 1886.

[10] See e.g. S. G. Bayme, 'Jewish Leadership and Anti-Semitism in Britain, 1898–1918', Ph.D. thesis (Columbia, 1977), 34–5.

[11] Israel Finestein, 'Arthur Cohen QC', in James M. Shaftesley, ed., *Remember the Days* (London, 1966), 283, 291–2.

This notion was to remain a central tenet of Conjoint thinking even when the evidence seemed all to the contrary.

Whether the congruence existed in the first place is debatable; all that matters here is that, in the mid-Victorian scene, it was perceived as existing. When Palmerston threw his weight around on behalf of Jews abroad—sometimes disarmingly so, as in the case of the Don Pacifico affair[12]—was he doing it on behalf of a personal Jewish interest or for some other principle, associated perhaps with Britain's 'unswerving and unfaltering championship of oppressed people'?[13] When, by extension, the Association founded Jewish schools or set up branches in Persia, Mesopotamia, Palestine, or India—anywhere, indeed, where British influence ruled supreme—was it simply availing itself of British security and protection, or was it consciously fostering British cultural, or even imperial, interests? The point is germane only in as much as it highlights the hazy area between perception and reality, a theme to which I shall return later.

Certainly in June 1878 the assumptions upon which an embryonic Anglo-Jewish foreign policy had been constructed had occasion to be put to the test. The Great Powers were convening under Bismarck's aegis in Berlin to determine the future of the Balkans in the wake of the Russo-Turkish War and the disintegration of Ottoman hegemony in the region. New states would be seeking international legitimization, and one in particular, Romania, had not only a large Jewish minority but also a well-known record of obstruction to granting them equal rights.[14]

The theorists of emancipation had a forcefully optimistic outlook on the future of society in general and on their less fortunate foreign coreligionists in particular. The fact that they used the term 'co-religionists' is itself significant. What they meant by this was that the rest of the (Jewish) world would eventually and inevitably become like themselves. This did not imply that Romanian Jewish emancipation, through the auspices of the Congress of Berlin, would be a walkover. The Anglo-Jewish bodies recognized, for instance, the need to convene with other Western European and American Jewish bodies with

[12] See Albert M. Hyamson, 'Don Pacifico', *TJHSE* 18 (1953–5), 1–39.
[13] The comment, which does not relate to any specific British action, is Lucien Wolf's in his Introduction to E. Semenoff, *The Russian Government and the Massacres: A Page of the Russian Counter-Revolution* (London, 1907), xxvii.
[14] Lucien Wolf, *Notes on the Diplomatic History of the Jewish Question* (London, 1919), 17–21; U. R. Q. Henriques, 'Journey to Romania', in *Century of Montefiore*, 230–53.

similar views, to bring maximum pressure to bear on their respective national delegations.[15]

Two things are implicit in their response. In the first place they were assuming that an 'export model' of their own British domestic achievement and aspirations would suffice and indeed be appropriate for the security and development of Romanian and all other non-emancipated Jewish communities. Secondly, they assumed that it would be British and other emancipated Western Jews who would, in consort with their respective foreign ministries, bring this to fruition. It was, in not so many words, a statement of manifest destiny.

The urgency for concerted action at Berlin led to some hard political bargaining between the two bodies. The Board, under the communal autocracy of Sir Moses Montefiore, had never reconciled itself to the competition, not to say the challenge, that the Association posed to its monopoly of communal wisdom, but at this stage to have simply ignored it would have been to see Goldsmid receive all the glory at Berlin. The Board's tenuous links to foreign affairs were in imminent danger of liquidation.

The subsequent compromise was reflected in the hybrid appellation of the Conjoint Foreign Committee. It would represent both organizations, have fourteen delegates—seven from each—and its meetings would be alternately chaired by its Board and Association presidents. The Board, jealous of its seniority, put in an additional proviso; the 'treaty' by which the Committee came into existence would be annually renewable.[16] In practice, however, two essentially self-selecting and oligarchic organizations had given a mandate to their respective Councils of Notables—in each case drawn heavily from the 'Cousinhood'—to develop and execute a 'politics of notables' with only the most passing reference to themselves.[17]

Sir Francis Goldsmid subsequently wrote a letter to Lord Derby, the foreign secretary, while his associate, Baron de Worms, petitioned

[15] See BDAI Papers, esp. Corr. box 5, for correspondence between Jewish organizations prior to the Congress of Berlin.

[16] Mowschowitch, 'Board of Deputies Foreign Affairs', MWS 23512–28; 'The Board', MWS 23534–42.

[17] The roll-call of the CJC presidents reflects this Cousinhood ascendancy. For the BD: 1878–80, J. M. Montefiore; 1880–95, Arthur Cohen, QC; 1895–1917, D. L. Alexander, QC. For the AJA: 1878–86, Baron de Worms; 1886–96, Sir Julian Goldsmid; 1896–1921, C. G. Montefiore. Leopold de Rothschild served both the BD and the AJA as vice-president of the CJC for most of the period, and many of the 'unofficial' representations went through him. See CJC minutes, 1878–1917.

Mr Disraeli, the prime minister. Specific clauses in the Treaty of Berlin followed. The sovereignty of the new states would be conditional on guarantees of full religious liberty and political equality for all their inhabitants. These would apply equally to Romania as they did to Bulgaria, Montenegro, and Serbia. The emancipatory principle had for the first time been clearly enunciated in Great Power protocol. For the Jews, said the Conjoint, 'it was a great charter of emancipation'.[18] Or so it seemed.

THE PROBLEM

The Conjoint interpretation of what happened at Berlin was naïvely simplistic.[19] Nor with hindsight did the event itself carry grounds for optimism. On the contrary, the partial replacement of the Ottoman Empire in Europe by new state entities dominated by one ethnic group and religious tendency generally marked a deterioration in the position of religious and ethnic minorities. Moreover, it heralded similar problems of much greater dimension as the territorial map of eastern and south-eastern Europe was further recast. The process continued with the Balkan Wars of 1912–14, and much more dramatically with the collapse of Russia and the Central Powers in 1917–18.

The development of the Conjoint was thus to a large extent shaped and indeed circumscribed within the forty-odd years between the Congress of Berlin, when the Jewish question first significantly appeared on the international agenda, and the Paris peace conference of 1919, when it was perceived as the most serious of the minority issues confronting the Allied peacemakers. One could argue that the key to an understanding of the Conjoint begins with the Romanian question at Berlin and culminates in Paris on essentially the same note.

Closer to 1878, however, not only did Romania not fulfil its obligations but the ability of the Great Powers to enforce them rapidly diminished.[20] The Congress of Berlin was in this sense a watershed,

[18] Wolf, *Notes*, 24.

[19] For a more accurate version of how the Great Powers were prevailed upon, particularly the behind-the-scenes role of Gerson Bleichröder, Bismarck's Jewish financial adviser, see Fritz Stern, *Gold and Iron: Bismarck, Bleichröder and the Building of the German Empire* (London, 1977), 351–93.

[20] See James Parkes, *Emergence of the Jewish Problem, 1878–1939* (London, 1946), 98–103; R. W. Seton-Watson, *A History of the Rumanians* (Boston, 1963), 346–52; Stern, *Gold and Iron*, 392–3. A documentary record of the diplomatic attempts and failures on this score is to be found in Wolf, *Notes*, 23–45.

8   *Introduction*

the last occasion on which the Great Powers were able to act in 'consort' on, among other things, the Jewish question. Thereafter the international fabric started disintegrating, and in little more than a decade it was replaced by two intensely rival power blocs.

It was a paradox that Western Jewish bodies like the Conjoint were emerging in this essentially post-liberal climate. The Alliance Israélite Universelle (of which the Anglo-Jewish Association was technically the English wing) had been founded in 1860 as a reflection of the consolidation and ascendancy of the French nation-state and saw its role in defending Jewish rights abroad very much in terms of *la mission civilisatrise*.[21] The role of the Hilfsverein der Deutschen Juden, formed in 1901, was the same from a German standpoint. All three organizations were proudly and enthusiastically 'patriotic'. In practice, however, their success in the international arena was entirely dependent on their close co-operation, amounting to a consensual approach. This had been essential to their success at Berlin. Its continuation was predicated not simply on the benevolence of their own states to these relationships but on an essentially harmonious relationship between the Great Powers themselves. In the poisoned and often tense atmosphere of alliances and *ententes* that ensued, this consensual Jewish politics ran against the grain of international realities. Alliance–Hilfsverein communication and co-ordination foundered on Franco-German rivalries. France's post-1894 *entente* with Russia practically silenced Franco-Jewish outspokenness on behalf of the tsar's Jews.[22]

Nor was the Conjoint itself free from the ramifications of this process. Since Britain remained initially peripheral to the bloc system, the Conjoint was in a position to balance the mutual antagonisms of the Alliance and Hilfsverein and lead them towards a more 'consistent Jewish attitude'.[23] However, its own freedom of manœuvre on behalf of Russian

[21] See André Chouraqui, *Cent ans d'histoire: L'Alliance Israélite Universelle et la renaissance juive contemporaine* (Paris, 1965); Michael R. Marrus, *The Politics of Assimilation* (Oxford, 1971), 81–8.

[22] Zosa Szajkowski, 'Conflicts in the Alliance Israélite and the Foundations of the Anglo-Jewish Association, the Vienna Allianz and the Hilfsverein', *JSS* 19 (1957), 29–50, and id., 'Jewish Diplomacy', *JSS* 22 (1960), 131–58. C. C. Aronsfeld, 'Jewish Bankers and the Czar', *JSS* 35 (1973), 96.

[23] Wolf to Kahn (Hilfsverein), 29 July 1913 (during Balkan War crisis) MWS 4148–9. See also Zosa Szajkowski, 'Nathan, Wolf, Schiff and the Jewish Revolutionary Movement in Eastern Europe 1903–1917', *JSS* 29 (1967), 3–26, 75–91. An example of the co-operation between the three organizations at the time of the 1905 Russian revolution was the publication of the *Russian Correspondence* simultaneously in London, Paris, and Berlin.

Jewry was clearly curtailed once the Foreign Office under Sir Edward Grey had decided in 1906 that it too would seek an *entente* with Russia.[24] It was doubly paradoxical that all this should have been happening at a juncture when, from the standpoint of Anglo-Jewish self-interest, a body with specific responsibility for foreign affairs was urgently required. Between 1881 and 1914, many hundreds of thousands of Jewish immigrants from Eastern Europe, mostly from Russia, flocked westwards, many to Britain. Indeed, the community jumped in size in this period from 65,000 to nearer 300,000.

The arrival *en masse* of distinctly alien, Yiddish-speaking Jews was perceived as threatening to 'swamp and transform the high English character of the community' and to drag it down in a wave of popular antisemitic resentment.[25] Neither development transpired. Nevertheless, the cultural and psychological gulf between the two communities, characterized in the distinction between the essentially well-off, fully assimilated, and religiously easy-going 'West End' of the capital and the slum-dwelling, Yiddish-speaking, and largely orthodox 'East End' was a profound one.[26] Communal efforts came increasingly to focus on how to stem the flow of immigration to Britain. None of the alternatives that immediately presented themselves—turning the immigrants back, creating organized settlement elsewhere through the Jewish Colonization Association (the ICA), or simply redirecting them to the United States—proved of much efficacy.[27]

[24] For the dramatic changes in the form, structure, and thinking of the Foreign Office in this period see Zara Steiner, *The Foreign Office and Foreign Policy 1898–1914* (Cambridge, 1969), esp. 46–55 for the new anti-Germanism and tilt towards Russia.

[25] Wolf, 'The Queen's Jewry 1837–1897', in Cecil Roth, ed., *Essays in Jewish History* (London, 1934), 359. On the growth of antisemitism in Britain see Bernard Gainer, *The Alien Invasion, The Origins of the Aliens Act of 1905* (London, 1972), esp. section on 'The Anti-Alien Mentality', 74–128; also Colin Holmes, *Anti-Semitism in British Society 1876–1939* (London, 1979).

[26] The relationship between Anglo-Jewry and the immigrant community is well documented. For a fine introduction see Todd Endelman, 'Native Jews and Foreign Jews in London, 1870–1914', in David Berger, ed., *The Legacy of Jewish Migration: 1881 and its Impact* (New York, 1983), 109–30. See also Lloyd P. Gartner, *The Jewish Immigrant in England, 1870–1914* (London, 1960); V. D. Lipman, *Social History of the Jews in England 1850–1950* (London, 1954); Black, *Social Politics*; Bayme, 'Jewish Leadership'.

[27] See Wolf letter, *Pall Mall Gazette*, 28 July 1900, 'Ever since 1882 the Jewish charitable societies have discouraged emigration to this country . . . they have transshipped large numbers of emigrants to the US and have dumped them there.' On the ICA and its redistribution efforts, particularly to Canada and Argentina, see Mark Wischnitzer, *To Dwell in Safety: The Story of Jewish Migration since 1800* (Philadelphia, 1948), 79–89; Theodore Norman, *An Outstretched Arm: A History of the Jewish Colonisation Association* (London, 1985).

Some other solution had to be found, preferably at source. The
causes of Jewish migration westwards were manifold. The conventional
wisdom of the period, however, perceived the root of the problem as
the restrictive legislation of tsarism, and particularly the confinement
of the majority of Jews within the Pale of Settlement.[28] In an increasingly reactionary climate in Russia, complete Jewish emancipation was
out of the question. Nevertheless, so the reasoning went, if the Conjoint Committee could bring its influence to bear with the regime
through the intervention of the Foreign Office, perhaps the Pale could
be dismantled and its Jewish inhabitants allowed to migrate internally
within the wider Russian empire.[29]

In fact, the transparent inability of the Conjoint to have any leverage
on the Foreign Office on Russian matters, even to assist in averting
threats of pogrom or expulsion,[30] only confirmed the tremendous gap
between its aspirations and reality. It was, moreover, beginning to
excite increasing scrutiny and criticism from disaffected elements on
the periphery of the communal establishment who saw its exclusivity,
secrecy, and unaccountability as symptoms of the community's failure
to confront the new challenges before it.[31]

Though the critics did not as a whole challenge the value of having a
communal foreign policy body and concentrated their attack instead on

---

[28] The major demographic and economic changes wrought by the collapse of the old
quasi-feudal economy in Eastern Europe were less understood or acknowledged than
the role of tsarist antisemitism. See e.g. Lucien Wolf, ed., *The Legal Sufferings of the Jews
in Russia* (London, 1912), and L. S. Greenberg, *The Jews in Russia* (New Haven, 1965).
Cf. Simon Kuznets, 'Immigration of Russian Jews to the United States: Background and
Structure', *Perspectives in American History*, 9 (1975), 35–124.

[29] For Wolf's proposals on behalf of the ICA for Jewish resettlement in Southern
Siberia see 'M. de Plehve and the Jewish Question', *The Times*, 6 Feb. 1904, Gaster to
C. G. Montefiore, 28 Oct. 1903, Gaster papers, laying out the advantages to Jews and
non-Jews of Jewish dispersion in the Russian empire.

[30] For the stock-in-trade rejoinder that intervention against Jewish expulsions from
Kiev 'would be calculated to cause irritation . . . as an unwarrantable act of interference
on behalf of a foreign government in the internal affairs of Russia' see e.g. Langley to
Wolf, 31 May 1910, MWS 449–50.

[31] The claim is made in 'Mentor' (the editor, Leopold Greenberg), *JC* 14 Mar. 1913.
On the CJC's working practices see CJC minutes, 1878–1917; on the score of unaccountability, the minutes for 12 Dec. 1906 certainly have D. L. Alexander, the BD
president, stating that the 'treaty' gave the CJC 'full executive powers'. See also Stuart
A. Cohen, *English Zionists and British Jews: The Communal Politics of Anglo-Jewry, 1895–
1920* (Princeton, 1982), esp. 69–76, 134–43.

ı

the personalities and methods involved,[32] it is debatable whether at this juncture one could call the nature of the Conjoint's work diplomacy. The Conjoint's importance, not to say independence, had been achieved, as Eugene Black has aptly remarked, 'by virtue of existing and being the medium through which most transactions went to the Foreign Office'.[33] More cynically, perhaps, its credentials rested on the ability of the group of highly acculturated and well-connected Jewish gentlemen who comprised it to put their case at the right time and in the right places. In practice this often implied dealings with peers of the realm and ministers of state with whom contact was established through London clubs and court circles, rather than direct contact with the Foreign Office *per se* (though of course official petitions and memoranda were submitted with great frequency). Ironically, though there was in this much of Montefiore's well-trodden path of intercessionary *shtadlanut*, it was less diplomacy than a refined form of pressure-group politicking.

The problem was that the Conjoint never really aspired to practise anything else. Its whole case rested on the essential consonance between British foreign policy and its own aims. As such, in the crisis years leading up to the First World War it was increasingly out of touch with its own constituency, and both out of step and out of favour with the Ministry in which it put so much faith.

The diplomatic breakthrough when it came was, in an important sense, a fluke, in that it rested on perceptions, or more correctly misconceptions, about the relationship of Jewish society to the wider world. In the critical years of the First World War, these misconceptions, held at the Foreign Office as elsewhere, not only provided the bargaining counters which were otherwise lacking but a window of opportunity with which to establish a genuinely resourceful and effective diplomacy. But its attainment also required leadership, some person or persons with natural or acquired skills in its art, who could not only recognize the opportunity for what it was, but seize upon and exploit it. One name of course immediately springs to mind: Chaim Weizmann. But not only was Weizmann not, strictly speaking, a member

---

[32] *JC* 19 June 1903, reporting AJA debate of 14 June 1903. On CJC's concern with 'prestige and tradition' see 'Mentor', *JC* 14 July, and *JC* 12 Dec. 1913, reporting AJA meeting of 7 Dec. 1913.

[33] Eugene Black, 'Lucien Wolf and the Making of Poland: Paris, 1919', *Polin*, 2 (1987), 6–7.

of Anglo-Jewry, or therefore of the Conjoint Committee,[34] he was quite out of sympathy with its basic aspirations or objectives. Indeed the many studies of his undoubted diplomacy in the period leading up to the Balfour Declaration in 1917 tend to examine the Conjoint exclusively in its adversarial role towards him.[35] Interest in the Conjoint's director, Lucien Wolf, follows a predictably similar pattern. The possibility that Wolf might have developed a distinctive diplomacy of his own at the Conjoint has thus gone by default. Indeed, as Simon Schama has noted, by opposing Weizmann, Wolf and his committee not only lost the cogency of their case but 'have been consigned by much of Jewish historiography to that dismal oblivion reserved for losing sides'.[36]

Even this statement begs serious questions about winners and losers. If Wolf and his committee were so clearly shipwrecked in 1917, how did they play such a crucial role in the evolution of the Minorities Treaties at the Paris peace conference, two years later? And how did they do so while holding to the same basic tenets of liberal emancipationist ideology which had inspired the Conjoint Committee's founders in 1878?

Here we seem to have a conundrum, and one moreover that on initial inspection is reinforced in the person of Lucien Wolf himself.

LUCIEN WOLF

A reading of Wolf's voluminous articles and correspondence shows his outlook to be firmly anchored in the mid-Victorian scene, and this despite the fact that he himself was not born until 1857.

The Jewish question at the present moment cannot be separated from the general political question . . . Any attempt to separate it would prove disastrous for the whole cause of reform . . . Russian Jews are fighting solely for the liberation of the whole Russian people and in harmonious and zealous concert with them. Properly speaking there are no Jews in this great struggle.[37]

[34] Weizmann's naturalization in 1910 would have technically made him eligible for membership.
[35] See most obviously Leonard Stein, *The Balfour Declaration* (London, 1961); Isaiah Friedman, *The Question of Palestine, 1914–1918* (London, 1973); David Vital, *Zionism: The Crucial Phase* (Oxford, 1987). Ronald Sanders, *The High Walls of Jerusalem* (New York, 1983), gives a blow-by-blow account.
[36] Simon Schama, *Two Rothschilds and the Land of Israel* (London, 1978), 200–1.
[37] Wolf letter, *The Times*, 18 Aug. 195.

Such remarks on the abortive Russian revolution of 1905, speak volumes about Wolf's commitment to an essentially Whig version of history and progress and the Jewish place within them. So, too, did his oft-repeated formula that 'economic forces' and 'the essentially economic bases of modern society' would make 'for the tolerance of the stranger and consequently for mixed nationalities'. In short, the approaching triumph of the forces and principles of liberalism, from which not even Russia or Romania could remain exempt, were for Wolf an article of faith.[38]

These deeply felt convictions were rooted in Wolf's immediate family history. Lucien Wolf was not a communal bigwig of some old Anglo-Jewish lineage, as was sometimes assumed,[39] but the son of a political refugee, albeit one from a relatively prosperous and well-connected business background. Edward Wolf had fled his native Bohemia after the failed revolutions of 1848.[40] His son's pronounced Anglophilia owed much to Britain's sympathy with the revolutionaries' aspirations and its willingness, in its wake, to offer them shelter, his father included.[41]

More crucially, the fact that Edward Wolf was a representative of those Central European Jews who had staked their commitment to liberalism on the barricades of Berlin, Vienna, Budapest, and Venice shaped Lucien's developing attitude towards the Jewish question. So much so that the revolutions of 1848 became for him the seminal event in the modern Jewish experience. Thus, when Lucien Wolf wrote about 1905, he did so through the prism of 1848.[42] Jews could only achieve equality and freedom by embracing the principles which would

[38] See Wolf, 'Zionism', *Encyclopaedia Britannica* (1901 edn.), xxvii, cols. 986–9; id., 'Anti-semitism', ibid. (1911 edn.), vol. ii, repr. in Roth, ed., *Essays*, 413–60; id., 'The Zionist Peril', *Jewish Quarterly Review*, 17 (Oct. 1904), 1–25.

[39] As Chaim Weizmann did in *Trial and Error* (London, 1950), 200.

[40] See 'Lucien Wolf: A Memoir', in Roth, ed., *Essays*, 3 (the memoir is not attributed but was written in part by Mowschowitch; Lucien Wolf, 'The Romance of a Bohemian Village', ibid. 55–9. For full details of Wolf's family see 'Miss Ruth Philips's Diary', Mocatta Lib., entry for 12 Sept. 1906 (Miss Philips was Wolf's personal secretary in this period); also Mowschowitch, 'Lucien Wolf, A Life', unpublished notes; Mowschowitch MS, 'Lucien Wolf and the Jewish Question' (Aug. 1932), MWS 253–78.

[41] Wolf, introd. to Semenoff, *Russian Government*, xxv; id., 'The Tsar's Visit, Liberals and Russia', *Morning Leader*, 30 July 1909.

[42] See id., 'The "Grenzboten" Jubilee', in Roth, ed., *Essays*, 52; id., 'The Jewish Vote', *Pall Mall Gazette*, 24 Nov. 1885; id., introd. to Semenoff, *Russian Government*, xxvii. On the relationship between 1848 and 1905 see Norman Stone, *Europe Transformed, 1878–1919* (London, 1983), 107–28.

free society as a whole, principles which in turn would make for Jewish acceptance and assimilation in those societies. No wonder so many of his Zionist opponents were eager to lambast him as the archetypal assimilationist who could not see beyond his own nose.[43]

But alongside Wolf the liberal ideologist *par excellence* there was also Wolf the pragmatist. This Wolf didn't like what he saw around him, but recognized that neither rhetoric nor commitment would resolve the Jewish question as it actually presented itself. This was a Wolf, moreover, prepared to countenance and support options which did not neatly dovetail with his convictions but which might offer practical assistance, perhaps even more thoroughgoing solutions, to specifically Jewish social and political problems.

In practice, this led Wolf at times in his pre-war career to endorse the forces of revolutionary socialism, territorialism, and even, in its initial stages, Herzlian Zionism.[44] His participation in communal affairs became clearly controversial. He outraged contemporaries like Joseph Cowen and Leopold Greenberg for his 1903 *volte-face* denunciation of Zionism.[45] He mortified his friends, including Claude Montefiore, the co-president of the Conjoint, for his co-founding, with the more obviously maverick Israel Zangwill, of the Jewish Territorial Organization, the ITO.[46] He even crossed swords, in 1906, with Lord Rothschild for supporting the Russian Jewish Workers' Bund instead of the constitutional parties. 'One could not pick and choose in times of revolution',[47] Wolf tersely told him.

If the controversial Wolf made both friends and enemies from within the ranks of the Anglo-Jewish establishment, in one sense his readjustment to the realities of his day was no more than a reflection of the establishment's own dilemmas. This may indeed be part of the reason why the fate of Lucien Wolf and Anglo-Jewry's foreign affairs body, the Conjoint Committee, are so inextricably linked.

The Conjoint Committee was run by well-meaning but essentially untutored amateurs. It lacked professional expertise. Wolf was the only

[43] S. B. Rubenstein letter, *JC* 1 Jan. 1909; Weizmann, *Trial*, 200.
[44] Josef Fraenkel, 'Lucien Wolf and Theodor Herzl', *TJHSE* 20 (1959–61), 161–88.
[45] Fraenkel, 'Wolf and Herzl', 182–4; Wolf, 'The Zionist Peril', *The Times*, 8 Sept. 1903, for his first major attack on Zionism.
[46] Letter from communal heads repudiating ITO, *The Times*, 8 Dec. 1905. For its development see Robert E. Weisbord, 'Israel Zangwill's Jewish Territorial Organisation and the East African Zion', *JSS* 30 (1968), 89–108.
[47] Reported in Wolf to Nathan Joseph, 11 Jan. 1906, MWS 2562–3.

person in the community who could supply this; indeed, his knowledge of the field was quite unrivalled.

Lucien Wolf was not a diplomat in the sense that he had a career in the Foreign Office or diplomatic service. These, before 1914, remained the preserve of a self-perpetuating aristocratic élite and were rarely open to outsiders, let alone Jews.[48] Nevertheless, he did have a truly remarkable insight into and understanding of the workings of European diplomacy, for having completed his education in Paris and Brussels in the mid-1870s—an education which made him as much the cosmopolitan, polyglot European as patriotic Englishman—Wolf chose to earn his living by working as a journalist. Some of this was with Jewish newspapers, notably the *Jewish World*, and it was through this ongoing journalistic connection that Wolf's involvement with the Jewish community grew. In communal terms the name of Lucien Wolf is thus associated with the Maccabeans (the debating club), the Jewish Literary Union, the Anglo-Jewish Association, and above all with the Jewish Historical Society of England, which he co-founded, with Israel Abrahams among others, in 1893. Indeed, it is in this capacity, as the first serious exponent of Anglo-Jewish history, that he is often best remembered today.[49]

Outside the Jewish scene, however, Wolf's professional career was not only progressing by leaps and bounds but also becoming increasingly specialized. Initially writing the occasional foreign affairs article for magazines such as the *British Mercantile Gazette* or the *St James Gazette*, Wolf had by the turn of the century established himself as the country's best informed and most astute observer of the international scene.[50]

As 'Diplomaticus' from 1895 for the *Fortnightly Review*, he had occasion to be described as the spokesman for Lord Salisbury.[51] Concurrently, as writer of the 'Foreign Office Bag' for the *Daily Graphic*, Wolf at times could claim to be less observing foreign affairs than instigating them. It was his personal boast that suggestions he had placed to the Russian ambassador Paul Lessar in 1898, with the

[48] Steiner, *Foreign Office*, 16–19.   [49] Roth, 'A Memoir', 4–5, 24–5.
[50] Ibid. See also biographical notes enc. with Wolf to Drummond, 8 Sept. 1917, FO 371/3085/175951. For an account of an early foray into the foreign affairs field see Wolf, *The Russian Conspiracy or Russian Monopoly in Opposition to British Interests in the East* (Birmingham, 1877).
[51] *DDF* 3rd ser., iii (Paris, 1929), no. 56, Fleurian (chargé d'affaires, London) to Poincaré, 30 May 1912.

approval of the foreign secretary, Lord Balfour, had been the basis for
negotiations which narrowly averted an Anglo-Russian conflict in
Manchuria.[52] Certainly later, in 1907, Sir Edward Grey, the then
foreign secretary, had to assure Count Metternich, the German ambassador, that his proposals for a North Sea and Baltic agreement had
nothing to do with Wolf's articles on the subject a few weeks earlier.[53]

Wolf was thus able to put at the disposal of the Conjoint both
formidable expertise and a truly encyclopaedic knowledge of foreign
affairs, founded on a reputedly vast filing system of articles and
papers.[54] Over and beyond this he was able to provide access to the
increasingly closed corridors of Whitehall.

Wolf's journalistic success had depended on his ability to find out at
any given moment what was going on in the embassies and chancelleries of Europe. This he had achieved through a carefully nurtured
network of contacts. With Sir Eric Barrington, Sir William Tyrrell,
and Francis Acland among the many senior British diplomatic officials
with whom he could claim to have excellent relations,[55] Wolf was in a
position to use these contacts on behalf of the Conjoint Committee.

Not that Wolf's involvement in the committee happened all at once.
It was as the specialist expert brought in to advise and write petitions,
as at the time of the Kishinev pogrom in 1903, that Wolf first made the
committee's serious acquaintance.[56] Certainly his standing with them
would have been enhanced too by his visit, on behalf of the ICA, a few
months later to V. K. von Plehve, head of the Russian Ministry of the
Interior, to discuss its proposal for Jewish settlement in Manchuria.[57]
Not until 1908, when crises developed into a state of permanence,

---

[52] Miss Philips's Diary, Mocatta Lib., entry for 12 July 1908; Wolf, 'Mr. Balfour at
the Foreign Office', *The Daily Chronicle*, 16 Dec. 1916.

[53] Grey to Count de Salis, 12 Dec. 1907, *British Documents on the Origins of the War,
1898–1914* (henceforth *BDOW*) (London, 1926–38), vol. vii, no. 125. See also de
Bunsen to Grey, 28 Dec. 1913, ibid., vol. xi, no. 184, reporting a conversation with the
Turkish ambassador to Vienna in which the latter proposed an Aegean islands settlement on the basis of Wolf's *Graphic* article, 11 Oct. 1913.

[54] Alexander Behr, 'Lucien Wolf, A Recollection', *The Jewish Monthly*, 4 (Aug. 1950),
260–1; Paul Goodman, *Zionism in England, 1899–1929* (London, 1930), 48.

[55] Wolf's personal correspondence files (MWS, folders 17–50), contain a wide
selection of contacts of this nature. Tyrrell, as Grey's private secretary (1907–15), was
clearly the most important of these in this period. Earlier, Barrington had been useful to
Wolf as private secretary to Salisbury and Lansdowne (1895–1905). Acland was a
parliamentary under-secretary in Grey's period. See also Steiner, *Foreign Office*, 119–20.

[56] For Wolf's participation at CJC meetings, see CJC minutes, 1878–1917.

[57] Wolf, 'M. de Plehve and the Jewish Question', *The Times*, 6 Feb. 1904.

did his advisory role start being transformed into one of executive direction; however, Wolf's arrival in this capacity does mark a major watershed in the history of Anglo-Jewish foreign policy. At a time when the Conjoint Committee was down on its luck and struggling against adversity, he was able to bring to it a professionalism and sense of direction which ensured it a new lease of life.

Under Wolf's leadership, the Conjoint Committee functioned for the first time as an authentic shadow Foreign Office, quite consciously imitating Whitehall's methods and procedures.[58] More important, it began to work strategically. No longer was the aim to achieve Romanian or Russian Jewish emancipation in one giant stride; that was clearly unrealizable. Rather, Wolf sought to exploit opportunities as and when they arose, particularly in 1908–9 at the time of the Bosnia–Herzegovina crisis and again in 1912–13 during the Balkan Wars.

Instead of seeing in these international crises grounds for despondency and inaction, Wolf sought to use them to reactivate international obligations relating to the Jewish question. Of course, this was no more than his predecessors at the Conjoint or contemporaries at the Alliance or Hilfsverein would have done. But whereas the traditional approach would have been to demand, for instance, Romanian's outstanding obligations raised to the agenda of any Great Power conference,[59] Wolf's manœuvres were always more subtle. Rather as at the time of the Bosnia–Herzegovina crisis, he requested only that the Foreign Office publicly acknowledge that the 'hopes expressed in 1880 of a more liberal disposition on the part of the Rumanian government towards the fulfillment of the views of the Powers signatories of the Treaty of Berlin have not been realised'.[60]

By attempting to draw the Foreign Office along the line of least resistance, Wolf sought to link British foreign policy with a Jewish interest without apparently committing the Foreign Office to anything.[61] Wolf hoped in this way to encourage it by degrees out of its intransigence and into a reassessment of its Jewish and indeed wider policy.

Yet Wolf's caution was at the same time a reflection of how limited

[58] Wolf, 'Notes on CJC Relations with the FO', MWS 25293–302.

[59] For Wolf's argument on this very point *vis-à-vis* the maximalist approach of Narcisse Leven, the AIU president, see Wolf to Montefiore, 8 Dec. 1913. MWS 2956–8.

[60] Wolf to Hardinge, 27 Nov. 1908, FO 371/511/11608.

[61] CJC memo encl. in Wolf to Hardinge, ibid. The ploy on this occasion failed, though Foreign Office diplomats were impressed by its astuteness; see Hardinge minute, 4 Dec. 1908, ibid.; Mallet to CJC, 3 Apr. 1909, FO 371/724/3158.

18 *Introduction*

the options were, how far the Conjoint had come from its assumption of a 'liberal' consonance between British and Jewish interests.[62] Added to this, there was in his directorship of the Conjoint a potentially fatal flaw. Wolf's journalistic association with the Foreign Office had been built up in the era of Lord Salisbury and 'splendid isolation' when Britain had eschewed all but imperial commitments abroad. He had been constructively critical of this policy, but never its adversary.[63] However, his increasing involvement with the Conjoint came at the time of a totally different Foreign Office rationale about continental commitments, culminating, in 1907, in the Anglo-Russian *entente*.[64]

Wolf was not alone in raising objections to this. All the great liberal commentators of the day deplored the accommodation with the tsar's reactionary regime, and said so.[65] What made Wolf's position quite distinct was a clear conflict of interests.[66] By day, he continued to earn his living in increasingly vitriolic and hard-hitting attacks on Grey and his ministry. Yet by night, so to speak, he was supplicating it in his part-time, purely voluntary capacity on behalf of the Conjoint. Perhaps Wolf believed the two roles could be kept in separate compartments. We know, however, from ministry minutes that ministry officials did not view it in that way, and were in fact increasingly at pains to keep him at arm's length, whatever the capacity in which he approached them.[67]

[62] Wolf to Emanuel, 18 Aug. 1908, MWS 19672–3: 'Unless we can show the Foreign Office that a situation of real gravity exists, not only will our representations lead to no result but I am afraid they will create the impression that we easily give way to panic and this would have a bad effect when we have a really serious case to bring to Downing Street.'

[63] See e.g. Wolf, 'Where Lord Salisbury has Failed', *Fortnightly Review*, Aug. 1898.

[64] Steiner, *Foreign Office*, 70–82.

[65] A. J. Anthony Morris, *Radicalism against War, 1906–1914* (London, 1972), esp. 60–9, 176–82, 250–70; A. J. P. Taylor, *The Troublemakers: Dissent over Foreign Policy* (London, 1957), 112–14; John A. Murray, 'Foreign Policy Debated: Sir Edward Grey and his Critics 1911–12', in L. P. Wallace and W. C. Askew, eds., *Power, Public Opinion and Diplomacy* (Durham, North Carolina, 1959), 140–71.

[66] See e.g. Wolf, 'Have We been Duped in Persia?', *Graphic*, 9 Dec. 1911; id., 'Sir Edward Grey's Stewardship', *Fortnightly Review*, Dec. 1911. On the difference between Wolf and the radical 'pacifists' see Max Beloff, *Lucien Wolf and the Anglo-Russian Entente* (London, 1951), 9.

[67] For the following exchange between Sir Eyre Crowe and Sir Louis Mallet 11 Mar. 1912, see FO 372/381/8978: Crowe: 'We must be very careful what we say to Mr. Lucien Wolf. He is not be trusted and for all we know may wish to use this information for the purposes of continuing his violent attacks on Sir Edward Grey.' Mallet: 'As regards as to Sir Eyre Crowe's observation, I do not think that Mr. Wolf is preparing an attack just now. His intention is all the other way as he wants to help to get the restrictions on the entrance of Jews into Russia removed. It is of no use to him to assail the Secretary of State until the latter has succeeded or failed in this.'

The contradictory nature of Wolf's relationship to the Foreign Office was reflected moreover in his position *vis-à-vis* the Conjoint. Wolf had no *de jure* standing on the Committee, having simply been co-opted at the instance of Claude Goldsmid Montefiore and David Lindo Alexander, its two long-serving presidents, and Leopold de Rothschild, its vice-president. These venerable gentlemen, moreover, continued to disguise the real leadership behind their own elected positions.[68] Not surprisingly, it all served to exacerbate a communal criticism which accused Wolf of being an *éminence grise* behind a Committee totally unaccountable to either of its parent bodies.

In spite of these seemingly intractable problems, Wolf's skill and tenacity not only kept the Committee's lines to the Foreign Office open but in the autumn of 1913 seemed to bring it to the verge of a breakthrough. The likelihood of a Great Power conference to legit-imize the territorial changes brought about by the Balkan Wars enabled the Conjoint to raise once again the question of Romania's unfulfilled obligations. The threat that the Balkan crisis would suck in the Great Powers, moreover, induced a spurt of diplomatic co-operation and power-broking reminiscent of 1878.[69]

Encouraged by the ministry's official confirmation that His Majesty's Government would consult with the signatories of the Berlin Treaty to reaffirm the liberties of religious minorities,[70] Wolf embarked on a major campaign. With the full and confident support of the Italian, French, German, and American Jewish bodies, he sought to co-ordinate diplomatic, journalistic, and financial efforts to force Romania's hand.[71] On 28 July, a month after the assassinations at Sarajevo and on the same day that Austria-Hungary declared war on Serbia, the Foreign Office reiterated its commitment. A week later, Britain was itself at war.[72]

---

[68] See CJC minutes, 20 Mar. 1912, 'It was left to Messrs. Montefiore, Alexander, and de Rothschild to decide what steps to be taken.' In fact, Wolf directed the CJC response to this particular crisis, the Beilis 'ritual murder' trial in Russia, from beginning to end. For further details see Zosa Szajkowski, 'The Impact of the Beilis Case in Central and Western Europe', *PAAJR* 31 (1963), 197–218.

[69] Steiner, *Foreign Office*, 149–50.

[70] Crowe to CJC, 29 Oct. 1913, FO 371/1742/1532.

[71] Wolf to Marshall, 17 June 1914, MWS 7540–3; Wolf to Morgenthau, 25 May 1914, C11/2/5; Wolf to Oscar Straus, 2 June 1914, ibid.; Wolf to Schwarzenfeld, 15 July 1914, ibid. For Wolf's parallel Italian *démarche* see Luigi Luzzatti, *God in Freedom* (New York, 1930), 486–90.

[72] Crowe to CJC, 28 July 1914, FO 371/2089/11207.

PART I

THE CHALLENGE OF WAR

East Central Europe before the First World War

I
The Challenge to the Community

The whole thing is so stupendous that it fairly staggers me. It is not only the carnage that will be frightful but the economic exhaustion and the starvation which will be infinitely worse and then when peace comes the desolation and certain revolution everywhere ... there will be no choice between the military dictator and the socialist ... how far Germany has made a mess of it I do not know but I am certain that we could not have done other than we have done.[1]

The outbreak of war in August 1914 marks a radical change in Lucien Wolf's life. It cut him off from most of his previous political and journalistic work and transferred him very much against his will to a new sphere of personal difficulties of a moral and material nature.[2]

The Anglo-Jewish establishment was inclined to blame its East European immigrant brothers for the sense of growing unease which afflicted it in the immediate pre-war years. Certainly the alien influx did bring greater and invariably hostile public attention to a community which had traditionally striven to avoid conspicuousness and blend into English society as smoothly as possible.[3] Riots against immigrant Jewish shopkeepers in Tredegar and other Welsh towns in 1911 unsettled the conviction that Britain was exempt from manifestations of continental-type antisemitism. Hilaire Belloc, Cecil Chesterton, and Leo Maxse used the occasion to charge that Jews were themselves responsible, through some innate inability to assimilate. Anglo-Jewish commentators declined to accept that but did concur that the difficulty of Anglicizing the immigrant population was at the root of the problem.[4] Lucien Wolf was not alone in advocating that the community itself should discourage immigration.[5]

The opponents of Anglo-Jewry, however, were much more concerned

[1] Wolf to Sir Henry Primrose, 7 Aug. 1917, MWS 3440.
[2] Mowschowitch MS, notes for chapter on 'Great War' in projected Wolf biography, MWS 297–32.
[3] Howard Brotz, 'The Position of Jews in English Society', *JJS* 1 (1959), 106–8.
[4] *JC* 25 Aug. 1911; Holmes, *Anti-Semitism*, 28, 71–2.
[5] Wolf to Meyerson, 19 Feb 1913, C11/5/2. For the wider Anglo-Jewish response see Black, 'The Struggle for the Aliens Act', in id., *Social Politics*, 271–301.

to bring attention to the community's supposedly highly acculturated 'English' élite and had particular reasons for doing so. Whether the British public liked it or not, the first decade of the century had seen a successful fraction of Jewry become extremely visible in high places, most notably at the court of Edward VII, as well as in the press, parliament, and in government. The route to this success had invariably been, directly or indirectly, through finance. It was the behaviour of Jewish banking houses and the interrelationship between them and Jews in high places which so exercised the minds of Maxse and others.[6] Through finance, they alleged, the Jews were in a position to manipulate society for ends beneficial to themselves but quite divergent from and indeed highly detrimental to the British nation. When in the winter of 1912/13 the government found it necessary to open two separate investigations into financial and commercial transactions undertaken on its behalf involving Jewish members of government and firms to which they were related, the allegation seemed on the point of being proven.

In the first government investigation it was Edwin Montagu, then under-secretary of state at the India Office, and his role in the purchase of silver bullion on its behalf which came under scrutiny. The purchase had been carried out through the auspices of Samuel Montagu and Co., a banking firm that belonged to Montagu's father, Lord Swaythling. Another partner in the firm was Montagu's cousin, Sir Stuart Samuel. Samuel was also an MP. There were connections here which implied rigging. Two months later, the exposure of underhand dealings involving the pre-flotation sale of shares in the government-sponsored Marconi concession added a new twist. Godfrey Isaacs, the managing director of the company involved, was brother to Rufus Isaacs, the attorney-general. Moreover the minister responsible for the concession in the first place was Herbert Samuel, the postmaster-general. He was also Sir Stuart Samuel's brother and Edwin Montagu's cousin.[7]

In fact, both Edwin Montagu and Herbert Samuel were entirely exonerated of any underhand dealings. They retained their government posts and the scandal blew over, but the community continued to

[6] Lipman, *Social History*, 162; Cecil Roth, 'The Court Jews of Edwardian England', *JSS* 6 (1943), 355–66.

[7] See Henry D'Avigdor-Goldsmid, 'The Little Marconi Case', *History Today*, 14 (1964), 283–6; Holmes's chapter, 'Our New Masters?', in id., *Anti-Semitism*, 63–8; Bermant, *Cousinhood*, 334–8.

reel from the shock. 'Mentor' in the *Jewish Chronicle* lamented, 'the May days of happy conditions for the Jews in this country are waning. The signs of anti-Jewish feeling are too marked and too obvious to be ignored.'[8]

The accusation of Jewish finance for Jewish ends struck hard at the ideological foundations of Jewish life in Britain, contradicting the community's pride in its British citizenship. There was, however, an extension of the Maxse-type argument which had an even more unsettling effect, one which, moreover, particularly because of the war, had potentially tragic consequences for the community. Jewish finance was considered to be not only powerful and manipulative but, like the Jews themselves, international and cosmopolitan. Not that this power was considered to be 'neutral' in global politics. On the contrary, it was 'the pro-German and pan-German tendencies of Jewish finance',[9] insisted Henry Wickham Steed, the leading *Times* journalist, which represented the real Jewish threat to Britain. In these terms, Jewish opposition to the Anglo-Russian *entente* suddenly became entirely explicable; it was not the condition of Russian Jewry which really concerned them—this was purely a camouflage. What was really at stake was the disruption that the *rapprochement* caused to German political goals and hence to Jewry's own international designs.[10]

Had these accusations been limited to the extreme and rabid right-wing press (Chesterton's *New Witness*, for example), Anglo-Jewry might have been better positioned to parry or otherwise dismiss them outright. But Maxse's *National Review* was considered to be a reputable journal, while Wickham Steed's elevation, in the spring of 1914, from Vienna correspondent to foreign editor of *The Times* added to those subscribing to these views the chief establishment organ of the land.[11] Moreover, the allegations were not so easily dismissable. Some of the Jewish banking houses were conspicuous in being owned by men of German birth or recent German origin. They included Sir Ernest Cassel, Sir Edgar Speyer, and Sir Alfred Mond. By the very nature of

[8] *JC* 14 Mar. 1913.

[9] Henry Wickham Steed, *Through Thirty Years: A Personal Narrative* (London, 1924), ii. 390.

[10] Ibid. 390–3. See also Maxse, 'The War against the Huns', *National Review*, Oct. 1914, on Russophobia as a German Jewish export.

[11] 'We should be blind if we failed to notice that since Mr. Steed became its foreign editor the anti-semitism that used continually to inform his messages from Vienna has been reflected in the leading columns of the journal'; Wolf leader, *Darkest Russia*, 10 June 1914.

finance, these houses did have international, including German, connections; Speyer, for instance, was a partner in a New York–London–
Frankfurt banking firm, and Cassel was heavily involved in German
commercial ventures.[12]

More to the point, some of the calumnies about Jewish–German
synonymity and political collusion did in a distorted sense contain an
element of truth. Jewish financiers did not welcome the *entente* with
Russia and did do all they could—albeit unsuccessfully—to attenuate
and ultimately reverse the economic, political, and naval rivalry with
Germany and its allies. Lord Rothschild publicly flew in the face of
government policy in early 1914 by floating a loan to Hungary. Cassel
did so more privately, negotiating with his German Jewish friend and
counterpart, Alfred Ballin, to promote Anglo-German co-operation on
the Berlin–Baghdad railway. It was they who with Edgar Speyer were
widely believed to be behind the official Haldane mission of goodwill and
reconciliation to Germany in 1912; and they again, this time with Mond,
who figured prominently in the Anglo-German friendship society which
aimed to find a peaceful solution to the two countries' quarrels.[13]

It was this Jewish refusal to flow with the tide of jingoistic anti-
German sentiment, and contrarily their tendency to join the movement
for the preservation of peace,[14] which ultimately enabled the community's enemies to indict it with corporate treason.

In late July 1914, as continental Europe plunged towards war, Lord
Rothschild, claiming to speak for the City, made strident efforts to
maintain Britain's neutrality. He interceded with both Lloyd George,
the chancellor, and Lord Northcliffe, the proprietor of *The Times*, in an
attempt to use Steed's absence to get his strongly worded leader
backing French and Russian mobilization cancelled.[15] Heartfelt opposition to British involvement was similarly expressed in the *Jewish
Chronicle*. 'We protest with all our might', ran a leader on 31 July,

against the mere thought of spilling blood or the squandering of British
resources in order that the Slavs may maintain their position against the

[12] Alfred Vagts, 'Die Juden im Englisch-Deutschen Imperialistischen Konflikt vor
1914', in Joachim Radkau and Immanuel Geiss, eds., *Imperialismus im 20 Jahrhundert:
Gedenkschrift für George W. F. Hallgarten* (Munich, 1976), 113–44, at 127; C. C. Aronsfeld, 'Jewish Enemy Aliens in England during the First World War', *JSS* 18 (1956),
275–83. Mond was of course primarily an industrialist.

[13] Vagts, 'Die Juden', 121–2, 127.

[14] *JC* report on Jewish Peace Society, 9 June 1914.

[15] Steed, *Through Thirty Years*, ii. 9, 14.

Teutons and an effete and barbarous autocracy be sustained on a tottering throne. We have no interest in the upholding of Russia and far less the debasing of Germany . . . with whom she [Britain] has no quarrel whatsoever.[16]

It was unfortunate that these Jewish appeals for neutrality coincided with actual German machinations to keep Britain strictly out of the war. At the beginning of August a telegram to the London office of the official German press agency, Wolff, carrying a manifesto from Ballin proclaiming Germany's peaceful intentions to Britain, was accidentally delivered to *The Times*. The telegram, which was to have been published in *The Times* but not until 3 August, after the massive German invasion of Belgium had already begun, was meant to give the German public the impression that *The Times* endorsed Ballin's sentiments. *The Times* did not publish the manifesto.[17] Nor did Britain abstain from war. The German entry on to Belgian soil represented a contravention of the 1830 Great Power protocol protecting its neutrality, and was moreover a threat to Britain's own security. Government indecision dissolved. On 4 August Britain joined France and Russia against the Central Powers.

The apparent link between Ballin's manifesto and the last-minute pro-neutrality efforts of Rothschild and others was not forgotten. Within a month, Maxse's first wartime edition of the *National Review* took the Ballin fiasco as excuse for a long and virulent polemic against what he termed the 'Potsdam party'; those who 'for financial or racial reasons' had attempted to manipulate the British Foreign Office for the benefit of Germany. It was German Jewish financiers, said Maxse, who 'in the interests of the Fatherland' had been responsible for the last-minute raising of 'the white flag of neutrality'. Though he went on to insist he had nothing against 'the national Jew who is a patriot', he immediately contradicted himself by asserting that 'the victory of Germany is for some reason a desideratum of almost the entire Jewish race'. In short, under the guise of attacking Cassel, Speyer, and Mond, Maxse lumped together English and German Jews indiscriminately in what amounted to a crude threat to the whole community:

German Jews here and German Jews elsewhere will be well advised in their own interests to avoid interfering with the arm of justice at the final liquidation. Even good natured, easy going Englishmen, immemoriably accustomed

[16] 'Neutrality and the War', *JC* leader, 31 July 1914.
[17] Steed, *Through Thirty Years*, ii. 16–25.

to be trampled on by the least desirable alien are growing restive under the odious Hebrew domination which has operated exclusively in the interests of Germany.[18]

Steed's view of the Rothschild neutrality bid as a 'dirty German Jewish international financial attempt to bully us into advocating neutrality'[19] determined that *The Times* would follow Maxse with insinuations that were if not as virulent, then at least as menacing. Casting aside Lord Rothschild's and Leopold de Rothschild's efforts to call a 'truce' on Jewish questions,[20] it ran extensive coverage in late 1914 and early 1915 of the alleged pro-German proclivities of Turkish crypto-Jews, and from Stephen Graham in Warsaw of the supposed intense Germanophilism of Polish Jewry.[21] At home, Israel Zangwill's attempt to counter allegations that pleas on the part of Jacob Schiff, the American Jewish financier, for a *status quo* peace was part of a wider German 'plot' brought forth a quite open threat in the letters column of *The Times* from something calling itself the Vigilance Committee against Jewish financiers who were attempting 'to influence American neutrality. . . . So far the pro-Germans in England and their organs in the Metropolitan press have been wisely quiet. They are the more closely being watched.'[22]

The very fact that such a piece had found its way into *The Times* at all, let alone in that form, says much for the emotional state of the country in the first months of the war. In the near-hysterical wave of jingoism and xenophobia that swept Britain at that time, Jews, whether Yiddish-speaking aliens from the East End or wealthy Anglo-Jews from the West End with foreign-sounding names, found themselves obvious targets for popular suspicion and popular wrath.[23]

[18] Maxse, 'The Fight against Germanism', *National Review*, Sept. 1914.
[19] Steed, *Through Thirty Years*, ii. 9.
[20] Montefiore to Wolf, 4 Nov. 1914, C11/2/5; Wolf to Isidore Spielman, 11 Dec. 1916, C11/2/10.
[21] Wolf to Montefiore, 5 Nov. 1914, C11/2/15, refers to 'Leo de Rothschild's complaints on this score'; see also Graham articles in *The Times*, 17, 29, 30 Oct. 1914, 19 Jan. 1915.
[22] 'Washington Despatch', *The Times*, 23 Nov. 1914; Zangwill reply, ibid., 28 Nov. 1914; Vigilance Committee letter, ibid., 26 Nov. 1914.
[23] Elkan D. Levy, 'Anti-Semitism in England at War, 1914–1916', *Patterns of Prejudice* (1970), 27–30. The 53,000-strong German community in Britain was of course specially targeted for chauvinistic attacks. See Panikos Panayi, 'The Bully Boys of Britain', *Weekend Guardian*, 5 June 1989, pp. 2–3. The Jews were in a sense doubly under threat, both as Jews and as supposed German sympathizers.

In spite of this, Anglo-Jewry responded with vigour to the war effort. Jews in all the belligerent countries were eager to use the opportunity of the war to prove their patriotism, whether to justify their citizenship, or substantiate their claim to it. On both sides they freely equated the justice of their national cause with the principles of Judaism,[24] and even French and Russian Jewry were able to reconcile their doubts about fighting with, or for, a reactionary antisemitic tsarist regime with the simple if facile solution that the alliance with the Western powers would sweep away its illiberal characteristics.[25]

Jews in Britain, led by the younger Rothschilds, flocked to the colours. A special committee was set up at the family's New Court business headquarters to encourage enlistment, and the *Jewish Chronicle* gave impetus to this development with its wartime slogan, 'England has been all she could be to Jews, Jews will be all they can be to England.'[26] But behind the trappings and proclamations of patriotism lurked a real sense of fear and insecurity, a fear engendered by the invective of the jingoist press and by the knowedge that Jews were constantly being watched, that one step out of line might spell disaster. The *Jewish Chronicle* frankly acknowledged the situation at the outbreak of war and advised its readers:

We Jews should be particularly careful at a time like this, by our conduct and demeanour . . . so that we shall not arouse a spirit of hostility, which at a time of national anxiety and stress such as that upon which we are entering, is a force . . . ready to assert itself at the slightest provocation.[27]

Jewish communal trepidation manifested itself in two main symptoms. The first was to deny or stifle all aspects of specifically sectarian behaviour which might lend credence to the idea that Jews put Jewish interests before national ones. 'At the present time,' Sir Francis Montefiore proclaimed when resigning his presidency of the English Zionist Federation in December 1915, 'the thoughts of all Englishmen should be for national questions.' David Alexander at the Board of Deputies agreed, overruling a suggestion earlier in the year that the

---

[24] See Chimen Abramsky, *War, Revolution and the Jewish Dilemma* (London, 1975), 9–11; also Jehuda Reinharz, 'Deutschtum und Judentum' in the Ideology of the Central-verein Deutscher Staatsburger Judischen Glaubens 1893–1914', *JSS* 36 (1974), 19–39.

[25] Abramsky, *War*, 11; Paula Hyman, *From Dreyfus to Vichy: The Remaking of French Jewry, 1906–1939* (New York, 1979), 50, 57; Leon Poliakov, *The History of Anti-Semitism*, vol. iv, *Suicidal Europe: 1870–1933* (Oxford, 1985), 162–3.

[26] *JC* 7 Aug. 1914; for an article on Jewish volunteers see *The Times*, 4 Dec. 1914.

[27] 'Mentor', *JC* 7 Aug. 1914.

question of interned enemy aliens be looked into, as 'open to the grave charge that the Jews placed their racial instincts before their patriotism'.[28] In the interests of self-preservation, it seemed, the communal leaders were prepared to wind up or whittle away at any form of separate communal expression which appeared to contradict the war effort. If necessary, the communal institutions would simply be frozen for the duration.

A second symptom which had even more stultifying effects on the communal institutions was clear indication of its nervous tension. Its vulnerability to right-wing press insinuations and hence a potential antisemitic backlash rested on its lukewarm if not downright hostile attitude to the war. This now underwent a hasty about-turn. Opposition to the war miraculously ceased. Anglo-Jewry, led by the *Jewish Chronicle*, which in a remarkable feat of amnesia turned in the space of a week from hostility to enthusiasm, became the war's convinced supporters.[29]

In the frantic desire to cover up past tracks, all murmurings of disquiet or dissent at the morality or conduct of the war had to be muzzled or quashed. Later, in 1916, this would express itself in a determined campaign by the communal heads, including Zionist leaders, to coerce the mostly Russian-born and hence dissenting immigrants into conscription; a campaign which if it failed, thought Wolf, stood to jeopardize the 'good name' of the community and spark off 'an explosion of anti-semitism'.[30]

It was the community's past behaviour in relation to the Russian *entente* which inevitably represented the weak link in its new posture. This did not stop Israel Zangwill, its *enfant terrible*, from denouncing the *entente* in a letter to *The Times* on 19 August 1914 as 'too high a price to pay even for safety against the German peril'.[31] His outspokenness, however, was not appreciated by the communal chiefs. Lord Rothschild had meanwhile been approached by Oscar S. Straus, the former American government minister and leading Jewish communal spokesman, with a perfectly logical scheme to solicit the Allies, in the

[28] On Sir Francis Montefiore's speech see *JC* 28 Dec. 1915; on BD meeting of 13 June see *JC* 18 June 1915.

[29] See *JC* leader, 7 Aug. 1914; also Levy, 'Anti-Semitism', 29–30.

[30] For Wolf's memo on the issue see MWS file 203 (unnumbered), 20 June 1916; for the views of Joseph Cowen, the EZF leader, and that of Greenberg on conscription, see *JC* 14 July 1916.

[31] *The Times*, 19 Aug. 1914; see also Joseph Leftwich, *Israel Zangwill* (London, 1957), 142–3.

interests of state policy, to persuade Russia to grant its Jews civil and political rights.[32] Rothschild's response was both to disown Zangwill and to dismiss Straus's scheme outright, arguing that the lot of Russian Jews would inevitably improve after the war. This became the new communal establishment line and even had its corollary in a new explanation of why Russia was antisemitic. Russian Jewry, noted the *Jewish Chronicle* in September, now saw that it had been 'the militarism of Russia's next door neighbour that has in the main been responsible for the reactionary spirit in Russia . . . With that system of blood and iron removed in Germany, Russia will be able to breathe and the last excuse for the bureaucracy will be gone'.[33]

It was with tortuous arguments such as these that Anglo-Jewry attempted to adjust itself to the war and so to avert the gaze of those who questioned its loyalty to Britain and its Allies.[34] But where did this leave its diplomacy? In absolving itself of guilt, the community had virtually abandoned Russian Jewry, the people at the heart of the wider Jewish question. Moreover, where did this leave Lucien Wolf, the man at the centre of the community's foreign affairs apparatus?

The problem was that Wolf was as much caught up in and constrained by developments on a wider communal level as anybody else. Indeed, he epitomized on the personal level the general tragedy which befell the community. In the pre-war years, Wolf had been the chief *bête noire* of those attempting to prove an anti-Russian, pro-German axis among English Jewry. Not surprisingly, unlike many of the more senior communal spokesmen who refrained from public polemic against the Anglo-Russian *entente*, the journalist Wolf had plunged in energetically. In the columns of the *Daily Graphic* and *Daily Despatch*, but more particularly in *Darkest Russia*, the weekly bulletin of Russian affairs which he created and edited from 1912, Wolf set out his case against the *entente*. The undemocratic and reactionary nature of the tsarist regime, he argued, posed real economic and political disadvantages, not to say dangers, to Britain.[35]

---

[32] Naomi C. Cohen, *A Dual Heritage, The Public Career of Oscar S. Straus* (Philadelphia, 1969), 235–7; Zosa Szajkowski, *Jews, Wars and Communism* (New York, 1972), 2 vols., i. 77.

[33] 'Mentor', *JC* 4 Sept. 1914.

[34] For more on the communal response see Aronsfeld, 'Jewish Enemy Aliens', 278–83; Levy, 'Anti-Semitism', 27–30; Black, *Social Politics*, 321–3.

[35] *Darkest Russia: A Weekly Record of the Struggle for Freedom*, Jan. 1912–Aug. 1914. *Darkest Russia* was underwritten by the ICA; see Lemarduchen to Wolf, 9 July 1914, MWS 10852–3.

His articles were hard-hitting and excited public attention. By the end of 1913, he could report to his ICA sponsors that *Darkest Russia* was growing in circulation and was increasingly used by radicals and labourites, inside and outside parliament, as a major source of intelligence for their own anti-Russian campaigns.[36] As a result Wolf made enemies, especially among those who saw merit in the *entente*. But he also in the process lost the sympathy of many high government and press patrons who now saw in the *rapprochement*, if not something desirable, then at least a necessary evil.[37]

Among his detractors the assumption grew that Wolf was a journalistic agent of the Wilhelmstrasse. The French embassy in London had long been convinced of this, ever since his sensational 1905 *tour de force* in *The Times*, 'Is Russia Solvent?', had produced something of a minipanic on the London and continental stock markets.[38] This view gradually gained a much wider currency among English journalists and Foreign Office officials after the signing of the *entente*. In 1909 Wolf considered bringing a libel action against Comyns Beaumont, the short-lived editor of the *Daily Graphic*, for asserting that he was a paid journalistic go-between and *agent provocateur* for the Germans. Beaumont in fact was forced to retract, his written statement of apology being widely circulated at the Foreign Office.[39] Privately, however, Beaumont stuck to his guns that Wolf was a German agent paid by 'a most influential and wealthy international house in the City'.[40]

The damage was done. For Beaumont, Maxse, W. T. Stead, and others, Wolf had become a key link in a German–Jewish financial–journalistic chain which, on the directives of the Wilhelmstrasse, operated to promote German political goals and conversely to disrupt the Anglo-Russian *entente*.[41]

Like the German-born financiers, Wolf was not well placed to

[36] *Darkest Russia*, half yearly report, 30 June 1917, MWS 10855–8; Wolf to Lionel L. Cohen, 23 Sept. 1913, MWS 10864–7.

[37] See e.g. Barrington to Wolf, 2 Jan. 1912, MWS 4321–2, on the necessity of the *entente*; and Wolf to Barnard, 24 June 1906, MWS 1804–6, on his losing work from the *Westminster Gazette* because of his opposition to the *entente* negotiations.

[38] *DDF* 2nd ser. (Paris, 1935 et seq.), vol. vi, no. 129, Cambon to Delcassé, describing Wolf as 'un journaliste israélite d'origine allemande à la fois germanophile et russophobe'; see also Aronsfeld, 'Jewish Bankers', 87–104.

[39] Wolf to Tyrrell, 16 Dec. 1909, MWS 4023; correspondence with *Daily Graphic* director Carmichael Thomas, Feb. 1909–Jan. 1910, MWS 3998–4008.

[40] Comyns Beaumont, *A Rebel in Fleet Street* (London, 1944), 45–6, 50–1.

[41] See Max Beloff, *Lucien Wolf*, 29.

scotch his detractors' allegations. His German-sounding name, often misspelt at the Foreign Office as Wolff or Woolf; his close continental connections, which went back many years to his school days in Paris and Brussels; his frequent visits to Wiesbaden in Germany, where he saw a specialist for his failing eyesight[42]—all conspired against him as being more a cosmopolitan Jew and less a patriotic Englishman.

Though Wolf was an independent-minded journalist who insisted on many occasions that he studied all political questions on their merits and vigorously denied any partisanship swayed by Jewish or other interests,[43] he undoubtedly did have Germanophile proclivities. In 1905, for instance, he privately expressed his preference for an *entente* with Germany rather than with France.[44] He was also an associate of Count Bernstorff, who as German ambassador in the first decade of the century had made some notorious attempts to manipulate the British press. In Wolf's case they were unsuccessful.[45] Equally, however, they were unnecessary: Wolf freely wrote flattering articles about the kaiser which were avidly read in Germany and Austria. His positive approach to Anglo-German relations was also reflected in his active role in encouraging the Haldane mission of goodwill to Germany in 1912.[46] Deteriorating relations between the two states were therefore bound to cause him trouble. Indeed, his July 1914 *Daily Graphic* articles on the growing continental crisis, for which he blamed not Germany or Austria but Serbia and the over-hasty mobilizations of Russia and France, were, once war had been declared, enough to spark off a minor witch hunt against him.[47]

Maxse led with a blistering attack in the September *National Review* on 'German' Jews who had 'rigged the news', 'wirepulled the press', and 'tottered out Russophobia'.[48] Though Wolf was not named in this

---

[42] See Miss Philips's Diary, Mocatta Lib., on Wolf's continental links.

[43] See e.g. Wolf to Kaminka, 28 July 1914, CII/2/11.

[44] Wolf to Bernstorff, 5 Apr. 1905, MWS 1853–4.

[45] See Wolf, 'Count Bernstorff's Failures', *Daily Chronicle*, 10 July 1915; Count Bernstorff, *The Memoirs of Count Bernstorff* (London, 1936), 60–3.

[46] See esp. Wolf, 'The Real Kaiser', *Daily Graphic*, 7 Jan. 1912; id., 'The German Grievance', *Pall Mall Gazette*, 6 Mar. 1906. For Wolf's speech at the Authors' Club, 10 Nov. 1913, at which Haldane and the German and Austrian ambassadors, Counts Kuhlmann and Mensdorff, were present as special guests, see also MWS 16–21. Wolf's letter of invitation to Kuhlmann, 30 Oct. 1913, MWS 2608 referred to it as 'a distinctly German affair'.

[47] Wolf, 'The Chancelleries and the Crisis', *Daily Graphic*, 27 July–1 Aug. 1914.

[48] Maxse, 'The Fight', *National Review*, Sept. 1914.

instance he was clearly implied, since Maxse went on to give a careful analysis of Wolf's July articles—carefully interspersed with the story of the Wolff telegraphic agency's misbehaviour—to give the impression that Wolf's pro-neutrality and Germany's official efforts to keep Britain out of the war were interrelated. The similarity between the names Wolf and Wolff no doubt also helped arouse sentiment against him.[49] At the *Daily Graphic* Wolf soon found himself being ostracized. He was deprived of his 'Foreign Office Bag' slot in the *Graphic* weekly, and finally, in November, he was bluntly informed that his services, after twenty-five years with the paper, were no longer required.[50] On one occasion, two Special Branch policemen appeared on his doorstep, on the basis of an anonymous denunciation of him as an unregistered alien and German spy; Wolf was forced to turn to Tyrrell at the Foreign Office to vouch for him.[51] Tyrrell did so, of course, but he could not undo the imputation of treason; nor could he restore Wolf's livelihood.

What was Wolf to do? Was he to stick by his pre-war pronouncements and thereby risk, in the uncertain climate of autumn 1914, further abuse, social exclusion, perhaps even lynching? Or was he to flow with the tide, in the way the rest of Anglo-Jewry was doing, by making patriotic utterances to signal his heartfelt conviction that Britain had justice on its side? Was there in fact any choice?

Other, non-Jewish, liberal journalists who had dealt with the coming of war in similar fashion to Wolf had also been bullied by Maxse. However, none had suffered quite as harshly materially as he had done as a result, nor were they so traumatized mentally as to be unable to stand by their views in the face of the stigma attached. Wolf, as an English Jew, was psychologically secure only in the knowledge that his Jewishness in no way interfered with or impaired his allegiance to the nation. He knew this, but in the climate of the times could not communicate it. He could either denounce the war and suffer the consequences, or stifle his reason and support the struggle. There was apparently no middle ground.

[49] See e.g. James W. Robertson Scott, 'Who Secured the Suez Canal Shares?', *Quarterly Review*, July 1949, 341–2, where Scott assumes Wolf was director of the Wolff agency.
[50] H. G. Charvel to Wolf, 28 Oct., MWS 2805–6; see also Wolf to Charvel, 31 Oct. 1914, ibid.
[51] Wolf to Metropolitan Commissioner of Police, 31 Aug. and 7 Sept. 1914, MWS 4626–7; Wolf to Tyrrell, 14 Sept. 1914, MWS 4027–8.

Unlike his fellow radicals who were not Jewish, Wolf found it impossible to continue public resistance to the war. He declined suggestions that he join the dissenting Union of Democratic Control, even though privately he sympathized with it. He refrained, too, from countering mischievous slanders against him in *The Times* and elsewhere.[52] Instead, his whole effort in the autumn and winter of 1914–15 was channelled into working his way back towards social acceptance, proving his innocence on treasonable accounts, and doing what he could to repair the tarnished image of Anglo-Jewry as one of good patriotic citizens. His response was very much a microcosm of the collective Anglo-Jewish state of mind.[53]

Wolf's concern to re-establish himself and his patriotism meant that like the *Jewish Chronicle* he was prepared to state publicly things which he believed to be false or inaccurate. Early in 1915 he wrote a pamphlet entitled *Jewish Ideals and the War*. Published under the auspices of the Jewish Historical Society and a new national committee to promote pro-Allied propaganda at home and abroad, it quite unashamedly blamed German antisemitic militarism as the root cause of the problems affecting the Jews of Russia. Wolf's ironic conclusion was that Jews, as Jews, were quite justified in fighting Germany as the only way to protect their political and civil rights and avoid a return to the ghetto.[54] But, as he confessed to Clara Melchior, his confidante, not only was this a rather remote justification for the war, it also did not help the Russian Jews:

We are in a tragical position of having to decide on a choice of evils. Whatever happens I am afraid the Jews of Russia will suffer and all we can do is to stem as far as possible the extension of anti-semitism westward. In the strong nationalist atmosphere that will exist after the war this is a grave peril.[55]

Thrust back on the defensive, Wolf's attention, like that of the rest of the community, was no longer drawn outward, expansively, to the plight of Jewry abroad, but inward, to Anglo-Jewry's now apparently extremely precarious relationship to British society at war. The whole

[52] Wolf to Ramsay MacDonald, 18 Sept. 1914, MWS 2676. For wartime radical opposition see Taylor, *Troublemakers*, 132–45; Michael Howard, *War and the Liberal Conscience* (London, 1978), 74–9.
[53] See e.g. Wolf's letters to George Prothero associating the Jewish Historical Society with the latter's Committee for Patriotic Organisations, Dec. 1914–May 1915, MWS 11129–49.
[54] Wolf, *Jewish Ideals and the War* (London, 1914).
[55] Wolf to Melchior, 15 June 1915, MWS 2525–6.

painstakingly constructed apparatus of Jewish foreign affairs, the Conjoint Committee—the pride of a confident community—seemed suddenly irrelevant. *Darkest Russia* was wound up in the first week of the war,[56] and the successful Romanian campaign brought to a rapid close. An enormous question mark hung over the future of Anglo-Jewish diplomacy.

[56] See last edition of *Darkest Russia*, 5 Aug. 1914, announcing its closure.

2
The Challenge to the Conjoint

We are . . . quite paralysed. We hope to make our voices heard when the time for peace negotiations and the construction of the New Europe arrives. Meanwhile not only can we do nothing, but we have definitely resolved to do nothing as we feel that all our energies must be devoted to the energetic prosecution of the war and that under any circumstances it would be improper of us to start discussions which might lead to friction between the Allies.[1]

Britain entered the continental conflict in August 1914 as an ally of Russia, France, and Serbia, and an enemy of Germany and Austria-Hungary. Within a year the Allies were joined by Italy, a year later by Romania.

What scope did this give to the Conjoint Committee? Successful Jewish action in foreign affairs had been largely dependent on a peaceful, harmonious Europe. This condition enabled free passage of information and ideas between one 'national' Jewish agency and another as well as the ability to co-ordinate actions in defence of Jewry without impairing or aggravating national interests. A divided Europe made this less possible. War made it less possible still.

From the specifically Anglo-Jewish viewpoint, the wartime configuration of forces could not have been worse. Europe's two most avowedly antisemitic powers, Russia and Romania—the powers that necessitated the existence of the Conjoint and like bodies in the first place—became allies of Britain, thus throwing doubt on whether the Conjoint could pursue a policy at all. True, it still had the option of working with the French Alliance, the Rome committee representing the Conserzio delle Comunità Israelitiche Italiane, the Romanian Union des Juifs Indigènes, and the semi-legal Petrograd Political Bureau, but if their joint considerations ran counter to the expressed desires of the Allies, this option became both improper and valueless.

Moreover, by dint of geography and the political situation prior to the war, the Conjoint Committee's greatest foreign asset in the pursuit of freedom for Jews in Russia and Romania had been close

[1] Wolf to Clara Melchior, 16 Nov. 1914, MWS 1122–3.

co-operation not with the Paris or Rome committees but with the Berlin-based Hilfsverein and the Vienna Allianz. Wolf had naturally had to pursue these relations with caution. His conspicuous alignment with German Jews could easily have been misinterpreted. There was the additional danger that embroilment in a joint Anglo-German venture for Russian Jewish emancipation might be exploited, if not by German Jews themselves, then by German newspapers or government for ends of a purely political nature. Nevertheless, it remains a fact that in the immediate pre-war years it was not Jacques Bigart at the Alliance but Armand Kaminka in Austria, and more particularly the German Jewish social democrat Paul Nathan, with whom Wolf worked most closely and whom he consulted for inspiration.[2] These relationships were now sundered.

This situation put in doubt not only the scope of the Conjoint's wartime activity but the very relevance of its continued existence. After all, it was founded on the particular premiss that British and British Jewish interests abroad were analogous and therefore could and might be pursued with the active co-operation of the British government. The Conjoint never saw itself as being disloyal or sectarian in presuming this, nor as putting its allegiance to Jews abroad before its duties and responsibilities as British citizens. Indeed, the fact that it was a British rather than a Jewish organization was acutely emphasized in its paradoxical exclusion, following the policy set by its parent organizations, of Jews who were not British-born or naturalized—though these were, in 1914, the majority among Jews living in Britain.

Some communal leaders saw the anomaly here. In an important debate at the Anglo-Jewish Association in April 1916, Rabbi Moses Gaster, the *haham* (head of Britain's Sephardi community), noting that there were some 10 million Jews outside Britain as compared with only 200,000 in it, crucially observed that the Conjoint Committee, being 'charged with seeing that justice was done to Jews throughout the world', had to consider 'not what suited them as English Jews but what suited the great majority . . . They could not view those questions solely from the point of view of English predilections.'[3]

[2] See Szajkowski, 'Impact of Beilis Case', 197–218. On Wolf's reluctance to get involved in Kaminka and Nathan's joint efforts on the Beilis case, see Wolf to Nathan 19 May 1911, Wolf to Montefiore, 23 May 1911, MWS 11060–1. On Nathan see Ernst Feder, 'Paul Nathan, the Man and his Work', *Leo Baeck Year Book*, 4 (1958), 60–80. For details of the Wolf–Nathan relationship see Zosa Szajkowski, 'Nathan, Wolf, Schiff', 3–26, 75–91; id., 'Nathan, Wolf and the Versailles Treaty', *PAAJR*, 38–9 (1971), 179–201.

[3] *JC* 7 Apr. 1916, reporting AJA meeting of 2 Apr. 1916.

The dilemma for Wolf and his associates was that there was little alternative. As Wolf half-sincerely confessed to the foreign secretary, Arthur Balfour, in January 1917, they hoped that there would be no dissonance between the interests of the Allies in the war and the interests of the Jews; but they realized that if such a dissonance arose, it was their duty to subordinate Jewish interests to the interests of their native country and of its Allies.[4]

To have put Jewish interests first, to have gone 'national' as the *haham*, Dr Gaster the Zionist, would have had them do, would have been not only to dismantle the whole ideological structure upon which the committee had been built but to open the committee and indeed the whole community, whose defence had now become its first priority over and above that of Eastern Jewry, to the very charges it was strenuously trying to avoid.

It was anxieties such as these which seem to have impelled the committee initially to do nothing, and where it did act to do so from a wholly negative viewpoint. No Conjoint meeting was in fact convened until November, three months after the war had begun, and even then only to deprecate vigorously a proposal by French Jews to defend their Russian co-religionists, denouncing it as bound 'to give credence to the assertion that Jews were cosmopolitan and only interested in their own interests and not in national allegiance'. This resolution had its counterpart in the attitude it decided to impart on the shaky subject of Russia: 'Russia is now the ally of England,' ran the Anglo-Jewish Association annual report. 'The success of her arms is longed for by every Englishman, all painful subjects of difference and dissension must for the time being be overlooked.'[5]

Three years earlier, Wolf had stressed to Claude Montefiore: 'If we once compromised on the question of the moral foundations of all politics, whether national or international, our case for our oppressed co-religionists wherever they may be will be gone.'[6] By acquiescing in the Russian alliance, Wolf was effectively eating his own words. From the moral standpoint it followed that the logical thing to do would have been to wind up the Conjoint altogether.

There were powerful pragmatic reasons which prevented this

[4] Wolf memo on interview with A. J. Balfour, 30 Jan. 1917, FO 800/210 (Balfour papers).
[5] CJC minutes, 4 Nov. 1914. Chief Rabbi Hertz was called upon to write to French chief rabbi Zadoc Kahn to this effect; see *AJA Report, 1913–14*, 6.
[6] Wolf to Montefiore, 16 Oct. 1911, MWS 2903.

happening. On the purely domestic level, the creation of a foreign
affairs vacuum posed the very real danger of having it filled with those,
Gaster for instance, who were liable 'to do all sorts of imprudent and
compromising things',[7] reviving in the process the arguments of
the community's detractors and dragging it down in a new wave of
suspicion and recrimination.

On the other hand, to do nothing invited contenders. Already in December 1914, Israel Zangwill and Leopold Greenberg had made their
own private and quite unauthorized representations to the Foreign
Office on the Russian and Palestine questions respectively,[8] thereby
undermining the credibility of the Conjoint and conversely strength-
ening the hand of the discontented Zionists, radicals, and others
disenchanted with the establishment who were set on either restruc-
turing or dismantling it altogether.

The war undoubtedly catalysed a new wave of criticism of the
Conjoint. Greenberg drew much attention in the *Jewish World* to its
outdatedness, its secrecy, the anomalous position of Wolf, 'the man
most responsible for its work' and yet by dint of his working in an
'honorary capacity . . . least amenable to either of the bodies that elect
the Committee'.[9] At the Board, and even in the more aloof Anglo-
Jewish Association, there were cries for the Conjoint to broaden its
membership and come forward with a policy. If it did not, warned
Nathan Laski, at a Board meeting in January 1915, Zionists, friendly
societies or other groups would. The Conjoint, in short, stood to be
displaced in very much the same way as the Board had been displaced
by the Association forty years earlier. Indeed, new grass-roots organizations, like the East End-based Workers' League for Jewish Emancipation, formed in 1915,[10] did directly challenge it. The challenge was made
all the more compelling by the fact that in America the following year, the
traditionalist and oligarchic American Jewish Committee was forced to
bow to demands for a democratic, popularly elected Congress.[11]

[7] Wolf to Alexander, 5 June 1916, CII/2/7.

[8] Wolf to Alexander and Montefiore, 7 Jan. 1915, MWS 7495–8.

[9] *Jewish World* leader, 9 Dec. 1914.

[10] Ibid., 18 and 25 Dec. 1914, reporting AJA meeting of 13 Dec. and BD meeting of
20 Dec., respectively. On the League's formation see Wolf to Alexander, 18 June 1915,
CII/2/6. It was, wrote Wolf, 'virtually intended to do the work of the Conjoint
Committee'.

[11] On American Jewish power struggles see Jonathan Frankel, *Prophecy and Politics:
Socialism, Nationalism and the Russian Jews, 1862–1917* (Cambridge, 1981), 509–41;
Oscar I. Janowsky, *The Jews and Minority Rights, 1898–1919* (New York, 1933),

If diplomacy was to continue at all, Wolf believed it had to be in the hands of those most capable and experienced at dealing with it, those who would continue to defend and improve Jewish rights abroad without jeopardizing them at home.[12] The war quickly proved that despite these disabling factors, Anglo-Jewish diplomacy was more necessary than ever.

Once it became apparent that the war, far from ending at Christmas as everybody had confidently predicted, was going to be a long-drawn-out affair, the likelihood of major changes, including territorial changes, increased. Already in August 1914, Grand Duke Nicholas, the Russian commander-in-chief in the west, had, in an attempt to maintain the loyalty of the Poles in whose territory much of the fighting was bound to take place, issued a manifesto in the name of his nephew the tsar promising them autonomy at the war's end.[13] This was bound to have major implications and long-term consequences for the Jews of the area, at between 10 and 15 per cent of the Polish population[14] the single largest concentration of Jews in the world, and not least because in recent years antisemitism had begun to play a major role in Polish politics. It had become a major plank in the nationalist campaigns of right-wing parties, leading after 1912 to a largely successful boycott of Jewish trade and commerce. At the outbreak of the war the boycott was still in operation.[15]

If the ultra-nationalist Poles were to be the inheritors of autonomy, or even independence, all the signs indicated that this would lead to an intensification of their anti-Jewish campaign. Even worse, if the Allies were to win the war, it was probable that German and Austrian Poland would be incorporated into the new, Russian-sponsored entity. A worst-case scenario might thus be a deterioration of the position of Jews in Congress Poland and a corresponding loss of citizenship rights for their brethren in Austrian Galicia and German Poznan and Pomerania.

161–90; Naomi C. Cohen, *Not Free to Desist: The American Jewish Committee, 1906–1966* (Philadelphia, 1972), 90–8; Cyrus Adler, *Jacob H. Schiff: His Life and Letters* (London, 1929), ii. 296–305.

[12] For his complaints on this score *vis-à-vis* the Workers' League see Wolf to Zangwill, 5 Oct. 1915, MWS 211 (unnumbered).
[13] Kenneth J. Calder, *Britain and the Origins of the New Europe, 1914–1918* (Cambridge, 1976), 22.
[14] This figure for 'Congress' Poland comes from Stephen Horak, *Poland and her National Minorities 1919–1939* (New York, 1961), 92.
[15] See Wolf's leader, 'The Boycott in Poland', *Darkest Russia*, 26 Feb. 1913.

42   *The Challenge of War*

Such departures might happen elsewhere too. In his early specula-
tions on likely consequences of the war, Wolf referred on a number of
occasions to a 'New Europe' arising; to the possibility of the Austrian
Empire becoming 'derelict'—even though in the early years of the war
this seemed rather remote—and to Romania, though in 1915 still
neutral, demanding her 'inevitable' share in its demise.[16] Romania's
recent record on the issue of citizens' rights was appallingly low. Jews
in Silistria and Dobrudja, formerly Bulgarian territories, had been deprived of such rights when Romania had appropriated them in 1913, in
the second Balkan War.[17] It was well known, moreover, that Romania
coveted Austrian Transylvania, which also had a significant Jewish
population. Romanian aggrandizement at the expense of Austria, like
Russian aggrandizement at the expense of that same empire in Galicia,
hardly boded well for Eastern Jewry.

There was, however, a saving grace. At the end of the war there
would inevitably be a peace congress. Both an independent Poland and
the territories granted to Romania, to say nothing of those gained by
force of arms in 1913, would have to be acknowledged and ratified by
international protocol. And this ratification, according to the precedent
set by the Congress of Berlin, would be conditional on the guarantee of
citizens' rights and religious liberty for all new subjects.

Far from meaning the Conjoint should cease existence, therefore,
the war demanded that it should preserve itself to meet wartime
exigencies and prepare itself for the presentation of the Jewish question at the peace. Indeed, the vast quantities of 'intelligence' and
information which would be needed in order to develop a coherent
picture of the requirements and aspirations of post-war Jewry demanded
that its apparatus be strengthened and extended.

This was not an easy task. The committee was not a permanent
bureau but a part-time group run by amateurs. Its budget was small. A
serious response would require the services of a full-time director, not
to say a permanent secretariat, if only to read and distil information
from the necessary foreign newspapers. All this would cost money.

It was a mixture of these requirements and the communal clamour
for change which finally forced the Conjoint, at the turn of 1914–15,
into something of an upheaval. To call it a revolution would be going
too far. Its structure was not changed, and nor was its essentially

---

[16] Wolf to FO, 23 Mar. 1915, FO 371/2448/16905.
[17] Wolf, *Notes*, 48–54.

aristocratic and limited membership. Indeed, the co-option in the following year of three additional leading Anglo-Jewish figures, Sir Leonard Lionel Cohen, Sir Matthew Nathan, and Lord Swaythling, served only to reinforce this fact.[18] Nor was the anomalous relationship of Wolf to the committee rectified, since his appointment as director was a purely private arrangement arrived at by Wolf himself in consultation with the Conjoint presidents and vice-president.[19]

Nevertheless, the January decision was significant inasmuch as the no-action policy was reversed and a special department was set up to put the committee on a wartime footing, with Wolf being paid to organize this on a full-time basis.[20] For the first time in its history, the Conjoint had a professional at its beck and call; but though he was in theory responsible to it, in practice he had been given *carte blanche* to do as he pleased. True, the committee continued to meet—more frequently, in fact, as the war revealed its surfeit of Jewish problems—but it did so now almost always to authorize decisions already made by Wolf, or to accept his future programme. Henceforth, the policy and methods of the Conjoint Committee bore his unmistakable stamp.

Wolf's tasks in early 1915, once he had brought the committee out of its torpor, were twofold: to forge links with the other 'allied' Jewish agencies for the eventual creation and co-ordination of a joint policy, and to receive the Foreign Office's sanction to do this. The first part proceeded almost naturally. By spring 1915, links with Paris, Rome, even Petrograd had been renewed. The last sent over a special envoy, Reuben Blank, to work with the Alliance and Conjoint, the supremacy of Wolf in the policy-making process being recognized in Blank's March message on behalf of the Alliance, 'L'Alliance suivra la politique du Conjoint Comité.'[21]

Getting the backing of the Foreign Office was both more vital and less easy. The Conjoint, in the final analysis, was totally dependent on the ministry for translating any policy it arrived at into actual peace

[18] CJC minutes, 17 May 1916. Cohen was president of the Board of Guardians, Nathan was vice-president of the AJA, and Swaything was president of the Federation of Synagogues. A fourth Anglo-Jewish representative, Lord Reading (Rufus Isaacs), the lord chief justice, declined co-option on the grounds of his official capacity as a government minister.
[19] Wolf to CJC presidents, 7 Jan. 1915, MWS 7475–8.
[20] Ibid.; Wolf to FO, encl. his credentials, 13 Jan. 1915, FO 371/2475/4800. It was surely not coincidental that Wolf's new post came hot on the heels of the loss of his full-time job at the *Daily Graphic*.
[21] Wolf to Blank, 2 Mar. 1915, MWS 468–52; Blank to Wolf, 7 Mar. 1915, C11/2/6.

diplomacy, a prerequisite which explains Wolf's strenuous efforts to work his way 'into the closest confidential relations with the Foreign Office'. Already in January 1915, he had got some way towards this: through the good offices of his friend Sir William Tyrrell and the outgoing permanent under-secretary, Francis Acland, he had gained access to Lancelot Oliphant, a Foreign Office official designated to deal with Jewish questions for the duration of the war.[22]

Gaining access was one thing but creating an ongoing relationship of mutual trust and understanding was quite another. Somehow Wolf had to convince the Foreign Office that he was not only *not* working for interests at odds with those of British diplomacy—a fact of which they were not likely to be easily persuaded given his past reputation—but actually pursuing a line responsibly in consonance with it.

But how could Wolf do this, except in negation? So long as Russia remained essential to the Allied war effort, pinning down the vast majority of German and Austrian troops in the east and forcing the Central Powers to fight on two fronts, British and French diplomats would do all in their power to maintain Russia as an ally. This by necessity precluded dissension on any aspects of her internal affairs, including Jewish ones. Certainly in these early months Wolf played down Conjoint interest in Russia proper. 'So far as the Russian question is concerned,' ran its very first wartime desiderata, which were sent to the Foreign Office for approval at the beginning of March, 'we see no prospect of any alleviation from the Peace Conference.'[23]

This did not mean he did nothing at all. He did initiate, through well-placed Jews in parliament and government—the MP Sir Charles Henry, and the head of the Local Government Board, Sir Herbert Samuel—a policy of 'private *viva-voce* representations' at high government level, the idea being to give Russia the hint, 'without giving offence . . . that the people of this country regard a solution of the Russian Jewish question on liberal lines as indispensable'.[24] However,

[22] Wolf, 'Notes on Conjoint Relations with the Foreign Office', n.d., MWS 25293–302; Wolf to CJC presidents, 7 Jan. 1915, MWS 7475–8; Wolf to Tyrrell, 18 Dec. 1914, C11/2/5. Lancelot Oliphant was the nephew of Laurance Oliphant, the Christian Zionist who had lent his support to a Russo-Jewish colonization scheme in Palestine.

[23] Draft letter to Bigart at the AIU, encl. with Wolf to Oliphant, 31 Mar. 1915, FO 371/2448/16905. Thus was initiated Wolf's wartime intention to submit all official correspondence to the FO's purview.

[24] CJC memo, 19 June 1915, encl. Report no. 1, n.d. (early 1915), MWS 4647–50; Wolf to Montefiore, 11 Feb. 1915, C11/2/6.

his actual proposals on this score proved very mild indeed; as suggested to Samuel in February, they amounted to no more than changes in the laws of domicile and education as they affected the families of Jewish soldiers and non-combatants in the war zone, to be effected not through British pressure but freely by the Russians themselves.[25] Rather, Wolf's focus was directed towards what the Foreign Office eventually might and could do: getting guarantees for the civil and religious liberties of populations in areas which had changed hands, and making such liberties a condition for the independence of a future Polish state, as indeed for the past territorial acquisitions of Romania.[26]

Romania, of course, being initially uninvolved in the war, still offered the opportunity in theory for Wolf legitimately to continue his campaigning and elicit Foreign Office aid for this. As he wrote to his friend and Romanian affairs adviser, David Mitrany of the London School of Economics, 'with regard to Russia we are bound to hold our tongues but so far no such obligation imposes itself upon us with regard to Rumania'.[27]

Romanian Jewish problems had not gone away with the advent of war. Indeed, increasing evidence from representatives of the official Romanian Jewish organization, L'Union des Juifs Indigènes, who had set themselves up in Switzerland to convey information to the Western Jewish organizations for its duration,[28] suggested that the war was aggravating them. In particular, a new law for the control of foreigners came into operation in early 1915, requiring individuals to provide documentary proof that they or their parents had been born in the country. Dr Labin, one of the Union's Swiss-based representatives, believed that as many 80 per cent of Romanian Jews were unable to furnish such documents, the result being expulsion, arrests, and an all-pervading sense of insecurity. The situation was of course worst in border areas. Dr Labin and his associates wanted the Conjoint and Alliance to do something about this; in the autumn of 1915 he proposed that they sponsor a pamphlet in French on the situation in Romania and initiate direct intervention with their respective

---

[25] Memo on interview with Samuel, 28 Feb. 1915, encl. with Wolf to Oliphant, 31 Mar. 1915, FO 371/2448/16905.

[26] Ibid., desiderata encl. in letter to Oliphant. For later desiderata see draft letter to Cyrus Adler (AJC), encl. with Wolf to FO, 7 Sept. 1915, FO 371/2446/155.

[27] Wolf to Mitrany, 16 Apr. 1915, C11/2/6.

[28] Union des Juifs Indigènes to AIU, n.d., Oct. 1915, MWS 19728–52.

foreign ministries as part of a renewed international effort to gain emancipation.[29]

Much of Wolf's pre-war work had been geared towards this goal, and nothing would have been more natural for him than to have taken up the request of the Union des Juifs with vigour. But he had in the meantime got wind of a new difficulty. The Allies and the Central Powers were by this time vying frantically for Romania's active support. The Allies were prepared to purchase this with vast territorial accessions at the expense of both Bulgaria, a party to the Central Powers after September 1915, and Austria-Hungary. As the contemporary historian Robert Seton-Watson noted, it was an increasingly common policy 'to pay almost any price for a new recruit so long as it was at the enemy's expense'.[30]

Wolf desired to see a British alliance with Romania no more than he had with Russia, and privately he said so.[31] But actively to encourage the Labin campaign carried with it the potential of wrecking the very negotiations which Britain and its allies were trying to pursue and hence an imputation of treason. Not for the last time, Wolf was faced with the appalling dilemma of whether to support something which he knew to be right and which held the opportunity for immediate Conjoint action, or whether to refrain in the hope that this would make a good impression on the Foreign Office and in the long term strengthen his hand with it.

Wolf's choice of the latter course proved him to be a ruthless pragmatist. He assured Labin in November 1915 that Romanian Jewish silence would not go unnoticed at the end of the war, that Allied policy was 'a policy of liberation for the oppressed', and its application to the Romanian Jews was 'stimulated by a fresh and special sense of obligation'.[32] The Foreign Office did in fact warmly approve this epistle,[33] and Wolf, perhaps employing the double-think which enabled him to stifle his public doubts on Allied post-war intentions, may in this way have seen light at the end of the tunnel. For Labin's people, however, the situation was less clear, and preparations for the pam-

[29] Labin to CJC, 28 Oct. 1915, MWS 19769–73.

[30] Seton-Watson, *Rumanians*, 490–1. The treaty was finally concluded on 17 May 1916.

[31] Wolf to Mrs Prothero (the wife of his Foreign Office friend, George Prothero), 28 Aug. 1916, MWS 4425.

[32] Draft letter to Labin encl. with Wolf to Oliphant, 4 Nov. 1915, FO 371/2443/165840.   [33] Oliphant minute, 19 Nov. 1915, ibid.

phlet continued. But Labin's resolve was matched by Wolf's own determination not to let the project proceed, and with Bigart's aid the publicity campaign was muzzled. Attempts to revitalize it in 1916 were met with the response that in the name of British and French civic duty it had to stop.[34]

These developments, undoubtedly viewed by the Romanian Jewish protagonists as a great betrayal (especially as they in effect terminated their chances of directly soliciting Allied support for the duration of the war), were an illustration of Wolf pursuing his diplomacy through negation. For Wolf, however, the problem was that with obstacles increasingly being stacked against him, he had to choose between evils simply in order to survive. He attempted to explain this to Montefiore in May 1916:

The whole of the ground we are treading on is very delicate and I do not want to give the Foreign Office any excuse for saying that we are creating unnecessary difficulties for them. The Rumanian business is of course very bad but the essential thing we have to concentrate on is the Russian question and in deviating from it, we always run the risk of compromising any chance we may have of dealing with it effectively. Rumania will not suffer in the long run, as a favourable solution of the Russian question will inevitably entail a similar solution to the Rumanian question. On the other hand, direct treatment of the Rumanian question at the present moment may end in our being rendered absolutely impotent on both questions.[35]

In the space of a year, Wolf had shifted his ground on the Russian question so much that far from being on the periphery of his vision it had become the very fulcrum upon which his wartime diplomacy at the Foreign Office depended. It now involved him in some highly complex and daring manœuvres, the stakes of which were partial if not total Russo-Jewish emancipation. This seemed to be strikingly at odds with his earlier self-imposed stricture not to pursue ventures which might

[34] Report on situation of Romanian Jews in CJC report no. 4, MWS 4967; Wolf to Bigart, 24 Nov. 1915, C11/2/7; Wolf to Stern, 4 July 1916, C11/2/9.
[35] Wolf to Montefiore, 30 May 1915, C11/2/8. This is the point at which I part company with Zosa Szajkowski who, in *Jews, Wars*, i. 41–92, argues that as Wolf's wartime career was essentially concerned with following the dictates of the British Foreign Office—a parallel being drawn here with the behaviour of German Jewish diplomats—it 'sacrificed the interests of the Jews of Eastern Europe'; see esp. *Jews, Wars*, i. 58–62, on the Romanian issue, 1915–16. My own conviction is that Wolf's official statements cannot always be taken at face value but were aspects of a subtle diplomacy in which the interests of Eastern Jewry remained paramount.

undermine his standing at the ministry. But in fact, the revitalization of the Russian Jewish question was not of his making.

Back in the autumn and winter of 1914/15, there had been considerable optimism among English and French Jewry that the Russians would solve their Jewish problem of their own volition. This would have ended the ambiguity they felt about the Russian alliance and spared them the guilt and embarrassment of having done nothing themselves for Russian Jews. There were propitious signs. Despite decades of persecution and discrimination, Russian Jews loyally rallied to the imperial cause in August 1914. N. M. Friedman, a Jewish deputy in the duma, made a much publicized speech promising that they would march to the battlefield 'shoulder to shoulder with all the peoples of Russia'. The *Jewish Chronicle* estimated that some two hundred thousand Jews were in fact with the Russian colours.[36] Such an effusive show of loyalty, it was widely believed, would be repaid with emancipation, and rumours were ripe soon after the manifesto granting autonomy to the Poles that a similar one would follow for the Jews.[37] The mood of expectancy was kept alive by Israel Zangwill's announcement, in *The Times*, soon after he had independently consulted the Foreign Office in September, that England looked upon the subject of Russian Jewish emancipation with sympathy.[38] Even though no manifesto appeared, the expectancy was kept buoyant by a new rationale. 'We believe', wrote Wolf in March 1915, 'that in view of the great liberal principles for which the Allies have been fighting, it will be impossible for the Russian government to maintain the present system.'[39]

The truth pointed in a drastically different direction. The tsar's government made no move to dismantle any of the aspects of the anti-Jewish regime; rather, the occupation of Austrian Eastern Galicia in late 1914 and the official proclamation by the reactionary Count Bobrinsky, its new governor, that it was to be Russified, suggested its extension.[40]

[36] Abramsky, *War*, 9–11; *JC* leader, 4 Sept. 1914. For the full text of Friedman's speech as reported in *Novoe vremya*, 9 Aug. 1914, see Frank Alfred Golder, *Documents of Russian History*, 1914–1917 (Gloucester, Mass., 1964), 36.
[37] *JC* leaders, 21 and 28 Aug. 1914.
[38] *JC* quoting Zangwill announcement, 18 Sept. 1914.
[39] Wolf to Oliphant, 31 Mar. 1915, encl. draft letter to Bigart, FO 371/2448/16905. The same sentiments are repeated in Wolf's report on the CJC–Zionist conference in FO 371/2448/51705.
[40] *The Cambridge History of Poland*, vol. ii, *1697–1935* (hereafter *CHP* ii), (Cambridge, 1951), 482. In fact, in April 1915, it was announced that Bobrinsky had sanctioned a scheme to deprive Galician Jews of citizens' rights and expropriate their property; see CJC report no. 1, MWS 4642–5.

Much more disturbing, particularly once the Germans had begun rolling back the Russian 'steamroller' advance into East Prussia at the battles of Tannenberg and Masurian Lakes in August and November 1914, were the reports that began filtering into London of a wave of virulently antisemitic acts. Perpetrated by the Russian military with the aid or connivance of right-wing Polish nationalists, their ulterior aim was to deflect culpability away from the tsarist army commanders on to the traditional scapegoat. By the summer of 1915, Wolf had accumulated, either directly from the Petrograd Bureau or indirectly through the censored Russian newspaper reports, a comprehensive dossier showing how this was being done.[41]

The Russian War Office and army commands were churning out proclamations, orders, and circulars castigating the Jews, whether Russian or Austrian subjects (as in the case of Galicia), as enemies of the Russian army; worse, they were a fifth column actively engaged in acts of espionage and sabotage on Germany's behalf. These were not charges levelled against isolated, particular individuals or people in particular zones, but were blanket charges aimed at indicting Jewry corporately. They were moreover so extensive as to cover every single aspect of army and civilian life. Jews were banned not only from working as trench diggers and engineers at the front, but from holding summer houses on the Baltic and Finnish coastline, hundreds of miles from the war zone. They were even banned from sanitary work in hospitals because they were believed to be spreading disease; more ludicrous still, an order issued on the southwest front in June 1915 warned against a German Jewish organization which was utilizing 'unclean' prostitutes in order to spread venereal disease throughout the army.[42]

Wolf had no doubt that these charges were fabrications. Jewish duma deputies had vigorously contested them, Friedman getting up in the duma in July 1915 and proclaiming them to be 'a revolting lie ... those who accuse others of treason are themselves guilty of treason'.[43] Nor were Friedman's charges lightly made. A team of enquiry led by Alexander Kerensky, the famous lawyer and Laborist deputy, only recently had investigated a charge of alleged corporate Jewish aid to, and sabotage on behalf of, German troops in the village of Kuzhi in Kovno province and had found it completely fraudulent. Yet the report

[41] CJC dossier, 'The Eastern War Zone: Illtreatment of the Jews', encl. with Wolf to Oliphant, 1 Sept. 1915, FO 371/2455/155.
[42] Ibid. see also CJC report no. 5, 27 Feb. 1916, MWS 4994–517. For lists of army orders affecting Jews see CJC report no. 9, 6 Feb. 1917, MWS 5629–63.
[43] Friedman's Duma speech, 26 July 1915, MWS 17783–92.

of these findings had not even been published. The Russian military censor seemed similarly biased: in late 1915, Wolf produced a Conjoint report showing that the censor was passing all anti-Jewish orders and calumnies while deleting any reference to Jewish bravery in the field or Russian–Jewish relations which might show the Jews in a good light.[44]

What was he to do? In 1907, in an introduction to *The Russian Government and the Massacres*, a book by the Russian exile E. Semenoff, Wolf had charged the tsarist government with responsibility for a whole spate of pogroms in the aftermath of the failed 1905 revolution.[45] Now, however, he could make no public statement to this effect without it rebounding on his head.[46] But the slur the charges cast on the good name and patriotic allegiance of Jews in Russia, and by implication everywhere, compelled him to do something. There was, moreover, by the summer of 1915 a further moral imperative.

A German breakthrough in the Carpathians in the late spring had led not just to the evacuation of Galicia but to the collapse of the Russian army along the entire front. German troops were able to occupy first Poland and then Lithuania, and by the summer they had advanced into the provinces of Kovno, Minsk, and Vilna. As the retreat of the Russian army gathered momentum so did the charges of Jewish conspiracy, justifying the army in holding hostages, perpetrating pogroms, and finally expelling Jews *en masse* from the extending war zone. By the autumn it was estimated that the war had ravaged three-quarters of the area of the Pale and had made half a million of its Jewish inhabitants refugees. Of these a majority left as a direct result of the expulsions,[47] fleeing east towards the Russian interior. In effect, the military had in a space of months caused the disintegration of an injustice which a hundred years of political and legal obstruction had sought to maintain. However, this process was not accompanied by any official alleviation of the disabilities and restrictions pertaining to the

---

[44] On the Kuzhi affair see Greenberg, *Jews*, 99–101. On the censorship issue see Wolf, 'Military Censorship and the Jewish Question', n.d., late 1915, MWS 13939–4038.

[45] See Wolf introd. to Semenoff, *Russian Government*. Historians today question the degree of government complicity in these events; see Hans Rogger, 'Jewish Policy of Late Tsarism: A Reappraisal', in his *Jewish Policies and Right Wing Politics in Imperial Russia* (London, 1985), 25–39.

[46] Chief Rabbi Hertz and Nahum Sokolov, the Russian Zionist, attempted to get Wolf to publish his documents in July 1915 but he argued that they would unleash 'a torrent of anti-semitic invective' and render his case at the Foreign Office impotent. See Wolf to Hertz, 27 July 1915, C11/2/6.

[47] See AJC, *The Jews in the Eastern War Zone* (New York, 1916).

Pale. On one level, all that had been achieved was a colossal human emergency, necessitating Anglo-Jewry, in response, to put aside its strictures on sectarianism in order to direct its energies into a massive relief effort.[48] On another, the Conjoint found itself forced by these events into a perilous confrontation with the Foreign Office.

Even to suggest that Britain's ally, Russia, was behaving in a less than fair way to its own subjects, let alone to accuse it of fabricating justifications for this ill-treatment, was to tread on dangerous ground indeed. The Foreign Office saw such claims as an attempt to cause friction between the government and its ally while at the same time deflecting attention from a concurrent British propaganda effort to publicize German brutality in Belgium.[49] Aware of this, when he first attempted to broach the subject of a 'cleverly arranged anti-Jewish campaign' in February 1915, Wolf did so more as an enquiry than a direct accusation. Moreover, when it came to presenting chapter and verse he used Leopold de Rothschild, who was on good personal terms with Sir Edward Grey, the foreign secretary, to do it.[50]

The seriousness of the charge did goad Grey to communicate Wolf's memorandum to Sir George Buchanan, the British ambassador in Petrograd, and thence to the Russian foreign minister, Sazonov.[51] The Foreign Office, however, was relieved to learn from Buchanan's reply the following month that 'there cannot be the slightest doubt that a very large number of Jews have been in German pay and have acted as spies during the campaigns in Poland. Nearly every Russian officer who returns from the front has stories to tell on the subject.' Buchanan backed up this statement with information obtained from Sazonov to the effect that Jewish soldiers volunteering for service in Polish hospitals 'had been carrying on a revolutionary propaganda among the wounded soldiers'.[52]

Though the ambassador could neither obtain material to disprove

---

[48] Petrograd Jewish Assistance of War Victims Committee to CJC, 6 Sept. 1915, MWS 7592–5: 'Relief of the war victims has become now the most important and urgent question of the Russian Jews which push in the shade all other problems.' For Anglo-Jewish 'Appeal for Russian Victims of the War' (note non-sectarian title), see *JC* 8 Oct. 1915.

[49] On the British propaganda effort see Z. A. B. Zeman, *A Diplomatic History of the First World War* (London, 1971), 166–9.

[50] Memo by Wolf encl. with Leopold de Rothschild to FO, 9 Feb. 1915, FO 371/2448/16905.

[51] Grey to Buchanan, 12 Feb. 1915, ibid. However, Wolf's name was deleted from the memo as presented to Sazonov, as it was known 'to give offence' in Petrograd.

[52] Buchanan to Grey, 10 Mar. 1915, FO 800/74 (Grey papers).

the massacres had taken place nor quote chapter and verse for Jewish culpability, it was his opinion that the case against the Jews was 'fully proved'. The Foreign Office accepted this statement at face value; indeed as far as they were concerned, there was little reason to doubt it. The Foreign Office did not need the anti-Jewish diatribes of *The Times* or *National Review* in order to be convinced that Jewry was 'internationally' Germanophile, though undoubtedly the 'informed' press helped reinforce their conviction. For many years prior to the war, His Majesty's diplomatic bags had been replete with the necessary evidence, the Constantinople embassy being particularly forthcoming. Since the Young Turk revolution of 1908, Sir Gerald Lowther, the ambassador, and J. H. Fitzmaurice, his chief dragoman, had been closely following the activities both of Salonikan crypto-Jews in the Committee of Union and Progress and German Zionists working in Palestine and Mesopotamia. They had come to the conclusion that it was all part of a German–Jewish plot to manœuvre Turkey into the Triple Alliance and so subvert British Near Eastern interests.[53]

With the outbreak of war, this focus shifted to Russia on the assumption that as Russian Jewry had been discriminated against by the regime, it would lend itself willingly to German designs. Certainly this seems to have been the latter's assumption. In August 1914, the German and Austrian high commands had drafted a proclamation inciting Russian Jews to insurrection in return for a promise of equal rights. The published version omitted the insurrectionary element, but official German and Austrian Jewish organizations had already opted to publicize this apparently emancipatory decree with their own leaflets.[54] Seeking to exploit German victories in the east for this end, Israel Bodenheimer, the prominent German Zionist, took a further initiative. Gathering together leading German Jews, both Zionist and assimilationist, he founded the Committee for the Liberation of Rus-

[53] See Lowther to Grey, 22 Aug. 1910, *BDOW* x, pt. I, no. I. Elie Kedourie's 'Young Turks, Freemasons and Jews', *Middle Eastern Studies*, 7 (1971), 89–104, is particularly acute in its assessment of Lowther and Fitzmaurice's pan-Judaic obsessions and fantasies. Crypto-Jews, or more correctly *Dönmeh*, were descendants of followers of the false messiah of Smyrna, Shabbatai Zevi, who had, under duress, converted to Islam in 1666. They remained an identifiable subgroup in Turkish society, esp. in Salonika. See Gershom Scholem, 'The Crypto-Jewish Sect of the *Dönmeh* (Sabbatians) in Turkey', in his *Messianic Idea in Judaism* (New York, 1971), 142–66.

[54] For German and German Jewish strategy on this score see esp. Egmont Zechlin, *Die Deutsche Politik und die Juden im Ersten Weltkreig* (Gottingen, 1969), 116–25; Fritz Fischer, *Germany's Aims in the First World War* (London, 1967), 141–3.

sian Jewry, which he hoped could work alongside the high commands. Though the committee's inflammatory name was quickly superseded by the more moderate-sounding Kommittee für den Osten, Bodenheimer made no bones about his belief that German victories would serve Jewish interests.[55] 'The Russian Jew has precisely the same interests as the German *reich* in a decisive German victory', he wrote to the influential American Jewish financier, Felix Warburg, while publicizing his conviction widely in the German press that 'Germanism would have strong support from the Jewish masses'.[56]

Quod erat demonstrandum. What the Foreign Office did not know or perhaps did not care to know was that the German and German Jewish efforts to incite the Polish Jewish masses had had little effect on the latter. This is not to deny that some Jews, like some Poles, might have been encouraged by German promises; the community, after all, was not monolithic in its political orientation, though the Foreign Office rarely understood this critical point. Likewise, the Foreign Office do not seem to have considered that as a vulnerable minority caught up in a war situation the best and possibly only course of collective action the Jews could adopt was that enshrined in the traditional rabbinic dictum *dina de-malkhuta dina*, 'the law of the land is law'. In practice this hardly provided a formula for Jews *qua* Jews challenging tsarist writ in Poland, either openly or covertly. On the contrary, it made for the classic Jewish response of continuing by all available means to avoid involvement in the struggle.

For Wolf, the dilemma was a truly agonizing one. To desist from denying the calumnies was to suggest that they were true; to carry on a campaign against them was to charge that Foreign Office personnel were lying.

In fact, what developed was a major battle of 'intelligence'. In September 1915, again through Leopold de Rothschild, Wolf presented the ministry with a 120-page dossier full of data, reports, interviews, and official circulars designed to scotch the anti-Jewish calumnies once and for all and prove them to be 'an anti-semitic invention . . . to distract attention from the former pro-Germanism of

---

[55] M. I. Bodenheimer, *Prelude to Israel: The Memoirs of M. I. Bodenheimer*, ed. Henriette Hannah Bodenheimer (New York, 1963), 237–8; Zechlin, *Deutsche Politik*, 126–38.

[56] Cited in Isaiah Friedman, *Germany, Turkey and Zionism, 1897–1918* (London, 1977), 205. See also Bodenheimer's *Kölnische Zeitung* article, n.d., 'The Jewish Language is a German Dialect', encl. in HO 45/10836/330094.

its authors'.[57] The Foreign Office replied with counter-information from its on-the-spot 'experts'.

In this way the controversy Wolf had got himself into in the first years of the Anglo-Russian *entente*, but which he had been strenuously trying to avoid since the beginning of the war, was freshly ignited. Professor Bernard Pares, an old sparring partner from those years[58] who was acting as a liaison between the English and Russian press during the war, personally visited Oliphant at the Foreign Office in June to assure him that the accusations against the Jews were quite correct, as were the actions of the Russian military in response to them. The point was soon endorsed by Stanley Washburn, *The Times* correspondent in Warsaw.[59] In January 1916 General Alfred Knox, the British military attaché with the Russian high command, waded in with his own comments. The German spy system in Poland, he unhesitatingly asserted, was Jewish-run. This 'necessitated' Jewish expulsion, though he went on to assure the Foreign Office, as had Washburn and Pares before him, that there had been few actual 'incidents' involving ill treatment of the Jews in the process.[60]

The ministry seems to have been delighted by this riposte, several of the more senior officials, including their 'chief', Sir Arthur Nicolson, wishing to use it 'to knock the anti-Jewish calumnies'. On 4 January 1916, Wolf indeed received a curt rebuttal of his case—though later the same day a telephone call from Oliphant informed him that it had been sent in error and should be regarded as cancelled. 'I conclude', he wrote, 'that the Foreign Office do not regard the report as a satisfactory confutation of our allegations and as a matter of fact it is not.'[61]

Wolf had won a minor victory, but the Foreign Office conviction that Jewry was pro-German remained unchanged; moreover there was

[57] Wolf to Oliphant, 1 Sept. 1915, 'Eastern War Zone', FO 371/2455/155.

[58] See Wolf, 'The Tsar's Visit, Liberals and Russia', *Morning Leader*, 30 June 1909; Pares's reply, 3 Aug., ibid., and Wolf's rejoinder, 4 Aug. 1909, ibid. Wolf's comment on Pares was that he was a 'sort of Cook's man' for 'official' visits to Russia; *Darkest Russia* leader, 17 Jan. 1912.

[59] Pares–Oliphant interview, FO 371/2455/155; Pares to FO, 22 June 1915, ibid. Washburn to Buchanan, 16 July, encl. with Buchanan to Cecil, 6 Aug. 1915, ibid.

[60] Knox to Oliphant, 10 Feb. 1916, FO 371/2744/4039. Knox's virulently antisemitic views resurfaced in the Russian Civil War; see Richard M. Ullman, *Britain and the Russian Civil War, November 1918–February 1920* (Princeton, 1968), 30, 113–14.

[61] A. Nicolson and H. O'Beirne minutes, 23 Feb. 1916, FO 371/2744/4039; De Bunsen to Wolf, 3 Mar. 1916, ibid.; CJC report no. 6, 17 May 1916, MWS 4451–2.

no sympathy for his subsequent reports of further pogrom rumours.[62] More importantly, by opening up old frictions and resentments the dispute was bound to have a long-term effect on his wartime relationship with the ministry.

Ironically, the avowed German–Jewish conjunction was hardly borne out in the relationship between Bodenheimer's organization and either the German Eastern Command or the German Foreign Office, the Auswärtiges Amt. True, joint projects were discussed, but the intimacy to which Bodenheimer aspired evaporated quickly once the Auswärtiges Amt realized that the Jews were not the key to power relationships in Poland.[63] On the other hand, Bodenheimer did at least enter into high-level negotiations; Wolf, by contrast, was clearly *persona non grata* at the Foreign Office. He was allowed access, but only grudgingly; and in late 1917, when expert departments were being set up, such as the Political Intelligence Department to which he would have been ideally suited, his application for a position was rejected. Other Jews, notably the Polish-born historian Lewis Namier, were admitted. Not Wolf, however. Hardinge's appraisal was blunt: 'not the sort of man who should be employed here'.[64]

The problem, of course, was not Wolf but the lack of synonymity in the early years of the war between British and Conjoint interests. Wolf had dextrously tried to avoid bringing attention to this by maintaining silence, biding his time until a consonance could be re-established. But wartime events outpaced him, rendering conflict unavoidable and seemingly irreversible.

[62] See H. O'Beirne minute, 13 Apr. 1916, FO 371/2744/4039; Barclay (Bucharest) to FO, 1 Dec. 1916, FO 371/2877/423608, has an HMG diplomat's typically hostile view on the Jews.
[63] See Zechlin, *Deutsche Politik*, esp. 125–7, 144–54.
[64] Wolf to Drummond, 8 Oct. 1917, FO 371/3085/175961, encl. offer of service and cv., and Oliphant quoting Hardinge comment, n.d. For further comments on embarrassment caused to FO by Wolf see Oliphant to FO, 27 May 1918, and Clark to FO, 6 Dec. 1918, FO 371/3396/13513. Szajkowski's suggestion that Wolf became 'an official adviser to the Foreign Office' (*Jews, Wars*, i. 62) is incorrect.

3
The Power of the Jews

A T the beginning of 1915, the Foreign Office suspended communication with *The Times*. Wickham Steed had written some highly contentious leaders in which he argued that Turkey's dramatic adhesion to the cause of the Central Powers in the previous November had had much to do with the misreading and mishandling of the situation by Britain's ambassador in Constantinople, Sir Louis Mallet.[1] The banishment, it was true, was only temporary. However, if the most important and powerful paper in the country, one which traditionally had excellent relations with the ministry,[2] could incur its wrath in this way, what chance had a weak, out of favour pressure group such as Wolf's?

By the yardstick of the *Times* case, Wolf's criticism of the Russian expulsions should have seen him to the door for good. Yet the Conjoint survived, and went on showing a remarkable capacity for survival. With so many factors working against it, this resilience requires explanation. Some of the answer paradoxically lies not so much with any intrinsic ability on Wolf's part but rather in the ministry's perception, or rather misperception, about what the Conjoint, as a Jewish body, represented.

As has already been suggested, the Foreign Office, like *The Times*, held firmly to certain assumptions about the nature of Jews in general. Few officials doubted that Jews were pro-German. On the other hand, the avowed Jewish corporate powerfulness, expressed through an ability to control and manipulate finance and large sections of the press, made them worthy of both awe and respect.

From the Jewish point of view, that this 'power' was wholly illusory had been amply demonstrated by their total inability to make Romania keep its 1878 promises on Jewish emancipation, despite conscious attempts 'to mobilise the press, stock exchanges and the politicians to

---

[1] *The Times, The History of the Times, 1912–1948*, vol. i, *1912–1920* (hereafter *History of the Times*, i), (London, 1950), 234–9.
[2] Steiner, *Foreign Office*, 190–1.

this effect'.[3] Likewise, although the American Jewish banker Jacob Schiff had certainly attempted to use loans to the Japanese at the time of the Russo-Japanese war in 1904 as a political instrument against Russian persecution, and although the English Rothschilds had tried to disrupt Britain's post-1906 moves towards *entente* by boycotting its Russian loan, their efforts to persuade other Jewish bankers to do likewise had dismally miscarried—and this despite Wolf's articles in the *Graphic* and *Darkest Russia* casting doubt on the safety of Russian investment. Indeed, subscribers to the loan included both the French Rothschilds and Bleichröder, the German financier. Jewish banking houses clearly did not have a Jewish political policy in common. Nor can Jewish financial pressure, where it was attempted, in any way be shown to have alleviated the pre-war condition of Russian Jewry. With *The Times* after 1912 producing a special Russian supplement geared towards commerce, and with English investment in the country steadily growing, Wolf was forced to conclude that 'as long as Russia is content to pay the price of dispensing with Rothschild's help in the shape of high interest and low price we are helpless'.[4] Yet the fact that Jewish bankers and journalists had acted as they had done only reinforced the popular myth, fully shared by the Foreign Office, that Jews could and would use their 'power' to channel political developments in their own favour.

The war gave a new thrust to this conviction. When it had begun in 1914, it was, despite the early Japanese involvement, still very much a European affair. But how long could this go on? Hemmed in by military stalemate, unable despite strenuous efforts to break it decisively, both belligerent blocs found themselves squandering their manpower, their industrial capacity, and their financial reserves. The obvious outcome under such circumstances might have been a search for a negotiated peace. But as the war intensified, as states staked their very existence on winning it, this option in itself became more remote. Instead, the belligerents joined battle, essentially a propaganda battle, to gain the adhesion of the one power that could tilt the balance: the United States.

[3] Stern, *Gold*, 392. For similar attempts to put financial pressure on the Romanians by drawing foreign investors' attention to the Romanian government's inability to pay back its borrowings see also *JC* 'Rumanian Bulletin' supplement, 15 Feb. 1903.

[4] Wolf to Montefiore, 9 Sept. 1912, MWS 2920–1. See also Wolf, 'Notes', *Darkest Russia*, 3 Jan. 1912; A. J. Sherman, 'German-Jewish Bankers in World Politics: The Financing of the Russo-Japanese War', *Leo Baeck Year Book*, 28 (1983), 59–73; Aronsfeld, 'Jewish Bankers', 89–92; Roth, 'Court Jews', 363–4.

In 1914, there were some three million Jews living in the United States. Most were recently arrived immigrants, or children of immigrants, living in desperately poor conditions in the great cities of the eastern seaboard. Culturally and socially linked to the Eastern European Jewish world and hence to fellow Jewish immigrants in London's East End or the Paris Pletzl, they had nevertheless been preceded to America by a Jewish community primarily of German origin. By 1914, this community was not only well established and acculturated but also, through some of its members, highly conspicuous in America's finance, press, and politics.[5] Indeed, three years earlier, they had shown themselves apparently capable of wielding considerable political clout by having the American Senate abrogate the commerce treaty with Russia on account of its discrimination against American Jewish passport holders. However, the ultimate aim of their campaign—to force Russia to review its discriminatory anti-Jewish policy—was very far from realized. On the contrary, it seems to have caused the Russian authorities to be more intractable than ever, exacerbating Russo-American relations in the process.[6] As elsewhere, however, the super-ficial success of the American Jews was well noted.

So too was their anti-Russian animus, an animus that was inter-preted by Sir Cecil Spring-Rice, Britain's ambassador in Washington (and perhaps significantly, a former ambassador in Constantinople), as proof of their pro-German sentiment. As early as November 1914 he was reporting to London that 'openly pro-German' Jewish bankers were 'toiling in a solid phalanx' to compass British destruction, a project, he claimed, they were able to undertake by manipulating American financial policy in an overtly German direction.[7] Spring-Rice singled out two names for particular mention: Paul Warburg, at the Federal Reserve Board; and Jacob Schiff, the senior partner in the banking firm of Kuhn, Loeb, and Schiff.

It was no secret that both men had German origins and connec-tions.[8] It was likewise no secret that Schiff had refused to participate in

[5] See Abraham G. Duker, 'Jews in the World War: A Brief Historical Sketch', *Contemporary Jewish Record*, 2 (1933), 7; Zechlin, *Deutsche Politik*, 460–4.

[6] Naomi Cohen, *Not Free*, 54–60; Gary D. Best, *To Free a People: American Jewish Leaders and the Jewish Problem in Eastern Europe, 1880–1914* (Westport, 1982), 190–200.

[7] See letter to Chirol and Grey, 13 Nov. 1914 in *The Letters and Friendships of Sir Cecil Spring-Rice*, ed. Stephen Gwynne (Boston, 1929), ii. 242–6.

[8] David Farrar, *The Warburgs* (London, 1975), 85–6; Adler, *Schiff*, ii. 181–200. The two 'dynasties' were connected by marriage.

the floating of a large American pro-Allied loan, and this despite the fact that the Anglo-French mission which arrived in New York in September 1915 to negotiate it was itself led by two Jews: Rufus Isaacs, later Lord Reading, and Octave Homberg, from the French Finance Ministry.[9] However, Schiff had not shown hostility to the Allied cause *per se*; he had offered to contribute to the loan if it only involved Britain and France, and promised to extend it to Russia as soon as the anti-Jewish laws began to be lifted. In the event, the abstention of Schiff's banking house and that of Speyer did not prevent the loan being raised by the pro-British banking house of Morgan; nor, moreover, did it prevent a personal contribution to it by Jacob Schiff's own partners, Otto Kahn and Mortimer Schiff.[10]

Curiously, though the mission helped pave the way for American finance and industry to be harnessed more firmly to the Allied cause[11]— and this a full year and a half before America ended its wartime neutrality —Spring-Rice was not alone in continuing to focus almost to the point of obsession on the importance of Jewish involvement in the American money market. More crucially, this involvement was now linked in the Foreign Office mind with the condition of the Russian Jews. 'It might be pointed out to the Russian Minister of Finance', wrote Lord Robert Cecil, its parliamentary under-secretary in January 1916, 'that antisemitism makes Jewish financial assistance to the Allies very difficult to obtain and this war may well turn on finance.'[12]

Lucien Wolf certainly did not agree with this assessment of the situation in its assumptions about either the importance of Jewish finance or the supposed pro-German proclivities of those in whose hands it was. Paradoxically, though, the Foreign Office's ideas gave him a bargaining counter which he would have been remiss not to exploit. If the Allies, and particularly the Russians, needed American Jewish finance, the only way they might procure it, Wolf could argue,

[9] Zeman, *Diplomatic History*, 173; 'Grande Bretagne, Emprunt Franco-Anglais aux État-Unis', 1915, MAE Guerre 1914–18, file 1464.

[10] Homberg to Ribot, 25 June 1916, MAE Guerre 1914–18, file 1464, fo. 156. On Sir Ernest Cassel's involvement in the mission in a private capacity to try and convince Schiff to participate in the loan, see Gueynard to Ribot, 24 Sept. 1915, fo. 60, ibid. The final sum raised—£100 million—was to be spent in the USA.

[11] Zeman, *Diplomatic History*, 173–4.

[12] Spring-Rice to Grey, 12 Feb. 1916, in *Spring Rice*, ed. Gwynne, ii. 311–14; Cecil minute, 6 Jan. 1916, FO 371/2744/4039. Cf. Cecil minute, 15 Feb. 1916, FO 371/1600/14562: 'Personally I think it is most regrettable that in view of the vast financial influence of the Jews, the Russians make so little effort to conciliate them.'

was by putting their house in order. The problem for the Foreign Office revolved around whether the overriding need to finance the war effort could ever outweigh the overriding principle of not antagonizing the Russians. In one sense, the summer of 1915 seemed a highly inappropriate time to consider such arguments. Russia was reeling from major defeats at Gorlice and Tarnow. The Central Powers had taken Poland and Lithuania. Rumours were rife that a separate peace was about to be negotiated.[13] Such circumstances required from Russia's allies not dissension but a clear show of solidarity.

In another sense, the time was in fact ripe for representations. The tsarist government responded to the calamities that befell it by replacing some of its more reactionary and incompetent ministers by more realistic men who recognized that changes might have to be initiated in order to see Russia win through. The minutes of the Russian Council of Ministers from this period in no way suggest that Russian Jews were suddenly seen in a more benevolent light; indeed, the old neuroses about the Jewish threat to the state were as openly voiced as before.[14] But the idea had clearly become implanted that if American finance was to be won, finance which would save Russia from economic exhaustion, the Jewish position would have to be alleviated—at least to some degree.

The *viva voce* representations initiated by Wolf in the spring of 1915 had much to do with this development. Through Leopold de Rothschild, perhaps also through Herbert Samuel, whom Wolf saw in February, influential government ministers, including Lord Crewe and Lord Lansdowne and, more importantly still, the war secretary, Lord Kitchener, were suitably briefed. They in turn impressed the point on the Russian finance minister, P. L. Bark, in his spring and summer visits to the West, in search of economic aid.[15] Eventually the message got back to the Russian Council of Ministers. At the meeting of 6 August, Bark, besides making much of 'the all powerful Leopold de Rothschild', observed: 'It is characteristic that Kitchener has re-

---

[13] Zeman, *Diplomatic History*, 84–8.

[14] *Prologue to Revolution: Notes of A. N. Iakhantov on Secret Meetings of the Council of Ministers, 1915*, ed. Michael Cherniavsky (hereafter *Prologue*), (Englewood Cliffs, NJ, 1915), 8–9; meetings of 4 and 6 Aug. 1915, ibid. 56–72. See also Raymond Pearson, *The Russian Moderates and the Crisis of Tsarism, 1914–1917* (London, 1977), 39–42.

[15] Reported by Wolf to Alexander, 3 June 1915, C11/2/6; CJC report no. 1, 1915, MWS 4643–5.

peated constantly that one of the most important conditions for the success of the war, is the amelioration of the lot of the Jews in Russia.'[16]

The Council on this occasion went on to debate concessions in response to the expulsions from the Pale, believing, significantly, that in doing so it was bowing to Jewish financial pressure. 'The knife is at the throat and there is nothing to be done,' lamented Alexander Krivoshein, the minister of agriculture, 'We are helpless, for the money is in Jewish hands,' chimed in Prince Scherbatov, the interior minister. Bark summed up, recalling his visits to the West: 'It is being openly hinted to me that we will not be able to extricate ourselves from our financial difficulties until some demonstrative steps are taken on the Jewish question . . . either we make some concessions to the Jews and re-establish our credit so that we can obtain the means to continue the war, or . . .'. Bark had no alternative solution.[17]

Pressure on the Council of Ministers, in the form of discreet private representations on the condition of the Jews in Russia, had come from another source too: the Foreign Office via Buchanan, their ambassador in Petrograd.[18] Here again, Wolf, through his intervention at the Ministry, was responsible. But in doing so, he himself had faced a dilemma. To have overplayed the financial card would have been to fall into the trap of agreeing that Jews did really wield such power, a confession which despite being untrue posed the danger of persecution for the Jews in the future. Wolf needed an alternative way of putting his case. Fortunately, there was another area of Foreign Office anxiety involving the Russian Jewish question which he could quite legitimately exploit.

Since the beginning of the war, the British had enjoyed an inbuilt advantage over the Germans in the propaganda war to win over neutral America: they spoke the same language, enjoyed a common cultural tradition, and, moreover, had control of the transatlantic cables. Through Charles Masterman's secret propaganda headquarters at Wellington House in London, the British attempted to exploit this situation to the full. Thus, the sinking of the Cunard liner *Lusitania* by a German U-boat in May 1915, an incident in which many Americans lost their lives, was used as an excuse to produce vast quantities of

[16] *Prologue*, 71–2.
[17] Meetings of 4 and 6 Aug., ibid. 60–1, 68. See also Rogger's comments on these meetings in *Jewish Politics*, 101–5.
[18] FO to Buchanan, 30 June 1915, FO 371/2445/155.

bloodcurdling material for American consumption alleging that the Germans had committed much worse atrocities in Belgium.[19] However, reports of expulsions and atrocities perpetrated by the Russian army against the Jews, as we have seen, cut right across this picture, playing into the hands of the German propaganda team in the United States led by Dr Dernburg in New York and assisted by Count Bernstorff, the German ambassador in Washington. They threatened in so doing not only to confirm American Jews in their worst fears but to infect much wider sections of American society with an anti-Russian animus.[20]

The effects of the expulsions on the American and American Jewish press were particularly striking. Whereas British censorship prevented publication of the atrocity stories in Britain, American papers were able to carry extensive reports. In March 1915, two-thirds of American Jewish papers signed a manifesto condeming the export of arms to Russia. In July it was much publicized that Hermann Bernstein, the influential journalist on the New York Yiddish paper *Der Tog*, had received the blessing of President Woodrow Wilson for his forthcoming trip to Europe to look into the truth of the atrocity stories. Not surprisingly, his articles passed a damning, accusatory verdict, one which, Wolf noted to the Foreign Office, would be considered in the United States as 'impartial'.[21]

Though the Foreign Office's wartime news department under Lord Eustace Percy, whose main task was the dissemination of pro-Allied propaganda in neutral countries, displayed some anxiety over these developments—seriously considering suggestions from distinguished American Jews, for instance, to alleviate the bad propaganda effects of the expulsions through Russian reform[22]—the ministry did not get unduly nervous. Thus, Cecil, a Foreign Office minister particularly bound up with the importance of the propaganda war, wrote to Buchanan of the reported pogroms in July 1915 'they are doubtless untrue or very greatly exaggerated and if we could be assured that such occurrences as have taken place, were due to some local or temporary cause which

[19] Zeman, *Diplomatic History*, 166–9.   [20] Ibid. 169.
[21] Percy minute, 14 Apr. 1915, FO 371/2488/16905; Wilson to Bernstein, 14 July 1915, encl. in AIU, Paris section, France, 11 D *bis* 36; Wolf to Cecil, 13 Aug. 1915, C11/2/7. On general American Jewish reaction to pogroms and expulsions see Szajkowski, *Jews, Wars*, i. 26–7, 65–7.
[22] Gottheil and Leon letters encl. with Spring-Rice to FO, 27 Mar. 1915, FO 371/2448/16905; Percy minute, 14 Apr. 1915, ibid.

is not likely to recur, that would probably, very largely meet the case'.[23] Bernstein's articles were met with similar scepticism. Attempts were made to get contradictory articles written, and even leading English Jews were considered for this role. Claude Montefiore, for instance, was to be inveigled in this way, his brief being to provide a more 'truthful' picture of Jewish conditions in Russia.[24]

The problem was that though Buchanan and other British 'intelligence' sources in Russia denied that the pogroms had occurred, they could produce no solid information to the contrary. By contrast, even if the Foreign Office chose to look askance at the substantial evidence Wolf had placed in their files, they could not ignore the efficacy of his argument that the effect the pogroms were having on the United States was doing and would continue to do 'infinite harm to the Allied cause'.[25]

In this way, despite the Foreign Office's animosity towards him for daring to contradict their assessment of the Russian situation, Wolf was able to keep his lines to them open. Indeed, in August he for the first time obtained an interview with Cecil, enabling him to take Cecil through material proving that the pogroms and expulsions had occurred—important duma deputies including Kerensky, Milyukov, and Tscheidze had recently denounced the Russian military's responsiblity for them—and emphasize how these events were playing into the hands of the Central Powers.[26]

Although Wolf here as elsewhere hinted at the political influence of the Jews in the United States, he left it entirely to Cecil and his colleagues to decide whether they wished to make a connection between the expulsions and the supposed political and financial pull of American Jewry in relation to the war. That Cecil certainly seems to have done this is evinced by his willingness, even before the Russian Council of Ministers' concessions of 3 September had been publicly announced, to contact Leopold de Rothschild with the news that 'the Russian government are alive to the importance of the (Jewish) question and are going to take it seriously in hand'.[27]

[23] Cecil to Buchanan, 27 June 1915, FO 371/2445/155.
[24] FO to Buchanan, 30 June 1915, ibid; Percy minute, 14 Apr. 1915, FO 371/2448/16905.
[25] Wolf to Cecil, 13 Aug. 1915, C11/2/7.
[26] Ibid. For Tscheidze and Dzubinsky's interpolations in the duma on the expulsions see also MWS 3862–9.
[27] Cecil to Leopold de Rothschild, 3 Sept. 1915, MWS 3526.

This 'seriously taking in hand' did not amount to Jewish emancipation, merely to permission for Jews who had been made refugees to
reside temporarily in towns beyond the Pale—with certain exceptions,
Petrograd and Moscow among them—and a further announcement
allowing them wider entry into gymnasia and universities. However,
the Pale had not been legally dismantled; although residence outside it
was now permitted by emergency ministerial decree, it could theoretically
be revoked at any time. Nor did the Council of Ministers see these
measures as the first stage in a programme of more sweeping reforms,
but rather as a deal between them and the Russian Jewish leaders in
return for the opening up of Jewish credit outside Russia, their entrepreneurial skills within it, and the use of their influence in 'quieting
down' the supposedly revolutionary Jewish masses.[28]

Nevertheless, the decrees of 3 September marked the first breach in
the tsarist anti-Jewish regime for more than thirty years and gave Wolf
and his committee a welcome fillip that fully justified in his mind its
continued existence. He wrote to Montefiore soon after: 'I suspected
all along that the Foreign Office had made energetic representations to
Petrograd after my interview with Lord Robert Cecil . . . looking back
and in the light of our present experience I can trace at least four of
these representations since the beginning of the war.'[29] On the role of
the Conjoint in these developments he was even more emphatic to
Emile Meyerson at the Alliance: 'the Conjoint has been very active
lately and I think I may say that the recent changes in Russia are in a
large measure due to it'. Wolf had further reason to be pleased when, a
month later, the Russian foreign minister, Count Sazonov, responded
to a further representation from Buchanan on the state of the Jews in
Russia by issuing a forceful denial of the charges of antisemitism. Even
though, as Wolf pointed out to Lord Rothschild's secretary, Archer,
there was little substance in the denial, 'it shows the anxiety of the
Russian government to shake itself free of the reproach of anti-
semitism'.[30]

Combined with developments in Russia in a broader sense, this
enabled Wolf to shake off much of the pessimism and frustration of the

[28] On Scherbatov's speech of 4 Aug. 1915 on the meaning of the decree see *Prologue*, 57–9.
[29] Wolf to Montefiore, 7 Sept. 1915, C11/2/7.
[30] Wolf to Meyerson, 16 Sept. 1915, C11/2/7. On Buchanan's representation and Sazonov's denial see Paleologue to Delcassé, 15 Sept. 1915, MAE Guerre 1914–18, file 1197, fos 99–101; Wolf to Archer, 7 Oct. 1915, encl. text of *démenti*, C11/3/1/1.

5

first year of his wartime work and to prepare at last a diplomacy which was positive in its content and direction. Russia had gone to war in July 1914 in a feverish wave of patriotic enthusiasm. This enthusiasm had overridden the dissent of liberals and radicals both within the duma and outside of it and for a time brought together tsar and country, reactionaries and moderates, in a *union sacrée*.[31] As the difficulties of running a semi-backward country for the promotion of a modern war effort increased, and as reverse followed reverse in the field, unrest grew, especially among the middle classes: unrest at the inability of the system to put itself on a war-footing, in an industrial-economic sense; unrest at the inefficiency and corruption of state bureaucrats; unrest at the incompetence of the army commanders. Even before the military disaster of the summer of 1915, therefore, the regime was having to make some concessions simply in order to calm disquiet. One result was the initiation at a local level of War Industries Committees, which gave industrialists and business people a first opportunity to participate in the adaptation of Russian industry to the war effort.[32] However, these concessions did not appease the country. On the contrary, as the regime showed itself increasingly incapable of adapting to the reality of war—of halting catastrophic price rises, food and munitions shortages, or declining productivity—the industrial community became a main focus of discontent, reviving and intensifying demands for not just economic but wider political change.

Throughout the summer of 1915, Wolf kept abreast of these developments via the Jewish Political Bureau in Petrograd and was able in his memoranda and dossiers to bring attention to the centrality of the Jewish theme running through them. Before the war, in *Darkest Russia*, he and his fellow-contributors had gone to considerable lengths to show how economic and other restrictions and disabilities imposed on Jews were holding up Russia's industrial development and indeed causing its stagnation.[33] A healthy, prosperous Russia, ran the message, was one where Jews were free to bring their particular entrepreneurial skills into play, a message Wolf was able to back up

[31] Pearson, *Russian Moderates*, 12–17.
[32] For War Industries Committees see Norman Stone, *The Eastern Front, 1914–1917* (London, 1975), 201–5.
[33] See Alexinsky, 'The Economics of Anti-Semitism', *Darkest Russia*, 27 July, 13 Aug., and 20 Aug. 1913; R. Blank, 'The Part Played by the Jewish Population in the Economic Life of Russia', n.d., 1908, MWS 12902–24.

with material from pre-war congresses of Russian trade and commerce supporting this contention. Now Wolf was able once again to focus on these congresses—the conference of *zemstvos* in early April, that of Russian industry and commerce later in the month, the conference of the Petrograd War Industries Committees in August—all of which called for the relaxation of Jewish disabilities as essential for putting Russia on a secure war-footing.[34]

In calling for Jewish reforms in Russia, Wolf could therefore argue that he was proposing neither more nor less than the most realistic elements in Russian society, an argument he could extend by pointing to formerly hostile antisemites such as Bobrinsky, Gurko, and Savenko in the duma who according to Reuben Blank were now demanding as a genuine necessity of state a policy of Jewish *revendications*.[35] By the same token, in contending as he did in June that the expulsions of the Jews were absorbing the army to the detriment of war operations, and hence contributing not only to the military defeat but also to untold chaos and disruption beyond the war zone, Wolf could claim that he was simply reflecting the anxieties of patriotic Russians who wished only to see their country win through.[36]

What happened as a result of the summer catastrophe in fact lived up to Wolf's best expectations. The most reactionary and antisemitic ministers and generals—the ones whom Wolf and Blank contended were the real enemies of Russia—were dismissed or transferred, and a new 'liberal phase', which saw among other things the decree of 3 September, was initiated.[37] Liberal the new government was not, but its willingness to build a bridge to the more moderate elements in the duma, grouped together in August in an alliance which became known as the Progressive Bloc, did at least present the potentiality for a further period of real liberalization. It was the formation of the Progressive Bloc which was in fact the cornerstone of Wolf's new optimism.

At the time of the first Russian revolution of 1905, Wolf still regarded the duma—the parliamentary machinery set up by the tsarist

[34] CJC dossier 'The Eastern War Zone', encl. with Wolf to FO, 1 Sept. 1915, FO 371/2445/155.
[35] Blank memo to AIU, 25 Oct. 1915, MWS 13649–51.
[36] CJC memo of 3 June 1915, handed in by Wolf and Blank at an interview with Oliphant, 2 July 1915, FO 371/2445/155. See also Wolf, 'The Russian Refugee Situation', 23 Feb. 1915, MWS 5044–62.
[37] Pearson, *Russian Moderates*, 39–42. The deposed ministers included Maklakov, the interior minister and Sukhomlinov, the War Office chief. Ianushkevich, the chief-of-staff in the west, was transferred to the Caucasus front.

regime—as a sop to the liberals that lacked any real political power or prerogative, and preferred to put his confidence in the revolutionaries who demanded a proper constituent assembly.[38] Once the revolution had failed and the opportunity for an alternative focus of opposition had ceased to exist, Wolf joined Russian Jewish leaders—he was by 1906 in touch with the Jewish Political Bureau in Petrograd[39]—in pinning his main hope for Russian Jewish emancipation on that body. Mostly because the duma was emasculated by the regime, this did not arise; but one of the parties represented in the duma—the Constitutional Democrats, otherwise known as the Cadets, who wanted parliamentary development in Russia along Western lines—did recognize it as an essential prerequisite for more general reform. Consequently it had the active allegiance of the vast majority of the Russian Jewish middle class.[40]

It was Paul Milyukov, the leader of the Cadets, who in August 1915 initiated developments leading towards the Bloc's formation and gave political expression to the public mood by advocating a ministry 'enjoying the confidence of the country'. It consequently grouped together not only moderate Cadets and Progressivists but more conservative Octobrists and even some Nationalists. The Bloc went on to formulate a legislative programme incorporating what it saw as the most urgent national requirements.

The programme's horizons were wide, including an amnesty for political prisoners and exiles, national rights for Poles and other groups, restitution of trade union rights, and demands for greater public involvement in the war effort. Point 5 of the programme called for 'the gradual reexamination of the restrictive laws and administrative regulations pertaining to the Jews'.[41]

This proposal, the result of Milyukov's convoluted manœuvres to ensure an understanding with the more conservative elements within

[38] See e.g. *Russian Correspondence*, 4 Oct. 1905, strongly endorsing the Bund's boycott of the October Manifesto constitution as a 'People's Representative Assembly without the People'.

[39] Mowschowitch's notes for Wolf Memorial Lecture, n.d., *c.* 1930 MWS 143–56; *JC* 22 June 1906, reporting telegrams from the Jewish duma group (Vinaver, Braudo, Sliosberg, *et al.*) to Wolf on Bialystok pogroms. For Wolf's support of constitutional reform programme in Russia see his *Darkest Russia* leader, 'Our Policy', 3 Apr. 1912.

[40] Michael F. Hamm, 'Liberalism and the Jewish Question: The Progressive Bloc', *Russian Review*, 31 (1972), 163–72.

[41] For Bloc formation and programme, 28 Aug. 1915, see Pearson, *Russian Moderates*, 49–51.

the Bloc, was less sweeping than other points in the programme, and fell far short of the traditional Cadet demand for immediate emancipation. In this sense it was a disappointment to the Bloc's Jewish supporters. Yet its very lack of definition meant that it was open to interpretation. This gave Wolf the option to surmise that if, as seemed possible, the Cadets became the driving force within a broad movement encompassing duma, State Council, government, and people, it would be a prelude to more thoroughgoing reforms. He wrote to Cyrus Adler of the American Jewish Committee in September, 'already there are great political changes in Russia and it is possible that the normal process of events may in this way render any special action on the part of the Jewish communities in the west superfluous'.[42]

However, Wolf did not remain inactive—he could not. The Bloc's programme gave him his first real opportunity to present the Foreign Office with an argument for Jewish emancipation which was consistent with actual Russian developments. Moreover, as American Jewish leaders had made it plain that their financiers' purse strings would remain tied until such time as the decree of 3 September passed into permanent law[43]—that is, through the duma—radical interpretation of the Bloc programme remained strikingly relevant. Wolf's duty in his diplomatic capacity lay in emphasizing this.

How he attempted to do this is made evident by his negotiations with Russian leaders. Hardly had the decree of 3 September been enacted when Bark was back in the West, presumably assuming that passage of the decree had opened up Jewish finance to Russia. Wolf did not see Bark himself but both the Conjoint presidents in England did, and likewise Baron Edmond de Rothschild for the French community a few days later. They all presented him with identical lists of suggested assurances which the Russian government might give if it wished to alleviate continuing American hostility. As drawn up by Wolf, these were (a) unrestricted rights of Jewish domicile; (b) unrestricted educational rights; (c) abolition of discrimination in the matter of passports; and (d) that all these reforms be enacted by law and not by ministerial decree. Bark, it seems, was shocked. The Russian government, he told Montefiore and Alexander, was behaving in a liberal manner; Ianushkevich, the Russian commander, not they, had been responsible for the expulsions. He returned to Petrograd,

---

[42] Wolf to Adler, encl. with Wolf to Oliphant, 7 Sept. 1915, FO 371/2446/155.
[43] Marshall to M. A. Gunzburg, the Russian Jewish leader, 23 Oct. 1915, C11/3/1/1.

however, empty handed, save for the four-point programme and the plain hint that, unless concessions were made, Western Jewish co-operation would not be forthcoming.[44]

That Wolf was exerting pressure on Russia's internal affairs was undeniable. It was also seemingly in contradiction to the statement he made to Alexander in April the following year that he was quite in agreement with Russian liberals, 'especially M. Milyukov', who said they could 'settle the Jewish problem themselves' and were quite opposed to 'foreign interference' if they could not.[45]

Yet Milyukov himself fell foul of Wolf's firmness when, leading a Russian parliamentary delegation to the west in June 1916, he discussed the Jewish question with him. Taking Milyukov to task for failing to persevere with the Bloc's programme for Jewish reform, Wolf warned that the question ought to be seriously considered, 'if only because of the grave embarrassments it was causing the Allies'. The English and French governments felt more deeply on the subject than Sazonov knew or imagined, he ingeniously added. Milyukov, like Bark before him, seems to have taken the hint, publicly reporting to the duma later in the month that if American–Allied relations were to be improved and more favourable conditions for borrowing American money found, the Jewish question would have to be resolved.[46]

The considerable pressure thus being applied to the Russians could be presented to the Foreign Office in quite a different light. Reporting to Cecil in September 1915 on the meeting with Bark, Wolf pointed out that the Conjoint had been both conciliatory, in that the proposals were no more than those being pressed for by the Bloc; and flexible, in that actually enacting them could be delayed until after the war, provided the Russian government declared its willingness to do so.[47]

This diplomatic tact was intended more than simply to impress Cecil. By underlining now his own proposals related to the Bloc's programme and hence to the whole spectrum of Russian liberal opinion, embracing apparently Jews in the Political Bureau in Petrograd and moderates in the government, Wolf was attempting to suggest the direction that the British government itself should be taking in regard to the Russian question. And by this Wolf meant not just its Jewish

[44] Wolf to Cecil, 1 Oct. 1915, C11/2/7; Bigart to Wolf, 6 Oct. 1915, C11/3/1/1, Wolf to Zangwill, 5 Oct. 1915, MWS file 211.
[45] Wolf to Alexander, 26 Apr. 1916, MWS 1724–5.
[46] Wolf to CJC presidents, 26 June 1916, MWS 1954–5.
[47] Wolf to Cecil, 1 Oct. 1915, C11/2/7.

aspect. As he explained to Lord Bryce, an old friend and the influential ex-ambassador to America, in May 1916:

> I am confident that if we do nothing to bind the Russian democracy to us now, the Russian alliance will not long survive the war and we shall find ourselves in a more precarious situation in Europe than we have ever been before. Let us not forget . . . how admirably Canning fortified the position of England by recognising the democratic affinity of France and by conciliating democratic sentiments throughout Europe. Pray forgive me for writing to you at such length but I have the matter very much at heart, on British, I assure you, even more than on Jewish grounds.[48]

The British government, by giving its full encouragement to such tendencies in Russia, enabled Wolf to foresee not only how Jewish emancipation might be brought about but also how his frankly embarrassing opposition to the Anglo-Russian *entente* might be reversed. A return to the old assumption of consonance between British and British Jewish foreign policy interests could thus be facilitated, bringing in turn renewed composure and dignity to the Anglo-Jewish community.

Wolf set to work with a will at the beginning of 1916 to promote his design. With the aid of his friend Israel Zangwill, who had agreed to a loose working arrangement with the Conjoint the previous year,[49] he attempted to have a collection of essays by leading non-Jewish Russian intellectuals endorsing a progressive attitude on the Jewish question translated and published in England. The essayists included such prominent figures as Paul Milyukov, Maxim Gorki, and Leonid Andreyev, and when published in Petrograd the previous year the collection had been a best-seller.[50] Now Wolf attempted to have Bryce write an introduction to the English edition, explaining to him that it would be useful to the Allies in neutral countries and pleasing to the Russian government. However, Bryce's readiness to help was thwarted by Foreign Office pressure, and the project lapsed.[51]

Wolf tried another tack. Since before the war he had been insisting that the removal of Jewish disabilities in Russia would be beneficial to

[48] Wolf to Bryce, 5 May 1916, CII/2/8.

[49] Zangwill to Wolf, 2 Aug. 1915, MWS file 211: 'the Jewish question should generally go through your hands as far as the Foreign Office is concerned'.

[50] For English translation see MWS 14809–87.

[51] Wolf to Bryce, 22 Mar. 1916, CII/2/8; Wolf to Bryce, 27 Mar. 1916, MWS 2050; Bryce to Wolf, 1 May 1916, CII/2/8. Szajkowski, *Jews, Wars*, i. 43, mistakenly gives the impression that the impetus for publication came from Zangwill and that Wolf, under Foreign Office pressure, blocked it.

British trade and commerce, not only providing British companies with excellent agents but also preventing the country falling prey to extensive German and Austrian economic penetration.[52] A 1915 circular from the Board of Trade, however, contradicted this, advising British companies trading with Russia not to employ Jewish agents on account of the restrictions imposed upon them.[53] This apparently official British endorsement of a reactionary Russian policy was also highly topical, as rumour was rife that the Americans were about to renegotiate their broken Russian commerce treaty and that American Jewish leaders had stipulated that the absence of racial or religious discrimination clauses would be critical in determining their own posture.[54]

Significantly, Wolf did not take the matter up directly with the Board of Trade but with Cecil at the Foreign Office.[55] Refurbishing some of his old arguments about the importance of the Jews to the British interest in the absence of a strong native middle class, he sparked off a new debate between British diplomats in Russia and Whitehall officials on this very point. In fact, only one British diplomat in Russia—Bruce Lockhart, the acting consul general in Moscow—readily agreed with Wolf on the economic utility of the Jews to the British cause; the rest rejected his position.[56] Cecil, however, had the final word. At his insistence, Wolf was received at the Board of Trade, where he obtained manifold apologies and the cancellation of the offending document.[57]

---

[52] Wolf, 'Notes', *Darkest Russia*, 29 July 1913; R. Blank, 'Economic Role of the Jews in Russia', n.d., 1914, MW6 12925–51. See also CJC, *A Memorandum on the Grievances of British Subjects of the Jewish Faith in Regard to the Interpretation of Articles i and ix of the Anglo-Russian Treaty of Commerce and Navigation of 12 January 1889* (London, 1912).

[53] Wolf memo on meeting with H. Fountain at the Board of Trade, 15 May 1916, C11/2/8.

[54] Wolf to Marshall, 28 June, C11/2/9; Marshall to Wolf, 8 Aug. 1916, ibid.; Marshall to M. A. Gunzburg, 23 Oct. 1915, C11/3/1/1. The occasion of the rumours was the appointment of a new US ambassador to Petrograd. The original commerce treaty had been abrogated by the US Senate in 1912 following an intensive campaign by the American Jewish community, which objected to discrimination by Russia against American Jewish traders; see Naomi Cohen, *Not Free*, 54–80.

[55] See Wolf to Cecil, 13 Jan. 1916, FO 368/1600/4562.

[56] Memos by R. B. Lockhart (26 Jan.) and H. A. Cooke (30 Jan.) encl. in Buchanan to FO, 2 Feb. 1916, ibid., fos 31–4. Lockhart was later on Britain's sole line of official communication with Bolshevik Russia in the civil war period. On the economic debate see also Pares's comments in *Novoe vremya*, 12 July 1916, on the dangers of German economic penetration in Russia: 'Unfortunately it is the intermediary Jew rather than the real Englishmen that is striving to fill the gaps.'

[57] Wolf memo to Board of Trade, 15 May 1916, C11/2/8.

But Wolf's efforts to involve the Foreign Office more fully in the question of Russian Jewish disabilities got no further. A joint attempt by the Conjoint and Alliance to resurrect the matter of British and French Jews denied access to Russia through passport restrictions, at the Inter-Allied Economic Conference in Paris in June 1916, never appeared on the agenda. Indeed, Wolf's memorandum on the subject provoked Oliphant to remark: 'I don't think Mr. Wolf should be encouraged to hurl Jewish propagandist memoranda at us as he seems to contemplate . . . I fear he is hard to defeat.'[58]

Wolf's real defeat was to come from another direction. The Russian 'liberal phase' of government about which Wolf had been so enthusiastic was moribund almost from its inception in September 1915. Opposition from the tsar led to the dismissal of all its more competent ministers in less than a year, with Sazonov, the foreign minister, being the last to depart in June 1916. As they were replaced by a succession of sycophants and incompetents, it became clear that reaction was once again firmly entrenched.[59]

As for the provisions of the September decree, the traditional police practice of interpreting such things in accordance with the size of the bribe proffered made them unenforceable. Reports of widespread Jewish harassment and expulsion continued. They were exacerbated by the refusal of Bark, the finance minister—the very minister who had pleaded with his ministerial colleagues for them on pragmatic grounds—to issue the necessary trading documents for Jews now living beyond the Pale, on the grounds that they did not tally with pre-September 1915 residential restrictions. Moreover, he showed his particular capacity for political survival in the new ultra-reactionary climate, by reviving his pre-war plans for the Russification of commerce: intended to block Jewish involvement in the purchase or possession of land or shares by joint-stock companies, Bark nullified at one stroke one of his own avowed justifications for the decree.[60]

The failure of reform in the Jewish or more general sense and the consequent inability to create a nexus between government and the

[58] Oliphant minute, n.d., in response to Wolf to Oliphant, 24 May 1916, FO 368/1600/4562. See also Bigart to Briand, 13 June 1916, MAE Guerre 1914–18, file 1198, fos. 13–17.

[59] Cherniavsky, *Prologue*, 245; Mowschowitch, 'On the Political Situation in Russia', n.d., early 1916, MWS 13367–81.

[60] 'The Extension of the Pale and its Application', n.d., unsigned, probably Mowschowitch, MWS 13291–310; 'Bark and the Jewish Question', MWS 13361–4, and 'Economic Restrictions', MWS 14360, both n.d. and unsigned, also probably Mowschowitch.

Progressive Bloc thus wrecked Wolf's slender hope of harnessing the British Foreign Office to the Russian liberal tendency. Nor did the survival of the Bloc into 1916 prove to be any consolation.

Milyukov turned out to be more interested in perpetuating its fragile existence, even at the cost of compromise with its more right-wing elements, than with pursuing a serious programme of reform. Confronting the government, in the duma or outside, was discountenanced, and the more salient features of the Bloc programme, including the Jewish proposals, were underplayed.[61]

But this in itself hastened the Bloc's disintegration. The Cadet Party buckled under the strain of a policy of stagnation, and its more radical elements demanded an alignment leftwards with Trudoviks and Mensheviks. The allegiance of its Jewish supporters became suspect.

This tense situation came to a head in the first sitting of the duma in March 1916. Friedman and Bomash, two Jewish deputies aligned to the Cadets, issued notice of their intention to bring an interpellation against the government. The occasion was the 'discovery' of two inflammatory government circulars—one from the Police Department of the Ministry of Interior, the other from the Ministry of Finance—which attacked the supposedly German-inspired speculatory or revolutionary behaviour of the Jews, and which in turn had precipitated an *oblava* or witch-hunt that had led to the arrest of several thousand Moscow Jews. When the two deputies turned to the Bloc to support their interpellation, however, they found that the Octobrist leader Count Kapnist insisted that the Jewish question should not be discussed for the duration of the war. Milyukov urged them privately to drop the matter or risk a negative vote and possible Bloc schism.[62]

While these developments hastened the ultimate demise of the Bloc, they also marked a major crossroads in the relationship of the Russian Jewish community to the duma and more particularly to the Cadets. True, a group of Jewish duma Cadets, led by Maxim Vinaver and G. B. Sliosberg, did attempt to shore up the traditional relationship to both duma and party. Friedman's dramatic secession from both, however, in June, paralleled by a stinging attack on party and Bloc by *Evreiskaia nedelia*, the traditional Moscow organ of Jewish Cadetism, perhaps more accurately reflected not simply the intensified frustration and disenchantment with Russian political life but the collapse of a

[61] Pearson, *Russian Moderates*, 88–9.

[62] Mowschowitch, 'On the Political Situation in Russia: The Jewish Question in the Duma', n.d., *c.* Apr. 1916, MWS 14100–22. See also Hamm, 'Liberalism', 163–72.

conventional wisdom.[63] Henceforth there could be no going back to the compromises of the Bloc programme—neither through Vinaver and the Russian Jewish leaders who maintained their allegiance to the Cadets nor through Friedman and those who now sought independent alliances with more radical groups both inside and outside of the duma. At least Wolf could be sure that in presenting to the Foreign Office demands for complete and immediate Russian Jewish emancipation, he would be doing no more than articulating the demands of the entire Russian Jewish community.[64]

This was of course of no value to Wolf's ambitious attempts to create a 'liberal' Anglo-Russian *entente* now that the wider conditions for that development were gone. But at least he could take cheer from another source: American in 1916 was still not in the war, and its Jews were seemingly as antagonistic as ever to supporting the Allied cause. There was still leverage for Wolf's wartime diplomacy.

[63] On Mowschowitch's retrospective view of the Vinaver and Sliosberg efforts see Mowschowitch, 'The Jewish Aspects of the Revolution', n.d., Mar. or Apr. 1917, MWS 14655–61. For Vinaver and Sliosberg's relationship to the Cadets via the Jewish *Narodnaia groupa* see Jacob Frumkin, 'Pages from the History of the Russian Revolution', in Jacob Frumkin, Gregor Aronson, Alexis Goldenweiser, eds., *Russian Jewry, 1860–1917* (New York, 1966).

[64] For the Russian Jewish duma realignment, see Mowschowitch, 'Jewish Aspects', MWS 14655–61, and Pearson, *Russian Moderates*, 98. In fact, while Milyukov was away in the west, Vinaver steered the Cadet Central Committee towards a demand for immediate legislation on Jewish rights.

PART II

WOLF AND THE ZIONISTS

4

Palestine as Propaganda

think we shall have a great success. That is of course the grievance on the
,ther side. They suspect that we are going to show that Jewry can be saved
,vithout Zionism.[1]

n the first part of 1914, Zionist aspirations to create a Jewish national
,ome in Palestine looked bleaker than ever. Herzl's turn-of-the-
:entury vision of conquering the land by direct diplomatic negotiation
,vith the Great Powers and the Ottoman Empire, of which Palestine
,ormed a small part, had proved unworkable. 'We stood before a blank
,vall which it was impossible to surmount by ordinary political means',[2]
ecalled Chaim Weizmann after the war. He might have added that the
lternative strategy, 'practical' Zionism, which, in the wake of Herzl's
leath in 1904 and his model's demise, had captured the movement by
,ropounding slow and gradual colonization, had also foundered, faced
,s it was by growing Turkish and Arab opposition to further Jewish
mmigration.[3]

What thus seemed like a closed letter was dramatically reopened by
he entry of Turkey into the war, on the side of the Central Powers, in
,Jovember 1914. The Ottoman Empire was generally held to be weak,
lecadent, and tottering on the edge of collapse, kept afloat only by the
raditional support of the Western powers. That support having been
,orfeited, the empire stood, if Turkey lost the war, to be partitioned
,etween the Allies; indeed, the British prime minister, Asquith, had on
, November 1914 given public notice of this intention by declaring
hat Turkey had rung her own death knell.

In fact, Asquith's speech was pure rhetoric. The British government
,ad, in 1914, no long-term plans for the dismemberment of the
,mpire; even when in April the following year the interdepartmental
le Bunsen Committee considered the matter further, the British

[1] Wolf to Abrahams, 30 Oct. 1916, MWS 1693.
[2] Weizmann's speech at the 12th Zionist Congress, 1921, quoted in Leonard Stein,
,alfour Declaration, 56.
[3] For the development of Palestinian opposition to Zionism see Neville J. Mandel,
,he Arabs and Zionism before World War I (Berkeley, 1976).

intention to preserve Turkey-in-Asia, albeit on a decentralized basis, was reinforced. However, this did not mean that Britain saw no consequences for a defeated Turkey.

Britain's 'vital interests' in the potentially enormous oil fields of Mesopotamia led the committee to envisage the predominance of British influence in that area, and in this context the port of Haifa on the Palestinian coast was discussed as a possible naval base and rail terminus connecting those 'interests' with the Mediterranean. But as for Palestine as a whole, Lord Kitchener was reported to have told a War Council meeting in March 1915 that it 'would be of no value to us whatsoever'.[4]

Even supposing that British intentions had been otherwise, there was no opportunity to advance such hypothetical goals by force of arms. The war showed the Turks to have considerable reserves of resilience and vigour; British attempts to undermine the empire's integrity with campaigns in 1915 in the Dardanelles and in Mesopotamia led to a quite considerable defeat at Kut-el-Amara and the evacuation of the Gallipoli peninsula. Not until 1917 were the Allies able to claim any substantial victories at Turkey's expense.[5]

These factors did not prevent interested British Jews, undoubtedly unaware of government reservations, from seeing in the situation not only a green light for a carve-up of the Ottoman Empire, but actual British sponsorship for Jewish developments in Palestine. Thus, at the very highest level, Herbert Samuel, the Jewish president of the Local Government Board, ventured in November 1914 to approach Grey on the subject, and on the possibility of Palestine becoming a Jewish 'centre'. Lower down the line, both Israel Zangwill and Leopold Greenberg, in separate initiatives, discussed the matter with Foreign Office officials the following month. None of these representations received anything more than the sympathetic interest of the ministry, Lucien Wolf being assured by Acland in January 1915 that the Palestine question was in 'no formal or informal sense under the consideration of the Foreign Office'.[6]

Both publicly and privately, Wolf had little interest in the issue, and undoubtedly would have preferred to steer well clear of it. True, the

---

[4] Quoted in Aaron S. Klieman, 'Britain's War Aims in the Middle East in 1915', *Journal of Contemporary History*, 3 (1968), 237–51.

[5] See Paul Guinn, *British Strategy and Politics, 1914–1918* (Oxford, 1965), 111–12, 217–19.

[6] Viscount Herbert Samuel, *Memoirs* (London, 1945), 140–5; Wolf reporting conversation with Acland to CJC presidents, 7 Jan. 1915, MWS 7475–8.

Conjoint had a duty to represent the Anglo-Jewish Association's Palestinian interests, in the form of the Evelina de Rothschild school in Jerusalem and other philanthropic projects. Its policy, however, did not extend to actually endorsing or sponsoring Zionist arguments for the transplanting of seven to eight million East European Jews, even supposing that in itself was feasible, to a semi-barren, extra-European backwater, albeit much cherished. Nor in fact did Wolf seem to have had any particular sentimental regard for the wartime fate of Palestine or Jewish Palestinians. When, for instance, at the beginning of the war, false rumours reached him, via the *Jewish Chronicle*, that Jewish refugees holding British nationality had been expelled from Palestine by the Turks and were to be shipped from Alexandria to Britain, Wolf tried to pre-empt this by writing to the Foreign Office suggesting they be sent to Cyprus instead.[7]

The growing pro-Zionist clamour amongst the Jewish immigrant masses, as reawakened by the war, and the threat this posed to the Conjoint Committee compelled Wolf to reconsider the issue, however. Already heavily under attack for failing to take the community into his confidence in relation to the Committee's wartime plans, Wolf in March 1915 departed from traditional Conjoint, not to say Western Jewish, practice by proposing a policy on Palestine. Writing to a presumably sceptical Bigart, at the Alliance, he attempted to justify this reappraisal thus:

Our present view is that the Zionist programme in Palestine can never offer any solution to the large practical questions which confront us in Russia, Poland and Rumania and hence it must be regarded as essentially a sentimental question. Nevertheless it is one which appeals to the historic sense of all Jews and also to the religious hopes of many non-Jews ... we feel ... it may be desirable to ask for special facilities for Jewish immigration and colonisation and the free development of Jewish institutions and Jewish cultural life.[8]

That could have been the extent of Wolf's wartime attention to the

[7] Wolf to Tyrrell, 27 Feb. 1915, C11/2/6. Fraenkel, 'Wolf and Herzl', 175–6, notes how Palestine always remained on the periphery rather than at the centre of Wolf's vision. He further speculates that his non-participation in the 'Maccabean' pilgrimage to the Holy Land in 1897 may have contributed to an emotional reserve on the subject not shared by those English Jews who had gone.

[8] Wolf to Bigart, 2 Mar. 1915, C11/3/2/1. Six months later Wolf reaffirmed these proposals with some amendments for the benefit of the AJC's Conference on Jewish Affairs. See Wolf to Cyrus Adler, 16 Sept. 1915, MWS 1713.

matter, if developments on the other side of the Channel, ironically enough involving his Alliance colleagues, had not taken a hand.

The French, like the British, were much concerned by the end of 1915 with the apparent pro-German tendencies of American Jewry, as anxiously reported by their ambassador in Washington, Jean Jules Jusserand. It was on the basis of his reports that they took the initiative, unlike the British, in attempting to do something about it. In the last months of that year, two French Jews were despatched to America with the remit to report on the situation and strike back at Bernstorff's pro-German propaganda effort.[9]

The first, Dr Nahoum Slousch, a Russian-born, French-naturalized professor of Hebrew at the Sorbonne, was a Zionist, and this had some bearing on his tour. Slousch believed that one way the Allies could calm American Jewish fears about Russia's treatment of its Jews was by issuing a declaration favouring an independent Jewish colony in the south of Palestine. To this end he approached the leaders of the American Jewish Congress, Louis Brandeis and Richard Gottheil, and addressed large public meetings.[10]

While Slousch was reporting these views to Paris, another Sorbonne professor, the distinguished liberal and Alliance member Victor Basch, was on his way to America. Basch was not a Zionist. Nor was he particularly concerned with public speaking; his *modus operandi* was to gauge discreetly the climate of American Jewish feeling by privately sounding out their leaders. His interviews with, at one extreme, the banker Schiff, and at the other, the socialist leader of the National Workmen's Committee on Jewish Rights, Dr Max Goldfarb, confirmed him in the view that even though some Yiddish papers such as the New York *Forverts* were receiving German subsidies, American Jewry were not as a whole enamoured with the German cause, nor by any means implacably hostile to the Allies. As Schiff assured him, if Russia could be made to reform, the whole spectrum of American Jewry, from left to right, would be behind the Allies to a man.[11] As a

---

[9] MAE Guerre 1914–18, file 1197 (Sionisme), which consists almost entirely of Jusserand's despatches to Delcassé on the German propaganda success with American Jews.

[10] Slousch, 'Notes sur les revendications des Israélites en Palestine', 15 Dec. 1915, fos. 116–18, encl. in Jusserand to Briand, 17 Dec. 1915, ibid.; Notes of M. N. Slousch, 22 Jan. 1916, ibid., fos 180–5. Slousch, like Basch after him, proposed a declaration on Jewish rights as a propaganda tool.

[11] Resumé des lettres de Victor Basch, n.d., Feb. 1916, C11/3/1/2. Extract of letter to Moutet, n.d., Feb. 1916, AIU/France, 1D3. See also Paula Hyman, *Dreyfus to Vichy*, 52–3.

result, Basch's proposals to Paris differed sharply from those of his predecessor. Civil rights, not Zionism, he argued, was the key to American Jewish support. Moreover, Britain and France could take a lead in this direction. They could, by acting in the tradition of Salisbury and Waddington at the Berlin Congress, simply declare their willingness to settle the outstanding issues of Jewish emancipation at the war's end.[12]

The contradictory information from Basch and Slousch must have perplexed the Quai d'Orsay, not least because Basch's emphasis on Jewish emancipation in Russia was something manifestly beyond the reach of Anglo-French diplomacy. Surprisingly, however, they wired back to him in February 1916 their endorsement of his proposal— perhaps assuming that Basch would take this as a hint to emphasize its Romanian, not its Russian potential. But their reply also evinced a cautious interest in the Slousch option. Basch's further instructions required him to pronounce that following Anglo-French–Russian discussions, the removal of the Turks from the Arab world would not see the liberty and extension of the Jewish colonies in Palestine forgotten by the Western Allies.[13]

Behind all this activity was the inauguration of a major French propaganda effort aimed at American Jewry. Its driving force, grandiloquently titled Le Comité Français d'Information et d'Action auprès des Juifs des Pays Neutres, had been created by the Quai d'Orsay's Comité de Propagande after consultation, in December 1915, with the Chamber of Deputies' Foreign Affairs Commission and Prime Minister Briand, no less. Presided over by Georges Leygues, an important member of the Foreign Affairs Commission, its mandate was primarily to work to Basch's recommendations.

The Comité contained many distinguished non-Jewish liberal deputies. Overwhelmingly, however, it was composed of French

---

[12] Basch, Resumé des lettres, C11/3/1/2; Jusserand to Briand, 12 Jan. 1915, reporting on Basch's proposals, MAE Guerre 1914–18, file 1197 (Sionisme).

[13] Berthelot to Basch, 12 Feb. 1916, MAE Guerre 1914–18, file 1197 (Sionisme), fo. 140; Slousch, in his 'Notes' (see n. 10, above) had been careful to delimit his colonizing plan to the south of Palestine, i.e. on the periphery, or outside a French area of immediate 'interest' in 'Syrie intégrale'. Despite the fact that the Sykes–Picot–Sazonov talks were well under way, there is no evidence to suggest that the three allies had discussed the Jews in relations to Palestine at this stage. Though both Friedman, *Question of Palestine*, 48–9, and Stein, *Balfour Declaration*, 219, refer to the Basch mission in their analysis of developments leading to the Balfour Declaration, neither mentions Slousch.

Jewish intellectuals drawn from the ranks of the Alliance. Bigart was to be its secretary, and it was he who informed Wolf of the Comité's existence, before the latter had even received details of Basch's mission.[14]

Patrioti tinged with hypersensitivity about the alleged pro-German, anti-Ally proclivities of their American-Jewish co-religionists seems to have had much to do with Franco-Jewish enthusiasm for the Comité. Wolf did not share this latter anxiety. True, he himself had emphasized to the Foreign Office the significance of the Russian atrocity stories in the American Jewish press in 1915 as a means of bringing pressure to bear on Russia in favour of Jewish concessions. In this sense he had only himself to blame if in the following year the ministry was not convinced by his assurances that the American Jews were 'not as black as they had been painted'.[15] On the other hand, he had evidence to suggest that their hostility to Russia was not an equation for a pro-German stand.

His own 1914 propaganda pamphlet, *Jewish Ideals and the War*, had sold well there and even received acclaim from Jews of German origin. Moreover, Louis Marshall, the leader of the American Jewish Committee, wrote in spring 1916 assuring him that the majority of its members were staunchly pro-Ally. A contemporaneous letter from Richard Gottheil, a British-born American Jewish professor, suggesting that many prominent committee members, including Cyrus Adler, were allied in secret machinations with Jacob Schiff to further the German cause, seemed, moreover, to be flatly contradicted by Basch's report that Schiff would willingly extend a loan to Russia as soon as there were signs of reform on the Jewish front. As for Adler, Wolf refused to accept the implied slander of an old friend. Rather, he proposed to Reuben Blank, who was to visit the United States that spring, that he double-check Gottheil's testimony.[16]

---

[14] Bigart to Wolf, 10 Dec. 1915, C11/3/1/2; Wolf notes on mechanism of Comité d'Action, n.d., early 1916, ibid.; draft of Comite d'Action aims, AIU/France, ID 3; Hyman, *Dreyfus to Vichy*, 51–2. AIU members included Jacques Bigart, Salomon Reinach, Eugene Sée, Emile Durkheim, Drs Basch, Netter, and Meyerson, and Sylvain and Israel Lévi. The latter was sent to Salonika on an identical mission to that of Basch.

[15] Wolf to Leopold de Rothschild, 21 June 1916, C11/2/9.

[16] Wolf to Montgomery, 5 Apr. 1915 for *Jewish Ideals and the War*, FO 371/2835/18095; Wolf to Montgomery, 15 May 1915, encl. letter from Marshall, FO 371/2817/787203. On Marshall's opposition to pro-German elements among American Jewry see Marshall to Lord Reading, 22 Sept. 1915, in Louis Marshall, *Louis Marshall: Champion of Liberty*, ed. Charles Reznikoff (Philadelphia, 1957), ii. 51. For Gottheil correspondence

Nevertheless, as a dutiful and patriotic Briton, Wolf felt bound to
'all in with Bigart's proposal that he form a parallel propaganda committee in London. He approached Cecil at the Foreign Office on the
:ubject almost immediately. His December 1915 'suggestions' for pro-
Allied propaganda in neutral countries[17] were a quite remarkable
leparture, however, from those being worked upon by the Comité in
'aris.

Wolf assured Cecil that American Jewry could be won over. Partly
his could be achieved by Basch-type arguments about Western
iberalism as opposed to German reaction, which had appeared in
Jewish Ideals and the War, and the liberal features of Russian society in
:ontradistinction to the Germanic court and bureaucracy. In addition,
:aid Wolf, Zionist sentiment might also be utilized, since latterly it had
ipparently captured American Jewish opinion.

How could this be done? 'This is the moment', Wolf insisted, for
the Allies to declare their policy on Palestine.' What they ought to do,
ie continued, would be to state their willingness, 'when the destiny of
he country comes to be considered', to guarantee equal rights for
'alestinian Jews with the rest of the population, reasonable facilities
'or immigration and colonization, a liberal scheme of self-government,
i Jewish university, and recognition of the Hebrew language. Such a
:cheme 'would sweep up the whole of American Jewry into enthusiastic
illegiance to the Allied cause'. Wolf's pseudo-Zionist proposition is
:trange, given his known background of public opposition to the
novement. In private he had reiterated his misgivings to Bigart in
March 1915 when he had suggested that if the Zionists really did gain
i Jewish state, their efforts would result in a fiasco which would
'ebound to the embarrassment of the Jewish world at large.[18] One
'eason for this, Wolf had proposed, at a Conjoint–Zionist conference
n April, could be inferred from the Zionist Inner Action Committee's
iwn estimates of the capacity for colonizing Palestine. In 1914, Zionist
:ettlers numbered only 35,000 out of a total population of 600,000,
ind owned only 2 per cent of the land. Even taking the most favourable

---

ee Gottheil to Wolf, 11 Mar. and 26 Apr. 1916, MWS 2339–41. For more on
Gottheil see Friedman, *Question of Palestine*, 40. On Basch report see C11/3/1/2,
3asch, Resumé des Lettres. For Wolf's comment see Wolf to Blank, 30 Mar. 1916,
C11/2/8.

[17] 'Suggestions for pro-Allied Propaganda in the USA', encl. Wolf to Cecil, 16 Dec.
915, FO 371/2579/18779.   [18] Wolf to Bigart, 2 Mar. 1915, C11/3/2/1.

reckoning and assuming that this figure could be increased to some 800,000 in a period of ten years, it would do no more than offset the natural growth rate of East European Jewry.[19] From the point of view of wartime propaganda, Wolf's proposal was a shrewd move. There was a growing movement in America for a nationwide Jewish Congress to formulate Jewish post-war desiderata, and this movement, following its main protagonist, Justice Brandeis, was deeply imbued with Zionism. By the end of 1915, all the signs suggested that grass-roots support would enable it to push through its preliminary conference, planned to be held in Philadelphia the following year, with or without the support of the American Jewish Committee.[20]

The Germans would want to capture the Congress. Propaganda-wise, they and their Austro-Hungarian partners were already at a clear advantage over the Allies as far as the situation in the East was concerned. They had sponsored Bodenheimer's Kommittee für den Osten; abrogated Russian restrictions in the territories they had occupied; encouraged Jewish cultural and educational schemes; favoured the representation of Jews on municipal councils; even appointed a Jew, Ludwig Haas, as head of the Jewish department of their civil administration in Poland.[21] The Auswärtiges Amt was also concerning itself with Palestine, intervening with their Turkish allies to prevent a wholesale expulsion of Russian Jews in 1914 and toying with Jewish rights there as a sop to American Jewish opinion. On this score, in November 1915, when Brandeis and his friends were preparing their resolutions for the coming Congress, the Auswärtiges Amt produced something of a *coup* by instructing its consuls in Turkey to aid Jewish and especially Zionist organizations in the empire, providing they did not conflict with Turkish interests.[22]

Here, however, was an area in which the Germans could be outbid. No German declaration on Palestine could be made without the Turks' prior agreement, and they certainly were in no frame of mind to hand over part of their empire to Zionists or anybody else. Moreover, Turkish blunders in Palestine were already a subject of embarrassment

---

[19] Wolf memo on CJC–Zionist conference, 14 Apr. 1915, encl. with Wolf to FO, 28 Apr. 1915, FO 371/2488/51705.
[20] For details of the preliminary conference see Janowsky, *Jews and Minority Rights*, 168; Zechlin, *Deutsche Politik*, 502–4; Frankel, *Prophecy and Politics*, 509–25.
[21] On Haas see Zechlin, *Deutsche Politik*, 204–10.
[22] Friedman, *Germany, Turkey*, 214, 246, 256–8; Zechlin, *Deutsche Politik*, 317–23.

o the Germans. The proposed expulsions of Jews from Jaffa in
December 1914 by Djemal Pasha, the local despot, had been more or
ess averted by German consular representations, but too late to pre-
'ent the British exploiting the affair from a propaganda angle. British
:ontrol of the Atlantic cables meant that when the story appeared in
America it had been magnified into a massacre of Palestinian Jewry.[23]
When Oscar Straus, the distinguished American Jewish Committee
eader, issued a statement in February 1915 protesting against the
slaughter of Jews by both Russians and Prussians and remonstrating
igaint their being 'plundered and expelled without cause' in Palestine,
Ambassador Bernstorff could only expostulate in reply that the Ger-
nans had in fact been protecting them.[24] British wartime interests
vere therefore served by comparing Turkish iniquities in Palestine
vith British benevolence; hence the permission granted to American
)oats laden with relief for Palestine to pass through the British naval
:mbargo on neutral shipping bound for belligerent shores.[25]

Wolf must have been aware that Turkey's behaviour in Palestine
vas a propaganda handicap to its allies, in the same way that Russian
)ehaviour in Poland and Galicia was an embarrassment to Britain and
France. Here too was an opportunity for Wolf to pay back his adver-
iary Bernstorff once and for all while demonstrating his patriotism and
showing the Allies how an initiative on Palestine would be a propaganda
victory over the Central Powers.

But the 'suggestions' also carried a more subtle insinuation. 'What
he Zionists would especially like to know', he argued, 'is that Great
Britain will become mistress of Palestine.' What they did not want was
an increase of Russian influence or an Italian annexation which would
ill the country with Sicilian peasants or an International Commission
vhich would be soulless, if it were not the hotbed of demoralising
ntrigues'. But, he added, Britain could not become mistress of Palestine
vithout French consent, and the impression he had received in Paris
n August was that the French insistence on assurances on Syria also
ook in Palestine. Wolf coyly noted that British mistress-ship might
:ause conflict with her ally.[26]

---

[23] Zechlin, *Deutsche Politik*, 319–20; Friedman, *Germany, Turkey*, 215.

[24] Cohen, *Dual Heritage*, 244–5. For reports of Straus's statement in *New York Times*,
. Feb., and reply, 11 Mar. 1915, see MAE Guerre 1914–18, file 1197 (Sionisme), fos.
:0–1.

[25] Friedman, *Question of Palestine*, 43.

[26] Wolf to Cecil, 16 Dec. 1915, 'Suggestions', FO 371/2579/18779.

What Wolf was proposing here, reading something less than between the lines, was that Britain could use Zionism to press forward
any claim to Palestine in the face of French counter-designs. That Wolf,
as a British patriot and a defender of Britain's commercial interests,
desired annexation is quite clear. As early as 1905, his infatuation with
ITO seems to have been motivated less by its Jewish aspects and more
by the asset that a flourishing Jewish colony in East Africa or elsewhere
would be to the British Empire.[27] By the same token, following the
conference with the Zionists in April 1915, he explicitly stated 'the
Conjoint Committee agree[s] with the Zionists that efforts should be
made to bring Palestine under the British Empire as being most
favourable to Jewish development in that country'.[28]

The threat to this potential outcome would come from France. Soon
after returning from a trip to Paris to co-ordinate closer links between
the Alliance and the Conjoint, Wolf received a visit from a Count de
Zogheb of the Syria Committee who insisted that the French wanted
Syria and Palestine. He proposed Zionist–Syrian co-operation to avert
this, and Wolf obligingly put him in touch with Joseph Cowen of the
English Zionist Federation. Wolf wrote to the latter as follows: 'I told
Count Zogheb however, that all Jews, whether Zionists or anti-
Zionists—excluding of course the French Jews—would be against the
annexation of Palestine by France and would clamour for an English
annexation and that they would have the overwhelming support of the
Protestant world.'[29] Ironically, in his zeal to outbid the French over
Palestine, Wolf pre-empted Basch's Palestine assurances by nearly
three months. Wolf saw Cecil on 16 December 1915; there is no
record of Quai d'Orsay clearance for Basch's assurance until February
1916.

But there were reasons closer to home why Wolf, in conversation
with Cecil, was cagey about wholeheartedly endorsing the Comité
d'Action programme. Doubting the influence that an official,

[27] Wolf–Zangwill correspondence in *The Times*, 5 Sept. 1905. Wolf proposed that the
colony should have a 'British rather than a Jewish autonomy'. See also similar statements
at ITO meetings on 6 and 27 Jan. and 23 Apr. 1906 in *JC* 12 Jan. 2 Feb. and 27 Apr.
1906.
[28] CJC reply to EZF, encl. in Wolf to Oliphant, 28 Apr. 1915, FO 371/2488/51705.
[29] Wolf to Cowen, 18 Aug. 1915, C11/2/7. This tends to contradict Friedman's
assertion in the *Question of Palestine*, 14, that Wolf, unlike Samuel, 'viewed the Palestine
question through a purely Jewish prism'. For French wartime pronouncements and
diplomatic demarches in relation to Palestine see W. W. Gottlieb, *Studies in Secret
Diplomacy during the First World War* (London, 1957), 72–3, 80–1, 101.

government-backed, French-speaking committee might have on
American Jews, he proposed as an alternative a series of propaganda
committees, first in London and later in all the Allied capitals, which
would be in closest confidential relations with their respective governments, yet would be 'unofficial and spontaneous'. Wolf offered his
services for this task.[30] Here, then, was Wolf's underlying intention.
This was at once a bid to get his committee patronized by the Foreign
Office and, by the same token, have the Foreign Office associated and
committed to whatever 'propaganda' plans he—albeit in Britain's
interests—might propose.

This was not the first time Wolf had attempted to catch the Foreign
Office by means of artful subterfuge. On several occasions prior to the
war he had suggested that they comment upon and amend his memoranda and publications while still in draft form, their comments thereby
appearing to give official sanction to his opinions though these were
very often at complete variance with government policy. In 1912, for
instance, he tried in this way to implicate the Foreign Office in his
memorandum calling for a reappraisal of the Anglo-Russian Commerce Treaty so as to counter discrimination against British Jews
travelling to or residing in Russia. Unluckily, Wolf's ruse was spotted
by the under-secretary of state, Sir Arthur Nicolson, who commented,
'it was adroit of Mr. Wolff [*sic*] to obtain from us observations and
suggestions as to the memorial—and make us thereby co-partners in
its authorship'.[31]

On this occasion, however, Wolf was fortunate in presenting his
scheme at a moment when the Foreign Office News Department was
much exercised with the problem of how exactly to influence American
Jewry. There were, too, recommendations from sources other than
Wolf. In January 1915, Vladimir Jabotinsky, the influential Russian
Jewish journalist and Zionist, had proposed the formation of a Jewish
Legion. Composed primarily of Russian Jewish *émigrés*, the Legion
would, he said, counter German propaganda in Russia and win enormous American support. By contrast, Horace Kallen, a Wisconsin
professor and influential figure in early American Zionism, wanted an

---

[30] Wolf to Cecil, 16 Dec. 1915, FO 371/2579/18779. The 'unofficial' aspect
stressed by Wolf was consistent with the softly-softly approach adopted by British
propaganda directed at America, as emanating from Charles Masterman's war efforts at
Wellington House; see Zeman, *Diplomatic History*, 166–7.
[31] Wolf to Norman, 27 July 1912, FO 372/381/8978; Sir Arthur Nicolson, minute,
n.d., July 1912, ibid.

Allied declaration favouring Jewish rights everywhere, and something he obscurely called 'nationalization' in Palestine. In particular, he ventured that Allied agents might be despatched to America to propagandize these proposals and thereby defeat the German agents with their Teutonic propaganda.[32]

The News Department was responsive to Kallen's suggestion. Lord Eustace Percy, the head of the department, agreed that someone ought to be sent out. Wolf, in many ways the ideal man for the task, was offering his services, but Foreign Office suspicions of his alleged German proclivities, now as on several vital occasions during the next few months, militated against him. Percy disparagingly minuted, 'I should be inclined to use his offer of service in the first place to find out if he can suggest anyone else.' Cecil seems to have had Claude Montefiore or Lionel de Rothschild in mind.[33]

Even while refusing to commit themselves to any aspects of Wolf's 'suggestions', including those relating to Zionism, the Foreign Office felt impelled to give Wolf some guarded encouragement. Cecil therefore gave him the go-ahead to contact Sir Gilbert Parker, who since the outbreak of the war had been in charge of propaganda in the United States, and also transmitted his 'suggestions' to Spring-Rice.[34] Cecil was of course anxious to pursue the propagandizing of American Jewry—indeed, he complained to Sir John Simon MP about Sir Arthur Nicolson's general lack of interest in the value of news and propaganda[35]—but he seems to have been as cautious as his Foreign

---

[32] For late 1915–early 1916 correspondence on 'Jewish Legion' see FO 371/2835/18095. See also Friedman, *The Question of Palestine, 1914–1918*, 43–7; Joseph B. Schechtman, *Rebel and Statesman* (New York, 1956), i. 225–32; Zimmern to Percy, 29 Nov. 1915, encl. Kallen to Zimmern, FO 371/2579/18779.

[33] Percy note, 5 Dec. 1915, FO 371/2579/18779; Cecil to Reading, 27 Feb. 1916, FO 371/2835/18095. It is not clear whether Wolf's offer of service preceded Percy's note. The record points to his offer being later, i.e. to Cecil on 16 Dec. 1915, and reiterated at his meeting on 27 Feb. 1916. It is quite possible, however, that Wolf made an earlier offer. The FO's willingness to utilize Montefiore or Lionel de Rothschild for propaganda purposes, the former in particular a close associate of Wolf's, tends to weaken Friedman's implication that Wolf was turned down because he was an 'assimilationist'; see Friedman, *Question of Palestine*, 50.

[34] Parker to Cecil, 16 Dec. 1915, FO 371/2579/18779; Cecil to Spring-Rice and Wolf, 29 Dec. 1915, ibid. There is no record of a meeting between Parker and Wolf.

[35] Cecil minute, 12 Dec. 1915, ibid. Cecil proposed Wolf should see Parker before he had actually seen Wolf himself. See also Cecil to Simon, 22 Dec. 1915, file 188244, cited in Mayir Vereté, 'The Balfour Declaration and its Makers', *Middle Eastern Studies*, 6 (1970), 71 n. 7.

Office colleagues about involving Wolf. It was therefore agreed that nothing further be done on Wolf's 'suggestions' until Spring-Rice had fully investigated them.[36]

Spring-Rice's reply, when it arrived a month later, severely deprecated any relations with Wolf or his proposed committee. Many years earlier, Spring-Rice had been in correspondence with Wolf over the latter's 'alleged Russophobia'. Now he warned that government involvement with the Conjoint Committee would give rise to major complications with Russia.[37] From the Foreign Office's point of view, Spring-Rice's warning was sound advice. The whole thrust of Wolf's diplomacy in 1915 had been towards the emancipation of Russia's Jews. If the Foreign Office had agreed to sponsor his propaganda plans, they would inevitably have been caught in an intriciate web whereby propaganda victories could only be won at the expense of actual concessions to the Jews from their Russian ally.

Ironically, in the six-week interval between his interview with Cecil and Spring-Rice's reply, Wolf had been busy realigning his project towards the goals of the French Comité d'Action. And they, taking their cue from Basch, were more interested in what could be done in Russia than in Palestine. Wolf moreover was under pressure from Reuben Blank, the Petrograd Political Bureau emissary. Blank was anxious that too much propaganda emphasis on the liberal forces in Russia, i.e. the Progressive Bloc, and their avowed commitment to solving the Jewish question, would only exacerbate a difficult situation there. On the other hand, Basch's news that the New York Stock Exchange was clamouring for a commercial *rapprochement* between Russia and America seemed to him a highly exploitable propaganda tool—that is, if a new treaty specifically excluding anti-Jewish restrictions could be negotiated. Blank was eager to travel to America to promote this option.[38]

Blank's proposal, as well as Wolf's four-point plan from the previous October for moderate concessions on the question of Russian Jews,

[36] Cecil to Spring-Rice, 29 Dec. 1915, FO 371/2579/18779; H. O'Beirne minute, 20 Dec. 1915, ibid.

[37] Spring-Rice to Cecil, 29 Jan. 1916, ibid.; Wolf to Spring-Rice (HMG ambassador, Teheran), 4 Apr. 1907, MWS 3917–18.

[38] Blank to Wolf, 18 Feb. 1916, MWS 1933–5; Basch letter to Moutet, n.d., Feb. 1916, AIU/France, 1D 3. Blank travelled to America after Wolf received FO sanction for a letter of introduction to the AJC; see Wolf to Cecil, 18 Feb. 1916, FO 371/2835/18095.

were discussed and endorsed when Wolf met in Paris with Leygues and his committee at the end of January 1916.[39] This meeting was highly significant, inasmuch as it seemed to provide the essentials for a joint Anglo-French policy for influencing Jewish opinion in neutral countries. It gained enormously from the presence of Philippe Berthelot, Briand's *chef de cabinet*, who promised to convey the gist of the Leygues–Wolf conversations to him.[40] This appeared to be powerful French government backing for Wolf's propaganda plans. Clearly, too, it could be used as considerable leverage to force the pace of the Russian concessions. Elkan Adler, a leading Conjoint Committee member, was just then on his way to Petrograd, and Wolf urged him to inform the Russian ministers he would meet that Jusserand was behind the French propaganda idea, and to impress on them the necessity of concessions if American opinion was to be truly placated.[41]

It was from a position of apparent strength, therefore, that Wolf presented his new propaganda proposals to Cecil on 18 February 1916. The French were behind him to the hilt, and Lord Reading, he claimed, had joined his propaganda committee. The Palestine 'suggestions' were relegated to third place on his list.[42]

Cecil's response was evasive; he approved the formation of the committee, but deprecated Anglo-French interference in Russian affairs. Wolf refused to be outmanœuvred. The Conjoint, he replied, were anxious to be in perfect accord with the government and to induce Jews in both Allied and neutral countries to be the same. But, he warned, British influence in America was waning, and he enclosed a report of Basch's mission as confirmation. Anti-Russian feeling on Wall Street was considerable: no aid would be forthcoming from there until Russia did something for its Jews. The recent German proclamations to Warsaw Jewry, to the effect that they would be emancipated once the Germans were masters of the situation, was again putting

---

[39] Wolf memo, 'Original Proposals of London and Paris Committees to Influence Jewish Opinion in Neutral Countries', n.d., Feb. 1916, C11/3/2/1.
[40] Wolf to Edmond de Rothschild, 14 Feb. 1916, MWS 3527; Wolf to Cecil, 10 Feb. 1916, C11/2/8.
[41] Wolf to E. Adler, 21 Jan. 1916, MWS 1712.
[42] Wolf to Cecil, 18 Feb. 1916, FO 371/2835/18095. Though Wolf was confident of Reading's support, a letter from Cecil to Reading on 17 Feb. 1916 (ibid.) led to him pulling out of the committee. See also Reading to Wolf, 23 Mar., C11/2/8; Wolf to Reading, 24 Mar. 1916, ibid., suggesting 'he might submit to you some grounds for reconsidering your decision'.

German propaganda into the lead in America. Once more, Wolf offered his services.[43]

Though the Foreign Office gave no response, Wolf continued to bombard them with the need for a campaign which would focus on the Jewish question in Russia. With this in view, he began preparing a series of pamphlets, including the collection of pro-Jewish statements by Russian intellectuals with an introduction by Lord Bryce.[44] On 2 March, he was again at the ministry, this time to see Oliphant and press him for a British commitment to the Comité d'Action approach. All the signs, he argued, showed the French to be interested in Russian concessions: Leygues, in his capacity as president of the Commission des Affaires Extérieures, favoured representations to Petrograd; Briand, for the sake of American public support, would agree. The government's active sponsorship of Basch's mission and the curious lack of interference in press reports of Russian Jewish affairs pointed in the same direction. With the interview concluded, Oliphant minuted:

> Mr. Wolf was disposed to view with considerable suspicion the lack of uniformity between the replies returned to the Conjoint Jewish Association (*sic*) by the British and French governments, which inevitably disposed his co-religionists to be suspicious of the real intention of the two governments.[45]

There is no indication to suggest Palestine had been discussed at this meeting. Yet the very next day, after Wolf had reiterated his points about the Comité d'Action, it quite unaccountably resurfaced in the form of a draft letter to Leygues submitted for Foreign Office approval. His Majesty's Government, Wolf wrote, did not approve of their February joint programme relative to Russia. Nor, in view of their efforts to gain Romania's adhesion to their side, could the first of Basch's proposals—an Anglo-French pledge to advocate Jewish rights, as in the Treaty of Berlin—be entertained. Wolf advised Leygues to drop these proposals for the present. But the second of Basch's proposals

[43] Wolf to Cecil, 18 Feb. 1916, FO 371/2835/18095.
[44] The proposed pamphlets included: 'What the Russian People Think on the Jewish Question', 'The Jews in the Russian Army', and 'The Legal Situation of Jews in German and Austrian Poland', see C11/3/2/1; Wolf to Bryce, 27 Mar. 1916; Bryce to Wolf, 1 May 1916, C11/2/8. The Comité d'Action had already prepared similar compilations; see Comité d'Action draft aims, n.d., Mar. 1916, AIU/France, 1D 3.
[45] Oliphant minute, 3 Mar. 1916, following Wolf–Oliphant interview, 2 Mar. 1916, FO 371/2817/42608; see also Friedman, *Question of Palestine*, 51–2, which is narratively similar on these events but follows a somewhat different interpretation.

(which as we have seen emanated not from Basch but from Slousch via the Quai d'Orsay) might be worked into a public announcement; Wolf submitted the following formula:

In the event of Palestine coming within the spheres of influence of Great Britain or France, at the close of the war, the governments of these Powers will not fail to take account of the historic interest that country possesses for the Jewish community. The Jewish population will be secured in the enjoyment of civil and religious liberty, equal political rights with the rest of the population, reasonable facilities for immigration and colonisation and such municipal privileges in the towns and colonies inhabited by them as may be shown to be necessary.[46]

Wolf's propaganda case at the Foreign Office rested on the argument that concessions in Russia would conciliate all American Jewish opinion. By the same token, the Foreign Office had shown no particular appreciation of, or commitment to, those parts of Wolf's December 1915 'suggestions' appertaining to Palestine. Why then, at this critical moment when Leygues was apparently receiving full French backing, did Wolf do an about turn?

Part of the answer may be sought in the actual presentation of the letter to Leygues. Cecil's refusal to countenance the joint 'Russian' proposals meant that Wolf literally had no room to manœuvre in that direction. Rather than drop the propaganda scheme altogether, he proposed alternative options. Thus, he outlined Basch's suggested peace conference pledge, only to drop it instantaneously; this was for the Foreign Office's benefit, not Leygues's. By suggesting that it would prejudice the Allied negotiations with Romania and adding that Grey's 1914 assurances to the Conjoint at the end of the Balkan wars obviated any urgency on the matter anyway, Wolf was really declaring his full approval of Britain's wartime diplomacy. By contrast, the Palestine element in the Leygues–Wolf conversation (which as we have noted from his December *démarche*, Wolf believed might be in Britain's interests) now came to the fore again as an effort by Wolf to demonstrate his patriotism and hence regain the Foreign Office's confidence. This is made clear by the fact that the formula was submitted to the ministry prior to being sent to Leygues. If they approved and then acted upon it in the interval, Leygues would be presented with a *fait accompli*, and one possibly detrimental to French Levantine intentions. Significantly, though Wolf had not consulted the Comité d'Action on

---

[46] Wolf to Leygues, draft, 3 Mar. 1916, FO 371/2817/42608.

this proposal, he now informed them of his willingness to have full relations with their bureau.[47] With the door closing on Russia, the Palestine initiative can be seen as a desperate effort by Wolf to regularize his committee's standing with the Foreign Office. But this alone cannot account for the precipitative urgency of his proposals. Two other factors came to coalesce here. The first was an incredible snippet of misinformation. On his return from the Comité d'Action conversations in Paris, Wolf wrote to Baron Edmond de Rothschild that the Zionists were 'taking advantage of our courtesy to push forward their plans without reference to us'. Wolf did not here specify who among the Zionists, or how they were doing this, but a letter he wrote to Lord Reading a few days later explains further. According to Wolf, Professor Basch had received reliable information in America, passed on via Leygues's committee, that 'Mr. Lloyd George has formally assured Dr. Weizmann, who is his "right hand man" at the Ministry of Munitions, that Great Britain will grant a charter to the Jews in Palestine in the event of that country coming within the sphere of influence of the British Crown.'[48] In fact, as Wolf learnt some months later from Weizmann himself, no such assurance had ever been made; Wolf wrote acidly to Bigart: 'I think you ought to bring this to the notice of Prof. Basch, as I understood from him that he had been informed in the U.S. that Mr. Lloyd George had given the assurance to Dr. Weizmann and I believe he even wrote to the Comité d'Action on the subject and asked M. Moutet to inform the French government. The facts ought to be made known to everyone who has been misled in this matter.'[49] Wolf had cause to be bitter, for Basch's misinformation had driven him into retaliatory competition with the Zionists, a process continually fed by false information on both sides, leading inexorably to the open confrontation in May 1917.

The second factor was an opportunity to scotch the Zionist challenge once and for all which presented itself at this juncture. The National Union of Jewish Rights, Wolf's invention to capture grass-roots Jewish opinion in the East End, had been in unofficial existence

---

[47] Wolf to Leygues, 20 Mar. 1916 (i.e. 17 days *after* submission of the draft to the FO), C11/3/2/1.
[48] Wolf to Edmond de Rothschild, 14 Feb. 1916, MWS 3527; Wolf to Reading, 24 Feb. 1916; C11/2/8.
[49] Wolf to Bigart, 12 Sept. 1916, AIU/Angleterre IJ 8. Wolf also sounded out Gaster to find out if he was responsible for the 'charter' rumours, but he hotly denied it. See Wolf to Gaster and vice versa, 30 Oct. and 3 Nov. 1916, CJC file, Gaster papers.

since January 1916, and its programme, drafted by Wolf himself, contained proposals on Palestine along the lines of his 'formula'. Its inaugural meeting was set for 12 March, only nine days after the presentation of the 'formula' to the Foreign Office. Wolf was therefore in frantic haste to get the government to declare itself on Palestine either before, or better still, at the meeting. Indeed, Wolf suggested this to Oliphant on 6 March, obviously envisaging that he himself would be the government's mouthpiece for this announcement.[50]

Though the Foreign Office denied Wolf this sweet victory, their response to the formula was serious and sympathetic. This was surprising, given that their interest in Zionism recently had been limited to keeping track of its apparent convergence with the ideas and development of the Turkish and Anglophobe Committee of Union and Progress. Thus, when Nahum Sokolow, an important Russian member of the Zionist Inner Actions Committee, had attempted in 1913 to reinstil their more positive turn-of-the-century approach, he had been unceremoniously shown the door. Sir Louis Mallet minuted, 'The less we have to do with the Zionists the better.'[51]

In the circumstances of the war, however, the Foreign Office's concern with what they believed to be the Germanophile instincts of Jewry, whether in the Levant, Russia or America, put Zionism in a new light. If Jewry were hostile, perhaps they could be won over to the Allied side through an act of benevolence at the expense of the Ottoman Empire. At least this offered more scope for manoeuvre than action at the expense of Russia. It all depended on whether Jewry would respond as a corporate whole to the Zionist appeal. When in December 1915 Wolf had implied as much in the case of American Jewry, the Foreign Office had not pursued the issue, presumably because at this stage they still lacked a coherent policy towards Zionism. Wolf's March 'formula' was however fortuitous in following on only a month after an initiative by Edgar Suares, head of the important Alexandria Jewish community. Suares had argued that 'with the stroke of the pen, almost,

[50] Wolf to Oliphant, 6 Mar. 1916, C11/2/8. Fraenkel, 'Wolf and Herzl', 187, speculates on how Wolf would have gone down in history if the 'declaration' had been sent to him rather than to Lord Rothschild in Nov. 1917. For the embryonic development of the NUJR see S. Cohen, *English Zionists*, 254–6. Note also the series of unanswered questions on Wolf's haste which ultimately led in the wrong direction in Friedman, *Question of Palestine*, 52.

[51] Mallet minute, 12 Feb. 1913, FO 371/1794/6584; Sokolow interview, 3 Mar. 1913, ibid.

England could assure to herself the active support of the Jews all over the neutral world if only the Jews knew that British policy accorded with their aspirations in Palestine'.[52] Wolf's 'formula' seems to have translated Foreign Office meditations on Suares's suggestions into active participation. Though Grey was away convalescing at the time, his stand-in, Lord Crewe, was ready to pursue the matter; 'the advantage of securing Jewish goodwill in the Levant and America', he surmised, 'can hardly be overestimated both at present and at the conclusion of the war. We ought to help Russia realise this.' However, another senior official, Hugh O'Beirne, who had been chargé d'affaires in Petrograd and Sofia from 1906 to 1915, deprecated pursuing the Russian aspects of the question.

The one ruling consideration . . . is . . . whether any suggestion put forward . . . would appeal to a large and influential section of the Jews throughout the world. If the question is answered in the affirmative and I believe it is so answered by good authorities, then it is clear that the Palestine scheme has in it the most far-reaching political possibilities.[53]

O'Beirne's enthusiasm carried the day amongst his more sceptical colleagues. It was decided to approach Britain's French and Russian allies with a view to their adhesion to the scheme on the basis of Wolf's formula, which was considered 'unobjectionable'. As O'Beirne, who emphasized how 'preponderantly hostile' world Jewry was to Britain, was left to draft the necessary letters, however, the scope of the proposal was widened to hold out the prospect of eventual Jewish statehood once the Jewish colonists had grown large enough in number to 'cope with the Arab population'.[54]

O'Beirne's belief that a bargain could be struck with the Jews over Palestine was shared by Sir Mark Sykes, the diplomatic troubleshooter, then in Moscow in his capacity as British representative in important three-Power talks which marked a crucial new stage in Allied intentions towards the post-war Ottoman Empire. As soon as Sykes received the news of Wolf's formula—telegraphed via Buchanan in Petrograd—he made energetic and quite unauthorized efforts to win

[52] Suares to McMahon, 23 Feb. 1915, quoted in Vereté, 'Balfour Declaration'.

[53] O'Beirne minute, 8 Mar. 1916, FO 371/2817/42608; also Crewe minute, same date. See also Keith Robbins, *Sir Edward Grey* (London, 1971), 332–3.

[54] O'Beirne drafts and letters to Bertie and Buchanan, 11 Mar. 1916, FO 371/2817/42608. For the 'Jewish world power' views which O'Beirne seems to have shared with Britain's dragoman in Constantinople, G. H. Fitzmaurice, see Sanders, *High Walls*, 333–5.

over Georges Picot, his French opposite number, to a scheme which
though referring to Wolf's was essentially of his own making: a Jewish
chartered company for land purchase plus full colonizing facilities in
an enlarged Palestine, excluding Jerusalem. Interestingly, though
Sykes had gone to Russia having read and memorized Samuel's
memorandum urging a British protectorate, at this stage he saw the
issue overtly as one of winning over malevolent Jewish forces. His view
of Jewry was in fact that of the Foreign Office *in extremis*. He saw 'Jews
in everything', and attributed to them a corporate will:

To my mind the Zionists are the key to the situation—the problem is how are
they to be satisfied—with 'great Jewry' against us, there is no possible chance
of getting the thing [the war] through—it means optimism in Berlin—dumps
in London, unease in Paris . . . if the Zionists think the proposal is a good
enough they will want us to win, they will do their best which means (*a*) calm
their activities in Russia, (*b*) pessimism in Germany, (*c*) stimulate in France,
England and Italy, (*d*) enthuse in the USA. This will be subconscious, unwritten
and wholly atmospheric.[55]

Significantly, too, Sykes, perhaps on the assumption that all Jews
were Zionists, mistook Wolf for one. The raising of the Palestine
question, he wrote to Nicolson, did not come as a surprise to him 'as
when we were in London I told him [Picot] to expect Zionists to move
in London when they knew he and I were at Petrograd'.[56] At this
stage, Sykes did not know any 'genuine' Zionists, but when later on he
met Gaster, he undoubtedly felt he had been duped by Wolf, for he
bitingly referred to him as one who 'has on more than one occasion
masqueraded as a Zionist'.[57] Whether Wolf had forewarning of the
Moscow talks is of course debatable. His journalistic career in foreign
affairs often provided him with a great deal of 'intelligence' from the
chancelleries of Europe. If this was the case on this occasion, Wolf
timed his *démarche* to a tee. More likely, especially considering that
Wolf was the principal loser from his action, it was wholly fortuitous.

London sharply rapped Sykes for his behaviour in Moscow—not for
his incredible statements on the Jews, but for indiscreetly discussing

[55] Sykes to Nicolson, 18 Mar. 1916, FO 800/381 (Nicolson papers). Printed in full
in Elie Kedourie, 'Sir Mark Sykes and Palestine 1915–1916', *Middle Eastern Studies*, 6
(1970), 340–5. See also Roger Adelson, *Mark Sykes: Portrait of an Amateur* (London,
1975), 204–7, for his view of the Jews as remembered by a Cambridge professor. See
also Sanders, *High Walls*, 352–3.
[56] Sykes to Nicolson, 18 Mar. 1916, FO 371/2767/938.
[57] Sykes to Graham, 28 Apr. 1917, FO 371/3057/84173.

the Samuel memorandum with Picot.[58] It was French susceptibilities, in fact, which killed the Wolf scheme. While Buchanan reported Sazonov's acceptance of it, Bertie in Paris communicated French indifference. 'Jews hostile to the Allies', ran the Quai d'Orsay reply, were 'inspired by motives which have nothing in common with Zionist aspirations, realization of whose goals will not make the former disappear.' The French suggested that the issue be dropped, at least until the Arab question had been resolved.[59]

At bottom, the French cold-shouldering can probably be attributed to their anxieties about Britain's real intentions in the Levant. Sykes and Picot had already tussled over the future of Palestine, and internationalization, as proposed by them in January, had been a compromise solution.[60] However, if Zionism, acting as a catalyst to a quick change of Jewish allegiance were really that crucial to the outcome of the war, as Sykes had suggested, the French would presumably have set aside their reservations and supported the scheme. Significantly their non-committal reply mirrors the information received from Basch and used by Leygues's committee, the very body which O'Beirne believed would back the scheme in the French interest.[61] Similarly, while not disputing that Jews were Germanophiles, some British diplomats were inclined to accept the French logic. Bertie, for instance, noted that the anti-*entente* Jews who really counted, such as Schiff, would not be impressed by a declaration on Palestine but might favour a Russian loan if Britain and France extracted Russian 'promises for the proper treatment of her Jews', though he went on to admit that this was something Britain and France could not guarantee. Likewise, Harold Nicolson, after viewing further Basch material, agreed that it showed 'the effect on Jewish opinion in the States which would be made by any

[58] Communicated by Nicolson to Buchanan, 16 Mar. 1916, FO 371/2767/938. Grey minuted (n.d.): 'Ask Sir George Buchanan to tell Mr Sykes to obliterate from his memory that Mr Samuel's Cabinet memorandum made any mention of a British Protectorate. Say that I told Mr Samuel at the time that a British protectorate was quite out of the question and Sir Mark Sykes should never mention the subject without making this clear.'

[59] Buchanan to FO, 23 Mar. 1916, FO 371/2817/42608; Bertie to FO, 22 Mar. 1916, ibid.; also in FO 800/176 (Bertie papers). For draft French reply see MAE Guerre 1914–18, file 872, fos. 40–1.

[60] Sykes-Picot talks 3 Jan. 1916, MAE Guerre 1914–18, file 871, fos. 148–64. See also Jukka Nevakiki, *Britain, France and the Arab Middle East, 1914–1920* (London, 1969), 13–44.

[61] O'Beirne minute, 8 Mar. 1916, FO 371/2817/42608.

98   *Wolf and the Zionists*

steps taken to restore Jewish confidence in Russia'.[62] The problem
was that British diplomatic pressure to bring about an amelioration of
the Russian Jewish condition could only lead up a veritable *cul-de-sac*.
Where did this leave Wolf? By proposing the 'formula', Wolf had
shown the British Foreign Office how to 'win' the Jews for the war
effort without upsetting the Russians. O'Beirne minuted:

> If it is the case that the Zionist scheme does not appeal to a large and
> influential section of the Jews throughout the world, who are now antagonistic
> to our case, then I agree that the whole scheme had better be dropped. But our
> information, so far as I know, is not to that effect.[63]

Thus, though temporarily defeated by the Quai d'Orsay, the British
now had an interest in Zionism, crystallized in their minds by the
'formula', which would eventually take them through to the Balfour
Declaration. Wolf, too, had inadvertently paved the way for Sykes, the
man most crucially involved in its fostering, to seek out the genuine
Zionists: Gaster and Weizmann.

This was all highly ironic from Wolf's point of view, amounting to a
gross and irredeemable miscalculation. Firstly, though his perspective
on the Jewish relationship to the war was completely at odds with that
of Sykes and O'Beirne, his 'formula' had served to reinforce their all-
embracing *Weltanschauung*. Secondly, he had in effect handed the
Foreign Office on a plate to his arch-rivals, the Zionists. Thirdly, in so
doing, not only did he not receive reward for his pains in terms of a
more tangible relationship with the Foreign Office but actually found
himself further distanced from the corridors of power.

Immediately after his *démarche*, Wolf was informed that his formula
was receiving, in consultation with the Allies, 'careful and sympathetic
consideration',[64] but after that no further response was forthcoming
until he himself approached the Foreign Office, three months later.
The events that followed served only to mystify Wolf. At the ministry
he was handed a letter that soothingly assured him that though an
announcement was inopportune at the present time, the 'formula'
would be borne in mind in the future. But Wolf was also told, on
authorization from Grey, that it had been the subject of consultations

[62] Bertie to Grey, 13 Mar. 1916, FO 800/176. For Bertie's views on Zionism see *The Diary of Lord Bertie of Thame, 1914–1918*, ed. Lady Algernon Gordon Lennox (London, 1924), ii. 104–5, 228–9. Nicolson minute, 11 Mar. 1916, commenting on Basch to Moutet extracts encl. with Wolf to Oliphant, 9 Mar. 1916, FO 371/2817/42608.
[63] O'Beirne minute, Basch extracts, 23 Mar. 1916, FO 371/2817/42608.
[64] Oliphant to Wolf, 9 Mar. 1916, ibid.

with the French, but the latter believed that it would 'not satisfy a very large body of Jewish opinion'. Wolf wrote to Bigart, 'I was given to understand that certain Zionists do not approve of the formula.'[65] Somehow Grey had managed to garble the French reply by making it seem as if the Zionists were behind their opposition to Wolf's project. In fact, at this stage, the Zionists still had no official standing with either the French or British governments, Sokolow having recently been yet again rebuffed by the Foreign Office and Gaster not yet interviewed. Wolf's mystification ran even deeper when he saw Briand, the French premier, a week later in Paris. Unknown to Wolf, Briand had interviewed Bertie on the scheme in March, but when Wolf now mentioned it to Briand, claiming on the authority of Baron Edmond de Rothschild that the Zionists would not object to it, the French premier preferred to suggest that no Palestine 'formula' had ever come before him. With no reliable information as to what was really going on, Wolf's worries about Zionist 'sabotage' now took full sway.[66]

Wolf meanwhile was contributing to his own alienation from the Foreign Office by continuing to feed it with Leygues Committee material that was diametrically at odds with its evolving pro-Zionist policy. 'What is so discouraging', minuted O'Beirne on Basch's letters, 'is that so much more stress is laid on the emancipation of the Russian Jews than on the Palestine question.' Oliphant commented, 'Certainly Mr. Wolf and his gang are bent on more material ameliorisation of

[65] de Bunsen to Wolf, 4 July 1916, ibid.; Oliphant note on interview, 4 July 1916, ibid.; Wolf to Bigart, 18 July 1916, C11/2/9. On Zionist 'sabotage' see Wolf to CJC presidents, 8 July 1916, C11/3/2/1.

[66] Sokolow memo, 12 Apr. 1916, FO 371/2817/42608; Gaster's 'unofficial' interview with Hardinge, 14 July 1916, ibid.; Wolf to Oliphant, 18 July 1916, encl. extracts from diary on visit to Paris and including meeting with Briand, 12 July 1916, ibid. On Bertie's interview with Briand see MAE Guerre 1914–18, file 872, fos. 40–4. One explanation for the French premier's silence may be sought in the 'Comité d'Action Française en Syrie' set up and approved by him in person on 30 June 1916 as a renewed effort to secure French interests in that part of the world, and only 17 days before the interview with Wolf. This committee, like the Comité d'Action auprès des Juifs des Pays Neutres, was sponsored by the French Parliamentary Commission on Foreign Affairs and housed in the same building: 243 Blvd. St Germain. Moreover, the two committees had members in common. Georges Leygues, president of the Jewish Committee, was a member of the Syrian Committee. Franklin-Bouillon, president of the Syrian Committee, was a member of the Jewish one. In other words, the Leygues Committee men could hardly have pressed for any Palestine solution inimical to France, while pursuing a contradictory policy in the Syria Committee; see *Paris-midi* report on the Syria Committee, MAE Guerre 1914–1918, file 873, fo. 127.

Jews in European countries rather than Zionism.' Justifying their actions to themselves with the argument that 'Mr. Wolff [*sic*] cannot be taken as the spokesman of the whole community', in April 1916 they dropped his projected propaganda scheme altogether.[67]

Though Wolf was undoubtedly defeated as far as his Zionist posturings were concerned, he nevertheless still had a valid case which the Foreign Office could not ignore. The summer of 1916 saw the war reach a new peak of intensity—Verdun, the Somme, the Brusilov offensive in the east; at any time one side might waver, peace feelers be made, and a European peace settlement negotiated. Wolf chose his moment well, at a time of considerable Foreign Office reshuffling,[68] not only to make his enquiries about the 'formula' but to remind the Allies that even if they were victorious the Central Powers might still be able to wrest advantage from the peace conference. In undoubtedly his shrewdest and most effective memorandum of the war, Wolf articulated how they would set about doing this.[69]

By contrasting Russia's continued ill treatment of its Jews with their own 'liberating' policies, he suggested, they would still be able to arouse sentiment in neutral countries in their favour. Drawing on his enormous knowledge of diplomatic history, Wolf enumerated the legitimate precedents they might utilize, 'all equally awkward to the Allies'. Wolf focused particularly on the American stance at the Bucharest Conference in 1913 when they had intervened on the question of racial and religious equality.[70] More recently, both Houses of Congress had jointly resolved to back the idea of a League of Neutral Nations to formulate a liberal peace treaty. What this might mean in practice, suggested Wolf, was that 'the Central Powers would speak and act

---

[67] O'Beirne, 14 Mar. 1916, FO 371/2817/42608; Oliphant, minutes, 23 Mar. 1916, ibid. The FO were inclined to put their own Zionist interpretation on the Basch mission. See Percy note, 16 Feb. 1916, FO 371/2835/18905: 'I believe the French are making some efforts to get hold of the [Zionist] movement, through a Jewish Sorbonne professor who recently went to the USA', Montgomery interview with Wolf, 3 Apr. 1916, FO 371/2835/18095. See also Crewe minute, 8 Mar. 1916, FO 371/2817/42608.

[68] The key change was that Hardinge replaced Nicolson as the FO permanent under-secretary at the end of June 1916.

[69] Wolf to FO, 14 June 1916, encl. memo, FO 371/2817/42608. Text in full in *The Peace Conference, Paris: Report of the Delegation of the Jews of the British Empire on the Peace Conference 1919* (London, 1920), (hereafter *RDJBE*), doc. 2, pp. 41–2. Parkes, *Emergence*, 106–7, describes the memo as 'admirably subtle and brilliant'.

[70] See Cyrus Adler and Aaron A. Margalith, *With Firmness in the Right: American Diplomatic Action Affecting Jews, 1840–1945* (New York, 1946), 135–7.

with American sympathy and support'. Having struck home, he daringly concluded with the suggestion that the whole question should be 'confidentially discussed by the Foreign Office and the [Conjoint] Committee, with a view to reaching a solution which would be equally satisfactory to the interests of the Allied governments and those of the oppressed Jewish communities'.[71]

The Foreign Office, despite its disapproval of Wolf, could not but agree that the 'embarrassments to the Allies' of which he warned were genuine. Arthur Nicolson, the outgoing under-secretary of state, therefore commanded him to furnish the committee's 'considered views', views which would be studied at the Foreign Office and which would lead to the committee receiving 'a further command'.[72] This was a considerable victory for Wolf, recognition that the Jewish question was relevant and that his views on the subject were worthy of respect. This seemed to be further endorsed when Oliphant telephoned the War Office to expedite Wolf's imminent journey to Paris—Wolf having hinted that 'the views' could not be ascertained without the concurrence of his friends in Paris and Petrograd—in spite of the fact that with the Somme offensive in full swing their priorities were strictly elsewhere. Oliphant's other news, that the Palestine 'formula' had finally been dropped, must have seemed to Wolf not much of a loss.[73]

Things at last seemed to be going the way Wolf had intended. But there was still need for urgent action. His associate David Mowscho- witch reminded him that at the Berlin Congress, Cremieux and the other Jewish 'diplomats' had settled everything by 'preliminary private arrangements'. Wolf would similarly need to have his recommenda- tions accepted and officially rubberstamped before the peace confer- ence and so, more importantly, before the Western Allies had a chance to renege on them.[74]

With this goal in mind, Wolf now bent all his efforts to ensuring the active support of the Alliance, the Rome Committee, and the Petrograd

---

[71] *RDJBE*, doc. 2, pp. 41–2.

[72] Nicolson minute, 19 June, FO 371/2817/42608; Oliphant minute, 16 June 1916, ibid.: 'There is considerable force in what he says about the enemy using the question as much as possible'; De Bunsen to Wolf, 23 June 1916, ibid. Cf. Friedman, *Question of Palestine*, 62, which comments on the failure of Wolf's 'formula': 'deprived of his last propaganda weapon, his policy was now in ruins'. The documentary sources, however, show that Wolf's policy was still exceedingly buoyant until the rejection of the 'con- sidered views' some six months later.

[73] Wolf to de Bunsen, 29 June 1916, FO 371/2817/42608; Wolf to CJC presidents, 8 July 1916, C11/3/2/1.   [74] Mowschowitch to Wolf, 27 July 1916, C11/2/9.

Bureau for his plan. 'Our case in its broad outlines' he wrote hastily to
Bigart, 'must be prepared almost at once, as there is a possibility of it
being taken into consideration by the Allied governments, at a very
early date . . . the object of my visit to Paris is to assure the identity of
your views with our own.'[75]

Wolf had his way. The Alliance hastily convened to discuss these
proposals with their English visitor and agreed to his maximum and
minimum programme for the emancipation of Russian Jews. When the
time came for representations, the Alliance promised they would make
a similar approach to the Quai d'Orsay. Angelo Sereni of the Rome
Committee, though not present at this parley, agreed through correspondence with the Alliance, to do the same *vis-à-vis* the Italian
government.[76] Wolf's headship of the Western Jewish organizations
thus seemed fully secure.

Significantly, though he had no direct control or power of veto in the
Leygues Committee, he was able while in Paris to get a promise of
their support, Leygues himself proposing to get the French Foreign
Affairs Commission to support the 'considered views'. It was also at
the instigation of another committee member, Deputy Moutet, that
Wolf was able to gain access to the French prime minister. Here again,
his hopes were raised when Briand agreed with him that the Jewish
question, especially the Russian Jewish question, was 'a serious
element in the diplomatic calculations of the Allies'.[77]

So far so good. Meanwhile, the slowness of the Petrograd response
was causing Wolf some consternation. The response had to be smuggled
out of Russia via Mowschowitch in Stockholm, and Wolf's original
stipulation to do nothing without their mandate gradually weakened as
the need for an immediate initiative grew.[78] However, as Romania's
entry into the war gave Wolf the pretext to deal with its Jewish question

[75] Wolf to Bigart, 5 July 1916, AIU/Angleterre 1J 8.
[76] On Wolf's visit to Paris see CJC Report no. 8, Sept. 1916, MW 5356–65. See also
Wolf to Oliphant, 18 June 1916, encl. 'Extracts of Diary', FO 371/2817/42608. The
'minimum' programme was an enlarged version of Wolf's 1915 four-point plan. At the
meeting Bigart had this extended to specifically include the abrogation of the 1881 May
Laws. The maximum programme was for total emancipation. See AIU to Rome
committee, 17 Aug. 1916, AIU/Angleterre 1J 8; Rome committee to Wolf, 17 Aug.
1916, MWS 5366–71.
[77] 'Extracts of Diary' encl. with Wolf to Oliphant, 18 June 1916, FO 371/2817/
42608.
[78] Wolf to Mowschowitch, 8 Aug. 1916, C11/2/9; Wolf to Bigart, 30 Aug. 1916,
ibid.

on the same basis as the other questions, the delay proved benevolent. Moreover, the Petrograd reply, when it did come in September, must have been particularly gratifying to Wolf. More than endorsing his programme, in a statement strongly reflecting the Western liberal approach to the Jewish question it repudiated the view that antisemitism had deep social roots in Russian life. It went on to affirm the Jews' rootedness in the Russian empire, 'to which they are bound historically, economically and culturally'.[79]

By the beginning of October, Wolf was ready to submit his 'considered views' to the government. His programme was a simple, straightforward argument for a liberal solution to the Jewish question on traditional Western lines. It demanded:

1. Total abolition of all political and civil disabilities which differentiated Russian Jews from their fellow countrymen.

2. The recognition of Jewish citizen rights in Romania, as recognized by article 44 of the Treaty of Berlin.

3. Guarantees that Jews living in the territories of the Central Powers would continue to enjoy their citizen rights should any part of these territories be ceded to Russia or Romania after the war.[80]

Significantly, the 'considered views' laid particular stress on the German and Austrian efforts to ameliorate the East European Jewish situation; Wolf backed this up with a revised copy of his June memorandum, claiming to show how this was aligning American sentiment towards the Central Powers. The embarrassing use of this propaganda weapon, Wolf argued, justified his view 'that the only solution which will meet the bare necessities of the case on the diplomatic as well as Jewish side, is emancipation'.[81]

There was also a fourth point: Palestine. This, however, came right at the bottom of Wolf's list. Simply a restatement of Wolf's March formula, albeit now as an aspect of Conjoint policy, it looked very much like an afterthought.

Although several months had elapsed since the Foreign Office's request for the 'considered views', Wolf seems to have been optimistic that Grey would keep his promise to address a further communication to the Conjoint once the 'views' had been 'received and studied'.

[79] Wolf to Bigart, 30 Aug. 1916, ibid.; CJC Report no. 9, Feb. 1917, MWS 5505–13. The Petrograd Bureau reply took ten weeks, arriving in late Sept. 1916.
[80] 'Considered Views', encl. with Wolf to Oliphant, 1 Oct. 1916, FO 371/2817/42608; see *RDJBE* 43–5 for full text; see also Parkes, *Emergence*, 107–8.
[81] 'Considered Views', FO 371/2817/42608; and in *RDJBE* 45.

While he did not expect the ministry to endorse the programme at face value, he believed it would be the basis for negotiations not only in London but also between the other Western Jewish organizations and their respective governments.[82] In this he was to be sorely disappointed.

Wolf could only expect British, French, and Italian endorsement of his plans if the Central Powers were overwhelmingly defeated: only then might the Allies be in a position to pressure a reluctant Russia on the Jewish question. Had the summer offensives succeeded, Wolf might have had a remote chance of getting his project carried, but by July 1916 the information he was receiving was pointing in a very different direction. On 6 July, Leopold de Rothschild was able to have an audience with Lord Hardinge, the new permanent under-secretary of state, to 'ask him for any messages he might have for Baron Edmond', which Wolf would convey to Paris. The interview, wrote Wolf, was disappointing:

Lord Hardinge said it was impossible for the British government to approach Russia on the Jewish question. Germany was ready to make peace with Russia and France at any moment and that being so, we could not afford the slightest difference with Russia. He said, besides, that France being the older ally of Russia, had a better right to speak than we had.[83]

In Paris, Wolf had this line confirmed by Baron Edmond himself; the Allies were 'afraid to talk' to an unstable ally like Russia. Pessimistically, Baron Edmond insisted that the best that could be hoped for, through continued Conjoint vigilance and perseverance, was stabilization of an otherwise deteriorating Russian Jewish situation, and perhaps the prevention of pogroms.[84]

In fact, even if the Foreign Office had wished to act in this matter, it was not well positioned to do so. Though Britain had provided a navy and considerable financial assets for the Allied war effort, it was not, in spite of conscription or the Somme offensive, in 1916, the country bearing the brunt of the fighting. France had truly been 'bled white', but even then it was Russia that first and foremost had to supply the Allied war machine with man-fodder, and it was consequently Russia

[82] de Bunsen to CJC, 23 June 1916, following Grey's request for 'Considered Views', *RDJBE* 43; Wolf to A. Abrahams, 30 Oct. 1916, MWS 1693; Wolf to Bigart, 29 Sept. 1916, MWS 7785.
[83] Wolf to Montefiore, 7 July 1916, C11/2/9.
[84] CJC Report no. 8, Sept. 1916, MWS 5359–60.

who sustained the greatest losses. With the catastrophic collapse of the initially successful Brusilov offensive, in the late summer,[85] and with the chances of a separate Russian peace with Germany thus greatly magnified, the British government was both less in a position to present Russia with demands and conversely more anxious not to do anything that might risk its defection. Moreover, even leaving aside the fierce antagonism of senior Foreign Office officials to the Jews,[86] a strong streak of hard-headed pragmatism convinced them that nothing they might do could help. 'The end will be that nothing will be done,' predicted Hardinge, 'as it is almost impossible to get Russia or Rumania to do anything for their Jews.'[87]

By December the Foreign Office had categorically decided not to pursue the matter, though the Conjoint was not informed. Wolf was growing restive. There seems to have been a communications break-down with the French and Italian Jewish committees, and he was fearful that neither committee had presented its own parallel representations.[88] Moreover, on 12 December, Theobald von Bethman-Hollweg, the German chancellor, made a formal peace offer to the Allies. Once again, Russia, on the point of exhaustion, was the most likely to consider the offer seriously. In fact, the offer was rejected, but Wolf seems to have sensed that these developments put paid to any diplomatic pressure Britain and France might be able to exert on their ally. 'We ought, I think,' he wrote to Montefiore, 'in common

[85] On the importance of the Brusilov offensive in Allied fortunes see Stone, *Eastern Front*, 246–50, 271–2.

[86] See e.g. Harold Nicolson minute, n.d., *c.* 5 Jan. 1917, FO 371/3092/4637: 'One would like to tell Mr Wolf that after the way the Jews in Russia and Rumania have behaved, it will be more than ever impossible to intervene on their behalf.'

[87] Hardinge minute, n.d., Oct. 1916, FO 371/2817/42608.

[88] Wolf to Bigart, 27 Nov. 1916, AIU/Angleterre IJ 8. See also Mitrany to Wolf, 20 Nov. 1916, C11/2/10, on AIU inactivity. Sereni to Wolf, 25 Dec. 1916, AIU/Angleterre IJ 8, did not mention a word about a joint representation, leading Wolf to write angrily to Bigart, 3 Jan. 1917 (ibid.): 'I was under the impression that you had informed Rome of what had been done and that you were concerting with our Italian friends, similar action in Italy and France.' There seems to be no evidence that either the AIU or Rome committee handed in representations. Stein, *Balfour Declaration*, 296, suggests that Briand asked the AIU to defer its memorandum, pending FO–Quai d'Orsay negotiations on the subject. One explanation as far as the Rome committee is concerned relates to their anger at the way Wolf fobbed off their urgent requests for a 'Congress' by claiming that all subsidiary points could be settled by correspondence while urging them to follow his lead on the 'considered views'. Possibly we have here a mini-Italian revolt against Wolf's hegemony. See Sereni to Wolf and vice versa, 17 and 30 Aug. 1916, AIU/Angleterre IJ 8.

prudence to prepare for the possibility of our suggestions not being acted upon.'[89] Unable to wait any longer, on New Year's Day 1917 Wolf pressed the Foreign Office for a reply to the 'considered views'. Their immediate answer was non-committal, regretting that it would not be possible 'to express any official opinion'.[90] This response reeked strongly of the ministry's pre-war sidesteppings of Wolf's representations to it. Wolf immediately pressed to find out if this was their final answer; he reminded them that it was they who had invited the Conjoint to furnish its views, and rather lamely threatened that if this was their final answer, the Conjoint would have to reconsider the whole situation. After further delay the Foreign Office wrote again, this time quite unequivocally. There could be 'no understanding now or in the immediate future' on the basis of the Conjoint suggestions.[91]

This was a bombshell for Wolf and the Conjoint. The Foreign Office was effectively dismissing the whole struggle for Jewish emancipation, which the Conjoint had so persistently though patiently fought for, and which now seemed on the verge of resolution, in a three-line letter. Wolf decided it could not be so.

I have a lingering belief at the back of my head that the situation is not as bad as it seems and if we only knew what it really is we might be spared any possible blunders in the future. I cannot imagine after the exchange of notes with the U.S. the government contemplate leaving the Jews in the lurch.[92]

Wolf here was referring to the Allied note replying to President Wilson's request to be furnished with the belligerents' war aims, which had been published on 19 January. *Inter alia*, it had pledged 'liberty and justice and inviolable fidelity to treaty obligations'. Now the Allies seemed to be cynically eating their words. Montefiore had an explanation: 'I fear that the Russians have hinted that if we say a word about the Jews, they will make peace with Germany.' Through the good offices of Montefiore and Leopold de Rothschild, however, Wolf was able by the end of January to discuss the Foreign Office reply with

[89] Wolf to Montefiore, 28 Dec. 1916, MWS 5559. See also Anthony Summers and Tom Mangold, *The File on the Tsar* (London, 1976), 217–18, on the highly secret German Imperial mission to Russia in December 1916 which attempted to intercede with the tsar to get Russia to quit the war.
[90] Wolf to Oliphant, 1 Jan. 1917, FO 371/3092/4637; Oliphant to Wolf, 5 Jan. 1917, ibid.
[91] Wolf to Oliphant, 6 Jan. 1917, ibid.; de Bunsen to Wolf, 20 Jan. 1917, ibid.
[92] Wolf to Montefiore, 24 Jan. 1917, CI1/2/11.

Arthur Balfour, the new foreign secretary. Prior to this encounter Wolf
was warned by Montefiore that Balfour was in the hands of Hardinge,
whom Montefiore claimed was 'anti-semitic and bureaucratic in the
German sense'; Balfour himself, according to Montefiore, had abstract
philosophical objections to the Jews. In the event, however, this did not
prevent a frank and wide-ranging interchange between Wolf and
Balfour.[93]

A month earlier, Wolf had abjured his wartime journalistic silence
and written a highly ingratiating article on Balfour's earlier involvements in foreign affairs in the *Daily Chronicle*.[94] The article laid
particular emphasis on Balfour's salutary role in the development of
the Triple *Entente* and on Wolf's own services to him in the 1898
China dispute with Russia. However, neither this nor Wolf's insistence
in the interview on the Conjoint's good behaviour in subordinating
their views to the war effort could deflect Balfour from reaffirming
what Wolf had already heard from the Foreign Office. The old problem resurfaced: 'We cannot appeal to the Peace Conference against
the Allies of our country.'[95]

In private Wolf gave full vent to his bitterness:

The enthusiasm for liberty cannot be very sincere if the Allies themselves
cannot secure humane treatment and the elementary rights of citizenship for
six millions of Jews within their own borders and cannot even agree that Jews
who are now free in German or Austrian Poland or in Transylvania, shall be
reduced to the terrible conditions of their Russian and Rumanian co-
religionists, when in the name of freedom for oppressed nationalities, their
provinces are transferred to Russia and Rumania.[96]

Wolf's policy was indeed in ruins.

[93] Montefiore to Wolf, 21 and 29 Jan. 1917, ibid.; Wolf memo on interview with
Balfour, 30 Jan. 1917, FO 800/210 (Balfour papers). The degree to which Balfour was,
or was not an antisemite has been the subject of some debate; Jehuda Reinharz, *Chaim
Weizmann, The Making of a Zionist Leader* (New York, 1985), 274, for instance, appears
to give him the benefit of the doubt. Sydney H. Zebel's *Balfour: A Political Biography*
(London, 1971), 237, 243–8, makes it clear that Balfour shared the general FO
assumptions about the cohesive nature and power of 'international' Jewry and its
significance, particularly in financial terms, for the outcome of the war.
[94] 'Mr Balfour at the Foreign Office', *Daily Chronicle*, 16 Dec. 1916: e.g. 'The
measure of the gratitude we thus owe to Mr. Balfour's grasp is sufficiently indicated to us
by our happy alliances in the present war.' On Wolf's role in the 1898 Manchuria
dispute see also 'Miss Philips's Diary', Mocatta Lib., entry for 12 July 1908.
[95] Wolf to Montefiore, 28 Dec. 1916, MWS 5559.
[96] Wolf to Leopold de Rothschild, 22 Jan. 1917, MWS 10508.

5
The Ideological Rift

The Conjoint Committee have their own formula, adopted partly as compromise with the Zionists, partly under the pressure of public opinion and in order not to show that they were dragged into Zionism by the event but on the contrary, they were leading. The formula is practically tantamount to the Basle programme though it differs from the point of view of principles.[1]

The Foreign Office's rebuttal of the 'considered views' served to heighten the tensions already existing between the Conjoint Committee and the Zionists. Within six months these had exploded in a major communal row which led to the committee's demise.

As soon as Wolf and his colleagues had clear evidence that the Weizmann group was negotiating with the government, a showdown was inevitable. The Conjoint, as the communal body authorized to speak on foreign affairs, felt jealous of its vested interests at the Foreign Office. The Zionist interlopers not only represented an unsubtle challenge to this special position but also, though holding no specific communal mandate themselves, brought into question the precarious foundations on which the Conjoint's communal legitimacy was laid. Nevertheless, to explain this as a communal 'power struggle' does not adequately explain the deep divisiveness of this controversy. When pressed, the Conjoint were ready to co-operate with the Zionists in submitting a joint scheme to the government. By the same token, Weizmann, as distinct from his many English Zionist competitors, was not interested in waging a campaign to bring Wolf down from his pedestal. In fact, the issue of communal authority was pushed more and more into the background as the real quarrel between the two parties crystallized. What essentially was at stake were two conflicting, indeed irreconcilable, world views.

Herzl's near-absolute hegemony of the early Zionist congresses and the primacy he gave to his own particular solution to the Jewish question tended to mask divergent currents within the Zionist ranks. Thus, Herzl's insistence on the creation of a Jewish state through the

---

[1] Mowschowitch notes, 30 Mar. 1917, MWS 24657–65.

active co-operation of the Great Powers generally speaking received its most uncritical support from Western European Jews who, like Herzl himself, already enjoyed the benefits of civil and political emancipation. Zionism in these terms was often a pragmatic response to the Jewish question as it was perceived to exist in Eastern Europe. Moreover, the attraction of securing and guaranteeing a national refuge for Eastern Jewry lay not only in that it might solve the problem of Jewish migration westwards. It also had something expansive and daring about it; Wolf himself was one of the very early proponents of this Herzlian vision.[2]

By contrast, much of the East European approach tended towards both fatalism and introspection. Conditioned by circumstances which increasingly seemed to militate against the likelihood of emancipation and assimilation on Western lines, the intellectual and nascent political leadership of Russian Zionism chose instead to reject the possibility or even wisdom of pursuing these goals in favour of an entirely auto-emancipationary creed. Redemption would come through Jews recognizing and making a virtue of their own national 'distinctiveness'. Logically, this could only happen through a Jewish reawakening which focused on the ancient home of the Jewish nation, Palestine. When Herzl's negotiations with the British led to the offer of a Jewish homeland in East Africa, it was Russian Zionei Zion supporters at the Sixth Zionist Congress in 1903 who thus most bitterly and stridently pronounced anathema upon it.[3]

For the spokesmen of emancipated Western Jewry, it was the ideas of this thoroughgoing, more all-embracing, Eastern European version of Zionism which represented a threat to the structure upon which their right to citizenship had been formulated and justified. Historically, this rested on developments reaching back to the Treaty of Westphalia which in 1648 had ended the Thirty Years' War and enshrined as statute the concept of religious toleration within states.[4] By the turn of the twentieth century, being a 'national' or 'citizen' of a state no longer, in theory at least, required one to be of a particular creed or race;

[2] See David Vital, *The Origins of Zionism* (London, 1975), 201–29; Fraenkel, Wolf and Herzl, 182–4.
[3] For the writings of early Zionists, see Arthur Hertzberg, ed., *The Zionist Idea. A Historical Analysis and Reader* (New York, 1969); Vital, *Origins*, 110–32. On the development of an anti-Herzlian opposition both before and during the Uganda affair see Vital, *Zionism: The Formative Years* (Oxford, 1982), 267–347; Reinharz, *Weizmann*, 167–210.
[4] Wolf, *Notes*, 2.

indeed, Western Jewry looked forward to states becoming multi-credal and multi-ethnic. As J. H. Levy, the political economist, wrote in 1901, 'Jews have no *locus standi* as citizens of a state in the main composed of other racial elements, except on the grounds of composite nationality . . . the great political hope of the future.' Liberal philosophy, too, confirmed the soundness of these developments; Lord Acton, for instance, in his famous lecture 'Nationality', agreed that the political nation might well be the sum total of many peoples and creeds.[5]

Henceforth, for Jews in England, France, and Germany, nationality connoted a purely political status. To be a Jew was strictly a matter of religion; to assume otherwise presupposed a Jewish state somewhere else. Jewish 'nationhood' had moreover been authoritatively denied by the Paris Sanhedrin of rabbis called together by Napoleon in 1807, and Western, including British, Jewry took this to be the last word on the subject.[6]

On several scores, therefore, Zionists themselves became an anathema to the mandarins of the Jewish 'liberal compromise'. By contesting that Jews could not be elements of the political nations of Britain, France, or elsewhere but were a distinct corporate national entity, they seemed to be both consciously undermining citizen rights already obtained and prejudicing the chances of those in Russia and Romania still without them. As J. H. Levy put it, 'If we proclaim ourselves aliens . . . I am at a loss to understand on what ground we can cry out that we are being unjustly treated as foreigners . . . the one thing which Zionism seems likely to attain is the manufacture of a logical basis for anti-semitism.' This, then, was the second point of issue. Max Nordau's proclamation at the Sixth Zionist Congress that all Jews were unassimilable, however much they attempted otherwise, played straight into the hands of those who argued that the Jews could never be dependable as citizens. While the protagonists of the 'liberal compromise' thus vehemently protested their record of patriotism and industriousness as proof of their allegiance to the state, the antisemites could simply turn to the Zionist 'national postulate' to reassert their case that this was simply a guise to hide the fact that Jews always worked for Jewish ends, and always, as Hamilton

[5] J. H. Levy letters, *JC*, 12 and 30 Aug. 1901; Lord Acton, 'Nationality', in *The History of Freedom and Other Essays* (London, 1907), 270–300. See also C. G. Montefiore, *Nation or Religious Community?* (London, 1917), originally (1899) an address to the Jewish Historical Society.

[6] See Simon Schwarzfuchs, *Napoleon, The Jews and the Sanhedrin* (London, 1977).

Fyfe had charged in 1903, 'put their original nationality before their adopted nationality'.[7]

If this was not enough, Zionist fatalism about the future of the Diaspora struck at the very moral foundations of the Western Jewish thought-system and seemed for people like Wolf to be a form of moral and spiritual degradation. After all, the struggle for emancipation, even in the West, had not all been plain sailing, and by the turn of the twentieth century the growth of reactionary and radical rightist movements threatened to perpetuate the struggle. But to accept defeat, 'to turn tail and run away', seemed to Wolf and his contemporaries a particularly dismal capitulation, especially when compared with the efforts of, for instance, the Bund in Russia to stand their ground and 'fight the good fight'. Besides, Jewry, following in the tradition of Moses Mendelssohn, had a mission to the world, one which could not be furthered if its people were bottled up in a corner of the Near East.[8]

Wolf's personal antipathy to the 'national postulate' was not as far-going as that of some of his associates. Unlike Claude Montefiore, for instance, a founder of Liberal Judaism in Britain, Wolf could not accept that being Jewish was purely a matter of religion, and that Jews were destined to intermarry as the principles of Judaism became more universal.[9] Wolf insisted that there was a Jewish racial identity and cultural distinctiveness, and that these were worth having. Later on, in his conversations with Weizmann, he agreed that the East European concept of nationality as an ethnic or cultural status might be applicable to Jews without injuring their allegiance as political nationals to a non-Jewish state. Nationality as such, Wolf concluded, was essentially a state of mind.[10] On the other hand, the more he studied the question,

[7] Series of letters by J. H. Levy, 'Anti-semitism and Zionism', *JC* 26 June–30 Aug. 1901; Hamilton Fyfe, 'The Alien and the Empire', *19th Century*, Sept. 1903 (to which Wolf referred alongside the Nordau speech in his letter on the 'Zionist Peril' in *The Times*, 8 Sept. 1903). For further examples of attacks on Jewish dual allegiance in Britain in this period see Holmes, *Anti-Semitism*, 12–17.

[8] Wolf to Zangwill, 27 Mar. 1903, CZA, A120/58 (Zangwill MSS). See also Wolf, 'Zionist Peril', 1–25; Laurie Magnus, *Aspects of the Jewish Question* (London, 1917); C. G. Montefiore and Basil L. Henriques, *The English Jew and his Religion* (Keighley, 1918); Stuart Cohen, *English Zionists*, 155–83; W. Laqueur, 'Zionism and its Liberal Critics, 1896–1948', *Journal of Contemporary History*, 6 (1971), 161–82.

[9] On Montefiore's anti-Zionism see Stuart Cohen, *English Zionists*, 163–8.

[10] Wolf to Zangwill, 27 Mar. 1903, CZA A120/58 (Zangwill MSS); also 25 Sept. 1903, ibid.: 'I have always been for the race . . . also most affectionately for the old customs on historical, ethnical and spiritual grounds but I see nothing in all this to

the more he became convinced that adoption of the 'national postulate' would be to the great detriment of Jews everywhere. Thus, in 1904 he had visited Romania and been received by Premier Sturdza, who candidly assured him on behalf of his Romanian co-religionists: 'If you have a nationality how can you come to us and say you want to be Rumanian citizens?'[11] This conjured up a twin nightmare for Wolf. On the one hand, it signified that Zionism could be exploited by East European reactionaries to justify the forcible removal of Jews *en masse* from their countries. On the other, and following on from this, it meant that the emigrants, barred for political and practical reasons from entry into Palestine, would seek refuge in the West, a development that the Jewish establishments in these countries feared would threaten their citizens' rights and security.

The 'national postulate' had thus by 1903 turned Wolf into one of the leading opponents of what he himself called 'the Zionist Peril'. A champion of the Jewish liberal compromise, Wolf became, as one of his communal critics put it, 'an adviser for the millenium [*sic*] of assimilation'.[12] Recognizing at once the appeal of Zionism to the immigrant and the threat it posed to the ideological structure upon which established Anglo-Jewry had confided itself, Wolf foresaw an eventual communal showdown. Following news of such a conflict in 1914 between the Hilfsverein and Zionists in Palestine, Wolf warned Lord Rothschild, 'the time is coming when leading Jews will have to make up their minds as to the side they will take'.[13]

Despite these prophecies, Wolf's 1916 Palestine 'formula' was produced in a spirit not of conflict but of compromise. Though clearly avoiding the Zionist 'national postulate', Wolf envisaged a scheme which, if accepted by the Allies, would give the Zionists the opportunity

---

prevent me from being a good Englishman or to make me wring my hands over the imbecility of my fathers in fighting and winning the battle of emancipation.' See also Wolf to Sokolow, 24 Nov. 1916, 'Notes on the Zionist Memo, 11 Oct. 1916', Gaster papers; Wolf to A. Abrahams, 20 Sept. 1917, MWS 1695.

[11] Wolf interview with Sturdza, *Jewish World*, 16 Oct. 1908.

[12] S. B. Rubenstein letter, *JC* 1 Jan. 1909.

[13] On the Hilfsverein–Zionist dispute, Wolf to Archer (Rothschild's secretary), 26 Jan. 1914, CZA A77/3c, (Wolf MSS). See Wolf to Nathan, 19 Jan. 1914, ibid. 3a: 'I have seen no reason to alter or modify my opinions. Nothing can tend more fatally to justify the theories of anti-semitism than the extreme nationalism of the Zionists.' See also Moshe Rinott, 'The Zionist Organisation and the Hilfsverein: Cooperation and Conflict, 1901–1914', *Leo Baeck Year Book*, 21 (1976), 261–78.

to build up in the course of time a state framework, even a local Jewish nation. Wolf said as much to Balfour in his interview with him in January 1917.[14] Nor was such a goal inconsistent with his previous reasoning. In 1905, for instance, Wolf had co-operated with Zangwill to form the Jewish Territorial Organization (ITO), which they hoped would provide for an autonomous Jewish territory, preferably in the British Empire. Wolf had then envisaged that autonomy would mean control of municipal affairs as well as immigration, leading, as the colony grew strong and resilient, to the sort of dominion status associated with Australia or Canada.[15] More recently, in 1913, he had urged on the Greek government a generous scheme of municipal self-government for the overwhelmingly Jewish city of Salonika. In both cases, however, Wolf had been careful to delimit the national aspects; for Salonika, pointing out that autonomy of itself did not require special privileges, and in the ITO stating that it 'in no way postulates Jewish alienship in Russia or Rumania or anywhere else'.[16]

What Wolf was after was a practical scheme which would please all parties. There were, for instance, strongly Zionist-orientated people in the Conjoint, notably Joseph Prag and Elkan Adler, who had been consistent members of the Chovevei Zion movement since its formation in England. The movement sought the development of Palestine through practical colonization projects, with an emphasis, unlike Herzlian Zionism, on gradualism. But Wolf's formula might also appeal to the Zionist Organization itself, especially as practical goals had in recent years become its dominant tendency, a reflection both of the political difficulties associated with Herzl's vision and the ascendancy of Eastern Jewry within the movement.

Leaving aside the wide divergences of opinion on how Palestine should actually be conquered, Wolf must have known that his personal interference in the issue was an enormous gamble. For one thing, the

[14] Wolf memo on interview with Balfour, 30 Jan. 1916, FO 800/210 (Balfour Papers). At the NUJR meeting on 12 Mar. 1917, Wolf insisted that they would not put obstacles in the way of the creation of a Jewish state; *JC* 17 Mar. 1916. Similarly, following *The Times* statement, Wolf wrote to Bigart: 'If you read our statement very carefully you will find that it concedes almost everything of any practical importance to the Zionists. It favours a Jewish settlement, it even engages not to oppose a national status for such a settlement, so long as the nationality is a local one. The only objections it raises are objections which relate to safeguarding the position of Jews in other countries'; see Wolf to Bigart, 5 June 1917, MWS 6001-3.
[15] Report of Wolf's ITO speeches of 27 May 1906 and 23 Apr. 1911, *JC* 1 Jun. 1906 and 28 Apr. 1911.
[16] Wolf's ITO speech, *JC* 1 Jun. 1906. Wolf to Gennadius, 17 Feb. 1914, C11/2/5.

1905 co-operation over ITO had not been wholly auspicious. Though the practical rather than ideological emphasis had brought in a wide spectrum of Zionists and assimilationists, it also left a good many influential figures outside and opposed to it. Moreover, as Wolf only a month prior to the scheme had been denouncing territorialism as 'a ridiculous fad', his miraculous *volte face* led the Anglo-Zionist leaders to believe they were witnessing a colossal deception; Cowen, indeed, insisted that the whole operation was an attempt 'to smash the Zionists'.[17] This engendered a great deal of ill-feeling and mistrust, and also boded ill for Wolf should he ever attempt further meddling with the Zionist movement. In 1916, Wolf did not consult the Zionists about his 'formula' because it was the subject of confidential negotiations with the Foreign Office; to the Zionists this appeared as a deliberate stab in the back.[18]

To succeed, therefore, Wolf needed quick government adhesion to the 'formula'; this would bring the Zionists into line and neutralize the 'national postulate' in the process. Preparing the ground for this, Wolf's National Union of Jewish Rights programme emphasized the importance of the practical Zionist goals of colonization and immigration. He sought, too, to co-opt the Zionist leaders and their sympathizers— Weizmann, Sokolow, Cowen, Chief Rabbi Hertz—and others on to the National Union platform for its inaugural meeting, alongside the Conjoint chiefs, in time to hear him announce government sponsorship for the 'formula'.[19]

When the announcement failed to materialize, Wolf was left in the lurch with a scheme which, when the Zionists found out about it— there are indications that Gaster knew as early as May—would have to be explained away as best as possible. Wolf's statement to the Anglo-Jewish Association in June 1917 that the 'formula' had been solely 'a

[17] Wolf interview on collapse of East Africa project, *JC* 4 Aug. 1905; Greenberg to Wolffsohn, 15 Dec. 1905; CZA W38 (Wolffsohn MSS). *JC* 13 Oct. 1905, reporting Bentwich speech at Maccabeans, 7 Oct. 1905; ibid., 19 Mar. 1909, reporting Cowen's speech at West Central Zionist Association, 14 Mar. 1909.

[18] Wolf to James de Rothschild, 31 Oct. 1916, MWS 7873–5: 'As you are aware the questions referred to are matters of confidential negotiations with the British government and we cannot make them public without the consent of the Foreign Office.' For Cowen's accusation against Wolf see Chaim Weizmann, *The Letters and Papers of Chaim Weizmann*, ed. Meyer W. Weisgal (Oxford, 1975), ser. A, vii, (hereafter *Weizmann Letters*), no. 286, to James de Rothschild, 30 Oct. 1916.

[19] Wolf circular to Zionist leaders, 3 Mar. 1916, C11/2/8. See also L. Resnik letter defending NUJR's practical Zionist goals, *JC* 25 Feb. 1916.

draft declaration recommended for purposes of propaganda', belied
the fact that it was modelled on the 1915 policy formulations and
appeared again in late 1916 as the basis on which the committee was
prepared to negotiate further with the Zionists; leading inevitably to
accusations that they were being asked to do so on the basis of a *fait
accompli*.[20]

If the motives behind the 'formula' were not wholly altruistic, nor
were they a conscious effort to deceive. Wolf had been in communication with the English Zionist Federation over the propaganda proposal,
and there is evidence to suggest that had it been given the government
green light he would have tried to co-opt leading Zionists, especially
Sokolow, in the same way as had happened over the Committee for
Russian War Victims.[21]

What Wolf first and foremost wished to avoid was the sort of public
discussion of the issue which stood to disrupt his wider diplomatic
goals. Zangwill's crowd-pulling charisma potentially posed the greatest
threat of havoc if, as Cowen and Greenberg hoped, he was roped in to
preside over the English Zionist Federation. At the beginning of the
war, however, Zangwill was closer in every way to Wolf, having by this
time rejected outright any theory of Jewish nationality.[22] The Anglo-
Zionist leadership presented another such threat. The *Jewish Chronicle*,
since Greenberg had bought the paper (with cash from the Jewish
Colonial Trust) in 1907, was its organ, and its wartime columns shared
the Cowen–Greenberg view that the Conjoint should extend itself, or
even better should give way to a more broadly based Anglo-Jewish
body, for the implementation of a publicly discussed, communally
agreed policy on Palestine.[23]

The opportunity to avoid this type of agitation came from an unlikely
source. In November 1914, Wolf was approached by Harry Sacher on

[20] Wolf to Montefiore, 15 Aug. 1916, C11/2/8, referring to a statement made by
Gaster at the AJA that Wolf had presented a 'mysterious' memo to the FO. Gaster's
informant may have been Sykes; report of BD meeting, 22 Oct., 'announcing' formula,
JC 29 Oct. 1916. See also Wolf memo on Gaster accusations, CJC minutes, 3 June
1917.
[21] Wolf to Cowen, 20 Jan. 1916, C11/2/8: 'I have great esteem for Mr. Sokolow and
should be very pleased to find myself working with him.'
[22] Weizmann to Greenberg, 20 Nov. 1914, *Weizmann Letters*, vii, no. 44; Weizmann
to Inner Action Committee Exec., 7 Jan. 1915, ibid., no. 95; Wolf to Zangwill, 19 Apr.
1915, CZA A77/3a (Wolf MSS).
[23] *Jewish Chronicle, 1841–1941*, 125–6; *JC* leader, 17 Mar. 1916, calling for amendment of BD constitution to create a real communal 'union'.

116 Wolf and the Zionists

behalf of a group of mostly Manchester-based English Zionists led by the Russian-born Chaim Weizmann. Sacher had two meetings with Wolf; he insisted that his group had nothing to do with 'the Greenberg–Cowen agitation' and also made proposals which seemed eminently reasonable to Wolf. Sacher told him that he was not interested in a Jewish state *per se*, but was concerned that they should gain the liberty to colonize Palestine and to develop a Jewish culture therein.[24] Lacking any reference to the 'national postulate', Sacher's propositions must have seemed to Wolf heaven-sent.

After years of interminable bickering, it appeared as if the most uncompromising adherents of Jewish nationality, of whom Weizmann was one, might be prepared, for the time being at least, to forgo their ideological idiosyncracies in the pursuit of a practical programme. Moreover, Sacher's 'cultural' suggestions were consistent with recent Zionist postures. The 'political' efforts to gain Palestine had faltered since the death of Herzl in 1904, and once the Young Turks had taken power in Turkey in 1908 and stated their centralizing intentions they had collapsed altogether. 'Political' Zionism was replaced by 'practical' Zionism, a readaptation of the pre-Herzlian Chovevei Zion creed to develop Palestine through gradual penetration and cultural regeneration. Some of Herzl's former Zionei Zion opponents were in the forefront of this new ascendancy; Weizmann, for instance was at this stage particularly associated with efforts to create a Hebrew University in Palestine, while 'politicals' like Cowen and Greenberg found themselves forced to take a back seat.[25] If Weizmann and his friends could be made to stick to their practical colonizing programme as set out in the Zionist Congress resolution of 1911, and if they would eschew all claims to a pan-Jewish nationality, Wolf foresaw the real possibility of finding 'a basis on which all parties in the community may unite'.[26]

The chance to do a semi-private deal with Weizmann had other obvious advantages too. A latecomer to the Anglo-Zionist leadership and removed from London-centred communal politics, his rapport

24 Sachar to Weizmann, 17 Nov. 1914, *Weizmann Letters*, vii. 44 n. 6.

[24] Sachar to Weizmann, 17 Nov. 1914, *Weizmann Letters*, vii. 44 n. 6.
[25] Reinharz, *Weizmann*, 377–401; Isaiah Berlin, 'The Biographical Facts', in Meyer W. Weisgal and Joel Carmichael, eds., *Chaim Weizmann: A Biography by Several Hands* (London, 1962), 29–31. Cowen and Greenberg were unimpressed with the university idea but lost ground to the 'Practicals' after the resignation of Herzl's lieutenant and successor, Wolffsohn, in 1911.
[26] Wolf to Zangwill, 25 Nov. 1914, CZA A120/51.2 (Zangwill MSS); Reinharz, *Weizmann*, 343.

with Wolf was not marred by the decade of acrimonious disputes which characterized Wolf's relations with Greenberg, Gaster, and others. Similarly, Weizmann's desire to work quietly, behind the scenes, gaining the adhesion of influential Jews and government figures, fitted in well with Wolf's own methods and temperament. Besides, Weizmann in 1914 to some degree needed people like Wolf. True, Weizmann already had some contacts in high places, including Herbert Samuel, Arthur Balfour, and Lloyd George, but his credentials as a Zionist leader were not particularly impressive. He was a member of the Berlin-based Larger Actions Committee, but not of its inner executive circle. He was, too, a vice-president of the English Zionist Federation but very much as the dark horse, on the periphery of an Anglo-Zionist leadership which was based in London. He might insist that he, rather than they, represented the Zionist Organization, but it was not until his diplomatic manœuvres brought him into closer association with the British government in 1917 that the mantle of leadership naturally followed.[27] This then enabled him to disregard 'unrepresentative Jews', including Wolf. In 1914, this eventual destination was still remote; Weizmann simply could not afford to alienate the traditional Anglo-Jewish leadership, whose influence and standing made it a useful if unloved ally.[28]

At this stage, these factors favoured Wolf. Knowing full well that Weizmann had no real authority to proceed without the Berlin executive—indeed, they sent out Nahum Sokolow as their representative to England—and knowing, too, that the executive itself was paralysed by the war, Wolf's response was leisurely. Weizmann, accompanied by Sacher, did come to see him in December to prepare the ground for preliminary negotiations between the Conjoint and the Zionists, but Wolf did not take this opportunity to discuss matters further with Weizmann. The Conjoint, said Wolf, would only negotiate with persons authorized to speak for the Zionist executive, namely Sokolow and his fellow delegate Dr Yechiel Tschlenow.[29] The outcome was that no further discussion took place between Wolf and Weizmann

[27] See Reinharz, *Weizmann*, 278–84. On Weizmann's Anglo-Zionist disagreements see Stuart Cohen, *English Zionists*, 100–23, 219–23.
[28] On Weizmann's efforts to also rope in Claude Montefiore and Philip Magnus see Weizmann to Dreyfus, 6 Dec. 1914, *Weizmann Letters*, no. 60 n. 6.
[29] Weizmann to Vera Weizmann, 10 Dec. 1914, ibid., no. 65 n. 4; Wolf to Archer, 11 Feb. 1915, C11/2/6. Implying the EZF's inability to act, Wolf noted that the majority of the Zionist Exec. were 'enemy aliens'.

until August 1916 when the political balance had tilted firmly in the latter's favour.

In retrospect, Wolf's 1914 indifference may be seen to have been fatal. Though he could not dictate to Weizmann, perhaps the latter's willingness to establish 'an entente' with the non-nationalist Jews, 'so as to appear before the Powers as a united body',[30] might have led to negotiations along the lines of Sacher's acceptable proposals. But Sacher's cultural plan was in itself a blind, masking Weizmann's real ideological stance. His attempts to come to a *modus vivendi* with Zangwill's ITO had just failed, due (according to Weizmann) to Zangwill's antagonism 'to any national view of the Jewish problem'. If he had discussed this issue with Wolf in 1914, it would have soon become so apparent that no common ground existed between them that negotiations would have most probably been abruptly terminated. In fact, at the time of the public row with the Conjoint in 1917 Weizmann made it abundantly clear that it was the issue of the 'national postulate' which rendered impossible any accord.[31] The Committee, he wrote to Harry Lewis, did not seem to realize one fundamental point.

We are an organisation which is nationalist in its fundamental view and if we give up one iota of our national programme, we cease to be the organisation which we claim to be . . . it is no mere accident that we have split on two questions, nationalism and the question of the charter.[32]

In 1914, however, the unfinished state of the Wolf–Weizmann business left a vacuum which at once gave Wolf grounds for hope yet at the same time gave credence to rumours that each side was pre-empting the other by presenting Palestine schemes to the government.[33]

There of course remained the official Zionist leadership in Britain. In April 1915, Alexander, Montefiore, Wolf, and Henry Henriques met in conference with Wolf's old adversaries, Cowen, Greenberg, Gaster, and Herbert Bentwich, for a full and frank exchange of views.

[30] Stein, *Balfour Declaration*, 178.
[31] Weizmann to Inner Action Committee Exec., 7 Jan. 1915, *Weizmann Letters*, no. 95; 18 Dec. 1914, no. 80.
[32] Weizmann to Harry Lewis, 1 June 1917, ibid., no. 432.
[33] Friedman, *Question of Palestine*, 35, suggests both parties were under a misapprehension in 1914. As for the rumours, within days of the Wolf–Weizmann meeting Weizmann quite mistakenly stated that Montefiore and others 'had hurried to present a memorandum to Grey'; see Weizmann to Vera Weizmann, 31 Dec. 1914, *Weizmann Letters*, no. 84.

Sokolow and Tschlenow, both Russians, were there on behalf of the Zionist Inner Actions Committee. Weizmann was absent. Tschlenow on this occasion led the Zionist presentation. The road to emancipation in Eastern Europe, he argued, was blocked. Palestine, however, could provide a home for millions of Jews. But how many exactly? The Zionist speakers themselves seemed to be at odds on what the country's actual absorptive capacity might be. Even Gaster's optimistic figure of one million in ten years, noted Wolf, could not, given Eastern Jewry's natural growth rate, substantially diminish the problem. Moreover, he had things to say about Tschlenow's pessimistic forecast for Eastern Europe. On the contrary, he rejoindered, things were moving 'towards a more enlightened and liberal polity'. True, Wolf agreed, 'the pace of moral and social assimilation must be slow in proportion to the magnitude and abnormality of the element to be assimilated', but the movements among Jews, especially in the universities and trade unions, showed that they were taking the matter into their own hands. Rounding off this survey, Wolf concluded, 'our faith in emancipation has at any rate, the support of precedent and of the upward political tendencies of the times, but the Zionist solution . . . runs counter to all experience and probabilities and is essentially reactionary'.[34]

Wolf, in making this charge, was referring specifically to two things which resurfaced at the conference. One was Tschlenow and Gaster's references to the Jewish 'nation'. In fact, Tschlenow, in particular seems to have been ambiguous here, referring to a Jewish commonwealth in Palestine rather than a national home. Nevertheless, for Wolf and his associates, any admittance of the 'national postulate' had to be repudiated:

It is no part of the business of the Conjoint Committee as such, or of its parent bodies, to promote the establishment of a Jewish commonwealth merely in fulfillment of Jewish national aspirations. Our sole aim and purpose is to secure the welfare of our co-religionists by obtaining for them full rights of citizenship in the lands in which they are still oppressed and by protecting them in the enjoyment of such rights where they are already in possession of them.[35]

The second area of controversy related to what Sokolow, Gaster, and Cowen envisaged if Palestine should come within the sphere of

---

[34] Wolf to Oliphant, 28 Apr. 1915, encl. report, 'Conference with the Delegates of the Zionist Org.', 14 Apr. 1915, FO 371/2488/51705.
[35] Ibid.

British influence or protection, namely, the formation of a chartered
company and special privileges for the Jewish settlers until such a time
as they came to be the majority in the land. For Wolf, the inadmissibility
of these two demands lay in that both ascribed to Jews an actual or
potential exclusivity. Thus if they were everywhere part of a dispossessed
'nationality', they would have to renounce their citizen rights in the countries in which they possessed them, or suffer the reproach that they had
been obtained by false pretences. Similarly, special economic and
political privileges in a chartered company in Palestine would make the
Jews there a privileged class and their Muslim and Christian neighbours
inferior and discriminated against. Wolf's emphasis on the injustice of
this proposal later convinced Weizmann that he was using it solely to
obstruct his efforts.[36] In fact, Wolf's argument was a logical and consistent defence of East European Jews. If the Arabs were denied equality
in their own home, or worse, evicted, then by the same token Polish,
Russian, and Romanian antisemites could do the same to their Jews.[37]

As it related to Britain and British Jews, Wolf's prognosis that Jews
would be turfed out if they declared themselves 'Jews first' bears
witness to wartime Anglo-Jewish establishment paranoia and insecurity. Yet though the finer points of the 'nationality' debate were lost on,
for instance, the Foreign Office,[38] tangible and substantial evidence
could be brought forward to endorse Wolf's case. Thus, there was a
marked sympathy for Zionism among those journalists who had been
most persistent in their accusations of corporate Jewish sabotage, disloyalty, and treason. Maxse rounded off his September 1914 *National
Review* tirade with the menacing prediction that 'the Zionist movement
which has hung fire of late years might develop on fresh lines, owing to
the irresistible demand for some sort of compulsory emigration to
Palestine'.[39] No mention of Jewish nationalism here, though Stephen
Graham, who had defended Russia's persecution of its Jews in *The*

[36] Weizmann to Brandeis, 23 Apr. 1917, *Weizmann Letters*, no. 351.

[37] 'Conf. with Delegates', FO 371/2488/51705. See also Wolf to James de Rothschild,
31 Aug. 1916, Gaster Papers, CJC file, which presents the fullest, most rounded outline of
Wolf's views on the inherent dangers of the Zionist programme. Wolf later wrote to
Zangwill: '(1) Principle: If the Zionists establish themselves in Palestine, it must be on the
footing of justice and fair play. (2) Expediency: If we evict Arabs, anti-semites in Europe will
evict Jews.' Wolf to Zangwill, 23 Dec. 1918, CZA A36/113 (ITO Archives).

[38] Oliphant minute, 20 Nov. 1916, FO 371/2817/42608. After reading both sides of
the protracted Weizmann–Wolf debate he despairingly wrote: 'When Jews fall out it is
none too easy to decide whether the Zionists or the anti-Zionists are in the wrong.'

[39] Maxse, 'The Fight against Pan-Germanism', *National Review*, Sept. 1914.

Times, suggested in February 1915 that there 'may be something in the possibility of the reestablishment of the Jews in Palestine as a nation'. Cecil Chesterton, an old adversary of Jewish financial 'power', agreed. He hoped for the dismantling of Jewish citizen rights in Britain and the establishment in their place of a two-tier apartheid system where special privileges would enable the Jews to contribute to the national interest without usurping it. With the creation of a Jewish state, he argued, the interests of the Jewish 'foreign' community in Britain would be naturally fostered and protected by their 'Palestinian' ambassador.[40] Finally, Henry Wickham Steed, the foreign editor of *The Times* and an obsessive believer in Jewish world manipulation, was another to profess a curiously strident enthusiasm for Zionist nationalism. It was perhaps not coincidental that when the Conjoint finally delivered its 'statement' against the Zionists in *The Times* in May 1917, the Zionist case received its most influential, if ambivalent, support from his editorial.[41]

Developments at the Foreign Office, too, convinced Wolf that the concept of Jewish nationality might be used to prejudice Jewish European security. In April 1916, Hubert Montgomery summoned him to the ministry to inform him of a recent despatch from Spring-Rice which held English and French Jews collectively responsible for the pro-German sentiments of their American co-religionists, and it was therefore the responsibility of English and French Jews, if danger was to be averted to European Jewry as a whole, to dissuade them from this course. Wolf angrily rejoindered:

I thought I detected both in the despatch . . . and in your observations, a tacit assumption of a solidarity apart from their confessional identity . . . this assumption finds some little justification in the mischievous and ill-considered doctrines of the extreme Zionists but it is none the less a fallacy. The Jews are a religious community, but . . . they have absolutely no international organisation either for religious or political purposes.[42]

[40] Graham, 'Russia and her Jews', *English Review*, Feb. 1915; Chesterton, cited in Holmes, *Anti-Semitism*, 118–19.
[41] Steed, *Through Thirty Years*, ii. 391–3; *The Times* leader, 29 May 1917, where Steed suggested Zionism might help weaken 'Jewish international solidarity' and give 'leading Jews everywhere the opportunity to make a public stand against tendencies which sometimes bring the Jewish race into disrepute'. Friedman, *Germany, Turkey*, 254–5, notes how German antisemites similarly favoured Zionism as a way of removing unwanted Jewish refugees from Eastern Europe.
[42] Spring-Rice to FO, 29 Jan. 1916, FO 371/2835/18095; Wolf–Montgomery interview and letter, 3 and 8 Apr. 1916, ibid.

Wolf's corrections went unheeded. A pervasive belief in Jewish cultural
and political oneness, which Wolf and his associates were constantly
trying to refute, existed with or without Zionism. Nevertheless, Wolf
was correct in assuming that Zionist ideology could be used to justify
discrimination at home and abroad.
Home Office co-operation with the ultra-right Polish National
Committee was a case in point. Towards the end of the war and at its
conclusion, the committee was able to provide certificates to Poles
living in Britain which denoted them as friendly aliens and thus spared
them any possibility of internment. Certificates were granted on an
ethnic basis. Jews, being automatically excluded, had to seek assistance
from a special Jewish committee. Sir John Pedder, a senior official at
the Home Office, justified its endorsement of this policy in these
terms: 'I have reason to believe the best Jewish opinion is not in favour
of any move towards treatment on the grounds of religion rather than
nationality.'[43]
The Home Office view had much to do with a negative appraisal of
Polish Jewish immigrants and their wartime behaviour, but the racial
test had a much wider application. Tadeusz Garszynski, for the Poles,
informed the Home Office in March 1919 that Jewish duplicity as to
the description of their nationality would make it very difficult to deal
with Jews who claimed citizenship in the new Polish state and yet were
also Zionists. In consequence, the option Garszynski offered Polish
Jews was either to produce evidence showing their aspirations and
interests were with Poland, or consider themselves members of the
Jewish nationality, whose home was in Palestine.[44]
It was fear that further developments of this sort would result from
Zionism, that led Wolf and his colleagues in the Conjoint to insist in
1915 that co-operation with the Zionists be pursued only 'on the basis
of the *ad hoc* elimination of nationalism and exclusive rights from their
programme'. These same conditions appeared again, in almost identical form, in Wolf's conversations with Weizmann in 1916, and again
when the Conjoint issued its manifesto in *The Times*.[45]

[43] Pedder minute, 4 Feb. 1919, HO 45 10889/352661/58.
[44] Garszynski memo, 7 Mar. 1919, ibid., file 83. For a full account and interpretation
of these developments see Norman Davies, 'The Poles in Great Britain 1914–1919',
Slavonic and East European Review, 50 (1972), 63–89.
[45] CJC to ZO, 27 Apr. 1915, Gaster papers, CJC file; Wolf to Sokolow, 7 Nov. 1916,
encl. memo on Wolf–Weizmann interview, 17 Aug. 1916; CJC letter, 'The Future of
the Jews', *The Times*, 24 May 1917.

Though after the conference both sides looked forward to eventual co-operation, and the Conjoint, 'to an approximation of views', the encounter tended to demonstrate the improbability of such an accord, and the matter ought to have terminated there. The Zionists resumed their liberty of action pending the suitable opportunity for joint representations, Wolf, returning to other issues, responded by pointing to the tactlessness of the Conjoint, as an exclusively British body, negotiating with an organization containing enemy aliens. Communication ceased.[46]

The possibility of coming into close confidential relations with the government by alluding to British control in a Jewish Palestine, something which the Zionists at the conference clearly desired to happen,[47] proved irresistible, however. Once the resulting 'formula' had become not simply a recommendation but Conjoint declared policy, Wolf had to search round for partners to accept its non-nationalist premiss. In many ways, Greenberg and Cowen would have been suitable since their Zionism excluded allegiance to any theory denying the value or continuing necessity of emancipation.[48] Their Herzlian state aims, moreover, differed very little in either content or form from those propounded by Wolf in the ITO. The gulf between them was fuelled less by ideological than by organizational dispute since the Federation contended for the communal role that the Conjoint, as offspring of the Board and Anglo-Jewish Association, possessed.[49] The repeated attacks on the Conjoint in the columns of Greenberg's papers in 1916—notwithstanding the charge that Wolf was personally unsuited to dealing with the Zionist problem—and the Federation's rush to accuse the Conjoint of sabotage once the 'formula' had become public knowledge ruled out any chance of renewed accord in that direction.[50]

This still left the unknown quantity, Weizmann. While the 'formula'

---

[46] Gaster papers, CJC file, ZO to CJC, 11 May 1915; Wolf to Sokolow, 11 June 1916, ibid.; Wolf noted to Zangwill, 19 Apr. 1915, that the conference was 'not likely to lead to any agreement'; see CZA A77/3a (Wolf MSS).

[47] Wolf to Oliphant, 28 Apr. 1915, encl. 'Conference with Delegates', FO 371/2448/51705.

[48] Wolf to Montefiore, 27 Nov. 1916, C11/2/10, in relation to news from Zangwill that Cowen had rejected the idea of *galut* nationality and expressed dissension from Weizmann and Gaster's essays in H. Sacher, ed., *Zionism and the Jewish Future* (London, 1916).

[49] See Bayme, 'Jewish Leadership', 313–15; Stuart Cohen, *English Zionists*, 69–76.

[50] See *Jewish World* leader, 18 Oct. 1916; *JC* leader, 20 Oct.; and ibid., 27 Oct., report of Wolf–Zionist exchanges at the BD, 2 Oct.

hung in the balance in the spring of 1916, Wolf had reason to believe that his support might still be forthcoming. The assumption rested on information received from two leading figures, one in Anglo-Jewry, the other in Franco-Jewry, both of whom were not only in contact with Weizmann but considered extremely sympathetic to the Zionist cause. Herbert Samuel had been the first to propound at high ministerial level the mutual advantages of a British protectorate over a Jewish 'centre' in Palestine. Certainly Wolf shared with him at least the desire to keep the French out.[51] As early as February 1915 the two men had discussed Palestine, and Samuel had on this occasion fully endorsed Wolf's limited cultural programme. When they met again, soon after the submission of the 'formula', Samuel, now home secretary, gave Wolf the impression that 'when it comes to the point the Zionists will be quite satisfied with the adoption of our formula'. This was important, Wolf reported to his Conjoint chiefs, 'as I know he is in continuous communication with Dr. Weitzmann' [sic].[52] Though enthusiastic for the Zionist cause, Samuel, himself a member of the Anglo-Jewish 'Cousinhood', was not likely to countenance any theory of Jewish nationality. Indeed, at a major Zionist get-together in February 1917, he had expressed reservations about Jewish nationality anywhere except in Palestine. Wolf could hope therefore that he would be a moderating influence on Weizmann and lead him towards co-operation with the Conjoint.[53]

Similar encouragement could be derived from Baron Edmond, the English Rothschilds' French cousin. Long-time spokesman of the Franco-Jewish community, he was also closely associated, through his philanthropic interest in Palestinian Jewish colonies, with Zionism. Baron Edmond favoured Wolf's formula, and like Samuel believed

---

[51] Wolf to Samuel, 10 Apr. 1916, MWS 3564, gives information on French interests in the Levant and suggests that Palestine had been earmarked for their takeover.

[52] Wolf note on interview with Samuel, 28 Feb. 1915, FO 371/2448/51705; Wolf to CJC presidents, 7 Apr. 1916, MWS 1771–2.

[53] Friedman, *Question of Palestine*, 232, on meeting in Gaster's house on 7 Feb. 1917. Views on the degree to which Samuel was a Zionist differ. Friedman argues that Wolf was mistaken in believing that Samuel agreed with him; according to Friedman, Samuel's March 1915 memo sought to blend 'political' and 'cultural' Zionism (ibid. 14). Bernard Wasserstein, 'Herbert Samuel and the Palestine Problem', *English Historical Review*, 91 (1976), 753–75, agrees that Samuel had Zionism at heart unlike most of his 'Cousinhood' relatives, but maintains that his approach was low key, cultural, and full of reservations. I do not see as wide a gulf between Wolf and Samuel as Friedman does.

Weizmann would not object to it.[54] In fact, it was at his prompting that a meeting was arranged in August 1916 at the English home of his son, James de Rothschild, a frequent host to the Weizmannites, to bring Weizmann and Wolf to some sort of compromise understanding.[55]

Baron Edmond was to be sorely disappointed. The fact that Wolf's 'formula' was here let out of the bag could have only confirmed Weizmann in the low opinion he held of 'self-appointed' leaders such as Wolf.[56] On the other hand, if Wolf had had hopes of doing a deal with Weizmann, these had already been irrevocably shattered by a recently published collection of essays, entitled *Zionism and the Jewish Future*. Both Weizmann and Gaster had contributed to the book, and as Leonard Stein notes, 'expressed themselves in language not calculated to narrow the gulf between the Zionists and their opponents'. It was in fact their specific statements which became the *'pièces justificatioins'* of the Conjoint's later 'manifesto'. The one by Gaster was a clear rebuttal of the traditional Anglo-Jewish stance as Jews by faith and Englishmen by nationality, according to Gaster, this was 'an absolute self-delusion'. Weizmann's misdemeanour was forcefully to proclaim the classic Zionist thesis of Jewish unassimilability. Assimilation and antisemitism, he said, were phenomena which went side by side. The position of the emancipated Jew was even more tragic than that of his oppressed brother, since his homelessness could only be resolved through the founding of a suitable home 'where the Jewish people could live and develop on the lines of its own national characteristics and ideals'.[57]

Despite these grievances, the two adversaries heard each other out. The ideological schism between them had not narrowed. Wolf pressed Weizmann to work on the basis of the original Sacher idea—peaceful penetration of Palestine—as encapsulated in the Conjoint 'formula'; if Jewish nationality and the charter were not discarded, he warned,

[54] Wolf to Oliphant, 18 July 1916, FO 371/2448/51705; extract from Wolf's diary of visit to Paris, ibid. See also Wolf to James de Rothschild, 31 Oct. 1916, MWS 7873–5; 'Your father definitely expressed his complete approval of the formula.'

[55] On how the de Rothschilds, father and son, related to Weizmann see Schama, *Two Rothschilds*, 192–202.

[56] For Weizmann's strangely ambiguous outburst against the CJC and esp. against Wolf see *Weizmann Letters*, no. 40, to Sacher and Simon, 28 Nov. 1914.

[57] Sacher, ed., *Zionism and the Jewish Future*, 6–7, 93; Stein, *Balfour Declaration*, 299–300. On Weizmann and Gaster's statements see extracts in MWS 5999–6005, Wolf to Bigart, 17 May and 5 June 1917.

there would follow 'a very angry controversy which would paralyse the efforts of the whole of Jewry'.[58]
Wolf's undisguised threat to 'make concessions or else', went unheeded. 'It is . . . impossible', insisted Weizmann to James de Rothschild, 'for us to yield on points of principle. Whatever we concede . . . they will and must work against us. Our interests clash and no paper formula can bridge over a gulf which is widening every day.'[59] Weizmann was right. Denied a solution on the basis of the 'formula' and fearing that the Zionists would leave them in the lurch, the Conjoint leaders, with Montefiore rather than Wolf this time at the helm, made preparations in September for an early manifesto against Jewish nationalism. The Conjoint was becoming truculent. 'There will be a devil of a row at the Anglo-Jewish Association and the Board of Deputies', said Montefiore, 'but are we to be ruined by our silence and fear of rows?'[60] The growing storm was fuelled further by James de Rothschild's transmission of copies of the confidential Wolf–Weizmann exchange of views, with their references to the 'formula', to other leading Zionists, which in turn precipitated accusations against Wolf. At the same time, Baron Edmond inexplicably reneged on his support for the 'formula', thus arresting all hopes of further mediation.[61]

Almost at the last moment, the decision to commence hostilities was arrested by Leopold de Rothschild's plea to the committee to preserve peace and search again for a fair compromise.[62] In a sudden about turn at the Board, Alexander offered to come to a compromise with the Zionists on the basis of the 'formula'. After a year and a half of noncommunication, Wolf wrote to Sokolow at Alexander's behest, requesting the resumption of the conference between the two parties and promising to explain the 'formula's' prior submission to the government as soon as negotiations recommenced.[63]

[58] Wolf to Sokolow, 7 Nov. 1916, Gaster papers, CJC file.
[59] Weizmann to James de Rothschild, 15 Oct. 1916, *Weizmann Letters*, no. 283.
[60] Montefiore to Wolf, 3 and 11 Sept. 1916; C11/2/9; Wolf to Montefiore, 3 Oct. 1916, ibid.
[61] Wolf to J. de Rothschild, 31 Oct. 1916, MWS 7873–5; Wolf to Cowen, 31 Oct. 1916, MWS 7878–9; Wolf to Leopold de Rothschild, 12 Nov. 1916, C11/2/9, on a letter from Baron Edmond 'which practically gives the lie to all my statements as to the Baron Edmond's assurances to me'. See also Weizmann to James de Rothschild, 30 Oct. 1916, *Weizmann Letters*, no. 286, n. 12.
[62] Wolf to Leopold de Rothschild, 18 Oct. 1916, C11/2/9.
[63] Wolf to Sokolow, 3 Nov. 1916, Gaster papers, CJC file; *JC* 27 Oct. 1916, reporting BD meeting, 22 Oct. 1916.

After a near-hysterical outburst at the Board, in which he contested
that the Conjoint had been secretly intriguing against the Zionists,[64]
Wolf proposed to the Conjoint chiefs that he stand down in any
further negotiations. The offer was refused.[65] Wolf attempted to present a further olive branch, this time to Weizmann, by replying to his
October letter in conciliatory terms. Nationality, he agreed, could be
conceived of in ethnographic and cultural terms, and so harmonized
with political allegiance to a non-Jewish state. Summarized, however,
Wolf's offer was both unsubtle and clearly transparent: emphasize all
points of agreement, avoid 'dwelling unnecessarily on points of disagreement', and so come to terms on the basis of the Conjoint's
'formula'.[66]

If this was conciliation, it could hardly postpone the final issue.
Wolf, moreover, was under pressure from Reuben Blank to take action
against what Blank deemed to be one logical consequence of the
Zionist argument, namely, the isolation of Russian Jewry.[67] In January
1917 Wolf wrote to the placatory Leopold de Rothschild:

I have no desire whatsoever to precipitate a controversy or a schism but . . . our
present policy of silence is not likely to make for peace and is leading to perils
infinitely worse than any public quarrel with the Zionists . . . in the higher
interests of the Jewish community we cannot leave the situation as it is. I am
absolutely certain that when the preoccupations of this war have passed away,
we shall find that the foolish things published by the Zionists will have
seriously compromised the situation of the Jews all over the world.[68]

Whatever Wolf might say to the contrary, he was now committed to
the fray.

[64] *JC* 27 Oct. 1916. Wolf to Leopold de Rothschild, 18 Oct. 1916, C11/2/9, argues
that the CJC 'intrigues' were 'a deliberate and malicious falsehood'. Clearly, Wolf was as
vulnerable to self-deception as anybody else.
[65] Wolf to CJC presidents, 3 Nov. 1916, C11/2/10; Wolf to Leopold de Rothschild,
7 Nov. 1916, ibid.; Alexander to Wolf, 5 Nov. 1916, ibid.
[66] Wolf to Leopold de Rothschild, 21 Nov. 1916, ibid.; Wolf to Sokolow, 24 Nov.
1916, Gaster papers, CJC file.
[67] Blank to Wolf, 21 Dec. 1916, C11/2/9.
[68] Wolf to Leopold de Rothschild, 3 Jan. 1917, C11/2/10.

6

Zionism versus *Bolshevism*

The claims of the Zionists that Zionism is the only solution to the Jewish question could give the pretext to the French, English and Italian governments, to do nothing on the Russian question as they would gladly prefer to give Palestine to the Jews rather than to quarrel with the Russian government.[1]

Wolf intended his Palestine 'formula' to be part and parcel of a much larger package in which the Conjoint's major post-war objectives for Eastern European and especially Russian Jewry would be satisfied. The Foreign Office could not do a deal on this basis, and therefore treated all Wolf's advances with extreme caution. As Cecil minuted in March 1916, 'if and when we are allowed by our allies to say anything worth saying to the Jews, it should not be left to Mr. Lucien Wolf to say it'.[2]

Even after the failure of the 'considered views', Foreign Office suspicions were confirmed by Wolf's persistent intrigues in this direction. Denied the direct and most legitimate channels of appeal, Wolf circulated the 'considered views' through the network of Anglo-Jewish Association branches to the colonial communities, with instructions to pressurize their governments to reopen the issue at the forthcoming Imperial Conference to be held in London in the spring of 1917. This in turn would give Wolf the opportunity of addressing and discussing the proposals with the Imperial delegates, ostensibly in the name not of the Conjoint Committee but of the communities that had apparently quite independently invoked their assistance. The ploy worked. The Australian, New Zealand, and Canadian prime ministers all promised, either to communal Jewish deputations or to Wolf in person, to petition for Jewish rights. Unfortunately for him, however, these efforts remained under the ever-watchful eye of the Foreign Office, which,

[1] Mowschowitch notes on the projected international Jewish conference in Paris, 30 Mar. 1917, MWS 24657–65.
[2] Cecil minute, 14 Mar. 1916, FO 371/2817/42608.

from beginning to end, knew that the colonial representations had been mobilized by Wolf himself.[3]

What the Foreign Office enthusiasts for a Zionist solution needed was a Jewish spokesman who eschewed the Russian quagmire altogether while endorsing their assumptions that Jewish 'power' could be drawn to and then anchored in the British orbit through Zionism. Their man was Chaim Weizmann. His advice to the Foreign Office ran diametrically counter to Wolf's.

If you give us a declaration in favour of Zionism, the declaration will make the Jews of the world understand that you are really friendly and that the friendship of the Jews of the world is not a thing to be blown upon, it is a thing that matters a great deal, even for a mighty empire like the British.[4]

Weizmann argued that what the majority of Jews, especially in America and Russia, cared most about was a Jewish state in Palestine. An Allied commitment in that direction would win them to the Allied cause, a proposal which by implication seemed to confirm the assumption prevalent in high places that Jewry was hostile to the *entente*. Weizmann's own pronounced Anglophilia—particularly because he was Russian born and therefore expected to be pro-German—served to augment his standing among British leaders, almost as a herald of mass Jewish defection to their side. Indeed, one diplomatic history of the period has quite erroneously noted 'the considerable achievement on the part of Chaim Weizmann' in having 'converted the Zionists from the German to the *Entente* cause'.[5]

More importantly, Weizmann played his cards right by refusing to be drawn on the Russian issue. This was the very concession the

[3] Wolf to AJA branches abroad, 28 Dec. 1916, C11/2/9; Wolf to Moss Davis, 29 Dec. 1916, C11/2/10; Wolf to Massey (New Zealand prime minister), 9 Jan. 1917, C11/2/11. See also Wolf to Oliphant, 4 Feb. and 1 Mar. 1917, FO 371/3092/4637; Oliphant minute, 4 Feb. 1917, ibid.

[4] Weizmann, *Zionist Policy: An Address* (London, 1919): this was his EZF speech of 21 Sept. 1919. (Cited in Abramsky, *War*, 14.)

[5] C. J. Lowe and M. L. Dockrill, *The Mirage of Power: British Foreign Policies, 1902–1922* (London, 1972), ii. 228 is interesting in that it conveys the FO's myopic interpretation of the Jewish wartime situation as historical truth: 'Until 1916, the Zionists worked for a German victory. The reasons were obvious. The traditional pogroms in Russia before the war and the wholesale expulsion of the Jews in Galicia by the Russian military in 1914–15, on the standard assumption that the Jews were German spies, was enough to convince any Jew in Russia, Germany or America that the only salvation lay in the victory of the Central Powers.' Note the interchangeability of 'Jew' and 'Zionist'.

Conjoint wanted from the Zionists when at the end of 1916 they attempted to renegotiate with them. Needing all the help they could get for the 'considered views', they insisted that co-operation in favour of Russian Jewish emancipation was imperative.[6] The traditional leaders of the English Zionist Federation were in fact in agreement with Wolf in desiring this objective. So too was Gaster—albeit from a national point of view—when as president of the newly resuscitated National Union of Jewish Rights he proposed at the beginning of 1917 that they work for general Jewish rights.[7] Weizmann begged to differ. The Russian Jewish question, he told Wolf in August 1916, was a question for Russian Jewry's own salvation. It was quite independent of the Palestine issue and, moreover, was unlikely to be on the agenda of any peace conference. Weizmann did not respond when the Conjoint publicly made their peace offer at the Board in October. Moreover, seconded by Sokolow, he quashed an English Zionist Federation proposal, put forward by Revd M. H. Segal on 11 February 1917, to create a representative Anglo-Jewish Congress which would formulate Jewish claims for the peace conference.[8]

Meanwhile, it can hardly be coincidental that four days prior to the Federation meeting, Sykes had met with the leading Zionists and confirmed British interest in a Jewish Palestine. This marked the real take-off for Zionist negotiations with the government—negotiations to be carried out henceforth not by Gaster (who up to this point had been Sykes's main Zionist contact), nor Bentwich, nor Cowen (still titular head of the Federation), all of whom were present as the nominated leaders of Anglo-Zionism—but by Weizmann and Sokolow.[9] Only they seem to have had an inkling of what was expected of them

[6] 'We want all sections of the Jewish community to unite in pressing forward a liberal solution to the Russian Jewish question as their first and most imperative duty. If that is agreed to by the Zionists, we are prepared to join them in urging upon HMG, or the Powers generally, a settlement of the Palestine question.' Such was Wolf's response to Newman's motion, 22 Oct. 1916, at the BD calling on the CJC to use its best endeavours to secure a legally guaranteed home for the Jews, see *JC* 27 Oct. 1916.

[7] Leader, 9 Feb. 1917, ibid. Greenberg argued that Russian Jewish hopes lay with Allied war aims. On Gaster at the NUJR, 4 Mar. 1917 see *JC* 9 Mar. 1917.

[8] Wolf to Oliphant, 1 Dec. 1916, FO 371/2817/42605, encl. Weizmann to Wolf, 3 Sept. 1916; Wolf to Sokolow, 7 Nov. 1916, Gaster papers, CJC file. *JC* 16 Feb. 1917, reporting Segal's motion at the EZF, 11 Feb. 1917.

[9] Notes on Zionist Meeting, 7 Feb. 1917, Gaster papers, CJC file; Sanders, *High Walls*, 457–62.

vis-à-vis the British government's wider political considerations, and only Weizmann seems to have understood how this could be effected to their reciprocal advantage.

Various factors seemed to be working in Weizmann's favour in the spring of 1917. The new Lloyd George government had marked pro-Weizmann tendencies; Lloyd George himself had made Weizmann's acquaintance through C. P. Scott, the influential *Manchester Guardian* editor, in January 1915, and had responded warmly to his Palestine aspirations. So too had Balfour, who renewed his acquaintanceship with Weizmann—they had first met in the backwash of the Uganda affair in 1906—at Lloyd George's suggestion, soon after. With Lloyd George as a near-dictatorial premier and Balfour as his foreign secretary, Weizmann suddenly found the corridors of power open to him. Even more important, perhaps, he found friends among the prime minister's private secretariat, an enormously influential body, which was, among other things in this period, busily denuding the Foreign Office of its rightful decision-making role. Here was not only Sir Mark Sykes but two other forceful and enthusiastic pro-Zionists, William Ormsby-Gore and Leopold Amery. Weizmann's direct access to and familiarity with them ensured the paramountcy of his position, leaving Wolf, *au fait* only with Foreign Office formalities and etiquette, very much in the cold. Moreover, the forthright, expansive, and essentially imperialistic pursuit of the war which the secretariat fostered, pushed cautious Foreign Office thinking on the Middle East centred on the Sykes–Picot agreement further and further into the background.[10] Direct British military intervention in Palestine became a distinct possibility. In April, General Allenby's forces, perched on the eastern edge of Sinai, did just that.

These developments by no means meant that Weizmann's goals, as opposed to Wolf's, were a foregone certainty. In December 1916, Wolf had intelligence of French moves to make a separate peace with Turkey, thus putting Palestine effectively beyond the orbit of the peace settlement. The British, especially when the invasion suffered major setbacks, made similar probes. Even then, once ensconced in Palestine, they did not necessarily need Zionism to legitimize their position there

---

[10] On Weizmann's relationship to Lloyd George and his secretariat see Weizmann, *Trial and Error*, 192–6, 226–31; Friedman, *Question of Palestine*, 125–7; Stein, *Balfour Declaration*, 137–40, 320. See also Roberta M. Warman, 'The Erosion of Foreign Office Influence in the Making of Foreign Policy, 1916–1918', *Historical Journal*, 15 (1972), 133–59.

since they had already given their blessing, albeit a confused blessing, to Arab designs in the area.[11] Moreover, Weizmann's increasing proximity to the government ought to have been utterly wrecked by the two outstanding and crucial events of the war: America's entry into it on the side of the Allies and the revolution in Russia. The reason the Allies had showered so much attention on American Jewry in the first place was that their hostility was understood to carry with it the ability to undermine financial assistance to the *entente* and even keep America out of the war. As Stein has noted, 'if they had all been reliable friends, there would have been no need to show them any special attention'.[12] Once America had declared war on Germany on 6 April 1917, any need for this special attention should have disappeared. Moreover, the collapse of tsarism a month earlier and the almost immediate promulgation by the new provisional government of emancipation for Russian Jews removed the main plank upon which American Jewish hostility to the Allies had rested. Moreover, as no-annexationist sentiment was now prevalent in both America and Russia, British justification for their involvement in Palestine on behalf of Zionism was correspondingly undermined.

The Zionists were caught on the hop, 'unaware and unready to meet such an emergency'.[13] Russian and American Jewry, led by their respective financial giants, Baron Gunzburg and Jacob Schiff, were rallying to bolster the Allied and particularly the Russian war effort with a massive 'liberty loan'.[14] Fortunately for Weizmann, however, these developments did not deter the Foreign Office from upholding its consistent *leitmotif* that the Jews were still working for a German victory and were still a factor in helping to carry this through.[15] If

[11] On suggested French moves see Wolf to Donald, 14 Dec. 1916, MWS 2868. On Capt. Herbert's proposed peace plan with Turkey see Drummond to Balfour, 7 July 1917, FO 800/206 (Balfour papers). The overlap of the promises made to the Zionists (Balfour Declaration) and the Arabs (MacMahon–Husayn correspondence) is of course the subject of bitter historiographical controversy; see Elie Kedourie, *In the Anglo-Arab Labyrinth: The MacMahon–Husayn Correspondence and its Interpretations, 1914–1939* (Cambridge, 1976).

[12] Stein, *Balfour Declaration*, 216.

[13] Mowschowitch notes, 30 Mar. 1917, MWS 24657–65.

[14] *Retch*, 3 June 1917, report of Petrograd Jewish Bureau's support of a 'liberty loan', MWS 15024–6. See also *Retch*, 28 Apr. 1917, MWS 14673, for Schiff's reported contribution of 1 million roubles.

[15] Harold Nicolson minute, n.d., *c.*1 May 1917, FO 371/3092/4637: 'there is ample evidence that the Jews in Russia and Rumania have been pro-German during the war . . . coupled with their exploitation of the internal economic situation'.

Jewish financial 'power' had up to 1917 been their main bogey, it was now the spectre of the revolutionary Jew that haunted the corridors of Whitehall.

Intelligence and news reaching the Foreign Office soon after the revolution tended to confirm these fears. Robert Wilton, Petrograd correspondent of *The Times* and a pronounced sympathizer with Russian ultra-reactionary forces yet also an agent for British Military Intelligence, filed a report in March blaming student unrest and peace agitation at the University of Dorpat on disruptive Jewish elements.[16] From the south the Foreign Office received a report from their acting consul in Nicolaiev that the Jews were working for a separate peace to pre-empt British commercial interests. This view was endorsed by the consul-general in Odessa: 'Everyone unites in affirming that Jews are working against England and are strongly in favour of Germany. Jewish agitators, all young, pervade every meeting in the towns and villages.'[17]

If many Foreign Office officials remained undecided as to the degree the Jews were responsible for these developments,[18] the Western Jewish communities lent credence to Wilton-type reports by their nervy response. Bigart petitioned Wolf to have the Conjoint co-operate with the Alliance and similar Western organizations to send a Jewish delegation headed by Sylvain Lévi to Russia to exercise 'une action moderatrice sur les masses juives et les amener à se grouper autour du gouvernement'. The Rome Committee wanted a joint message to the Russian Jewish community along similar lines. But considerations of whether to act or not were overshadowed by a series of American Jewish personal and public telegrams to Russia, the most remarkable being from members of the American Jewish Committee to the new Russian foreign minister, Milyukov. American Jewry, it stated, 'is alarmed by reports that certain elements are urging separate peace negotiations between Russia and Central Powers', and convinced, the

[16] Dorpat report, *The Times*, 28 Mar. 1917. On Wilton see *History of the Times*, i. 284–9; Mangold and Summers, *File on the Czar*, 102–3; Sharman Kadish, 'Bolsheviks and British Jews: The Anglo-Jewish Community, Britain and the Russian Revolution', D.Phil. thesis (Oxford, 1986), 25–6, 160–2.

[17] Bagge (Consul-General Odessa) to FO, 16 May 1917, FO 371/2996/811, also encl. Brown (Acting Vice-Consul Nicolaiev) to Bagge, 23 Apr. 1917.

[18] Hardinge minuted (n.d., May 1917, FO 371/2996/811) that German intrigues were probably financed by Jewish money, but Lindley's report, encl. in Buchanan to FO, 29 Apr. 1917, ibid., said that Wilton's accusations against the Jews were 'injudicious' and 'unfair'.

telegram added, that 'Russian Jews are ready to make sacrifices to support the present provisional government'.[19]

The implication that the Jews were chiefly responsible for the growing radical left-wing opposition to the provisional government's continuing pursuance of the war—a vital necessity at this stage if the Allies were to pull through—became the conundrum for which the Foreign Office was desperate to find a solution. Weizmann offered it in the form of Zionism, Wolf disputed its veracity. The last stages of the Wolf–Weizmann conflict therefore became very much a clash of information, with Weizmann endorsing and amplifying British anxieties and Wolf denying them their basic premiss.

Wolf did not accept that the majority of Russian Jews, whether left-wing or conservative, were out to disrupt the provisional government. On the contrary, their best defence against counter-revolutionary pogroms, he maintained, was to support and uphold it. After the Dorpat accusations, he made his own enquiries to the traditional head of the Russian Jewish community, Baron Gunzburg, and to the leading Jewish Cadet, Maxim Vinaver, to get to the truth of the matter. Gunzburg's reply came first, at the end of May. It was edgy, reflecting conservative disquiet at Jewish prominence in radical departures. The Dorpat students, he agreed, were very troublesome; 'we do our best to persuade them that every conspicuous Jewish action would be disastrous to us'. Wolf and his Conjoint colleagues were at first inclined to accept his account. They felt, moreover, that they should do what they could, without directly intervening, to assist in the 'orderly evolution of Russia', going so far as to put themselves at the Foreign Office's disposal for this purpose. However, Vinaver's reply, a week later, was of different mettle. *The Times*'s accusations, he stated, were completely and maliciously untrue; the spectrum of Jewry, from liberal supporters of the Cadets to left-wing Bundists, was imbued with political moderation and support for the provisional government's defensist war policy. Vinaver urged Wolf to inform British society of *The Times*'s misinformation, which threatened to provoke 'unpleasant feelings in Russia'. Wolf's response was to try to have both Gunzburg's and Vinaver's

[19] Bigart to Wolf, 22 Apr. 1917, MWS 5821; Wolf to Bigart, 26 Apr. 1917, AIU/Angleterre 1J 8; Rome Committee to CJC, 30 Apr. 1917, MWS 5824; *Retch* report on Marshall, 24 Apr. 1917, MWS 14670–1. For other telegrams from Schiff to Kaminka, Gompers to Jewish Labour Groups, etc., see Szajkowski, *Jews, Wars*, i. 255–6. Mowschowitch blamed the AIU for the AJC *démarche*; see Mowschowitch to Wolf, 28 Apr. 1917, MWS 24704–7.

statements published in the paper, suggesting he was still unsure as to which statement contained the greater corpus of truth. *The Times* declined to publish.[20]

Information received from Russia in the following weeks and months tended to confirm Vinaver's view of the situation. Leading papers, including Kerensky's *Dyelo naroda*, strongly protested against Wilton's Dorpat 'distortions'; indeed, the Russian Council of Journalists publicly accused him of aiding the enemies of the new regime by stirring up 'the basest passions'. All the indications suggested that reactionary elements were attempting to magnify Jewish involvement in the revolution, especially in the Petrograd Soviet of Workers' and Soldiers' Deputies, in order to give the revolution, in Blank's words, 'un aspect juif', and thereby incite opinion against the provisional government.[21]

Wolf did not and could not deny the very sudden and highly disproportionate prominence and activity of Jews in Russian political life. Statistics collated by his assistant, David Mowschowitch, showed that among the 41 members of the important Executive Committee of the Petrograd-based Soviet there were 7 Jews, and 8 in the 17-strong Menshevik Central Committee. The elections to the Petrograd Town Council had resulted in 28 out of 102 councillors being Jews, even though the Jewish percentage of the city's population was a negligible 5 per cent. Leading Jewish politicians, notably Vinaver, Bramson, and Dan, were in close proximity to the provisional government and had only declined government posts for fear of presenting their coreligionists as targets to the enemies of the new regime.[22] Wolf obdurately contested that their high incidence in radical and revolutionary groups implied that the Jews were working for the most extreme ends.

While there were Bolshevik Jews like Zinoviev and Kamenev in the Petrograd Soviet working for an end to the war, the regular analyses by Mowschowitch that Wolf forwarded to the Foreign Office could point

[20] Wolf to Oliphant, 10 Apr. 1917, FO 371/2995/811, encl. statements of Gunzburg, 29 Mar., and Vinaver, 6 Apr. 1917. *The Times*, 10 Apr. 1917, published a note stating that the Jewish community did not agree with Dorpat report. Vinaver and Gunzburg's letters were published on the same day in the *Daily Telegraph*.
[21] Russian Council of Journalists' denunciation of Wilton, 26 Mar. 1917, MWS 5813; *History of the Times*, i. 248; Braudo message via Gunzburg, n.d., June 1917, MWS 6088–93, urging Western Jewry to get their press to counter anti-Jewish attacks; Wolf to Oliphant, 31 July 1917, FO 371/3012/102649, encl. Blank to Wolf, 7 July.
[22] Mowschowitch's reports on 'The Jewish Aspects of the Revolution', 30 Apr. and 21 July 1917, MWS 14688–715 and 14770–1: Gregor Aronson, 'Jews in Russian Literary and Political Life', in Frumkin, *Russian Jewry*, 293.

to the many more prominent radicals who were stressing moderation. One was Mark Liber, the Bundist who had defended the war effort at a Soviet General Conference. The Bund itself had become largely aligned to the minimalist Mensheviks rather than the maximalist Bolsheviks under Lenin, but the Mensheviks, claimed Mowschowitch, had excluded the celebrated Jewish leader Martov from their Central Committee for being too radical. Further to the right, the Laborist Bramson and the Cadets Sliosberg and Vinaver (the latter now chairman of the party), had criticized Jewish maximalists and anarchists as 'renegades' to Judaism. Mowshowitch claimed that in taking this position as well as in strongly defending the regime they reflected the 'majority' Jewish view. Moreover, he insisted, of all the 'national' groups in Russia, the Jews alone were 'busily engaged in helping the Provisional government and endeavouring to avoid causing any trouble whatsoever'.[23]

Retrospectively, this view was fully endorsed by Kerensky, the last and most important of the provisional government premiers:

99% of the Russian Jews were against the Bolsheviks and during the whole of the revolution the Jewish intellectuals and the Jewish masses . . . were . . . faithful . . . to the revolution . . . and although numerous Jews are to be found among the Bolshevik leaders they are renegades . . . no longer representative of Russian Jewry.[24]

By contrast, Lloyd George's *Memoirs* make strange reading:

Russian Jews had become the chief agents of the German pacifist propaganda in Russia. By 1917, the Russian Jews had done much in preparing for the general disintegration of Russian society . . . it was believed that if Great Britain declared for the fulfillment of Zionist aims in Palestine . . . the effect would be to bring Russian Jewry to the cause of the *Entente*.[25]

[23] Mowschowitch's reports on 'The Political Situation in Russia', 13 Apr. and 13 June 1917 MWS 14663–4, 14730–65 (also encl. in Wolf to Oliphant, 10 May 1917, FO 371/3012/102649). The Mowschowitch analysis of Jewish Bundists and Mensheviks, as moderates is supported in Leonard Schapiro, 'The Role of the Jews in the Russian Revolutionary Movement', *East European and Slavic Review*, 40 (1961–2), 148–67; in Robert J. Brym, *The Jewish Intelligentsia and Russian Marxism* (London, 1978), 73–86, which relates Jewish Bolsheviks such as Kamenev to their essentially Russian background; and in Zvi Y. Gitelman, *Jewish Nationality and Soviet Politics: The Jewish Sections of the CPSU, 1917–1930* (Princeton, 1972), 61–5. However, Bernard K. Johnpoll, *The Politics of Futility: The General Jewish Workers Bund of Poland 1917–1943* (New York, 1967), 61–5, is more critical of the degree to which Liber and the Bund were wholly 'defensist'.
[24] Cited in Johnpoll, *Politics*, 61.
[25] Lloyd George, *War Memoirs* (London, 1936), ii. 721, cited in Ram Marom, 'The Bolsheviks and the Balfour Declaration, 1917–1920', *Wiener Library Bulletin*, 29 (1976), 20.

The key to this remarkable statement was in the persistent, one might say wilful, misreading of the situation by the British government, and more particularly by the war secretariat. Ormsby-Gore wrote in April: 'In Russia it would appear the Jews are taking the extreme line probably in the hope of splitting Russia into fragments.'[26] Eschewing the Wolf–Mowschowitch reports, which were accurate and reliable but psychologically not what they wanted to hear, the government's experts took themselves to Weizmann who was more willing to accommodate himself to their presuppositions.

Weizmann's standing at this time was receiving a considerable boost in government circles, as a result of Balfour's American mission. Here the British foreign minister met several high-placed Jewish figures who were rumoured to have great influence with President Wilson and Colonel House, his foreign affairs adviser—Judges Brandeis and Mack, Professor Frankfurter, and others. These were not simply influential people but also Zionists who had broken with the Berlin executive's wartime neutrality and were now ready to back Weizmann's argument for a British protectorate in a Jewish Palestine.[27] As Weizmann's prognostications about American Jewry were thus apparently reliable, it was natural that he should be sought out on the Russian question too.

In May, Weizmann was interviewed by Hardinge, Cecil, and Graham, senior Foreign Office officials who were especially anxious about the anti-British activities of young Russian Jewry. His response was to suggest that Sokolow, or failing him as he was then in Paris, Boris Goldberg, another Russian Zionist, be sent out to Russia to influence the coming Zionist conference there in an Anglophile direction. At a Federation meeting two weeks later, he made the following suggestive statement, previously passed by the Foreign Office without comment. 'It will be I am sure an honourable task for the Zionist organisation all over the world and especially for our friends in Russia to contribute as much as is in their power to the stabilisation of conditions in Russia.'[28] A month and a half later, Weizmann's American associate, Frankfurter, following a rendezvous with him in Madrid, sent a telegram to the American State Department, amplifying more explicitly what was in

[26] Ormsby-Gore to FO, 14 Apr. 1917, FO 800/198 (Cecil papers).

[27] Zebel, *Balfour*, 243–4; Friedman, *Question of Palestine*, 200.

[28] FO interview with Weizmann, 11 May 1917, FO 371/2996/811; Graham to Ormsby-Gore, 9 June 1917, FO 371/3012/95206, on Goldberg. In fact, Goldberg did not get beyond Copenhagen. For Weizmann's EZF speech see *JC* 25 May 1917.

Weizmann's mind: 'F.O. greatly disturbed by the chance of alleged peace activity of Russian Jews. Zionists most important organise Jewish forces in Russia and F.O. are very anxious Zionists, especially Americans go at once to influence Jewish opinion by means of Zionists.'[29]

Only a few months earlier, Weizmann had been openly saying that internal Russian affairs were outside the scope of British Zionist negotiations. Now, doing a skilful about-turn, he strove to prove to his British patrons that the Zionists represented the aspirations of nearly all Russian Jewry and therefore, if the British declared themselves on Palestine, their best, most reliable allies in Russia. Weizmann had some information at hand to corroborate this thesis. Writing to Sir Ronald Graham in June, he pointed to developments at the all-Jewish Congress in the south of Russia, representing some two million Jews, which had adopted a Zionist platform by 333 votes to 36. 'Considering that the whole of Poland and part of Lithuania are occupied by the Germans, we can take it that more than half the actual Jewish population of Russia have declared for Zionism.' Drawing on extra-Russian developments, Weizmann concluded that opposition came from only a small oligarchy of Jewish *haute finance* and a fraction of Jewish socialists. However, this also would disappear as soon as Zionism became 'a tangible political reality'. But Weizmann warned that the Germans were attempting to use the Zionists for the purposes of peace agitation, and even possible peace negotiations. German and Austrian papers, moreover, were beginning to present the advantages of a Jewish Palestine to the Central Powers.[30] The message was implicit; if the British did not take advantage of the most powerful force in Jewry, the Germans would.

Again, Wolf's information clashed. Like all his Western Jewish colleagues, Wolf at this juncture was anxious about the growing Russian resentment of Allied and especially British behaviour and intentions during the war. In particular, he was concerned about the hostility of Russian Jewish socialists towards Britain for attempting to negotiate an agreement with the provisional government whereby Russian Jews living in Britain who refused conscription would be 'repatriated' to Russia.[31] Moreover, the information he received from

---

[29] For Frankfurter telegram, 8 July 1917, see Szajkowski, *Jews, Wars*, i. 282.

[30] Weizmann to Graham, 13 June 1917, encl. and commented on in FO 371/3058/123458, Graham to Hardinge, 12 Oct. 1917; see *Weizmann Letters*, no. 432.

[31] Wolf to Oliphant, 25 July, HO 45/10821/318095/371, encl. Vinaver statement, n.d., June, and Mowschowitch letter, 3 July 1917.

Mowschowitch suggested that the Russian situation would deteriorate with or without the Jewish factor: the peace movement would get stronger, the food question would not be solved. As for the revolution, it was, Mowschowitch prophetically stated, 'not yet final'. Wolf agreed. 'I see no prospect', he wrote to Montefiore, 'of a wholehearted Russian co-operation in the war.'[32]

Though refusing to be bludgeoned into hasty action, Wolf recognized, especially after receiving appeals from Russian Jewish leaders for Anglo-Jewish aid, that something ought to be done 'to give a more active support against the anti-English propaganda'.[33] His proposal to the Foreign Office was to send out to Russia an English Jew who had the confidence of Cadets and Jewish socialists. Wolf surely had himself in mind.[34] In 1905, he had edited the *Russian Correspondence*, a weekly paper which gave support and encouragement to the Russian revolution of that year. The Bundists had been particularly well publicized, since information received suggested they were in the vanguard of the revolt.[35] In 1917, Wolf again laid considerable emphasis on the Bund, helped by Mowschowitch's reports that they were once more the most active of the Jewish elements involved in the struggle. If the British wanted to influence the section of Russian Jewry with the most political muscle, it was the Bund, he argued, to whom they should address themselves.[36]

As for the Zionists, Wolf contested their value. 'The Zionists *qua* Zionists have no political importance and are inferior in numbers to the other parties',[37] he wrote to the Foreign Office in May, at a time

[32] Mowschowitch, 'The Present Position in Russia', 18 Mar. 1917, MWS 14902–10; Wolf to Montefiore, 11 May 1917, MWS 6063–4.

[33] Wolf to Oliphant, 25 July 1917, HO 45/10821/318095/371.

[34] Ibid. The statement proposed Wolf as the person most likely to be able to influence Russian Jewish journalists and 'give them a proper idea of the consequences involved in 1 [*sic*] propaganda against England and France'.

[35] See *Russian Correspondence*, 4 Oct. 1905–17 Feb. 1906, 17 issues, esp. no. 1, on leading' role of Bund. On Wolf's personal involvement with the Bund in 1905 see David Soskice Papers, WO1–13, House of Lords. Wolf also had the dubious distinction of being named in Count Lamsdorff's proposed 'Anti-Semitic Triple Alliance' as a fund-raiser and publicist for the Bund's fighting groups. For Lamsdorff's Jan. 1906 memorandum see Wolf, *Notes*, 57–62. Wolf did actively support the Bund's self-defence groups, though he was unable to organize an Anglo-Jewish committee for this purpose as Lamsdorff claimed he had. See Wolf to Soskice, 27 June 1906, Soskice papers WO8.

[36] Wolf to Blank, 17 Apr. 1917, MWS 1922: 'the middle and upper classes of the Jews are with us. The danger comes from the socialists and bundists.'

[37] Wolf to Oliphant, FO 371/3012/102649, encl. memo. to CJC presidents and Mowschowitch report on 'The Russian Jewish Situation', 18 May 1917.

when Weizmann was telling them exactly the opposite. In support of his claim, Wolf noted that the manifesto of the Central Zionist Executive recently issued at Copenhagen, which called on Russian Jewry to employ their new status to promote national regeneration in Palestine, had led to socialists at the preliminary conference of the all-Russian Jewish Congress roundly warning them of impending obstruction if they tried to have it included on the agenda. These themes were reiterated a few days later when Wolf saw Rex Leeper, an important Political Intelligence officer at the Foreign Office. Asked by him if a Palestine declaration would make Russian Jews more friendly to England, Wolf 'did not think that anything that might be said would alter the political aspects of the situation. The Zionists would no doubt be very enthusiastic but their political influence *qua* Zionists was inconsiderable.' Ingeniously, he added that a declaration on Palestine might in fact backfire, as Jewish socialists, who viewed Zionism as reactionary but who had 'far more political influence at this moment than the Zionists . . . would regard it as an interference against themselves and would resist it accordingly'.[38]

Claude Montefiore tried similarly to impress these points on Lord Milner, an old friend and major figure in the War Cabinet, when he saw him some days prior to Wolf's soundings from Leeper. Montefiore was relieved to discover that the government's immediate interest in the question had been dampened by delays in the actual Palestine campaign. On the other hand, he surmised, they were still interested 'insofar as it may affect Russian Jewish opinion in Russia'. 'It has obviously been represented to His Majesty's Government', Montefiore concluded, 'that the Russian Jews are all enthusiastic Zionists.' Montefiore seems to have had a greater impact on Milner than Wolf did on Leeper. He tried to demonstrate that Zionism was by no means representative of all Russian Jewry, and expressed his hope that the government would be very careful how it committed itself to Weizmann and Sokolow. Milner recognized that Montefiore was 'tremendously anti-Zionist', but was inclined to agree with his impassioned logic: 'if, as Weizmann says, all the Russian Jews are very revolutionary, anti-monarchical, anti-annexation and anti-British, they are hardly likely to be converted to a better frame of mind by any message we could send them, even about Palestine'. As for Montefiore's doubts

---

[38] Note of interview with Leeper, 21 May 1917, C11/3/1/3; on the Preliminary Conference dissensions see *Dielo pomoschotschi* report, 25 Apr. 1917, MWS 14790–1.

about Weizmann and Sokolow, Milner accepted that these were impelled 'by an honest conviction that they are not reliable guides'.[39]
Only with hindsight can we weigh up the validity of Weizmann's
and Wolf's conflicting arguments. Undoubtedly, Wolf's predisposition
to the Bundists led him to overestimate their importance in Jewish
political developments. Thus when it came to actual voting for delegates to the Russo-Jewish Congress in early 1918, the Bundists gained
a mere 9 per cent as compared with the Zionists 57 per cent.[40]
Mowschowitch too, as a member of the socialist 'autonomist' party, the
Farainigte, would have had an anti-Zionist ideological axe to grind.

On the other hand, despite the very dramatic increase in Zionist
shekel-holders in the summer and autumn of 1917 (the Russian organization claimed three hundred thousand members in October),
Weizmann's assertion that the Zionists spoke for all Russian Jewry and
therefore wielded considerable political clout was a gross misrepresentation. The congress to which Weizmann referred and which had
elected an overwhelmingly Zionist platform, had taken place in what
had been the southern part of the Pale. Here a traditional orientation
towards Zionism reflected the increasingly marginalized nature of an
impoverished Jewish *petite bourgeoisie*. 'Tottering on the edge of
collapse',[41] a situation which emancipation in itself could not ameliorate, their vote for Zionism was a vote for an escape route, however
utopian, from their socio-economic *impasse*. By contrast, other parts of
the Pale then under German control, notably Poland and Lithuania,
had a very different occupational structure. A much larger proportion
of Jewry was proletarianized and hence more closely affiliated to
socialist groups, notably the Bund.[42] Weizmann preferred to presume
that the objections of these 'fractions' to Zionism would abate after the
British had declared themselves on Palestine. There is no evidence to
suggest that this happened. Moreover, as the Zionist leaders were
more interested in Palestine than in Russia, and as their rank and file
were politically passive, their profile on the wider Russian political
scene was low. This situation was reflected in their failure to elevate

---

[39] On Montefiore interview, 16 May 1917, see Milner to Cecil, 17 May 1917, FO
800/198 (Cecil papers); for Montefiore note on proceedings (16 May 1917) see MWS
5968–72.
[40] Stein, *Balfour Declaration*, 34; Gitelman, *Jewish Nationality*, 78, breaks down the
figures for the 1918 elections as Zionists 60%, Socialists 28%, Orthodox 10%.
[41] Gitelman, *Jewish Nationality*, 71.
[42] Ezra Mendelsohn, *Class Struggle in the Pale* (Cambridge, 1970), esp. x–xi.

Palestine to anything more than last place on the agenda at the preliminary Russian Jewish Congress in April,[43] and then only as a
grudging compromise on the part of the socialists. It also has to be
remembered that the Russian Zionist leaders themselves were not
necessarily enamoured with Weizmann's efforts, particularly as they
flouted the Copenhagen policy on 'neutrality'. Weizmann had in fact
considerable difficulty trying to win them over from their caution—
something, of course, which he did not publicize to his Whitehall
patrons.[44]

But, as Stein has so accurately noted, 'the British government was
not much interested in the internal strains of Russian Jewry'.[45] Montefiore considered it a pity that Milner in his early 1917 trip to Russia
had made no effort to contact representative Jewish leaders; if he really
wanted accurate information on the Russian-Jewish situation, Montefiore urged him in May, he should contact Vinaver. Wolf similarly
bewailed the fact that no Jew had been able to join the French and
English socialists who visited Russia soon after the Revolution.[46] But
by this time, it was too late: the government had already committed itself
to the Weizmann course. Thus, reading one of Wolf's denials of Russian
Zionist power, Graham could only comment, 'Dr. Weizmann is always
positive that the vast majority of the Jews in Russia are Zionists.'[47]

What makes this rigidity all the more amazing in retrospect is the
fact that the information supplied by Wolf, who was never able to
shake off the stigma of disloyalty and whose information was in consequence treated with the utmost caution, was corroborated by no less

[43] Wolf to Oliphant, 18 May 1917, FO 371/3012/102649, encl. Mowschowitch
report on 'The Political Situation and the Jewish Aspects of the Revolution'. Again, this
view is supported by Brym, *Jewish Intelligentsia*, 70–2; Stein, *Balfour Declaration*, 431;
and Gitelman, *Jewish Nationality*, 70–84. Gitelman notes the strength of Bundists on the
Berdichev Soviet and the success of their wider proposals for national autonomy at the
July 1917 Congress of Soviets. Zionist historians would disagree. J. B. Schechtman, for
instance, in 'The USSR, Zionism and Israel', in Lionel Kochan, ed., *The Jews in Soviet
Russia since 1917* (Oxford, 1970), 99, claims that the Bolsheviks on seizing power found
'a powerful, dynamic, deeply-rooted Zionist movement'.

[44] Weizmann to Tschlenow, 1 Sept. 1917, *Weizmann Letters*, no. 489, complaining of
Russian Zionists being too much 'under the banner of the Soviet of Workers deputies'.
Weizmann went on to admit that 'very little can be done [in Russia] in the wider political
field'. On Tschlenow's consistent neutrality see Stein, *Balfour Declaration*, 347.

[45] Stein, *Balfour Declaration*, 347.

[46] Montefiore to Milner, 16 May 1917, FO 800/198 (Cecil papers). Wolf to Blank,
17 Apr. 1917, MWS 1922.

[47] Graham minute, n.d., *c.*18 May 1917, FO 371/3012/102649.

a figure than Buchanan in Petrograd. Asked in April to comment on
the possibility of 'countering Jewish pacifist and socialist propaganda'
by Zionism, Buchanan replied that his information suggested that
there was no great enthusiasm for it, especially since the overthrow of
the old tsarist regime; and that as far as he knew, only the Jewish far
left was pacifist. He concluded, 'I doubt very much whether an expression of sympathy with Jewish national aspirations will help.'[48]

Yet Sykes, whose business it was 'to estimate as objectively as he
could the value of Zionism as a political asset', chose to dismiss this
information out of hand. Already a convinced Weizmannite, Sykes
implied that Buchanan did not know his own job; he insisted that the
real situation could only be ascertained through Weizmann, Sokolow,
or Jabotinsky. As we have seen elsewhere, the view Sykes had of
Zionism was as some sort of *ex machina* agency capable of deflecting
hostile forces 'and transmuting various pacific tendencies into friendly
political elements'. Extreme he may have been, but Ormsby-Gore
shared his view that British diplomats in Petrograd really did 'under-
estimate the power of the Jews in Russia'.[49]

Shorn of alternative interpretations, the government could forge
ahead to secure full political advantage from their connection with
Zionism—the only means, presumed Graham in June, of reaching the
Jewish proletariat. Convinced by Weizmann that Zionism was their
only chance of averting revolution by the Bolsheviks or disrupting
German inroads into the Ukrainian grain trade to feed their starving
home front, the government's decision to isssue the Balfour Declaration in November 1917 was motivated primarily by a near desperate
belief that it would avert Russia's withdrawal from the war.[50] In this it
was to be disappointed.

[48] FO to Buchanan and vice versa, 24 and 27 Apr. 1917, FO 371/3053/84173.
[49] Sykes to Graham, 28 Apr. 1917, ibid.; Ormsby-Gore to Graham, 30 May 1917,
FO 371/3012/102649.
[50] Graham to Hardinge, 31 Oct. 1917, FO 371/3058/123458. On the 'Russian'
motives behind the Declaration see CAB 23/4/261, 31 Oct. 1917, Cabinet minutes.
For Balfour and Cecil's reasoning, esp. on Jews and the Ukrainian grain supply and the
'internationalism' of Jews such as Trotsky, see ibid. 304, 21 Dec. 1917. Even after the
Bolshevik takeover the British seem to have hoped that the Zionists would be able to use
their influence on Trotsky to prevent a separate German–Russian peace. See Marom,
'Bolsheviks', 21; Stein, *Balfour Declaration*, 573–4; Zebel, *Balfour*, 247–8. See also Kadish,
'Bolsheviks', 208–26, 233–44, which comes to approximately the same conclusions on the
causes of the Declaration and Weizmann's role therein. By contrast, Sanders, *High Walls*,
pays curiously scant attention to the Russian revolutionary connection.

Even then, Mowschowitch was busy filing an eleventh-hour report to Wolf, statistically confirming from an authentic Bolshevik source that Bolshevik 'maximalism' was proportionally weaker in the Pale than in some other areas, while Menshevik 'minimalism' was proportionately very strong there. The report, presented by Wolf to the Foreign Office soon after the declaration was issued, fell on deaf ears.[51]

In the final analysis, Wolf's penchant for the truth in 1917 was no match for Weizmann's skill in deception. The Allies were reaching a critical stage in the war and welcomed tangible support from wherever it came. Weizmann offered them this, on a basis which fitted in with their distorted preconceptions of Jewish traditional roles and wartime behaviour.

The clash of information had one other result. By late spring 1917, the Conjoint, under heavy communal fire and desperate to maintain its credibility, wanted in earnest to rebuild its bridges to the Zionists. But leaving aside the 'national postulate' issue, to accept a new *modus vivendi* would have required Weizmann to jettison his Russian information, or at least adjust it beyond recognition. With this, his strongest argument with the Foreign Office, no deal with the Conjoint was conceivable. The Conjoint's approaches thus shunned, the communal controversy was one step nearer.

[51] Wolf to FO, 26 Nov. 1917, FO 371/3019/226666, encl. a report by Mowschowitch (21 Oct. 1917), based on a Bolshevik Stockholm weekly. The statistics showed the Bolsheviks strongest in the 'pure' Russian areas, notably Central Russia, and the Mensheviks strongest amongst the 'nationalities'. These figures were paralleled by the background of Bolshevik and Menshevik deputies in the preliminary parliament. After showing the report to Cecil, Wolf noted that 'from the interest he took in it . . . he had been under the same misapprehension as M. Clemenceau'; Wolf to Bigart, 26 Nov. 1917, AIU/Angleterre IJ 8. A year later, Mowschowitch complained to Wolf: 'I have good reason for believing that the FO have a very faint idea of what is going on in Russia . . . they ought to have two or three good correspondents who ought to be attached to the embassy.' Mowschowitch to Wolf, 29 Aug. 1918, MWS 10625–8. Wolf's attempt to get Mowschowitch attached to the FO's Russian 'intelligence' failed; see Wolf to Mowschowitch, 21 Sept. 1918, MWS 10593–4.

7
The End of the Conjoint

I F the Zionists believed they were on the path to British sponsorship in the spring of 1917, the Conjoint still felt it was their due to be consulted, as the 'legitimate' spokesmen of the community, before the government arrived at any decision on Palestine. Wolf had made this clear in his 'considered views' the previous autumn.[1]

Moreover, until almost the last moment, the Conjoint chiefs were confident that their usefulness to the government on Jewish matters would make for the continuation of Conjoint–government relations. They had evidence to support this supposition. In the summer of 1916, for instance, both the Foreign Office and the Home Office, in the latter case in the person of Herbert Samuel, the home secretary, had called on Wolf's assistance, not vice versa, to try and find a solution to the problem of unnaturalized Russian Jews in Britain who refused to join the colours.[2]

Samuel had got himself into deep water in a Commons speech by threatening the dissidents with transportation back to Russia. This had sharpened the resolve of the dissidents, and their radical English supporters, to resist; but it had underscored popular resentment, especially in the areas of heavy immigrant concentration, against an unloved minority group whose members had somehow been favoured with exemption from the recent military conscription act. The Home Office feared that to leave the matter alone would be to fuel that ill-feeling. The Anglo-Jewish establishment was, unsurprisingly, in full accord with this view, sharing the governments' disdain of the immigrant's lack of patriotism and pressing for determined action to avert a more general anti-Jewish backlash.[3]

[1] *RDJBE* 47.
[2] Wolf to Montgomery, 22 May 1916; FO 371/2835/18095; Wolf memo, 'Russian Jews and Military Service', 15 May 1916, MWS 5449–59.
[3] For Samuel's speech in the Commons, 29 June 1916, see HO 45/10818/318095/32; for Wolf's view that the dissenters' 'unwise and discreditable attitude threatened to compromise the whole work of the Conjoint Committee in Eastern Europe' see Wolf, 'Russian Jews', MWS 5449–59. For a study of aspects of the issue from the immigrant standpoint see Julia Bush, *Behind the Lines, East London Labour 1914–1919* (London, 1984), 171–84.

Wolf found himself in a position where he was able to play a considerable role in shaping the Home Office response, which was to provide for a preliminary voluntary enlistment scheme until 30 September 1916 and the announcement of penalties only after that date. Acting as an intermediary between the ministry and the East End Russian Jewish representatives, he saw the necessity to encourage the 'voluntary' scheme not through the 'establishment' War Services Committee, based in Rothschild's New Court premises, but through one closer in spirit to the East End. With this in view, he helped in the formation of a special committee which aimed to propagandize the East Enders to enlist; and despite his poor relations with Weizmann and Sokolow he successfully co-opted them on to it.[4] When this committee proved to be unsuccessful, Wolf more or less on his own initiative, approached Jabotinsky; his ideas for a 'Jewish Legion' were anathema to him, but he hoped to channel his enthusiasm into the enlistment efforts. Through Wolf's influence, Jabotinsky was also able to bring his close associate, Meir Grossman, a Russian Jewish journalist then in Copenhagen, to come and assist with these efforts in Britain.[5]

In fact, the voluntary scheme was a dismal failure, and the Home Office throughout the rest of the war was left unable to decide whether or not to use its ultimate means of compulsion, deportation.[6] These developments did not reflect on Wolf in a bad light, however. On the contrary, his recognition that the Zionists might be most suited to do the work in the East End and his encouragement of their schemes were evidence of his desire to compromise, for the sake of 'the national interest'.[7] Moreover, the lukewarmness of their efforts served only to

---

[4] Wolf, 'Russian Jews', MWS 5449–59; Wolf to Samuel, 17 and 21 Aug. 1916, C11/2/9. The East End committee was under Gregory Berenson, managing director of the Russian and English Bank. The scheme provided for immediate naturalization for those who enlisted.

[5] Wolf to Samuel, 1 Sept. 1916, C11/2/9; Wolf to Jabotinsky, 4 Sept. 1916, ibid. A Home Office official, Henderson, minuted on 2 Sept. 1916: 'Mr. Wolf said the Zionists needed him and asked us to give instructions for his journey', HO 45/10819/318095/76. See also Fraenkel, 'Wolf and Herzl', 187.

[6] The Home Office efforts culminated in a government decision, never carried out, to place the dissenters in concentration camps in Hull and Aberdeen prior to deportation. See War Cabinet meeting, 22 Jan. 1918, CAB 23/5/329.

[7] Wolf to Henderson, 6 Sept. 1916, HO 45/10819/318095/172, complaining against the censor's deletion of part of his *Daily Chronicle* article of the same date, 'The Aliens and the Army', suggesting that Jews might serve in Home Service or labour battalions in Egypt where 'the Zionists are rather keen on serving'. Weizmann favoured this solution. See Henderson memo, 19 Sept. 1916, HO 45/10818/318095/92.

magnify the traditional Anglo-Jewish leadership's reliability as government agents. For this Wolf received the Home Office's thanks.[8]

Almost a year later, in May 1917, Wolf's services were again urgently requested, this time by the Foreign Office—and, significantly, over Weizmann's head—with regard to reports that anti-Jewish outbreaks in Palestine were imminent. The ministry officials wanted German Jews to make representations to their government to make the Turks desist from this action but were unsure as to how exactly to contact them. One way, noted Wolf, was through the Zionist offices in Copenhagen; but he deprecated this, fearing that the situation in Palestine was in part due to the 'great publicity which had recently been given to the Zionist negotiations with the Allies'. The Foreign Office accepted his alternative, which was to telegraph to Dr Ehrenpreis, the pro-German chief rabbi of Sweden, and provide him with the necessary facilities to do so.[9]

Though this was in a sense a moral victory over the Zionists, it was also one of Wolf's last major acts in his Conjoint capacity. The Committee might consider itself indispensable to the government, but all the signs suggested that the government in its resolve to negotiate with the Zionists was now prepared to dissociate itself from it.

That the Zionists had attained an intimacy with the government that enabled them to ignore the Conjoint's renewed plea for renewed talks between them was abundantly clear to Wolf from the tenor of their recent correspondence with him. To Wolf's suggestion that a fresh agreement could be reached on the basis of the Conjoint's 'formula', Sokolow replied in March 1917 that this could only be reached on the basis of the Conjoint's prior acceptance of the Basle programme, that is, 'the establishment for the Jewish people of a legally secured and publicly recognised home in Palestine'. Its nationalist overtones obviously made this a non-starter for the Conjoint, and Wolf responded by threatening that unless these conditions were withdrawn within the next fortnight, the Conjoint would regard the negotiations for a resumption of the conference at an end. Sokolow hedged, pleading

---

[8] See letters from Wolf to Henderson, 21 and 27 Aug. 1916, HO 45/10819/318095/76, which also advise the Home Office to rely on the New Court people as Berenson's committee was 'not very much to be trusted'. For a view of the issue reflecting Wolf in a less sympathetic light, see David Yisraeli, 'The Struggle for Zionist Military Involvement in the First World War (1914–1917)', *Bar-Ilan Studies in History* (Ramat Gan, 1978), 197–203.

[9] Wolf to Montefiore, 7 May 1917, MWS 2985–6; Wolf to Ehrenpreis (telegram), 4 May 1917, MWS 5921.

absence from London to delay an immediate response to this
ultimatum. For a crucial month, communication between the two
parties was severed.[10]

What Wolf did not know was that Sokolow's 'absence' represented a
major diplomatic advance in the fortunes of the Zionists; he was in
Paris with Sykes, negotiating for French support for a Jewish Palestine.
In mid-April, however, Wolf received news of these developments
from Bigart. The French, he learnt, had in principle accepted Jewish
national aspirations in Palestine, their right to free immigration and
self-government. Sokolow had also told them, said Bigart, that
Britain favoured a chartered company to administer Palestine from
London, though the French had pointed out that they would not
accept this particular feature should Palestine come under their
influence.[11]

The knowledge that both the French and the British were at one in
desiring to promote Zionism, apparently along the 'national' lines
considered so grave a threat to the Conjoint's work, was the final factor
driving Wolf to belligerency.[12] Nevertheless, he first attempted to
apply pressure to bring the Conjoint back into negotiations with the
government and at the same time to bring the Zionists to heel. Though
the committee would still be ready to resume negotiations, Wolf informed Sokolow, 'they must now resume their full liberty of action',
including 'the right of publishing the correspondence relating to the
conference and negotiations with your organisation, whenever they
may see fit'. To the Foreign Office, Wolf sent Bigart's report, more or
less demanding to know if it was accurate and forcefully reminding
them of the consequences of an agreement with foreign Jews who
for the most part did not co-operate with community affairs (here
Wolf was obviously intent on drawing a parallel with the enlistment
issue). He warned that to proceed along these lines with those who
had no right to speak for the native Jews of Britain and without the
Conjoint's participation would not only 'be a great injustice to the

[10] Wolf to Sokolow, 8 and 26 Mar., Gaster papers, CJC file; Sokolow to Wolf, 8 and
30 Mar. 1917, ibid.
[11] Bigart to Wolf, 16 Apr. 1917, MWS 5948–52, encl. report of AIU meeting with
Sokolow, 14 Apr. 1917. For Sokolow's diplomacy in Paris see Friedman, *Question of
Palestine*, 150–1; Stein, *Balfour Declaration*, 399–404.
[12] Wolf informed Bigart that negotiations with the Zionists had been broken off 'and
the Conjoint will shortly have to decide what attitude they will take in regard to the
Palestine question', see Wolf to Bigart, 26 Apr. 1917, AIU/Angleterre, IJ 8.

Anglo-Jewish community', it would also incur the risk of 'very serious mischief'.[13]

The Foreign Office baulked at the prospect. One official, Lord Drogheda, agreed that they were not yet definitely committed to Zionism and that all sections of the British Jewish community should have the opportunity to express their views on the question. Graham drafted a conciliatory letter to Wolf to the effect that 'the government . . . are sincerely anxious to act in all matters affecting the Jewish community not only in its best interests but with a due regard to the wishes and opinions of all its sections and will not depart from this guiding principle'. No agreement, he insisted, had been reached on Palestine.[14]

Wolf was not so easily appeased. At the end of April he suggested to Cecil that he might call on him to explain the Conjoint's views. Perhaps, he added, the Zionist–Conjoint correspondence might have to be published. This veiled threat put the Foreign Office on edge; Oliphant, as well as leading Zionist sympathizers including James de Rothschild, requested him to think again.[15] But Wolf was clearly not in a conciliatory mood. Moreover, he seems to have recognized the damage he might now inflict by a spoiling action, not necessarily through publication of the correspondence *per se* but through the generation of a public debate which would upset or possibly even indefinitely postpone the declaration which the Zionists sought.[16] Though on 2 May he reassured Oliphant that the Conjoint did not contemplate a public polemic with the Zionists, in the next breath he reiterated that publication of a 'statement' on government–Zionist negotiations was inevitable both 'for the information of the Jewish community and the vindication of the Conjoint Committee'. 'Whether

[13] Wolf to Sokolow, 26 Apr. 1917, Gaster papers, CJC file; Wolf to Oliphant, 26 Apr. 1917, FO 371/3092/4637. See also Wolf to Montefiore, 9 Apr. 1917, MWS 2981, where Wolf links the need for a manifesto 'repudiating and reprobating the bad influences at work among the foreign community' to disturbances in the East End.

[14] Drogheda minute, 25 Apr. 1917, FO 371/3092/4637; Graham draft, 25 Apr., and Graham to Wolf, 27 Apr. 1917, ibid.

[15] Proposal to Cecil conveyed in Wolf to Oliphant, 30 Apr. 1917, ibid.; Oliphant minute, 30 Apr. 1917, ibid. Wolf suspected Weizmann of being behind the Zionist sympathizers' appeals. See Wolf memo, n.d., encl. in CJC report no. 10, May 1917, MWS 5959-62.

[16] Cowen to Wolf, 3 May 1917, Gaster papers, CJC file. Cowen argued that publication 'would be prejudicial to the interests in which we are both concerned . . . we should be glad to have due notice from you before you proceed'.

the statement should take the form of a public declaration or a private representation to His Majesty's Government', he concluded, 'must depend on the form in which the plans of the Zionists come before the Committee.'[17]

By leaving the Foreign Office in suspense as to when, or even if, the 'statement' would take place, Wolf was insinuating that the price for preventing a controversy was Conjoint involvement in the negotiations. In other words, Wolf's manœuvres at this juncture were an attempt to reassert the primacy of his committee's relationship to the Foreign Office over that of the Zionists, whom he cast in the role of poachers. There were limits, however, to the pressures that Wolf could exert at the ministry. To alienate them completely was to lose all, as further access would simply be blocked. Moreover, the Conjoint had traditionally (but particularly during the war) sought to impress the Foreign Office with their sense of responsibility by acting with caution and with manifestations of being in full accord with government policy. 'Considerations of loyalty play a great part in all that the Conjoint are doing and sometimes they have put the Foreign Office in surprise by expressions of loyalty in forms which are monstrous', noted Mowschowitch. It is, he added, 'a kind of special wisdom with English Jews to be as docile and submissive as only good children should be'.[18]

Wolf thus failed to goad the Foreign Office into including the Conjoint in the discussions, but he did receive assurances in person from Cecil that no Palestine arrangement would be made without taking into account the whole of Jewish opinion. With this in mind, Wolf wrote to Oliphant on 15 May agreeing to withhold the Zionist–Conjoint correspondence from general publication, but with the reservation that the Conjoint would still use it to defend themselves against Zionist attacks at the Board and Anglo-Jewish Association. As for the 'statement', Wolf took great pains to explain why they were going ahead with it. 'They feel it is impossible for them to remain silent any longer, not only because their silence is being misrepresented . . . but also because their constituents are clamouring to know what their views are and it is clearly their duty to give such guidance as in their power.'[19] The 'statement', therefore, was no longer directed at the Foreign Office, and Wolf offered to come and personally discuss it

[17] Wolf to Oliphant, 2 May 1917, FO 371/3092/4637.
[18] Mowschowitch notes, 30 Mar. 1917, MWS 24657–65.
[19] Cecil–Wolf interview, 8 May 1917, FO 371/3092/4637; Wolf to Oliphant, 18 May 1917, FO 371/3053/84173.

with Cecil prior to publication. This was consistent with the committee's usual approach. But in the event, the 'statement' only arrived on Cecil's desk a day after it had been published in *The Times*, on 24 May, Wolf lamely explaining that publication had been a 'little hurried'.[20] It seems that Wolf's highly untypical lack of courtesy was precipitated not by a desire to present the ministry with a *fait accompli*, for in the long-term little could be gained from such an action, but by communal developments. In April, following the British invasion, the *Jewish Chronicle* had openly challenged the Conjoint to declare its position on Palestine, adding that if it did diverge from Jewish national sentiment, the Board would intervene to prevent it from jeopardizing the Zionist–government negotiations. The challenge was taken up by both the Association and Board, at the latter in the form of a resolution by Rabbi Samuel Daiches on 20 May calling for British recognition of Jewish historical claims to Palestine. Though this had been narrowly defeated, the fact that the Board had departed from its usual traditions of not debating such contentious issues, and indeed without Conjoint consultation, suggested that a determined effort was afoot to undermine the committee's decision-making authority.[21]

Already before Rabbi Daiches's defeat, in fact on 17 May, the Conjoint had decided by majority vote to publish the 'statement'.[22] Even then, the whole thing may have been a bluff on Wolf's part. Hertz, the strongly pro-Zionist chief rabbi, had been present at the meeting, at Conjoint invitation, and Wolf had suggested to him that the 'statement' could still be rendered unnecessary and a new Conjoint 'formula' devised if Weizmann and Gaster 'could be induced to modify or otherwise explain away their public statements'. Unfortunately, Hertz passed this information on to Greenberg, who himself claimed 'no authority whatsoever to speak for the Zionists', but who as a result was forewarned of the committee's plans.[23] Greenberg was thus in a position to expose Wolf's manœuvres in his papers, and indeed on 23 May, the *Jewish World* hinted that the Conjoint would openly oppose

[20] FO 371/3092/4637, conveyed in Wolf to Oliphant, 18 and 25 May 1917.
[21] For Cowen, Newman, and Daiches's notice of motions see *JC* leader, 18 May 1917; on BD debate on 20 May see *JC* 25 May 1917.
[22] CJC minutes, 17 May 1917; 'Statement on Palestine Draft', July 1917, MWS 5973–84. The voting went 12 to 2, with 7 absent. The dissenters were Joseph Prag and Elkan Adler.
[23] Hertz to Montefiore, 30 May 1917, MWS 2994–6; Wolf to Montefiore, 1 June 1917, MWS 2997–9.

152   *Wolf and the Zionists*

the British government's views on Palestine. Wolf interpreted this as a violent attack on the Committee and saw worse to come when the *Jewish Chronicle* came out two days later. Convinced that nothing could be done to bridge the ideological gap, Wolf pleaded to Montefiore that if the Jewish community were to receive an 'unprejudiced judgement', clearance must be given for immediate publication.[24]

The irony of the matter was that if Wolf had known the actual state of British–Zionist negotiations, he would have found the issues which necessitated the 'statement', namely the 'national postulate' and the charter, much less threatening than he imagined. A month earlier, the charter scheme, which Sykes had so enthusiastically sponsored, had been quietly dropped. Following an interview with Brandeis in America, moreover, Sir Eric Drummond had noted that though their long-term objective was a Jewish national home, the immediate goal was 'equal opportunity for Jews in Palestine', a framework remarkably similar to Wolf's own 'formula'.[25] Weizmann himself publicly said as much at a Federation meeting only four days before the 'statement's' publication. 'States', he said, 'must be built up slowly, gradually, systematically and patiently . . . while the creation of a Jewish commonwealth is our final ideal . . . the way to achieve it lies through a series of intermediary stages.' Indeed, when Weizmann and Sokolow put forward their proposed format for a British declaration on Palestine, it said nothing about a Jewish state nor charter nor anything of colonization or immigration, aspects which Wolf had taken pains to include in his 'formula'.[26] 'The more the question is studied,' he wrote to Montefiore in May, 'the less the Zionists will get and in the end people will see that the anti-Zionists with their formula were really the better Zionists.'[27]

The correctness of Wolf's prediction in fact enabled him, when the Balfour Declaration was finally announced in November, to greet it not altogether unsympathetically. 'The elements of a good bargain exist', he told Montefiore. Though he had had no direct leverage on the matter for some six months, a fierce rearguard action was fought by leading 'establishment' Jews, including Montefiore and more particularly, in the government itself, Edwin Montagu, the secretary for India. The result was provisions which specifically safeguarded non-Jewish

[24] Wolf to Montefiore, 23 May 1917, MWS 2991–3.
[25] Drummond memo on interview with Brandeis, 24 Apr. 1917, FO 371/3053/84173.
[26] *JC* 25 May 1917, reporting Weizmann's Federation Conference speech, 20 May.
[27] Wolf to Montefiore, 23 May 1917, MWS 2991–3.

rights in Palestine and Jewish political rights outside it, and which thereby alleviated Wolf's worst fears.[28] All he needed in making representations to Downing Street in November was an 'emendation' of the phrase 'a national home for the Jewish people', or an explanation of it which would 'rob it of all dangers for the future'. He suggested as an alternative 'a Jewish national home in Palestine', which, turned round, did not carry the same connotations as the original text of Jewish alienness from the countries in which they otherwise resided.[29] The very vagueness of the declaration, in fact, paved the way for a multiplicity of interpretations, not always to the Zionists' advantage.[30]

The convergence of the two sides' formulas in May does not however signify that a consensus could have been realized if Wolf had known of the erosion of the Zionist scheme. As a matter of principle, Weizmann felt negotiation with those who rejected the 'national postulate' was impossible. More importantly, to have agreed to a 'broad front' including the Conjoint for representation to the government would have risked the disruption of his arguments as to the nature of American and Russian Jewry so vital to the success of his diplomacy. Time and time again, he insisted that what he wanted was not joint action with the Conjoint, but a demarcation line so that the two groups would not clash.[31] For this very reason, he opposed attempts at the Board to make for reconciliation. Joseph Prag, one of the two men who had voted at the Conjoint meeting against the 'statement', noted perceptively after its publication, 'the whole conduct of the negotiations by the Zionists was done in a curious manner and gave me the impression that while professing to be anxious for an *entente* they were not averse from avoiding one if it were at all possible'.[32]

If, however, the Conjoint chiefs believed that the carrot and stick

[28] Friedman, *Question of Palestine*, 259–63. For statements by Montefiore *et al.* to the government, Oct. 1917, see Stein, *Balfour Declaration*, 524–6.

[29] Wolf to Montefiore, 30 Nov. 1917, CII/2/II. On 30 Nov. 1917 Wolf wrote to Marshall: 'I have made further representations to Downing street and I feel convinced our interests will not be neglected'; see Wolf to Marshall, 30 Nov. 1917, Adler papers.

[30] Stein, *Balfour Declaration*, 524. The final text of the declaration ran: 'His Majesty's Government view with favour the establishment in Palestine of a national home for the Jewish people and will use their best endeavours to facilitate the achievement of this object, it being clearly understood that nothing shall be done which may prejudice the civil and religious rights of existing non-Jewish communities in Palestine or the rights and political status enjoyed by Jews in any other country.'

[31] Weizmann to Sieff, 17 Oct. 1916; *Weizmann Letters*, no. 284; Weizmann to Lewis, 1 June 1917, no. 411, ibid.   [32] Prag letter, *JC* 1 June 1917.

method—frightening the Zionists with threats of publication, yet offering willing co-operation if their points could be met—would bring Weizmann round, they made a bad mistake.[33] What it did, in fact, was to awaken a hornet's nest within Anglo-Jewry. Its communal heads— Lord Rothschild, Chief Rabbi Hertz, and the *haham* Moses Gaster— all spoke out against the statement publicly, an embarrassment which could not be offset even by a counter-letter of Anglo-Jewish notables supporting it.[34] Wolf's request to the normally pliant Alliance to publish a similar statement in the French press was declined because of France's 'situation spéciale en Turquie', and a host of protests came in from colonial communities, notably from the South African Jewish Congress. At home, the *Jewish Chronicle* took the opportunity to call on the Board and the Anglo-Jewish Association 'to sweep away for once and for all the Conjoint Committee, which has brought discredit on the community and with which Anglo Jewry had been encumbered only too long'. In fact four of the Committee's number, including the long-serving Elkan Adler, resigned.[35]

What folllowed has become one of the most celebrated episodes in Anglo-Jewish history. At a meeting of the Board on 17 June, the best attended in its history, a motion censuring the Conjoint action was passed by 56 votes to 51. This led in turn to the resignation of the president, David Alexander, his vice-president, Henry Henriques, and the treasurer, Joshua Levy.[36] More significantly, perhaps, the Board went on the following month to annul the annual 'treaty' with the Anglo-Jewish Association. In the minds of many Board delegates, the high-handedness of the 'statement' was the hallmark of the Association's élitist, undemocratic methods and behaviour. Technically, the Conjoint had ceased to exist.[37]

[33] CJC letter, 'The Future of the Jews', *The Times*, 24 May 1917. See also Wolf to Bigart, 5 June 1917, MWS 6001–7, where Wolf insists the 'statement' was conciliatory.

[34] Letters in *The Times*, 27 May 1917, opposing the 'statement', and 29 May 1917 endorsing it. The 'notables' included Lord Swaythling, Laurie Magnus, Leonard Cohen, Henry Henriques, and Sir Lionel Abrahams. They later became the core of the anti-'nationalist' League of British Jews. See also S. Cohen, *English Zionists*, 238–9, 303–10.

[35] Wolf to Bigart, 5 June, MWS 6001–3; Bigart to Wolf, 21 June 1917, MWS 6006; *JC* leader, 1 June 1917; CJC minutes, 6 June 1917.

[36] *JC* 22 June 1917, reporting BD meeting, 17 June 1917. Wolf suffered the humiliation of having the Board vote endorsed by the congregation at Woolwich, for which he was a deputy; 'Mentor', *JC* 13 July 1917.

[37] *JC* 20 July 1917, reporting BD meeting, 15 July 1917. Officially the 'treaty' did not come to an end until the AJA reconvened after the summer recess to ratify it. On AJA

Weizmann's path to the Balfour Declaration, in its last crucial phase, was now uninterrupted. Though his diplomatic adversary Wolf had assured the Foreign Office in June that the Board vote of censure showed only that the parties were 'more evenly balanced than supposed', and would lead to constitutional changes not 'to the advantage of the Zionists', ministry officials were glad to note that Wolf was 'in decline' and to assume that further consultations with his committee would hence be unnecessary.[38] Denied his last, desperate effort to resume negotiations, and despite conceding all by suggesting that neither side 'insist on the preliminary acceptance of any formula by the other', Wolf had nothing left with which to deter the Zionists.[39]

But it would be a mistake to assume that these developments marked a decisive communal victory for the Zionists, as many contemporaries and later historians have suggested.[40] If this had been so, Wolf would have been banished from the centre of communal power and left to lurk for the rest of his 'active' political life in the wings. Incredibly, Wolf's communal position was ultimately strengthened by these events.

As Stuart Cohen has admirably shown, factors other than Zionism, essentially to do with provincial dissatisfaction with the Board's outdated, overcentralized, and undemocratic habits, played a considerable part in the censure vote.[41] Certainly there was also dissatisfaction with a sometimes overcautious and seemingly unimpressive Conjoint diplomacy, and this did contribute to the Committee's downfall.[42] But if the

---

meeting, 9 Sept. 1917, see *JC* 14 Sept. 1917. Mowschowitch suggested that the conflict, though ostensibly between the BD and the CJC, was in substance between the BD and the AJA.

[38] Mowschowitch, 'The Board', MWS 23534–42, 7 Sept. 1943. Nicolson minute, 18 June 1917, FO 371/3053/84173. See also Graham minute, n.d., *c.*24 July 1917, FO 371/2884/72706: 'Mr. Wolf has ceased to speak in any name but his own as the Conjoint Committee has been dissolved.'

[39] Wolf to Cowen, 4 June 1917, Gaster papers, CJC file. There were some weak efforts to resume CJC–Zionist negotiations (see Herman Landau's speech at the AJA on 3 June, reported in *JC* 8 June 1917) and, by Wolf, to continue disrupting Weizmann's closing accord with the Zionists; see Wolf to Cowen, 12 June and 2 July 1917, Gaster papers, CJC file.

[40] A Zionist interpretation of the vote (sometimes referred to as a 'Whig' interpretation) can be found in Friedman, *Question of Palestine*, 239–40, and Bermant, *Cousinhood*, 260–1. This interpretation has been effectively dismantled by Stuart Cohen, 'The Conquest of a Community? The Zionists and the Board of Deputies in 1917', *JJS* 19 (1977), 157–84 and by Bayme, 'Jewish Leadership', 258–9.

[41] See S. Cohen, 'The Conquest', esp. 158–9, 166, 172–5.

[42] For Board complaints of 22 Apr. against CJC see *JC* 27 Apr. 1917.

solution appeared to be dispensing with the Conjoint and setting up a foreign affairs committee run and elected exclusively by the Board, very large practical problems soon presented themselves. A month prior to the Board's vote of censure, Wolf had enjoyed a major and tangible success. Baghdad Jews residing in Britain had since the beginning of the war been suspected of Turcophilism, leading to restrictions on their trade and movement. With the 'liberation' of Baghdad by British forces in March, Wolf, using arguments concerning the interests of British Near Eastern and Indian trade, was able to have these restrictions removed.[43] His pragmatic handling of the question, and hence its favourable outcome, was very much a consequence of years of tactful diplomacy in dealing with government. If the community desired responsible and astute action in the field, it entailed dependence on Wolf. Joseph Prag said as much in public when he noted that the dissolution of the Conjoint at a critical time for the community might lead to the men with experience in Jewish foreign affairs being overruled by those with none. Wolf, in private, agreed. 'The Board, while thinking that it has liberated itself,' he told Montefiore, 'has really created great difficulties for itself.'[44]

Indeed it had. While the Board dithered over what to do about foreign affairs in the future, leaving it to their Law and Parliamentary Committee to decide, the Association reasserted its traditional interest in the matter by quickly appointing its own foreign affairs executive committee. This consisted of not only practically all the leading lights in the old Conjoint but many influential figures in their own right, including Montefiore, Swaythling, Prag, Elkan Adler, and Leonard Cohen. It contained others too, notably Harry Lewis and Leonard Stein, with marked sympathies for Zionism, suggesting a wider spectrum of opinion than the old Conjoint. The Board committee was no match for it, nor, as Henry Henriques later admitted, for its new permanent secretary, Lucien Wolf.[45]

Unhindered by Board–Association wrangles and with the luxury of not having to deal with Palestine, Wolf was, in his new committee, able to surge ahead and tackle issues very much nearer to his heart. In fact,

[43] Langley (FO) to HO, 7 May, HO 45/108339/33037/7; Wolf to Henderson, 21 May, and vice versa, 5 June 1917, ibid.

[44] Prag letter, *JC* 19 Oct. 1917; Wolf to Montefiore, 16 July 1917, CII/2/11.

[45] AJA Foreign Affairs Committee, Interim Report, 25 Oct. 1917, CII/2/12; on formation of alternative Board committee led by Sir Stuart Samuel see *JC* 21 Oct. 1917; for Henriques' comments at BD meeting, 22 June 1919, see *JC* 27 June 1919.

it was at this stage that a new policy, especially on Romania and Poland, was formulated at Wolf's behest, transforming the community's approach to foreign affairs and preparing the ground for their efforts at the peace conference.[46] However, the existence of two Jewish foreign affairs committees working in parallel yet separately was something which could not continue indefinitely. It made for absurd overlap—for instance when the Greek premier, Venizelos, on his visit to London, received two deputations who said the same thing—and for mystification and annoyance at the Foreign Office. Moreover, if they were going to compete, it was the Board committee which would inevitably lose out, for it was Wolf who had the contacts and influence. Indeed, as soon as the Association committee came into existence, it received the acknowledgement not only of the relevant foreign Jewish bodies but also of foreign diplomats.[47]

Therefore, it was the Board chiefs, led by Sir Stuart Samuel, their new president, who were most earnest in making moves providing for a new 'treaty', moves which were easily carried, despite the spirited harrying of the Zionist deputies and the vituperations of the *Jewish Chronicle* against the restoration of the 'old system'. Following a round table conference, a new 'Joint Foreign Committee' was inaugurated in December 1917.[48] True, some of the old idiosyncracies of the Conjoint which had most grated on its opponents, including the separate minute book of the committee chiefs, which had epitomized the 'inner camarilla' control, were removed. In addition there was now a stipulation giving both Board and Association members the right to refer any voting matter back to their parent bodies. In nearly all other respects, however, the implicit advantage to the Association remained as before. It continued, despite its non-elective basis, to have eight out of seventeen (as opposed to eight out of sixteen) members on the committee, a situation which remained virtually unchanged until 1937. Moreover many of the Board delegates, such as Henry Henriques and Sir

[46] AJA Interim Report, 25 Oct. 1917, C11/2/12.
[47] Ibid. The deputations to Venizelos (BD on 18 Nov., AJA on 23 Nov. 1917) were connected with issues of compensation following the fire in Salonika in 1917 which destroyed most of the old Jewish quarter; see Letters to the AJA Committee from Zaleski, Misu, *et al.*
[48] Terms of treaty between AJA and BD, 19 Dec. 1917, C11/2/12. On AJA meeting of 13 Jan., see *JC* 18 Jan. 1918. See also 'Mentor', *JC* 25 Jan. On Samuel and the Board's 'sell-out' see *JC* leader, 22 Feb. 1918.

Adolph Tuck, continued to hold their Association membership, thus serving the committee in a dual capacity. There is no indication from a review of the members of the new committee that the old authority of the 'Cousinhood' was undermined, nor, despite the involvement of vociferous Zionists such as Daiches and Bertram Benas, of a new, pro-Zionist orientation. Moreover, the executive powers of the committee, in the event of emergencies, remained untouched; and as Montefiore, who re-emerged as co-president, noted, most matters were ones of routine urgency. Finally, Wolf's own position, which had been so anomalous and controversial while at the Conjoint, was now regularized. Though having to vacate his Association and Board positions, he was at last recognized as the committee's and hence the community's 'foreign secretary', a post he continued to hold without challenge until his death in 1930.[49]

Practically on every score, therefore, Wolf's position had been strengthened. If there had been inroads, they were mostly due to causes other than Zionism—for instance, the death in June of one of the Conjoint's most valuable assets, Leopold de Rothschild. True, Wolf's relations with Sir Stuart Samuel, the new Board president and Conjoint co-chief, whom the Zionists and Board radicals hoped would democratize the organization, were at first shaky; certainly they were never as harmonious as those with David Alexander, his predecessor. Samuel, however, soon proved himself accommodating to the Conjoint method. In 1919, when the 'treaty' was again under attack from Zionists and others demanding majority rule, it was Samuel who staunchly defended the Board's traditional relationship to Jewish foreign affairs. The attack was soundly routed.[50]

Even on the Zionist issue, Wolf was by no means vanquished. The League of British Jews, of which he was a co-founder, continued to press for a clarification of the Balfour Declaration, as outlined by him in *The Times* manifesto. Though one of the original stipulations of the 'treaty' was that the new committee should not deal with Palestine, even this was subsequently waived, enabling it to make its own policy formulations on the issue.[51] It was a measure of the Board's accept-

[49] Terms of treaty, 19 Dec. 1917, C11/2/12. Mowschowitch, 'The Board', 7 Sept. 1943, MWS 23534–42.

[50] *JC* 27 June 1919, reporting BD meeting 22 June. See also *Jewish Opinion*, 8 (July 1919), on defeat of Zionist attack on the 'treaty' by 104 votes to 3.

[51] On lifting of BD ban *vis-à-vis* Palestine, see Joint Foreign Committee (hereafter JFC) minutes, 3 Dec. 1918. See also JFC, *Palestine: Statement of Policy* (London, 1919).

ance of Wolf and his committee's right to speak on this that their proposals, though in some respects running counter to those of the Zionists—for instance, in denying the right to economic preference—were carried at the Board and subsequently presented to the peace conference. It was Wolf, too, who, on this occasion, submitted an English Zionist Federation petition favouring a British Palestine. The highest irony, however, was yet to come. In 1921, following anxious rumours that Dr Motzkin, the 'ultra' Zionist, was campaigning in England for the admission of the Jewish 'nation' to the League of Nations, Wolf was instructed by Lord Rothschild on behalf of the Joint Foreign Committee and Zionist Organization to call on the Foreign Office and to repudiate Motzkin's 'dangerous views'. A ministry official briefly minuted 'Curious that Mr. Lucien Wolf should call on behalf of the Zionist organisation.'[52]

[52] On BD support for JFC Palestine proposals, 16 Feb. 1919, see *JC* 21 Feb. 1919. On EZF petition to Paris peace conference see *RDJBE* 50. For Wolf's role in the repudiation of Motzkin see Wolf–Adam interview, 16 Feb., FO 371/6392/2115, and Adam minute, 17 Feb. 1921, ibid.

PART III

THE JEWS AS A NATIONAL MINORITY

8

National Autonomy

The problem of dealing with religious or national minorities has acquired a new significance through the Russian revolution and the Committee is now confronted by demands which go far beyond the old situations based on a simple equality of political and civil rights.[1]

This statement, part of a new revised statement on war aims announced to the Anglo-Jewish Association Foreign Affairs Committee meeting on 25 October 1917, ushered in a remarkable new phase in Wolf's wartime decision-making. The Russian Revolution, he told his audience, had created new entities—the Ukraine, Poland, Lithuania, Finland—'and might go on to create more federal units of the new Russian state'. Each had distinguishing characteristics of its own; traditional 'emancipation' politics could not answer for the Jewish problem within each.

This was not merely a recognition of the failure of the 'considered views', but a statement of those views' obsolescence. Events in 1917 had so outstripped Wolf's normal terms of reference that totally new guidelines had to be created, something which went beyond the simplistic equation of Jewish emancipation with Jewish security and prosperity. The solution marked a radical new departure: national autonomy.

The Western ideology of emancipation had been founded on two profoundly linked late-eighteenth- and nineteenth-century developments. First, the transformation of society into modern nation-states ensured that Jewish communities within those states could no longer lead an existence divorced from their political realities and requirements. Jews henceforth were, willingly or unwillingly, citizens of Germany, France, or Britain. Secondly, the triumph of capitalism and its theoretical adjunct, economic liberalism, provided the vehicle by which those same Jews were enabled to integrate socially and culturally into the wider non-Jewish society. Adopting and identifying with these new dominant (and of course, secular) norms, the nineteenth-century leaders of Anglo-Jewry insisted that they were Englishmen of the

[1] AJA Interim Report, 25 Oct. 1917, C11/2/12.

164   *The Jews as a National Minority*

Mosaic persuasion; their German counterparts equally saw themselves as *Deutscher Staatsburger Judischen Glaubens*.[2] It was the overall success of this process in Western Europe which more or less predetermined that the diplomats of the Hilfsverein, Alliance, or Conjoint should seek the emancipation of their Eastern co-religionists in these terms.

In the multi-ethnic Ottoman, Russian, and Austro-Hungarian empires, a fragment of the Jewish financial and commercial class which had broken loose from its political and economic chains was indeed able to follow this pattern. In the vanguard of nineteenth-century developments transforming peasant feudal economies into neo-capitalist ones, these Jews were encouraged, favoured, and sometimes ennobled by their imperial masters, and they in response adopted the culture of their milieu and identified with its aspirations. Barons Gunzburg thus encouraged all Russian Jews to Russify; in Congress Poland a small but successful class of assimilated Jews persisted in their efforts to Polonize their Yiddish-speaking brethren; in Hungary, ennobled Jews became Magyar nationalists.[3]

In many respects it was logical that this process should be carried through among the great bulk of Eastern Jewry. A distinct socio-economic class, with its own language and culture, Eastern Jewry lived as compact pockets in a sea of peasantry, 'in a maelstrom of warring nationalities and fragments of nationalities'.[4] A trading and commercial intermediary, the Jew had little ground for identification with Slovak, Ukrainian, or Romanian peasants bound together only by imperial rule, but did have cause for allegiance to an empire opened up to his entrepreneurial skills.[5]

The preconditions for this progression, however, did not materialize.

[2] See Jacob Katz, *Out of the Ghetto: The Social Background to Jewish Emancipation 1770–1870* (New York, 1978); C. A. Macartney, *National States and National Minorities* (London, 1934), 13–16.

[3] Greenberg, *Jews in Russia*, 62; Gitelman, *Jewish Nationality*, 21–3. On the Warsaw *Gmina*'s assimilationist leaders see Frumkin, *Russian Jewry*, 59–62; also Wolf, 'M. de Plehve and the Jewish Question', *The Times*, 6 Feb. 1904, on 'the attempts of the Polish Jewish *couches-supérieures* to promote Polish amongst their poorer Jewish speaking co-religionists'. On Hungarian Jewish assimilation see William O. McCagg, *Jewish Nobles and Geniuses in Modern Hungary* (New York, 1972), 89–98.

[4] Wolf to FO, 3 Oct. 1918, encl. memo on 'the Polish–Jewish Question', FO 371/3286/5737.

[5] S. Poliakov, 'Russian Jewry and the League of Nations', n.d., 1919, MWS 7970–5: 'Morally and economically the Jews are interested in the unity of the Russian empire . . . dismemberment would be a big blow to them.' Had it not been for national autonomy, Poliakov argued, the Jews would have been fierce centralists.

The failure to sustain an intermediary role in the face of a collapsing feudal economy—a situation accentuated by a general but more particularly Jewish demographic explosion and the refusal of the regime in Russia to assist by liberating them from the confines of the Pale— forced Jews into new modes of production within limited (in fact, decreasing) geographical parameters. The increasingly proletarianized or pauperized Yiddish-speaking communities inevitably turned more and more in on themselves.[6]

If economic stagnation and political deprivation provided the bedrock for cultural revivification, the Jewish proletarian parties which emerged in the 1890s gave it its political forum. This involvement was significant, inasmuch as it gave this nascent Jewish nationalism, as Wolf later acknowledged, a form and direction quite distinct from Zionism.

These parties, notably the Bund, were primarily interested in the position of Jews not as Jews but as an exploited proletariat, the destruction of whose bondage could only be achieved through a general proletarian upheaval embracing Jews and non-Jews alike.[7] Close links were thus forged with other proletarian class parties. The Bund was already closely aligned with the Russian Social Democratic movement and despite a split in 1903 over the autonomy issue continued to have links with the Mensheviks. The Jewish Socialist Workers' party, better known as Serp or the Sejmists, co-operated often with the Russian Social Revolutionaries and indeed a leading Yiddishist, Chaim Zhitlowsky, was a co-founder of the latter movement.[8] From the first, therefore, these groups assumed the Jews to be part of, and to have a role to play in, a wider Russian revolutionary scene, and hence implicitly to have a Russian future to look forward to after the struggle; a view rejected out of hand by the Zionists.

The 1901 Bundist Congress resolution may have stated that national feeling was 'the only cloud hanging over the consciousness of the

[6] Salo W. Baron, *The Russian Jews under Tsars and Soviets*, 2nd edn. (New York, 1976), 43–9; Brym, *Jewish Intelligentsia*, 25–38. For a Marxist analysis see Abram Leon, *The Jewish Question: A Marxist Interpretation* (2nd edn.) (New York, 1972), 197–207. For demographic changes see the tables in Paul R. Mendes-Flohr and Jehuda Reinharz, eds., *The Jew in the Modern World* (New York, 1980), 526–9.

[7] For the development of the Bund, see Frankel's definitive study, *Prophecy and Politics*, 171–257; Mendelsohn, *Class Struggle*, 55–64; Gitelman, *Jewish Nationality*, 27–31.

[8] Frankel, *Prophecy and Politics*, 282–6. For an interview with Zhitlowsky see *JC* 4 July 1913.

Jewish proletariat', but such a view, while reflecting the ideological preferences of its educated and Marxist-oriented leadership, became inreasingly untenable as the party became immersed in the Jewish milieu in which it worked and yet at the same time recognized the rights of other ethnically and linguistically non-Russian nationalities to local autonomy within the empire. The early years of the twentieth century thus saw Jewish national rights being acknowledged by the Bund as part of their platform.[9]

Their formula for achieving this was national–personal or cultural autonomy. What this meant was that political allegiance to the state and personal allegiance to one's cultural/ethnic group would be removed to two separate planes, thus avoiding the requirement for Jews or other nationalities to live in a distinct territorial unit. While the political (state) framework would continue as before, the national (ethnic) framework would provide for that nationality's control of those institutions most vital to the preservation and fulfilment of its cultural and social life, with particular emphasis on schools.

The degree of control envisaged among the various parties that formulated this programme varied enormously. The Bund believed in self-administration, and the rights of taxation for such purpose, at an essentially local level. The official use of Yiddish was to be provided for where required—in legal documents, courts, government organs, and in schools—though the state ultimately would have supervisory control of school curricula. The Folkspartei, led by Simon Dubnow, the great autonomy theorist, proposed to tackle the issue through the restoration of the traditional *kehillot*; reformed as secular entities they would form a network of Jewish community and local councils. The doctrinaire socialist Sejmists, more thoroughgoing still, formulated elaborate plans for an all-embracing national–political structure, to include electoral *curiae*, proportional representation, and a national diet. In 1917 they united with a like-minded group, the Zionist Socialist Labour Party (a name which belied the fact they were interested in creating a Jewish territory *within* the empire) to form the Farainigte.[10]

The emphasis, however, at least as propounded philosophically by Dubnow, continued to be less on the political and more on the personal aspects of nationality. The Jews, Dubnow argued, had outlived the

[9] Frankel, *Prophecy and Politics*, 215–27. The Bund did not officially endorse national autonomy until 1906.

[10] Gitelman, *Jewish Nationality*, 48–52; Janowsky, *Jews and Minority Rights*, 114–30.

politico-territorial stage in their national development and were evolving through what he termed the cultural-historical to the spiritual stage. Dubnow made his point forcefully: 'As a Jew I utter the word "national" with pride and conviction because I know that my people, because of the special conditions of its existence in the Diaspora, is not able to aspire anywhere to primacy and dominance. My nationalism can only be purely individualistic and hence completely ethical.'[11]

The philosophy of Dubnow and the approach taken by the Bund had aspects in common that gave Wolf in 1917 an opportunity to attempt a reconciliation of the concept of national autonomy with traditional Western Jewish goals. In an article in the *Edinburgh Review* entitled 'The Jewish National Movement',[12] he openly acknowledged that the necessary conditions for full assimilation on Western lines were not available in the east; but even so, he contended, Jewish national autonomy was consistent with wider developments on the East European scene because 'the principle of self-government and equal rights for all nationalities has taken its place as a necessary corollary of the principle of individual freedom and equal rights for all the many varieties of Russian citizens'.[13]

The Yiddishist autonomists, therefore, in desiring to take their place 'among the other secular sub-nationalities of the Russian empire',[14] were simply acting in consonance with the Ukrainian, Finnish, Polish, and Georgian intelligentsia. Rejecting Zionist aspirations to create a Jewish extra-Diaspora form and culture centred around the artificial revival of an élite language, Hebrew, they insisted on the veracity of their traditional *patois* and their rootedness in the local milieu.

The implicit assumption that the empire would continue, albeit in a federal and decentralized form, was again consonant with Wolf's reasoning, inasmuch as it still offered Jewry its best hope for geographical mobility and hence economic advancement. With time this would undoubtedly lead to a diminution of the Yiddish ghetto-based culture associated with the Pale. Moreover, this was not incompatible with Dubnow's thesis. Certainly, Dubnow believed in the normality of the Diaspora but as something onward-going, not static. The constancy

[11] Koppel S. Pinson, 'The National Theories of Simon Dubnow's *JSS* 7 (1948), 335-8.
[12] Wolf, 'The Jewish National Movement', *Edinburgh Review* (April, 1917), 303-18.
[13] Ibid. 314; see also Wolf memo, 'The Polish Jewish Question', CJC minutes, 17 Sept. 1918.
[14] Wolf, 'Jewish National Movement', 309-11.

of distinctive features, such as the Yiddish language, would, for instance, 'be dictated by the dynamic forces of Jewish life and the special
conditions prevailing'.[15] Such a conception harmonized well with
Wolf's fundamentally positivist approach to Jewish Diaspora existence.
National autonomy could thus be presented to his more sceptical
colleagues as a logical and necessary sequence in Eastern Jewry's evolution and a corollary to what Western Jewry had achieved 'unfettered'
by nationalism; namely assimilation and 'pure Judaism'.[16]

The movement for national–cultural autonomy was crystallized by
the Russian revolution of 1905. Indeed it took so strong a hold of the
Jewish masses that even the Russifying middle class 'League for the
Attainment of Equal Rights', as well as the Zionists at their Helsingfors
Congress in 1906, were forced to acknowledge it as an element in their
manifestos.[17] With the full restoration of the tsarist regime, however,
and the subsequent clampdown on radical movements, the autonomist
surge diminished into near insignificance. Throughout these events
there is no evidence to suggest that Wolf, despite his public utterances
on behalf of the Bund, showed any particular sympathy for national
autonomy. Indeed, despite growing friction between Poles and Jews
after 1912, he continued to proclaim the merits and advisability of
Polonization.[18] No ideological change of stance leading to 'the Jewish
National Movement' is discernible, until immediate political considerations and the prompting of David Mowschowitch forced Wolf to
change tack, some time in late 1916. Meanwhile, the traditional

[15] Pinson, 'National Theories', 339.
[16] Wolf, 'Jewish National Movement', 316–17: 'Whether improvement is to be
affected in that direction [Russia] must come from the progress of general emancipation
and more particularly from the national autonomy movement in Russia. The movement
is a national movement entirely in harmony with its Russian environment and with the
conditions of modern political life and it offers a complete and practicable solution for
the Jewish problem so far as it is a political problem.'
[17] The initiative for acceptance of cultural autonomy by the League for the Attainment of Jewish Rights came from the Vilna programme devised by Vinaver and Sliosberg. Subsequently they founded the Folksgruppe in 1906. Poalei Zion, the socialist
wing of Russian Zionism, as distinct from the mainstream Russian variety, was more
closely aligned to the ideas of national political autonomy; see Frankel, *Prophecy and
Politics*, 157–69; Gitelman, *Jewish Nationality*, 46–8; Janowsky, *Jews and Minority Rights*,
91–113.
[18] See *JC* 10 Mar. 1905, reporting Wolf at the Maccabeans, 5 Mar. 1905. On Polish
Jewish patriotism see *Darkest Russia* leader, 'The boycott in Poland', 21 Feb. 1913 and
again his deprecating leader on A. Walters, 'The Ideal of a Federation of Autonomous
Peoples', ibid. 10 Mar. 1913.

assumptions about eastern Jewish emancipation were, regardless of ideological stance, having to be reconsidered in the light of extra-Russian developments.

There were strong economic reasons why the autonomists in Russia should seek the preservation of the empire. Traditionally, Jewry's overwhelming involvement in local, regional, and international trade and finance had prospered not only by dint of a vast network of family/commercial contacts but also through unimpeded access to markets. The empire favoured this state of things. Fragmentation did not. Yet this latter tendency, if not especially apparent in Austria-Hungary or Russia at the outbreak of the Great War, was already quite marked in a decaying Ottoman Empire. It was the dissolution of the European rump of that empire, in the Balkan wars in 1912–13, which brought home to the Western Jewish diplomats the necessity to protect, paradoxically, specific Jewish interests. The focus came to centre on Salonika. Here was the major port of the Aegean, in which some 70,000 of a total population of 113,000 were Jews.[19] Occupationally diversified, with Jewish porters, dockers, shopkeepers, businessmen, and politicians, the Salonika community presented to the outside world a picture of flourishing economic, political, and cultural life, a symbol of the possibilities and potentialities for Jewish existence in the Diaspora.

Yet this situation was dependent on the maintenance of certain conditions. First and foremost, a Turkish administration which favoured Jewish economic life over and above that of the Bulgar and Greek Salonika communities. Secondly, uninterrupted continuity of links with Salonika's overseas markets. Finally, the maintenance of a special relationship with the port's Macedonian hinterland,[20] amounting in effect to an economic monopoly. The Balkan wars, however, succeeded in disrupting all three. The Turks were removed and Macedonia shared out between the Serb, Bulgar, and Greek partners in the anti-Turkish coalition. Salonika itself became a divided city, occupied by both Bulgarian and Greek troops pending an international decision on who should have sovereignty.

[19] Florentin, the editor of the Salonika Ladino paper *El Avenir*, gave the figure of 70,000 in a letter to the Zionist Organization Executive in Berlin, 15 Dec. 1912; quoted in N. M. Gelber, 'An Attempt to Internationalise Salonika, 1912–1913', *JSS* 17 (1955), 115. The *Encyclopedia Judaica*, xiv, cols. 702–4, gives 80,000.

[20] Florentin letter quoted in Gelber, 'An Attempt', 115. See also M. P. Argyropoulos, 'Le Problème juif à Salonique pendant les premières années de l'occupation hellenique', n.d., *c*.1919, AIU/France ii DIO.

What were the Salonika community—and by the same token, the Conjoint, Hilfsverein, and Alliance—to do? Were they to sit tight and hope that the Balkan allies would come to an equitable solution satisfactory to the Jews? This seemed a very great risk, especially as all the signs pointed to their falling out over the spoils. Were they to petition the Great Powers, and thereby become prey to international intrigues? Were they to support one side against another in the hope that the side supported would protect their interests?

Both the Greeks and Bulgars had a clean slate as far as civil and religious rights to their native Jews were concerned, but economically there was a distinction favouring annexation by Bulgaria as the lesser of two evils. Bulgaria was still essentially an underdeveloped peasant economy. No native middle class had emerged to challenge the Jewish intermediary role. Moreover, Sofia's control of Salonika would be advantageous to an enlarged export of Bulgarian grain, a development easily encompassed through Bulgaria's Sephardic merchant community with its close Salonika ties.[21]

Greece, by contrast, had its own long-standing commercial class; moreover as the Greek nation expanded, it would desire in the national interest to Hellenize commerce further still. Whether Salonika Jewry could or would want to be integrated fully into this system, on a basis quite unlike that which had aided their fellow Jews in the West, was questionable. In Romania, the growth of national consciousness had in the late nineteenth century led to considerable efforts to Romanize commerce and finance, a process definitely unfavourable to Jewish entrepreneurs that had led many to seek Austrian consular protection.[22] Besides the likelihood of a similar process occurring in a Greek-occupied Salonika, there was also the fact that as the Greeks already had an overseas trade outlet at Piraeus, Salonika would simply be 'excess baggage', with its Jews competing against the Greek system.[23]

These factors inclined Western Jewish diplomats, notably Paul Nathan, to support the contention of Bulgaria's Chief Rabbi Ehrenpreis

---

[21] Gelber, 'An Attempt', 113; Ehrenpreis interview, *JC* 30 May 1913.

[22] N. Spulber, *The State and Economic Development in Eastern Europe* (New York, 1966), 109–10. Spulber cites in particular attempts to set up a specifically Romanian *Banca Nationala*, thereby countering Jewish-owned banks such as the Masmorosch bank.

[23] Wolf argued that division of Macedonia would mean that Salonika would 'assuredly be strangled by customs barriers and even if it is annexed to Greece, this will not help it for all its northern trade will have gone and its markets will be supplied and worked by other Greek ports'; see Wolf, 'Foreign Office Bag', *Graphic*, 4 Jan. 1913.

that Salonika must be adjudicated to Bulgaria. But, as Wolf noted, to openly espouse this would be to 'cause dissension among the Balkan allies'. Moreover, if the Greeks 'had to win Salonika in the face of international Jewish opinion', it would give them an 'abiding grievance' which would reverberate against Salonika and Greek Jewry.[24] What, then, was the alternative?

The Turks and the Austrians, who both had politico-economic interests in the town, mooted the idea of Salonika's internationalization.[25] This was a solution which Wolf and many Jewish commentators considered well chosen to Jewish needs. Wolf responded:

If as seems possible Salonika becomes a free and self-governing port, its character as a Jewish autonomy would be automatically settled by the numerical superiority of the Jewish residents over other denominations ... if Salonika should be adjudged to Greece which saving its retention by Turkey is the only alternative, I do not see that the Jews can do anything more than protest on the grounds of their being excluded from the benefits of the principle of nationalities by which the recasting of the map of the Balkans is being regulated.[26]

Here then was an acknowledgement, possibly an unconscious one, that Jews could be seen as one of many distinct national ethnic groups in the Balkans. They had interests of an economic and cultural nature which differentiated them from other groups. Subsequently, identification and assimilation with Serbs, Greeks, Bulgars, or whoever could not be achieved by some 'Western' formula. Nor, for that matter, was it necessarily desirable.

Wolf continued to pursue this line of thought after the Greeks had wrested Salonika from the Bulgarians during the second Balkan war. In conversations with Ionnis Gennadius, the Greek ambassador to London, Wolf insisted on supporting Salonika Jewry's own desiderata. These called for a wide degree of economic and municipal autonomy; the right of communal taxation; educational liberty, with the budget of Jewish schools to be in part covered by the public treasury, as was the case under the Ottomans; the protection of the Sabbath, and hence Sunday trading; and exemption from military service for a given number of years. These proposals, intended to protect and perpetuate as far as possible the community's distinct cultural, economic, and social life

---

[24] Ehrenpreis interview, *JC* 30 May 1913; Wolf to Montefiore, 28 Nov. 1912, MWS 2922–3.

[25] Gelber, 'An Attempt', 105–6; Interview with H. E. Rousso Bey, *JC* 16 May 1913.

[26] Fragment of Wolf letter as reported by Zangwill, *JC* 22 Nov. 1912.

(and nearly identical to those drawn up by Rabbi Ehrenpreis in the expectation of a Bulgarian annexation of the port),[27] were tantamount to an acceptance of Jewish autonomy at least as thoroughgoing as Wolf asked for at the 1919 peace conference.[28]

While Salonika was to some degree a special case, Wolf's *Graphic* commentaries on the development of the Balkan Wars evince a constant concern and disquiet at the way ethnic minorities rights were being eroded in the states which had replaced the Ottoman Empire. In March 1913, for instance, he cited the way Bulgarian schools and churches were being closed and Bulgar names prohibited in predominantly ethnically Bulgarian regions in the new Serbia. This, Wolf argued, was indicative of all the victor states' schemes of 'so called assimilation', schemes which threatened the national habits, customs, and characteristics of the alien populations.[29]

It was a short step from noting the dangers of forced Serbization, Romanization, or Hellenization of distinct linguistic and ethnic peoples and urging guarantees protecting their cultural and scholastic autonomy to favouring similar clauses for the Jews as well. Such guarantees could still in 1913 be garbed in the language of religious toleration, especially as ethnic feuds between Greeks and Bulgars, for instance, could be expressed in terms of religious Patriarchist–Exarchist schism.[30] Thus, Wolf wrote to the Foreign Office:

In the new conditions of mixed races and creeds which confront those states and in the face of the symptoms already apparent of an accentuation of the

[27] 'Desiderata of Salonika Jewry', given by Wolf to Gennadius, n.d., *c*.Dec. 1913, MWS 2285–90. For the legal and cultural rights suggested by Ehrenpreis see Gelber, 'An Attempt', 113.

[28] Gennadius expostulated in reply: 'to ask us to make special distinctions or grant special privileges would be to upset the very principle of equality which is on the other hand demanded of us . . . you cannot ask us fairly or consistently to consider our Jewish fellow citizens differently than they are considered in England, nor has any other creed or nationality thought of requesting . . . a system of capitulations in Greece'. See Gennadius to Wolf, 11 Feb. 1914, MWS 2283–4.

[29] Wolf, 'The Position of Foreign Affairs: The New Bondage in the Balkans', *Graphic*, 7 Mar. 1914.

[30] Wolf was in fact asked by Ehrenpreis to solicit Great Power support for the scholastic and religious rights of Balkan minorities; see Bulgarian Consistoire Central Israelite to Conjoint, 22 Aug. 1913, MWS 2457–60. This followed the failure of the US representation to have a specific clause on this score incorporated into the Treaty of Bucharest, due to outright rejection by the victors of the second Balkan War. For protocol of Bucharest Treaty, 27 July 1913 see Wolf, *Notes*, 47. Pressure for such a clause also came from other sources; see Luzzatti, *God in Freedom*, 470.

long standing interconfessional bitterness and strife, they [the Conjoint] prefer not to relinquish the international obligations by which the rights of their coreligionists have been secured. In this view they find themselves supported not only by the Jewish communities of the Balkans but by all the religious minorities in the dominions which have recently changed hands.[31]

Still concealed within the traditional formula of civil and religious liberty, Wolf's memorial to the Foreign Office contained the germ of an innovatory conception: ethnic diversity within the modern nation-state.

[31] CJC memo encl. in Wolf to FO, 13 Oct. 1913, FO 371/1742/1832; also in Wolf, *Notes*, 48–51. At the Paris Peace Conference Wolf acknowledged that the JFC's efforts on behalf of cultural autonomy were not new but 'had been alluded to in the negotiations of 1913–14'; see *RDJBE* 22–3.

9
The Breakup of Empires

IN the early stages of the war, Wolf showed no signs of shaping Conjoint policy along the lines implicit in his memorials on the Balkan war. Nor was there any driving stimulus to do so. Britain's enemy was Germany; it was the defeat of German 'militarism' which was the primary objective. Though the war was also being fought against Austria-Hungary, its removal and replacement by new and unknown 'national' entities was no part of British policy. This cautious conservatism was reflected in the Conjoint's agenda. Some territorial changes were to be expected, but the essential thing was to make sure that the civil and religious rights of exchanged populations, especially those which might be lost to Russia, were guaranteed. Even the early wartime reference to the probability of Romania demanding a share in 'the derelict Austrian empire' did not lead Wolf to speculate further on the consequences of its complete demise.[1]

It was reflected, too, in Wolf's preference to leave national autonomy as a vague, undefined afterthought in the Conjoint's post-war plans. In early 1916, Wolf was challenged on this point by Joseph Finn, the veteran Jewish trade union leader. What was needed, Finn wrote, was not 'paper rights' for Russian Jewry but concrete safeguards, encapsulated within a federal system. These should include local educational and taxation autonomy, Jewish governors, and officially recognized local Jewish militias. Wolf replied that equal rights once obtained, 'the Jews would have leverage from which to claim the administrative reforms which would suit their special conditions'. A few days later, Wolf did however agree that 'the direction of all effective reform must be that of decentralisation'.[2]

Even if Wolf believed he could stand aside from the issue, European developments demanded his attention. The military balance between the Allies and the Central Powers presented the prospect of a very long and indecisive war. After initial failures to force the issue on the

[1] Wolf to FO, 3 Mar. 1915, encl. desiderata, FO 371/2448/16905.
[2] Finn to Wolf, n.d., Mar. 1916, MWS 2214–23; Wolf to Finn, 29 Apr., MWS 2223–34; Wolf to Finn, 1 May 1915, C11/2/8.

battlefield, both sides searched for alternative routes to victory. One method was to seek new allies; another was to attempt to sabotage the internal fabric of the enemy camp. The possibility of appealing to the subject peoples of Europe and Asia Minor had advantages on both these scores, acting as a powerful stimulus to propaganda campaigns in neutral countries and providing through latent nationalism the ammunition for the destruction of the enemy's unity and cohesion.

The Allies began cautiously, the Russian Grand Duke Nicholas's August 1914 manifesto promising Polish autonomy being essentially a defensive measure to keep the Poles in line. The Germans, however, in their ambitions to create a *Mitteleuropa* dominated by themselves, were keen to foster nationalist sentiment in tsarist Russia. The aim here was not to create independent national states on Germany's eastern border, and certainly not a strong Poland, but a system of vassal entities—states would probably be too strong a word—to fit in with areas such as the Baltic province of Courland intended for direct annexation.[3]

The Central Powers' declaration in November 1916 of an independent but extremely limited Polish state thus failed to engender Polish enthusiasm. But the apparent support for self-determination implied in Chancellor Bethman-Hollweg's reference to a 'League of Russia's Foreign Peoples' in a Reichstag speech in April 1916[4] did hold opportunities for other weaker ethnic groups. Among these was Polish and Lithuanian Jewry.

The German and Austrian occupation of these territories acted as a stimulus for the re-emergence and crystallization of their demands for national autonomy, demands which the creation of a Polish state, however weak, with all the concomitant Polonizing tendencies, threatened. Bodenheimer's early awareness of these dangers led him in August 1914 to urge on the German military authorities in Poland a plan for a federation of national autonomies, including the Jews. Though Bodenheimer's plan broke down in negotiations with the Polish 'club', an élite circle of Poles willing to talk to the Germans, the Germans themselves, once their hold on Poland had been tightened the following year, continued to be receptive to Jewish autonomy ideas.[5]

[3] Fischer, *Germany's Aims*, 237–8. On German efforts in the Ukraine and Georgia see Zeman, *Diplomatic History*, 93.

[4] Fischer, *Germany's Aims*, 237–8.

[5] Bodenheimer, *Prelude*, 234, 255–62. Cf. Ezra Mendelsohn, *Zionism in Poland: The Formative Years 1915–1926* (New Haven, 1981), 39–45, which acknowledges the rise of

In June 1916 General Hindenburg, after some hesitation, recognized Yiddish as an official language. Five months later, the *Verordnung* provided the framework for national–cultural autonomy by allowing Jewish communities at a district level to have their own governing bodies and rights of self-taxation. The proposal had limitations. Community was defined in strictly religious terms and therefore excluded the wider, secular purposes of non-orthodox groups—those most interested in autonomy. One-third of the governing council's seats were to be filled by appointees of the German governor-general rather than by election, which impeded any real independence. Nevertheless, the development tended to involve a wider spectrum of Jewry in the movement towards national consciousness, a movement considerably aided by the support it received from German Jewry.[6]

If German moves in the East appeared beneficial to Jewish autonomy, British plans tended to be less so. The fragmentation of the Austro-Hungarian Empire had no great appeal to the diplomats of the Foreign Office, who foresaw in it the conditions not for future peace and security in Europe but for increased turbulence. Ministry memoranda proposing its dismembering into new states were put aside. As late as November 1917, in unofficial talks in Geneva aimed at attempting to get Austria to break away from Germany and sign a separate peace, Smuts insisted to Count Mensdorff that the British object was not to interfere in Austria's internal affairs but help her to make a 'liberal' empire.[7]

Nevertheless, by the end of 1916, a new tendency was infiltrating government thinking. It was fed by the journal *New Europe*, whose leading lights were Henry Wickham Steed and Robert Seton-Watson. The *New Europe* line was drastically different from that of the old Foreign Office chiefs. It demanded total victory in the war, which meant not only the defeat of Germany but also of Austria-Hungary, Bulgaria, and Turkey. What would follow would be the radical re-

---

Jewish national consciousness in this period but plays down the degree of real political support it received from the occupying powers. On Studnicki's pro-German Polish state club see *CHP*, ii. 467–8.

[6] Wolf to Cecil, 16 Jan. 1918, encl. Mowschowitch report, 2 Jan. 1918, on 'Polish Jewish Situation', FO 371/3277/3361; anonymous *American Hebrew* article, 24 Nov. 1916, on *Verordnung*, MWS 16101. See also Archduke Friedrich's declaration favouring Jewish political and cultural rights in the occupied Austrian sector, reported in *Djen*, 21 Mar. 1916, MWS 17402–3; Zechlin, *Deutsche Politik*, 199–209.

[7] See *History of The Times*, i. 319–20.

organization of Europe, the principles of self-determination providing the framework for the new states which would be created.[8] Seton-Watson and Steed were unusually influential. In part this was because of their first-hand and informed knowledge of areas of Europe of which British decision-making circles were totally ignorant. Also, however, they were able to back up their contentions with articles from 'liberal nationalist' academics who were at this juncture finding their way as East European specialists into government advisory roles: Lewis Namier, James Headlam-Morley, Alfred Zimmern, Rex and Alexander Leeper were all crucial figures in what came to be the Political Intelligence Department of the Foreign Office. It was their 'intelligence' which became a significant factor in the movement towards a 'nationalist' revision of the East European map as part of Britain's essential war aims.[9]

If the Foreign Office was reluctant to commit itself wholeheartedly to fully independent Polish, Czech, or South Slav states, external factors were forcing its hand. One was the need to appease American public opinion, and more specifically to respond to President Wilson's note of December 1916, calling for the principle of self-determination to be amongst the belligerents' war aims. In reply, the Allies the following month promised European reorganization 'based at once on respect for nationalities and the right to full security and liberty of economic development possessed by all peoples great and small'.[10] If this was a vague rhetorical gesture to get America into the war,[11] the prospect of Russia pulling out of it gave East European nationalism a new vital dimension.

Without a strong centralized Russia, the traditional obstacle to Germany's eastern designs was removed. Even before the Bolshevik

[8] Zeman, *Diplomatic History*, 153; Calder, *Britain*, 92–8, 113–19.

[9] Harry Hanak, *Great Britain and Austria-Hungary during the First World War: A Study in the Formation of Public Opinion* (Oxford, 1962), 178–88; V. H. Rothwell, *British War Aims and Peace Diplomacy, 1914–1918* (Oxford, 1971), 17; Sir James Headlam-Morley, *A Memoir of the Paris Peace Conference 1919*, ed. Agnes Headlam-Morley et al. (London, 1972), xx. The Political Intelligence Department had its origins in the Wellington House propaganda bureau, was subsequently merged in Beaverbrook's Ministry of Information in 1917, and became part of the Foreign Office in April 1918. Seton-Watson and Steed were also employed in Beaverbrook's Department of Propaganda (Austria-Hungary Section). [10] Calder, *Britain*, 103–7.

[11] Both Seth Tillman, *Anglo-American Relations at the Paris Peace Conference* (Princeton, 1961), 26–30, and Calder, *Britain*, 126, emphasize the reply as propaganda for American consumption rather than as a fixed aspect of British policy.

takeover, Russian disintegration was manifesting itself as Finns, Ukrainians, Poles, and other national groups asserted their independence from Petrograd. What gave real justification to the *New Europe* radicals, therefore, was the need to build up a new barrier against Germany. Hence, the Allies' commitment in 1917 to an 'independent and indivisible' Poland, and so too to an expanded Romania.

For Wolf these were disturbing departures. If there was to be in place of the Russian and Austrian empires a bloc of independent national states, what would be the fate of the multitude of ethnic minorities within their midst? Would they be forcibly assimilated to the dominant national language and culture, or would the state be polyethnic? Seton-Watson had, in 1916, foreseen the dangers of such a development but was assured 'that those racial minorities whose separate existence reasons of geography and economics render impossible, will attain guarantees of full linguistic and cultural liberty'.[12] Wolf saw no reason for such complacency. All his reasoning and experience pointed to the behaviour of what he referred to as 'jumped up nations' being both despicable in domestic affairs and a danger to international peace and order. Romania's flouting of the international protocol of the 1878 Congress of Berlin which provided for Jewish citizenship rights was one such long-standing grievance. Wolf's observations, however, were not confined solely to injustices perpetrated against Jews. Italy's annexation of Tripolitania in 1911 was, he argued, during the continued fighting for the former Ottoman province the following summer, a veritable scandal for the European *ménage*,[13] while the Serbian, Greek, and Bulgarian compact to carve up the European rump of the Ottoman Empire soon thereafter was confirmation of his worst suspicions. Proclamations emanating from the belligerents in the ensuing first Balkan war that this was a war of liberation were, Wolf angrily rejoindered, simply a hollow sham resulting 'in the creation of a whole series of new and abominable captivities . . . the affranchisement of oppressed nationalities has been turned into a game of shameless grab in which all national rights have been cruelly and cynically trampled in the dust'.[14] A year later, when tension between Austria-Hungary and

[12] Hanak, *Great Britain and Austria-Hungary*, 33, quoting Seton-Watson, 'German, Slav, and Magyar' (1916).

[13] Wolf on the new Mediterranean agreement, *Daily Graphic*, 8 July 1912.

[14] Wolf, 'The New Bondage in the Balkans', *Graphic*, 7 Mar. 1914.

Serbia mounted following the Sarajevo assassinations, Wolf not surprisingly made it quite clear where his allegiance lay:

> If such a war is waged against Austria [by Russia] on behalf of the Serbs, it will run decidedly counter to our sympathies if not our interests. Austria has always been a good friend of ours and we could not view without sorrow any attack made upon her doing anything that she is legitimately entitled to do.[15]

That Wolf in 1917 considered the preservation of the empires in the interests both of European peace and Jewish survival, is made manifestly clear in 'The Jewish National Movement'.[16] Starting out from Lloyd George's recent pronouncement that Allied victory would create one emancipated land from the Urals to the Atlantic, Wolf sought indirectly to remind the decision-makers of the 'many unsuspected national problems' which would reveal themselves. One such problem was the Jews who, despite no fixed territorial base, constituted, after the Poles and the Ukrainians, Eastern Europe's largest ethnic group. With an intense national consciousness of their own, and comprising, for instance, in a reconstituted Poland, 40 per cent of the urban population, Wolf warned of the perplexity these national claims would present to the peace congress.

After examining the development of this movement and the social and political conditions making for divergences both from Western-style Judaism and Zionism, Wolf offered a solution not only to the Jewish but also the wider East European national problem. His solution rested on conclusions borrowed and freely acknowledged from *The Struggle of the Austrian Nations for the State*, an influential book by Rudolf Springer, the Austrian jurist.[17]

Springer was an advocate of national–personal autonomy; a nation,

---

[15] Wolf, 'The Chancelleries and the Crisis', *Daily Graphic*, 27 July 1914.

[16] Wolf, 'Jewish National Movement', 316–17. Friedman, *Question of Palestine*, 229, has pointed to the appearance or reappearance of anti-Zionist tracts at the same time as Wolf's article (Montefiore's *Nation or Religious Community?*, Magnus's *Jewish Action and Jewish Ideals*), to propose that this was part of a concerted effort to castigate the Zionists. Though it is true that Wolf does compare Zionism unfavourably with the autonomy movement, the article is only tangentially an attack on it. In the main it represents a stage in Wolf's persistent efforts to come to terms with changes in Eastern Europe itself. The article originated with a lecture given at the St John's Wood Liberal Synagogue, 11 Mar. 1917; see *JC* 16 Mar. 1917.

[17] Wolf, 'Jewish National Movement', 312–13. For details on Springer (the alias of Karl Renner) and the influence of his 1902 book on Jewish autonomists see Janowsky, *Jews and Minority Rights*, 32.

he said, 'is a union of like-thinking and like-speaking individuals, a collectivity with common political, cultural and economic interests'. But he was at pains to emphasize that this was quite compatible with a wider political union, as, for instance, in the Austro-Hungarian empire. As outlined by Wolf, Springer's plan was to decentralize the state on a federal basis. Each national group in a given administrative 'circle' would be represented proportionally in national diets, and would be further protected by national electoral *curiae*. Scattered frag-ments of the group—and here Wolf, presumably thinking of the Jews, noted how economic necessity required freedom of movement and domicile within the wider union—would be cared for by their national diet under special treaties with other national diets.

The diet itself, Wolf continued,

deals with all questions in which national interests are involved or in which national idiosyncracy expresses itself—political rights, public worship, justice, emigration, interior colonisation, education, literature, art, the theatre and so forth, all being subject to a uniform minimum scheme of essentials laid down by the Federal State. Each diet is empowered to levy taxes and is supplied with a responsible ministry presided over by a Secretary of State, who among other functions represents the Nationality on the imperial or federal councils.[18]

In putting forward the Springer plan, Wolf was advertising his con-viction that the peace, stability, and progress of Eastern Europe was served not by an appeal to the fragmentation of empires but by a reordering and democratic revitalization of the *status quo*. As such, it was counter-nationalistic, implicitly refuting Seton-Watson and Wickham Steed's contention that an end to oppression for Czechs, Poles, or, for that matter, Jews could only be achieved through national sovereignty.

Consistent it was too with the utterances of British liberal-radicals, whose attitudes Wolf had tended to reflect in pre-war days. If Noel Buxton, H. N. Brailsford, E. D. Morel, and other distinguished mem-bers of the Union of Democratic Control had previously been partisan to, and sometimes actively involved in, the struggle for self-determination in the Balkans, their distaste at the behaviour of the second Balkan League's redistribution of the spoils in 1913 led them to deplore any proposals for the dissolution of Austria-Hungary as an invitation to chaos.[19] What would result, warned H. N. Brailsford, was

[18] Wolf, 'Jewish National Movement', 312–13.
[19] Hanak, *Great Britain and Austria-Hungary*, 136–7; Howard, *War*, 75–84. Brails-ford had fought with the Greeks for the liberation of Crete from the Turks in 1897.

a situation where the Powers would be forced to intervene to impose, in the face of the fanatical opposition of 'half-crazed nationalists', a whole charter of linguistic and cultural rights for minorities.[20] Ironically, these erstwhile nationalists who now put forward federal schemes similar to Wolf's were flying in the face of the government's ostensibly liberal policy, a policy which was in reality dictated not by liberal sentiment but *realpolitik*. Indeed, one of the few genuine liberals at the Foreign Office, Robert Cecil, opposed it throughout.[21]

If Wolf's liberalism propelled him to advocate national autonomy, he still had the problem of squaring it with traditional Conjoint policy. In practical terms, to gain his committee's endorsement he would have to prove to them firstly that Eastern Jewry wanted it, and secondly that it was a feasible proposition. Despite his extensive knowledge of East European Jewish affairs, Wolf nevertheless lacked the specialist knowledge which would have enabled him to come to such a decision of his own accord. In short, he needed advice.

Wolf's traditional aides, however, tended to be markedly prejudiced against the autonomy idea. For instance, Emile Meyerson, the ICA administrator and Polish Jewish affairs expert, Polish-born but living in Paris, was strongly antipathetic to any tendency which sought to undermine the Polonizing efforts of the leaders of the Warsaw Jewish community. In 1912, however, their advice to Jewish residents of Warsaw to support the Polish Concentration candidate, Jan Kucharzewski, in the elections for the duma (as spelt out in their organ, *Nowa gazeta*) was largely ignored. This was because Kucharzewski had refused to take an explicit line on equal Jewish rights until these had been achieved in Russia as a whole, so the majority of Warsaw Jewry

[20] For Brailsford's *New Republic* proposals (16 Dec. 1916 and 31 Aug. 1918) for Poland to be federalized with Austria-Hungary see Hanak, *Great Britain and Austria-Hungary*, 139–40.

[21] 'Whether a new Europe with two or three additional Slav states will be more peaceful than the old, seems to me, I confess, very doubtful. If it had been at all possible to make Austria the head of a Central European Confederation in which the Slav elements would have been placed in an absolute equality with the Germans and Hungarians there would have been much more to be said for such a settlement', Cecil FO memo, 7 Aug. 1918, BM Add. MSS 51105 (Cecil papers). Cf. Trevelyan, *From Liberal to Labour*, 1921, quoted in Howard, *War*, 84: 'When Europe began to be repartitioned at Paris and a dozen new oppressions were substituted for the old ones, there was no protest in the name of principle or justice or liberalism against the fate of Germans annexed to Poland, Austrians to Italy and Czechs, Serbs and Hungarians to Rumania . . . the liberal war to end all wars has closed with an imperialist peace to perpetuate national injustice and armaments.'

responded by voting instead for Wladyslaw Jagello, his Social Democrat opponent. The third candidate, the ultra-right Roman Dmowski, took advantage of the situation to call a highly effective boycott of Jewish shops and trades. For Meyerson, the lesson from these events was clear. If only for the sake of expediency, he wrote to Wolf, Jews in Poland had to identify with the Poles—a view shared and fully endorsed at the time by Wolf himself.[22]

The advice of Reuben Blank, the man sent out by the Petrograd Political Bureau to liaise with the Western Jewish communities during the war was similar, though from a different angle. Blank was part of that small fragment of Jewry which had been able to assimilate fully into Russian society, identifying himself—by contrast with the Polonizing work of Kazimierz Natanson, Samuel Dickstein, and A. Eiger—with the Russifying efforts particularly associated with Baron Gunzburg. Speaking to Wolf in late 1916, he denied the existence of any national claims of the Polish and Russian Jews 'with regard to Poland'.[23]

But Wolf had reason to believe Blank's information was incorrect. His source was his assistant David Mowschowitch, a young Russian Jew and former secretary of the Petrograd Bureau. Mowschowitch had initially come to London in 1915 to deal with Russian relief questions but had subsequently, from Stockholm, provided Wolf with invaluable information on the Russian situation compiled from Russian papers and sent on to him in regular reports. Though Mowschowitch's nationalism had not been initially welcomed by Wolf, his information and advice eventually became the overriding factor that caused Wolf to more or less disregard Blank's advice and espouse national autonomy.[24]

Mowschowitch provided Wolf with some of the answers he was

---

[22] Meyerson to Wolf, 14 Feb. 1913, MWS 2847–54; Wolf to Meyerson, 19 Feb. 1913, Wolf to Meyerson, 21 Feb. 1913, MWS 2859–60. See also Wolf leader, 'The Boycott in Poland', *Darkest Russia*, 26 Feb. 1913. Meyerson was at the time collaborating with Wolf on *Darkest Russia*.

[23] Cited in Mowschowitch to Wolf, 4 Jan. 1917, MWS 10362–3.

[24] On Wolf's initial problems with Mowschowitch see Wolf to Montefiore, 14 May 1915, MWS 2963. Just before the Peace Conference Wolf wrote to Mowschowitch: 'It would have been of great value to me if I could have had your assistance, more especially as direct communication with the Russian Jewish organisations is not practicable. Dr. Blank has informed me that he represents the organisations and we have asked him for a statement on their behalf but he has told me nothing that we did not know already'; Wolf to Mowschowitch, 20 Dec. 1918, MWS 10672. There is evidence to suggest that the Wolf–Blank relationship deteriorated with the ascendancy of Mowschowitch; see again Wolf to Montefiore, 21 Dec. 1916, MWS 2963.

seeking. He was able to show that, contrary to what Blank was saying, there was a growing movement for national autonomy among Russian and Polish Jewry. Even before the Russian Revolution, he reported that Vinaver, 'the most moderate and careful leader of the most moderate Jewish party in Russia', was showing tendencies in this direction.[25] If these were tentative prior to the February revolution, after it Mowschowitch was able to bombard Wolf with material proving that autonomy was not only being demanded by a broad spectrum of Russian Jewish leaders themselves but recognized as their right by non-Jewish progressive forces.

In the late spring and early summer of 1917, congresses of Social Revolutionaries, of Cadets, and of the Petrograd Soviet resolved for Russian federalization and for national self-determination of the people within it. Kerensky at a conference of the Laborists did the same.[26] The more conservative secular elements in Jewry were swept up in the tide. In June, the Petrograd community's resolution of support for the provisional government also included a note in expectation that Russia 'will secure for the Jewish people the rights of national self-determination', while Vinaver and Sliosberg's newly reformed Narodnaia Groupa (the Folksgruppe) put forward its own extensive programme for national–cultural autonomy. This included not only the right to local democratically elected self-government and taxation but also to a recognition of the public–legal character of Jewish communities. They would have a right to claim state or regional subsidies, even to be represented by a general Jewish council before the government. Clearly, in the wake of the revolution, a general radicalization was permeating Russian Jewish life.[27]

That Mowschowitch chose to focus Wolf's attention on the behaviour of the Folksgruppe rather than, say, his own Sejmist party was a shrewd move.[28] Prior to and during the war, Wolf's main contact with

---

[25] See reports of Vinaver's 'nationality' speeches, *Retch*, 27 Apr., MWS 138851–5, and *Evreskaia nedelia*, 4 Dec. 1916, MWS 16107–12.

[26] *Evreskaia shisn*, 7 May 1917, MWS 11410–11; *Retch*, 8 Apr. 1917, encl. with Wolf to Oliphant, 10 May 1917, FO 371/3012/95062.

[27] *Retch*, 3 June, MWS 14722–3; *Evreskaia nedelia*, 4 June 1917, MWS 14724–9. See also Mowschowitch, 'Some Remarks on Baron Gunzburg's Letter on Jewish Affairs in Russia', n.d., June or July 1917, MWS 6103–13, notes a general reorganization and democratization of the former oligarchic community structure.

[28] Specific references to Vinaver's Folksgruppe effort appeared in Wolf's foreign affairs contribution to the *AJA Report*, no. 46 (London, 1916–17), 11, and in Wolf to FO, 3 Oct. 1918, encl. memo 'On the Polish Jewish Question', FO 371/3280/5393.

Russian Jewry was through Folksgruppe members—Braudo, Sliosberg, Vinaver—in their capacity at the Petrograd Bureau, which was
itself closely aligned with moderate Cadet-style liberalism. In presenting national autonomy to his committee and to the Foreign Office,
Wolf was therefore in a position to argue that it had not only extensive
support but responsible leadership.

Mowschowitch was also able to show Wolf that Jewish autonomy
could be speedily implemented in a modern secularized form. An
apparatus of local government, the *zemstvos*, had existed in Russia since
1864 and had been extended to Poland (though not to the Jews) in
1913. Though the pre-modern unit of Jewish self-administration, the
kehilla, had been theoretically disbanded in 1844, central committees
for statistics, health, and finance continued to function, as did the
Supreme Rabbinic Commission, which dealt with certain civil matters
as well as with questions of religious administration. As for education,
the May 1914 Law on Primary Education acknowledged in theory at
least the right of local groups to form their own autonomous schools,
and, due to duma pressure, the right to use their own languages. This
was also to hold good for Yiddish. The problem was that the tsarist
government refused to include the schools in a wider state supervisory
framework, thus ruling out state subsidies and in turn weakening
educational standards. Mowschowitch concluded optimistically that to
implement national autonomy 'would be a matter of putting right a
thing which exists rather than creating anything new'.[29]

Most important, however, Mowschowitch was able to demonstrate
convincingly that identification with Russifying or Polonizing tendencies,
whose advantages were proclaimed by people like Gunzburg or
Dickstein, was incompatible with the changed nature of Eastern Europe.
Not that Mowschowitch was not prepared to acknowledge the logic of
the Gunzburg case. For instance, he agreed that if Galicia were to be incorporated in a unified and liberal empire, it would greatly strengthen
Jewry's cultural and economic ties. In 'Congress' Poland this was
already the case where Litvaks—Russian Jews domiciled there—held
some 80 per cent of the bonds connecting the two countries.[30] But if
Poland, the Ukraine, or other areas became totally independent, as
seemed likely in 1917, the Jews would no longer be a considerable

[29] Mowschowitch notes, 'Educational Developments in Russia', n.d., Mar. 1917,
MWS 24708–11; report by Dr Braude of Lodz, 'Jewish Schools in Poland', n.d., 1919,
AJC Marshall papers, Peace Conference and Poland, box 1.
[30] Mowschowitch report on Polish question, n.d., 1917, MWS 16175–81.

minority of six million in a big empire but, as one contemporary commentator, S. Poliakov, noted, 'a series of small minorities in many little countries.'[31] How were the Litvaks, stranded in Poland yet identifying with a Greater Russia, going to accommodate to that? Indeed, would they be allowed to accommodate?

At the root of the problem, Mowschowitch blamed the shortsightedness of Gunzburg's Russification policy, which had given Poles, and in the future would give Finns, Lithuanians, and others, the opportunity to claim that the Jews were attempting to Russify them also. On the other hand, if this seven-million strong, united community were overnight to be converted into Poles, Tartars, Ukrainians, and Georgians, they would become 'the prey of local rivalry and local patriotism'. 'Events have shown', said Mowschowitch, 'that it is much safer for the Jews in Poland to be simply Jews.'[32]

Such was Mowschowitch's reply in April 1917 to Gunzburg's assertion to Leopold de Rothschild that Yiddishist demands for autonomy amounted to 'a separatist calamity for Russian Jewry'.[33] The reply was incorporated in the next Conjoint report. The convergence of views which amounted to tacit alliance between the Gunzburgs and the Conjoint had come to a close.

[31] Poliakov, 'Russian Jewry', MWS 7970–5.

[32] Mowschowitch, 'Some Remarks on Baron Gunzburg's Letter', MWS 6103–13.

[33] Gunzburg to Leopold de Rothschild, 30 Apr. 1917, MWS 6099–101. Gunzburg was specifically complaining about Yiddishist efforts to use Anglo-Jewish relief funds sent to the Petrograd Jewish Relief Committee for non-religious purposes. For the background to this dispute see Steven J. Zipperstein's interesting article, 'The Politics of Relief: The Transformation of Russian Jewish Communal Life During the First World War', *Studies in Contemporary Jewry*, 4 (1988), 22–400.

IO

The Struggle with the Polish National Committee

THE particular focus of Mowschowitch's anxieties was Poland. Competition between the Central Powers and the Allies for Polish support had been intense since the Austro-German 'Two Emperors' pronouncement in November 1916 declaring their intent to create an autonomous, though at that stage undefined, Polish state. The post-revolutionary provisional government in Russia had acknowledged the principle of self-determination. President Wilson, moreover, in January 1918, had unambiguously declared a free and independent Poland with access to the sea to be one of his 'Fourteen Points' for a post-war settlement. It was clear, therefore, that a Polish state of some sort would emerge at the end of the war. At least two million Jews would be included within this entity, amounting to possibly some 14 per cent of the population.[1]

As the existence of a reformed Poland would have to be acknowledged and ratified by any future peace conference, Mowschowitch insisted that the Western Jewish organizations must ask for international guarantees which specifically included the recognition and protection of Jewish national rights.[2] In early 1917, Wolf showed signs of responding to this logic and planned to raise the Polish question at a conference of French, Italian, and British Jewish representatives to be held in Paris in March. Due to the Russian Revolution, however, the conference never took place. Wolf's opportunity to lead the Western Jewish organizations in a fresh approach was stillborn.[3]

At home, too, Wolf made probes in accordance with Mowschowitch's suggestions. He had already intimated to Balfour, in an interview with him in January, the value of national autonomy as the basis for a liberal solution of the Jewish question. Learning in April that Balfour in-

[1] Zeman, *Diplomatic History*, 342–7; Calder, *Britain*, 145–52; Wolf, 'Jewish National Movement', 303.
[2] Mowschowitch, 'Notes on Projected Conference', 30 Mar. 1917, MWS 24657–65.
[3] Wolf to Bigart, 2 Apr. 1917, AIU/Angleterre, IJ 8.

tended to make a statement on the Polish question in the Commons, he followed this up by proposing that he include in his speech a reference to the rights of Jews, Lithuanians, Ruthenes, and other minorities. A mere formula of equal rights would not meet the case; what was important, echoing Mowschowitch to a word, was that 'the Poles should be made aware that Western Europe is not ignorant of, or indifferent to, the grievances of minorities'. The Commons speech, however, transpired to be a false rumour, and Wolf's new departure was again frustrated.[4]

Wolf seems to have been reluctant to pursue the matter further with the government. To espouse the idea of Jewish autonomy, as he did in 'The Jewish National Movement' was one thing; actually to make a policy which insisted on the government intervening to enforce Jewish national rights in a new Poland was quite another. For one thing, the Foreign Office would probably point out that the matter related to the internal affairs of the state and hence was beyond their scope. While the protocols of the Congress of Berlin might be invoked as precedent to protect religious and civil rights in the new states, no such framework existed for national rights. Balfour had implied as much to Wolf when he told him that the reference in the Allies note of January 1917 to the rights of nationalities was meant to refer to 'compact territories' not 'people'. When Wolf pressed the point a week later referring to how a recent Lloyd George statement that victory would create 'one emancipated land from the Urals to the Atlantic shores' would be interpreted by oppressed Russian nationalities in a Wilsonian sense, the Foreign Office's response was to 'ignore' the letter.[5] Wolf decided not to press the Foreign Office further with the issue. He had reasons, moreover, for hoping that his committee would not need to do so. For one thing, the Russian provisional government, and in turn the Russian Jews themselves, seemed to be actively concerned that any transference of power by Russia to an independent Poland would involve guarantees for minorities. The provisional government had indeed declared itself favourable to Polish independence, but with provisos guaranteeing Polish subnationalities their national existence. They had

---

[4] Wolf memo on interview with Balfour, 30 Jan. 1917, FO 800/210 (Balfour papers); Wolf to Balfour, 1 Apr. 1917, MWS 4283–4; Balfour to Wolf, 7 Apr. 1917, ibid. 'Notes on Interview with Lucien Wolf', 28 Apr. 1917, MWS 24704–7: 'The suggestion in question was made to Wolf by me and Mr. Wolf handed it over to the Foreign Office.'

[5] Wolf memo, 30 Jan. 1917, FO 800/210 (Balfour papers); Wolf to Balfour, 4 Feb. 1917, ibid.; Drummond minute, 5 Feb. 1917, ibid.

given the job of liquidating Russian affairs in Poland to Alexander
Lednicki, who, though a Pole himself, was also a close associate of
Vinaver's in the Cadets. Lednicki favoured a liberal reconciliation of
Poles, Jews, and other national groups. He was also in full accord with
the liberal 'tendencies' of the Russian provisional government. With
Lednicki in charge, an independent Poland would be likely to remain
in Russia's orbit to the mutual advantage, thought Mowschowitch, of
both states.[6]

The maintenance of good relations between the provisional government and Lednicki's Commission would therefore be Russian Jewry's
best guarantee for the safety and well-being of their Polish brethren.
Even if this failed, Russian Jewry, unfettered by restrictions and themselves a pillar of the new regime, were now in a position to exert their
own influence on the matter. With a proposal for securing the rights
of Jews outside Russia on the all-Russian Jewish Congress agenda,
Wolf could look forward to a prospect where instead of the Conjoint
having to take the initiative on Romania or Poland, the Russian Jews,
supported by their government, would be the ones to do so,[7] leaving
the Conjoint to bring up the rear.

Negotiations with Polish 'liberals' supported Wolf's further hypo-
thesis that an equitable internal settlement could be achieved without
external prompting. As early as January 1915, he had met with two
leading members of the liberal-orientated Polish Progressist party,
Stanislaw Patek and August Zaleski, who had satisfied him that they
favoured a liberal solution of the Polish Jewish question.[8] The actual
form this would take seems to have been vague at this stage, but this
apparently did not worry Wolf; he had great faith in Polish liberalism.
Zaleski, in particular, he characterized as 'the most liberal minded
Pole I know',[9] and it was he whom Wolf met again in July 1917 to try
and thrash out some framework for Polish–Jewish coexistence.

Zaleski proved amenable to the Mowschowitch programme for
national autonomy which Wolf presented to him. He agreed that the

[6] Mowschowitch to Wolf, 31 Mar. 1917, MWS 10366–9 reported that the provisional
government's declaration on Poland was 'a great victory of the Russian Jews for the
cause of Polish Jews'. See also Mowschowitch report on Polish situation, n.d., late 1917,
MWS 16175–81; *CHP*, ii. 468–70. On Lednicki see Calder, *Britain*, 160, 162.

[7] Mowschowitch to Wolf, 10 Oct. 1917, MWS 10460–3.

[8] Wolf memo on interview, 30 Jan. 1917, MWS 4688–90.

[9] Wolf, 'Diary of the Peace Conference', 23 Apr. 1919, fo. 211. This comment was
endorsed by Israel Cohen, who described Zaleski as 'one of the few liberally-minded
statesmen of pre-war Poland'; quoted in Davies, 'Poles', 68.

parties of the left would accept cultural self-determination and proportional representation in state elections, but advised that the official
use of Yiddish 'would not find favour with any section of the Polish
people'.[10] This was something of a set-back, especially for Mowschowitch who had been insisting all along (echoing a 1915 article by the
Russian Zionist theorist Julius Brutzkus), that the key to the Polish
situation was the use of Yiddish. This, Brutzkus had said, was not a
luxury but a necessary condition of Jewish cultural and economic
development. Without it there could be no liberty of meetings or
school education, no political life, no justice or legal protection.[11]

Despite this damper, Wolf continued to place his hopes in Zaleski,
whom he rightly saw as being in line with developments asociated with
Lednicki in Russia. Indeed, further correspondence with him yielded
details of the second Polish Democratic Congress held in Petrograd,
where Polish centre, liberal, and leftist parties coalesced under
Lednicki's leadership in favour of a radical platform which included
non-Polish national rights. Wolf took this to be the foundation of the
future Polish state.[12]

By aligning himself to these tendencies, Wolf was doubly flying in
the face of his own government. Firstly, though Zaleski was a pronounced Anglophile and the acknowledged wartime head of the Polish
community in Great Britain, he was by 1917 out of favour with the
Foreign Office, indeed under constant police surveillance. The ministry's main reason for distrusting him lay with his being a representative
of the leader of the Polish Socialist party, Josef Pilsudski, the man
behind whom Polish leftist groups had originally coalesced at the
outbreak of war. Pilsudski, like Zaleski, had no quarrel with the
Western Allies but saw the defeat of Russia as being the prerequisite
for the liberation of all Poland, including those parts controlled by
Austria and Prussia. A pragmatic and limited co-operation with the
German and Austrian forces of occupation hence followed, and indeed
when they set up an advisory Polish Council of State in January 1917,
Pilsudski agreed to serve on it.[13]

---

[10] Wolf memo of interview with Zaleski, 6 July 1917, encl. with Wolf to FO, 3 Oct.
1918, FO 371/3280/5373; Mowschowitch proposals 'On the Polish Question', 9 July
1917, MWS 16133–9.

[11] Brutzkus article, *Evreskaia shisn*, 6 Dec. 1915, MWS 11205–12.

[12] Report of Second Democratic Congress encl. with Wolf to Cecil, 21 July 1917, FO
371/3019/226666.

[13] Davies, 'Poles', 68–72; Calder, *Britain*, 82, 161–2.

As it was assumed that Pilsudski and his English-based agent Zaleski were pro-German—more incredibly, Lednicki was also suspected— the Allies had to search elsewhere for Polish support. Here again Wolf found himself in deep water. The Allies' search took them to the Polish National Committee. A coalition of *emigré* individuals, groups, and parties of the right, the committee was not formed until after the Russian Revolution, in the summer of 1917, and, significantly, beyond the reach of Lednicki, in Lausanne, Switzerland. It represented the most reactionary elements in Polish life, the complete antithesis of both Lednicki's Congress and Pilsudski. In Britain and France, however, these aspects did not work to the committee's disadvantage. On the contrary, its aristocratic composition tended to endear it to officials with similar backgrounds or inclinations. Foreign Office Catholics such as Gregory, Drummond, and Clerk were amongst its staunchest supporters.[14]

If the committee was a disparate coalition, it also contained one dominating element: the leader of the National Democrats, Roman Dmowski. What made his credentials so unimpeachable was the fact that having early in the war openly supported tsarist plans for Polish autonomy, he now threw in his lot quite unequivocally with the Western Allies, an approach which seemed to contrast most favourably with the cautious expediency of Pilsudski or the declared neutrality of Zaleski.[15]

Dmowski's apparently untarnished record meant that he was well-positioned both to insist on his own reliability and conversely to denigrate Zaleski (and indeed all other groups outside the Polish National Committee) as pro-German—the reason, he implied, why they could not for the present be included in his committee. As such, the Foreign Office was not inclined to dispute his claim to Cecil in September 1917 that the National Democrats represented 90 per cent of the Polish population, despite the recent counter-claims by Zaleski to the effect that the majority were behind the Polish Council of State.[16]

[14] Paul Latawski, 'The Dmowski–Namier Feud, 1915–1918', *Polin*, 2 (1987), 37–49; Calder, *Britain*, 159–64; *CHP*, ii. 472, 490–2; Davies, 'Poles', 82. Polish National Committee bureaus were set up in Britain, France, and the USA; according to Davies (ibid. 82), Gregory characterized one of their leaders, Count Sobanski, as 'one of the best types an ancient social order in Eastern Europe can produce'.

[15] On Dmowski see *CHP*, ii. 406–7; Latawski, 'The Dmowski–Namier Feud', 37–49.

[16] Cecil memo on interview with Dmowski, 3 Sept. 1917, FO 800/205 (Balfour papers); Davies, 'Poles', 72–3; Calder, *Britain*, 160–1.

Moreover, they seemed equally willing to overlook the fact that a greater Poland as envisaged by him would include as many non-Poles as Poles. The important thing, and here one could make distinct parallels with Weizmann, was that Dmowski offered them whole-heartedly Polish support, and, in the long-term, given the probable collapse of Russia, a strategic bulwark against the Germans.[17]

There was another important aspect in Dmowski's policy: his anti-semitism. If his party took power in Poland, the Jews could expect nothing less than political discrimination and economic strangulation. Dmowski's reasoning was explicit. He wanted an expanded, homo-geneous, Catholic, intensely Polish Poland. The Jews were a distinct alien element, spoke a foreign language, in the case of the Litvaks represented Russification, were not Catholics, and most importantly of all, dominated both domestic and external trade and commerce. The Polonization of the country's economic life was the *sine qua non* of Dmowski's Jewish policy. There could be no room for a gradualist accommodation; they would simply have to emigrate.[18]

Dmowski already had a long record of translating his Jewish policy into practice. It was his organ, *Dwa grosha*, which in 1912 had called the still-continuing economic boycott. It was *Dwa grosha* again, during the war, which accused Polish Jewry of pro-Germanism, espionage, financial manipulation, and general sycophancy. The boycott, it urged, must become more effective, so that Jewish emigration would in turn increase.[19]

This antisemitic notoriety meant that Dmowski was well known to Wolf even before his association with the Polish National Committee. In 1915 and again the following year, Wolf, in conjunction with the French propagandizing Comité d'Action, was able to get meetings and lectures planned by Dmowski and his associates in Britain and France curtailed or cancelled.[20] But at that time Dmowski's

[17] In Wolf to Montefiore, 24 Oct. 1917, CII/2/12, Wolf reports that Sir George Clerk had frankly confessed to Zaleski that moral questions *vis-à-vis* Dmowski had not been considered; the government had opted for him purely for his practical value to the Allies.

[18] Memo on Polish Jewish question encl. with Wolf to FO, 3 Oct. 1918, FO 371/3280/5373.

[19] Cecil memo on interview with Dmowski, 3 Sept. 1917, FO 800/205 (Balfour papers); reply to *Dwa grosha* attacks, *Hazefira*, 5 July 1917; MWS 16623–48; statement (unsigned), 'Poles and Jews', n.d., MWS 16077–85.

[20] Meyerson to Wolf, 2 Mar. 1916, MWS 2866; Wolf to Meyerson, 30 Mar. 1916, ibid.

standing was still tenuous, and the likelihood of his receiving official acknowledgement from the British was remote. In October 1917, however, this is exactly what did happen: Britain followed France in recognizing the Polish National Committee as an official Polish organization.

In a sense this was less devastating than it sounded as it still left the door open to accredit other 'official' organizations. Nevertheless, Sir George Clerk, in conversation with Zaleski, had implied that when the Russian Constituent Assembly declared Poland independent, the Allies would recognize the Polish National Committee as its *de jure* government. As the French had already authorized the formation of a Polish army, presently under French command, it was conceivable that in the not too distant future this would become the Polish National Committee's instrument for some vast 'pogrom' of both Progressists and Jews.[21]

Wolf was thus faced yet again with his old dilemma: was he to acquiesce as a good patriot in the government's decision, or was he to take up arms against it? Zaleski favoured the latter course and proposed that the Progressists and Anglo-Jewish Association—this was the period of Wolf's interim committee secretaryship—should unite in an open campaign against the Polish National Committee.[22] If Wolf accepted this suggestion, it would be tantamount to a Jewish organization politically aligning itself against its own government. Wolf drew back. He proposed instead that the two groups work in parallel though independently of each other, and wrote to the Alliance and the American Jewish Committee to persuade them to adopt a similar approach to their own governments.[23]

This discreet approach failed to have much impact. Wolf proposed to Balfour in couched terms that the government make known its disapproval of Dmowski's antisemitic policies. Members of both the House of Commons and the House of Lords were also approached, the former to raise questions on the government's decision, the latter to threaten a rumpus. However, Cecil and Balfour

[21] Wolf to Montefiore, 24 Oct. 1917, on Clerk–Zaleski interview, CII/2/12; Calder, *Britain*, 156.

[22] Wolf to Montefiore, 24 Oct. 1917, CII/2/12.

[23] Wolf to Marshall, 30 Oct., ibid.; Wolf to Bigart, 30 Oct. 1917, AIU/Angleterre IJ 8: 'in view of what has happened we cannot possibly remain silent'; Mowschowitch, 'Notes on the Diplomatic History of the Jewish Question, 1917–1950', n.d. MWS 24901–47.

were able to thwart these efforts by invoking the 'public interest'.[24] Wolf could obviously not let the matter rest there. To recognize Dmowski was to recognize his antisemitism, an open invitation to reactionaries in other states coming into being on the Russian hinterland to seek British support. The seriousness of the situation galvanized Wolf to declare his new war aims: national minority rights. It also forced him to recognize that, if 'friendly' political elements like Zaleski were to be reinstated with the Allies, it was up to the Jews to eschew timidity and declare for them.

Zaleski gave Wolf the opportunity to do so. He proposed that Wolf and other Western Jewish representatives should meet in a neutral country with representatives of Lednicki's Polish Democratic Concentration and hammer out a definite scheme of settlement on the Polish Jewish question.[25] In a sense, Wolf had no right to do this as he was as yet without any mandate from the Polish Jews themselves, but it was a good tactic to use at the Foreign Office. In an interview with Cecil in November, he informed him why it was necessary that the government should give him the option to go. It was impossible, he said, to negotiate with Dmowski. Nor would the prospect of a Dmowski government in Warsaw make for the internal stability of the new Poland. But if a definitive settlement could be arrived at on the Jewish question, it would make for orderly development, and would also mean that the Jews forced into 'political solidarity' with the liberals would continue to hold the ring in Polish politics to the advantage of the democratic forces.[26]

This was daring indeed; a sharp and unqualified jab at the British government for having tactically blundered in backing Dmowski and an open invitation to reverse or at least rethink their Polish policy in a leftist direction. The effect was to cause something of a minor storm in the Foreign Office. Cecil, sticking to his guns on the need to conciliate

---

[24] Mowschowitch, 'Notes', MWS 24901–47. On the withdrawal of the parliamentary questions tabled by Hoare, Whyte, and Lord Weardale on Dmowski's antisemitism see also Wolf to Balfour, 31 Oct. 1917, C11/2/12.

[25] Wolf note on interview with Zaleski, 22 Nov. 1917, C11/2/12; Zaleski to Landau, 28 Nov. 1917, ibid. Hermann Landau, one of Wolf's committee members, acted as intermediary in these negotiations. This is interesting as Landau, himself Polish-born, was one of the few members of the Anglo-Jewish élite who understood and sympathized with the Yiddish-speaking immigrant milieu and recognized the importance of the linguistic divide, whether between Yiddish and English or Yiddish and Polish; see Black, *Social Politics*, 61–2, 88–9.

[26] Wolf to Cecil, 26 Nov. 1917, FO 371/3019/226666.

the Jews as a powerful political force, agreed that not only would Dmowski's antisemitism 'wreck all chance of a successful independent Poland . . . but [would] greatly embarrass us in other places. It is Rumanian anti-semitism that makes it so difficult to secure a South Russian block.' Wolf had warned that if he did not participate in the discussions, the American and Russian Jews certainly would, and British interests would subsequently be ignored. For expediency's sake if nothing else, Cecil insisted that he must go. Gregory, however, entirely disagreed. Convinced by the Dmowskites that Zaleski and others were indeed pro-German or Austrian, he argued that to sanction the meeting was to encourage a *rapprochement* with those favouring a compromise with the Central Powers. This argument was enough to overrule Cecil and scotch the Wolf–Zaleski project.[27]

Far from deterring Wolf, this provoked him to be quite blunt about what he was proposing. He sent on to Cecil the Zaleski material on the Lednicki Congress in Petrograd. This had recognized not only the independence of Poland but that of the Ukraine, and possibly of Lithuania and White Ruthenia too. Failing that, all minority rights would be safeguarded. The Congress had also insisted—a glance here at the Dmowski people—that all other Polish political organizations should place themselves at the disposal of the Polish State Council in Warsaw. This organization, argued Lednicki, was neutral in the present hostilities but would soon be the vehicle of future statehood.

By way of commentary, Wolf proposed that if, as he felt confident, Lednicki was going to be the winning force in Poland, it was in Britain's interests to support him. Moreover, he continued,

a friendly combination of Poland, Lithuania and Ukrainia is quite possible on the Lednicki basis of the independence of each of these countries and of national autonomy for the minorities within their frontiers, while such a powerful combination is excluded by all the essentials of M. Dmowski's policy. The point I think is worth bearing in mind and at a given moment should be made the starting point of discreet negotiations for an *entente* with M. Lednicki. If in this connection I can be of any use to His Majesty's Government, I shall be very pleased to place myself entirely at their disposal.[28]

This was in fact Bodenheimer's 1914 'Federation of Minorities' scheme

[27] Gregory, 29 Nov. and 10 Dec. 1917, ibid.; Cecil minutes, n.d., and 19 Dec. 1917, ibid.

[28] Report of Second Democratic Congress encl. with Wolf to Cecil, 29 Dec. 1917, ibid.

tailored to suit British foreign policy. Wolf meant it sincerely: an attempt to build up not a network of fragmented ultra-nationalist states but an alliance of self-governing units, which, through people like Lednicki, would still be associated with a liberalizing and perhaps, in time, revitalized Russia. It was a plan to preserve the European peace, create an obstacle to Germany, and, last but not least, save the Jews.

In proposing it, Wolf was once again stating that British and Jewish 'foreign' policy still could have mutual interests, and that these interests could be brought together by Wolf himself working in conjunction with the liberals at the Foreign Office. This was not altogether far-fetched. Cecil was on this score entirely in accord with Wolf. Moreover, when the Political Intelligence Department came into existence the following spring, it produced other figures, notably the Jewish and Galician-born Lewis Namier, who adopted a similar approach. There is also evidence to suggest that Wolf helped scotch insinuations by Dmowski to the effect that both Namier and Rex Leeper were pro-German.[29]

The upper echelons of the Foreign Office, however, for the most part remained distinctly pro-Dmowski, being indeed advised on Polish affairs by an affiliate if not an actual associate of Dmowski, Jan Horodyski.[30] Wolf's proposal remained a dead letter.

Paradoxically, following a logical trend Wolf was unable to resist, the necessity to pursue the issue further was eased, temporarily at least, by developments initiated by the Central Powers. In the East, in the early part of 1918, they were in the ascendant. Russia was out of the war, the peace of Brest-Litovsk extended German influence into its hinterland, the Ukraine was a client state, and both Lithuania and Russian Poland, though nominally granted independence, were in reality ruled by German governor-generals. While attempting to conciliate these prospective *protégés*, German interests were best served by keeping them divided and weak. National autonomy fitted into this pattern.[31] Jewish fortunes, which had been subject to considerable oscillations

[29] See Cecil and Gregory minutes, 29 Dec. 1917, ibid.; Namier and Toynbee memo on Jewish Nationality, 15 Nov. 1918, FO 371/3414/181911; Lady Julia Namier, *Lewis Namier: A Biography* (London, 1971), 128–9; R. A. Leeper's letter of thanks to Wolf, 26 June 1918, C11/3/1/3.
[30] See Zaleski–Wolf interview, 22 Nov. 1917, C11/2/13. For Horodyski's influence on FO men, including Clerk, Drummond, and Tyrrell see Davies, 'Poles', 65. Latawski, 'The Dmowski–Namier Feud', 41–2, is more sceptical of Dmowski's degree of influence.
[31] Fischer, *Germany's Aims*, 375–6, 456–66, 487.

under Central Power occupation, as a result showed signs of marked improvement.[32]

A new German Jewish umbrella organization, known by its initials as VJOD, created to formulate a Jewish agenda for the peace conference, was officially acknowleged by the Auswärtiges Amt. In January 1918, it was received by Baron von dem Bussche-Heddenhausen, the German deputy foreign secretary, who made two important public statements. One was an offer of immigration and settlement in Palestine (a propaganda response and counter to the Balfour Declaration), and the other was a clear endorsement of Jewish minority rights.[33]

This *démarche* was soon dramatically superseded by the Austrians. At the beginning of February, a delegation of Jewish Austrian nationalists was received by President Seidler and Count Toggenberg, his interior minister. They agreed to consider sympathetically the nationalists' 'maximum' demands: not only Jewish self-administration and official recognition of Yiddish, but the right to proportional representation, a national chamber, and their own secretary of state.[34] If the Austrian desire to please was partially out of a desire to save the empire from within rather than having it dismantled from without, it also carried with it important consequences for Polish Jewry. It was widely known that Austria favoured Polish integration into the Dual Monarchy, possibly by extending it into a tripartite monarchy consisting of Austria, Hungary, and Poland.[35] If this did materialize, the nationalist Polish capacity to oust the Jews would be considerably diminished.

The same lesson could be drawn in reverse from the German controlled provinces known as the Ober-Ost. The easternmost of these provinces, Courland, was earmarked for direct annexation, but its neighbour, Lithuania, if enlarged, would serve as a useful land-

---

[32] Mowschowitch, 'Austrian Policy and the Jews in the East', n.d., 1918, MWS 16129–32, notes the ambiguous behaviour of the Austrians, on the one hand favouring cultural autonomy, on the other, imposing forced labour and undermining the Jewish tobacco monopoly. A similar situation existed in the German Ober-Ost. See also Mendelsohn, *Zionism in Poland*, 39–45.

[33] On the formation and structure of the VJOD (Vereingung Judischer Organisationen Deutschlands zur Wahrung der Rechte der Juden den Osten) see Zechlin, *Deutsche Politik*, 221–3, and Friedman, *Germany, Turkey*, 394–5. For report on Bussche interview with Soberheim, Warburg, and Hantke see Mowschowitch to Wolf, 17 Jan. 1918, C11/2/13.

[34] Report on Seidler–Straucher interview, Jewish Press Bureau (Stockholm), 6 Feb. 1918, C11/3/1/3.

[35] *CHP*, ii. 407–8.

bridge to it. As the Lithuanians themselves had no overall majority in the proposed state but were balanced out by considerable minorities, particularly of Poles and Jews, the Germans were in a position to divide and rule through encouraging national autonomy.

In every respect this favoured the Jews; allied with the Lithuanians against the Poles, they could arrest the latter's expansionist designs in the area and safeguard the great Jewish economic and cultural centres of Vilna, Grodno, and Bialystok.[36] A framework for full Jewish national–personal autonomy had, moreover, already been formulated by the Ukraine. Newly created and entirely dependent on the Germans, the Ukraine had, as a result of the Treaty of Brest-Litovsk, absorbed the Polish province of Chelm.[37] This emphasized the fact that not only in an eastern *pax germanica* were the Poles to be territorially hemmed in, but that if they desired to protect Polish nationality rights in ceded provinces, they would have to recognize the same rights for national minorities within their own boundaries.

The reports Wolf received on Poland itself seemed to reflect this pattern, with, for instance, the transference of the school system under German auspices, in late 1917, providing for Jewish educational self-administration at a primary level.[38] There were, too, some disquieting developments, relating particularly to the plans announced in February 1918 for the future Polish State Council. Created and controlled by the Germans, the Regency Council's members would be in part their direct nominees and in part elected. As this would not be on the basis of proportional representation, and given the probability of gerrymandering, the Jews were expected to receive a mere 2 out of its 110 seats. As Mowschowitch sardonically noted, the Poles were forced to do the German bidding, except on the Jewish question.[39]

If the situation remained in flux, however, with the Germans refraining from imposing a solution to the Polish Jewish question in its entirety, Wolf nevertheless remained hopeful that the Poles in control

[36] Fischer, *Germany's Aims*, 450–60, 464–72; reports on declaration by von Falkenhausen (Imperial Commissioner, Ober-Ost) to VJOD delegation on Jewish minority rights in Lithuania, 10 July 1918, MWS 21045–8. On situation in Ober-Ost and Lithuania, 17 Sept. 1918 see also MWS 8187–93.

[37] *CHP*, ii. 473; Fischer, *Germany's Aims*, 485–7; on declaration of national autonomy by Ukrainian Rada see Jewish Press Bureau (Stockholm), communiqué, 13 Feb. 1918, C11/3/1/2.

[38] Text of Polish school system regulations, 12 Sept. 1917, MWS 16141–2.

[39] Jewish Press Bureau (Stockholm), *communiqué* 16 Feb. 1918, on Polish State Council, C11/3/1/2; Mowschowitch to Wolf, 10 July 1918, MWS 10531–2.

in Poland were receptive to the idea of a liberal internal settlement. In February, Premier Kucharzewski made public assurances to Warsaw Jewish editors along these lines, and although Mowschowitch insisted that he was an antisemite in the Dmowski mould, information from Zaleski suggested to the contrary, that he was an adherent of Lednicki. Wolf, who had doubted the virulence of Kucharzewski's alleged anti-semitism at the time of the 1912 Warsaw elections, endorsed Zaleski.[40]

The possibility of Kucharzewski making a successful internal settlement—information already suggested that the assimilationist group headed by Professor Dickstein and Wladyslaw Natanson had come to such an arrangement 'without co-operation or assistance from outside'[41]—seems in fact to have undermined Wolf's resolve to pursue national autonomy. Concurrently, Mowschowitch's hold on Wolf seemed to be diminishing. Wolf expressed his doubts to him as follows:

The difficulty is to obtain some authentic expression of the wishes of the Polish Jews as a whole. If they wish us to stand out for national autonomy we will do so but if there are serious differences of opinion among them on this question I am afraid we shall have to leave them to fight it out among themselves and limit ourselves to a demand for equal rights.[42]

In reply, Mowschowitch confessed that the hold of the Polish assimilationists on the Yiddish-speaking masses was not vanishing as fast as in Russia. But he went on to expostulate:

The duty of the Conjoint Committee (*sic*) as I understand it, is to be neutral in the international struggle between the Jewish parties but not in the struggle between the Jewish minority and the Polish majority. If the gentlemen of your committee are unable to grasp the thing for which the whole of Eastern Europe agonises, let them at least support the demand that in the Polish Constitution should be inserted a stipulation according to which a general Congress . . . of Polish Jews organises culturally and religiously the Jewry and represents it through its organs before the government as a whole.[43]

If Mowschowitch's efforts were enough to have convinced Wolf that

[40] Mowschowitch to Wolf, 21 Jan. 1918, MWS 10428–35; Wolf to Mowschowitch, 8 Feb. 1918, MWS 10460–5; Zaleski to Wolf, 30 Jan. 1918, C11/2/12 (also encl. in Wolf to Cecil, 16 Jan. 1918, FO 371/3277/3361).

[41] Report from *Die Zeit*, 3 Feb. 1918, MWS 16203–6.

[42] Wolf to Mowschowitch, 25 Feb. 1918, MWS 10467–8.

[43] Mowschowitch to Wolf, 21 Mar. 1918, MWS 10471–5. This was consistent with efforts by the various Jewish secular parties in Poland to create an all Polish Jewish conference to place Jewish desiderata before the Polish authorities; see Mendelsohn, *Zionism in Poland*, 91–2.

the pronounced assimilationism of the Dickstein people would not be able to overcome the Jewish dilemma in Poland, he was not prepared to commit himself further to Mowschowitch's demands until the degree to which the Jews in Poland were themselves committed to national autonomy had been resolved.[44]

An article by Adam Sutherland that appeared in May in *Prawda*, the Zaleski-oriented Polish-language journal published in London, offered an alternative approach. Sutherland was concerned to draw out the distinctions between the various Jewish parties in Poland. At one end he noted 'the Circle of the Polish Patriots of the Mosaic Persuasion', that is, the Dickstein people, were so insistent on putting Polish national interests before all else that they agreed that Jews who did not identify with this, in spirit and sentiment, should emigrate. At the other end, Sutherland lumped together Zionists, nationalists, and populists as wanting various degrees of national autonomy—he noted that Polish Zionists accepted that not all Jews would be able to go to Palestine—and were also, in varying degrees, hostile to Polish statehood. All wanted the Jewish question to be dealt with internationally. This obviously did not augur well for a 'liberal' internal settlement. There were, of course, too, the Bundists, allied at present with the Polish socialists, but their opposition to the bourgeois Jewish parties and their revolutionary Russian tradition put them outside the scope of any 'broad' settlement.

But, suggested Sutherland, this still in a sense left out the great mass of orthodox Jewry, traditionally non-political yet represented through organizations like Agudas Yisroel. This, he argued, was the body with which the Polish government ought to negotiate, the one which would accept a programme of religious toleration and full civil rights and in return would promise allegiance to the state. The effect would be to get the vast mass of Jewry behind this arrangement and, in so doing, undermine the autonomist rationale.[45]

Wolf seems to have taken the cue that Jewish national autonomy, at least as far as Western Jewish diplomacy was concerned, was better left alone. Taking up an appeal by Reuben Blank in June that the Allies complement the Balfour Declaration with one proclaiming Jewish civil,

---

[44] The strength of the anti-autonomy lobby is attested to in Janowsky, *Jews and Minority Rights*, 243, which notes how the Warsaw and Lodz assimilationists were able to prevent communal elections on a popular franchise basis until after the German departure.

[45] Sutherland article in *Prawda*, 18 May 1918, C11/3/1/3.

religious, and political rights as among their essential war aims, Wolf in his first major initiative at the Joint Foreign Committee made no mention of national autonomy except in so far as it had been used by the Germans and Austrians as a 'specious bribe' to the Jewish masses of the East. A declaration of civil and political emancipation would, he argued, counter this. Mowschowitch was furious.[46]

But if Wolf felt in June he could sidestep the issue, by August he was back at square one. Having taken cheer from what was happening under the auspices of the Central Powers, he had forgotten about the situation in the Allied camp. On the verge of military disaster in the spring, the Allies, reinforced with American troops, had by the late summer recovered sufficiently to be considering their post-victory intentions. The Polish National Committee, despite the doubts of liberals and the efforts by people such as Namier to reinstate Zaleski, still represented their key to post-war Poland—indeed in the last days of the war they invested it with real power by giving it political authority over General Haller's French-based Polish army.[47]

The outlook from the Jewish point of view was bleak, especially as the committee had made no effort to accommodate itself on the Jewish question or even to conceal its antisemitic prejudice. Wolf's hopes on this issue were rudely shattered by the uncompromising reply made to Sutherland by *Tygodnik polski*, Dmowski's London organ. Mass Jewish assimilation was neither possible nor desirable, said Leon Brunn, the journal's protagonist, in July. The Jews had two options; to declare themselves Poles without reservation and agree to the solution of the Jewish question from the point of view of Polish national interest, or declare themselves unequivocally as Jewish nationalists.[48] Either way, it boiled down to one thing: emigration.

This was exactly the line which the committee was pursuing with the British Foreign Office in relation to the distribution of certificates

[46] Wolf to Bigart, 21 May 1918, AIU Angleterre, iii, D 49; Wolf to Oliphant, encl. memo, 18 June 1918, FO 371/3386/856. The AIU made similar successful representations; see Nathan Feinberg, *La Question des minorités à la conférence de la paix* (Paris, 1929), 39–40. For Mowschowitch's outrage see Mowschowitch to Wolf, n.d., June 1918, MWS 10582–5.

[47] *CHP* ii. 477, 491–2 on the Allies, the PNC, and Haller. For Political Intelligence Dept. doubts on PNC see Intelligence Dept. memo on National Democrats, 25 June 1918, BM Add. MSS 51105 (Cecil papers); Calder, *Britain*, 197–9; Rothwell, *British War Aims*, 231–2.

[48] Leon Brunn, 'Insincerity on the Polish Question', *Tygodnik Polski*, 14 July 1918, MWS 16230–6.

registering Prussian and Austrian Poles as friendly aliens. Originally, in 1915, the administration of this had been in the hands of the English-based Zaleski-orientated organization, the Polish Information Committee. The following year, however, this had been displaced by another committee, called Polish Exiles Protection (Opieka Polska), with the help of British sympathizers, notably Miss Laurence Alma-Tadema, which was working in the Dmowski interest.[49] One of the cardinal aims of the new committee was to exclude political opponents from receiving certificates; another was to discriminate against Jews on a racial basis. When the administration of certificates was handed over to the Polish National Committee in 1918, these terms of reference continued to apply: Jews could not be classed as Polish nationals. Both the Foreign and Home Offices concurred.[50]

At face value the British government's response represented a stigmatization of Polish Jews living in Great Britain. Sir Stuart Samuel at the Board led the Jewish protest, shrewdly warning that their continued support for Dmowski was 'entirely neutralising the good effect produced by the Balfour Declaration'.[51] But from Wolf's point of view, the Polish National Committee's stance had a much wider application. It was not simply a question of whether a compromise could be reached by providing certificates through an alternative Jewish committee, as Samuel had proposed as one solution, but whether Polish Jewry in a new and sovereign state would or would not be excluded from the body politic.[52]

Wolf sought assurances. In July, two high-ranking members of the Joint Foreign Committee, Henry Henriques and Lord Swaythling, met with a leading Polish National Committee spokesman, Count Sobanski, and were indeed assured that in the future state all citizens would 'be equal before the law'.[53] Far from appeasing Wolf, however, this statement galvanized him, after more than a year of prevarication, finally to submit to the Foreign Office, in October 1918, his definitive case on the necessity of Jewish national autonomy in Poland.

[49] On displacement of the Polish Information Committee see Waller memo, 12 Nov. 1915, HO 45/10836/330094; Davies, 'Poles', 72.
[50] Moylan (HO)–Clerk (FO)–Sobanski–Kozicki (PNC) meeting, 8 Jan. 1918, to discuss administration of certificates; HO 45/10889/352661/4. Gregory concurred with the PNC's view; see Gregory minute, 28 Apr. 1918, FO 371/5280/5373.
[51] Copy of S. M. Samuel to HO, 6 Mar. 1918, encl. with FO 371/3280/5373. See also Rothwell, *British War Aims*, 231–2.
[52] Wolf–Moylan interview, 8 July 1918, C11/3/1/3.
[53] Details of Sobanski–Henriques–Swaythling meeting, 23 July 1918, encl. with Wolf to FO, 3 Oct. 1918, FO 371/3280/5373.

Wolf recognized that the government would be reluctant 'to do anything which would run counter to the wishes of M. Dmowski and his committee'. Nevertheless, taking as his starting point the apparent convergence of interests between the Dmowskites and the British government, Wolf boldly outlined why the Sobanski formula would simply not safeguard Polish Jewry. In particular, he pointed to a major precedent in the 1862 Act of Emancipation which, while having given the Polish Jews equality before the law, had done so on the stipulation that they renounce the use of their own Yiddish language in speech, writing, contracts, and court procedure. This linguistic provision had, at the time, been overridden, but the fact that it had not been repealed meant that it could, he argued, still be utilized as the basis for future disenfranchisement.

Evidence to this effect, said Wolf, was already at hand. The Warsaw Town Council had in the autumn of 1916 invoked the 1862 Act against the use of Yiddish or Hebrew and thereby defeated an attempt to set up a separate Jewish school system. If now a general law were to make Polish the only legal language, 'the Jewish disability would be maintained without any technical derogation from the principle of equal rights'.[54]

While Wolf noted other ways in which the Jews might be deprived of their political rights while still technically holding them, primarily through the gerrymandering of parliamentary constituencies to maintain them in a constant minority and the enactment of a Sunday rest law to deprive them of their economic livelihood, it was to the linguistic question that Wolf most insistently returned. Drawing heavily from Mowschowitch's arguments, and in turn from Brutzkus,[55] Wolf explained why the Joint Foreign Committee would have to defend Yiddish as the necessary corollary of equal rights. It was idle, he argued, to discuss whether or not a 'Yiddish' consciousness ought or ought not to exist:

It exists as a very formidable outcome of ineluctable historical conditions and cannot be altered in the least by the disapproval of foreign Jewish communities whose historical, social and political lines have fallen in pleasanter places and have enabled them to pursue a different and perhaps wiser course. The only question is whether these foreign communities will refuse to aid their Polish brethren with which they are threatened on account of their attachment to

[54] Wolf memo on 'Polish Jewish Question', 3 Oct. 1918, ibid. For submission of memo to the JFC see JFC minutes, 17 Sept. 1918.
[55] Brutzkus article, *Evreskaia shisn*, 6 Feb. 1918, MWS 11205–12.

Yiddish. However much we may despise the jargon as it is called, it is after all the vernacular of 6 million of Jews, the growth of 700 years of separate Jewish history, the medium of a considerable and highly respectable Jewish literature, the spontaneous dialect of the Polish Jew in his home and in the market place and an indispensable element in the intricate social and economic relations of the Jewish community which lives in great masses and which would be completely disorganised without it. To deprive them of it would be a great cruelty and since in that case they would be suffering as Jews, they would certainly seem to be entitled to the support of their Jewish brethren in other lands, even though Yiddish has no attraction for them.[56]

The question Wolf pragmatically pursued was entirely independent of considerations of whether Jews were a religion or a nationality. The Polish Jews, he agreed, were themselves divided on that issue, the assimilationists being in fierce disagreement with the separatists. For the Joint Foreign Committee, as a Jewish body to interfere, therefore, was to risk a possible impropriety. Nevertheless, 'if national or cultural autonomy is, in any form, conceded to other Nationalities in Poland and denied to the Jews, it will probably be necessary for the western communities to take the risk of resisting such an injustice'.[57]

In conclusion, Wolf summarized his points:

1. Recognition of Jews as Polish citizens
2. Repeal of the 1862 linguistic provisions
3. Autonomous management of Jewish religious, educational, charitable, and other cultural institutions
4. Sunday labour/Saturday rest

A month and a half later, with the war ended and the peace conference about to commence, Wolf formally presented the Foreign Office his new proposals for a liberal settlement of the Jewish question in Eastern Europe. 'What is called national autonomy has been adopted as a fundamental principle by all the democratic parties in Great Russia and a scheme to give effect to it was embodied in the Constitution by the republican *rada* of the Ukraine.'[58] Point 3 of his submission to the Foreign Office on Poland, that relating to Jewish autonomy, Wolf now reiterated as a necessary condition for the safeguarding of Jewish rights throughout Eastern Europe. The Joint Foreign Committee was, it seemed, publicly committed to national autonomy.

[56] Wolf memo on 'Polish Jewish Question', 3 Oct. 1918, FO 371/3280/5373.
[57] Ibid.
[58] Wolf to Balfour, 2 Dec. 1918, FO 371/3419/199696; repr. in *RDJBE* 73–4.

I I

The Art of Compromise

Agreement by diplomacy implies compromise and compromise implies that you will get less than you think right. The alternative however is not to reach agreement, that is, to get nothing at all.[1]

The hard facts of the collapse of Russian Jewry in 1919 and the exigencies of political prudence and moderation compelled Wolf, acting as he did on behalf of Western European organisations, to ask for no more than ethical, religious and linguistic minority rights.[2]

Wolf may have desired that the Jews in Eastern Europe received everything for which Mowschowitch said they were striving. It was quite another matter, however, to assume that the Poles, the Romanians, and the rest would gracefully accept this challenge to their new-found or enlarged sovereignty, and unrealistic to hope that the Foreign Office would indeed back up such demands against the wishes of their East European 'clients'.

But before confronting these obstacles, Wolf had the much more parochial problem of persuading his own colleagues of the autonomy idea. British-based Jewish socialists had already clearly enunciated their positive appreciation of the autonomy idea, and as early as 1916 Wolf had striven to gain their support by, among other things, including national autonomy rights in his National Union manifesto.[3] He was cognizant, too, of the success of the Poalei Zion at the International Socialist Dutch–Scandinavian Committee in Stockholm in 1917. Poalei Zion's resolution for Jewish national–personal autonomy had been passed and assimilated into the committee's Peace Manifesto, for 'international application'.[4]

[1] A. J. P. Taylor, 'Old Diplomacy and New', in id., *Europe, Grandeur, and Decline*, Pelican edn. (London, 1967), 366.

[2] 'Wolf: A Memoir', in Roth, ed., *Essays*, 22.

[3] *JC* 28 Jan. 1916, reporting NUJR manifesto, point 2: 'To obtain "national rights" in the sense of communal and more especially educational autonomy whenever such rights may prove to be necessary.'

[4] Mowschowitch to Wolf, 21 Oct. 1917, C11/2/12, reporting Poalei Zion success as a 'great victory'; Poalei Zion declaration to Dutch–Scandinavian Committee 6 Aug. 1918, MWS 11417–33; see also Janowsky, *Jews and Minority Rights*, 197; Macartney, *National States*, 213–19.

Furthermore all the signs suggested that a mixture of Zionism and socialism would prevail at the American Jewish Congress when it finally met in December 1918, leading to the formal adoption of similar aspirations.[5]

Wolf, under Mowschowitch's guidance, had latched on early to the autonomy idea, but the communal establishment seems to have been a good deal slower in grasping its meaning or significance. In mid-1917, the *Jewish Chronicle* had dismissed national autonomy out of hand as an effort to undermine 'true' Palestine-orientated nationalism, while the joint Foreign Committee, Mowschowitch complained to Wolf in early 1918, was still prevaricating over the issue.[6] Indeed, Wolf's impassioned plea for Yiddish as the basis for East European Jewish existence, which was at the heart of his memorandum on the Polish Jewish question in September, was as much an attempt to convince his own committee as the Foreign Office, to whom it was ultimately addressed. Anglo-Jewry had scant sentimental regard for what they considered to be an uncultured jargon; they were embarrassed by it and bent their efforts to extirpate it as quickly as possible among East European Jewish immigrants. Wolf's 1906 efforts as editor of *The Jewish World* to increase its readership with the addition of a Yiddish supplement[7] may not have gone down well with the stricter adherents of this view.

To insist on the official recognition of Yiddish as the cornerstone of his Committee's peace conference agenda for the amelioration of the East European Jewish condition, Wolf had to move tactfully. Private letters to the committee chiefs, in an attempt to assuage their fears on the subject, thus preceded the formal submission of these proposals before the rest of the committee.[8] 'I do not think', he told Montefiore, 'that there is any danger of the Yiddish-speaking Jews ignoring Polish. What they want to do is to be able to use Yiddish as a medium of instruction in their schools but of course they will also teach Polish.' The overt emphasis on national rights diminished.

---

[5] On Jewish Workers' of America proposal to Dutch–Scandanavian Committee for national autonomy see *JC* 29 June 1917. See also Parkes, *Emergence*, 110–11.

[6] *JC* editorial, 29 June 1917; Mowschowitch to Wolf, 21 Mar. 1918, MWS 10471–5.

[7] See Chaim Bermant, *Troubled Eden: An Anatomy of British Jewry* (London, 1969), 56; Black, *Social Politics*, 110.

[8] Thus Wolf to Montefiore, 12 Sept. 1918, C11/4/1/(3), suggested that Montefiore, Samuel, and himself should confer 'to settle how much we are to tell them [the FC] about the Polish Jewish question as otherwise they may come to the wrong conclusion and may blame us for keeping them in the dark'.

What at all costs we ought to insist upon is that in the constitution of the new state, citizen rights shall be granted to all natives of Poland without any linguistic test or indeed any other test which under the guise of uniformity would exclude any specific religious communities, race or linguistic groups. If we get that we may safely leave the Polish Jews to fight their own battles as once they are full citizens they are sure to find other parties in the state and other sub-nationalities ready to act with them for purely party or sub-nationality ends.[9]

Sensing the need to find a formula which would at once appease those members of the committee who would object to Jewish non-integration in the state and yet at the same time satisfy the aspirations of Jewish autonomists, Wolf turned to Mowschowitch's conciliatory March suggestion which had referred only to cultural and religious self-administration.[10] 'All religious and cultural minorities', ran his December submission, 'should be secured in the autonomous management of their religious, educational, charitable and other cultural institutions.'[11]

The proposed clause was in many ways weak and vague. It failed to specify the degree to which schools and other institutions were to be subject to the general law of the state, or whether the state was obliged to support them.[12] The term 'national' had been studiously omitted, because, as he explained to Louis Marshall and Jacques Bigart, it would 'only lead to discussions and controversies among ourselves. The Jews of Eastern Europe will, I believe, be quite satisfied with the term "cultural" which they will be able to interpret as they please.'[13]

The vagueness also meant that it would be open to abuse should the new states choose to misapply it, but this was a chance Wolf felt compelled to take. What mattered was, firstly, that it could be accepted by a broad spectrum of 'political' Jewry, from Zionists to assimilationists, who might interpret it as they wished; and secondly, and following on from this, that it might be the basis for a realistic, unified Jewish programme at the peace conference.

By repeating the motions of his 1916 Palestine 'formula', by attempt-

[9] Wolf to Montefiore, 12 Sept. 1918, CII/4/I(3).

[10] Mowschowitch to Wolf, 21 Mar. 1918, MWS 10471–5.

[11] Wolf to Balfour, 2 Dec. 1918, FO 371/3419/199696.

[12] Criticisms voiced by Malkin, the FO legal adviser; see his memo on definition of a national autonomy, 26 Feb. 1919, FO 608/151/493/1/1.

[13] Wolf to Marshall, 28 Nov. 1918, CII/2/13; Wolf to Bigart, 29 Nov. 1918, AIU/ France ii D7.

ing to find consensus on the basis of the lowest common denominator, Wolf was again laying himself open to allegation and incrimination: from the Zionists for pusillanimity and betrayal, from the assimilation- ists for extremism and an irrevocable deviation from tradition. Cer- tainly in the ranks of the Joint Foreign Committee accepting the formula, there seems to have been little enthusiasm accompanying it. At the parley of Jewish delegations at Paris in April 1919, its approach was very low key indeed; Sir Stuart Samuel, for instance, used the opportunity to berate Jewish linguistic and actual segregation from the Poles and other nations and by contrast to extol the advantages of assimilation.[14]

If Wolf's committee colleagues were lukewarm (or perhaps more accurately, failed to comprehend his scheme), the Alliance approach ranged from apathetic to downright hostile. Without a Mowschowitch to help them along, their leaders seem to have confounded the national movement in Poland with Zionism; Wolf made little headway in Paris in explaining to them the difference.[15] In a sense this was strange as they were busy in early 1919 preparing *revendications* for Salonika Jewry for submission to the peace conference, which specifically in- cluded provisions for cultural and educational autonomy.[16]

But their response in this instance was purely pragmatic. The Salonika schools were mostly in their hands, and they wanted them to remain that way; the Greeks wanted to Hellenize them. Autonomy as such represented an obstacle to their encroachments. The Alliance, however, failed to apply these same pragmatic standards to the Polish Jewish situation, and at no stage evinced sympathy either for the concept of autonomy or for the perpetuation of the Yiddish language.[17] At best Wolf was only able to elicit a negative sort of concurrence for his plan:

[14] 'Abstract of Report of Meetings of Representatives of Jewish Organisations', 6 Apr. 1919, fo. 107, Adler papers, Peace Conference box., encl. Peace Conference Diary.

[15] For Wolf's efforts to convince Sée, Salomon Reinach, and others see his Paris Diary, 17 and 18 Jan. 1919, fos. 13, 20–1. The AIU's mental block is perhaps not altogether surprising given that the Zionists were both the most politically conspicuous Jewish group in Poland in early 1919 and pressing for full national autonomy; see Mendelsohn, *Zionism in Poland*, 91–5.

[16] AIU to Pichon, 12 Feb. 1919, AIU/France ii D7.

[17] For the official AIU statement, 6 June 1919, opposing national minority rights as creating dividing walls between Jews and their fellow citizens, see Alliance Israélite Universelle, *La Question juive devant la conférence de la paix* (Paris, 1919), 38.

Meyerson... agrees with me that if we allow the Polish Jewish nationalists to have their way, the national movement will soon disappear, whereas if we put obstacles in their way and frown on their scheme for national and linguistic autonomy we shall only martyrise them and the Polish-Jewish question will go on indefinitely.[18]

The perpetuation of the old partnership between Wolf's committee and the Alliance was therefore bought with a further attrition of his cultural programme, providing for the Polish language to be 'made an obligatory subject of instruction' in the Jewish schools.[19]

If the association with the Alliance proved to be an impediment to consensus with the other Jewish delegations who were to appear on the scene in Paris, this failure was balanced by the positive gains Wolf achieved in being able to sell his 'moderate' plans to the British delegation and in turn to the principal peacemakers.

The Allies were in late 1918 still seemingly committed to the Polish National Committee and hence to the creation of a large and vigorous Poland. They were reluctant to rock the boat, Wolf surmised, with schemes ostensibly undermining Polish sovereignty.[20] National–personal autonomy as Wolf described it in 'The Jewish National Movement' need not have represented an infringement of that sovereignty, but the British (at least in their *Daily Review of the Foreign Press*) seemed either unable or unwilling to endorse the distinction. Indeed, Wolf spent some considerable effort attempting to enlighten Colonel Wake, the *Review*'s head of Intelligence, on these points.[21]

The Foreign Office was tied up in knots on the problem. On the one hand, many of the more traditional diplomats wished to avoid the issue altogether. Not only was it without precedent, but it would also involve them in serious complications with newly created states. On the other, the more astute and knowledgeable planners in the Political Intelligence Department recognized that if the minorities issue was not tackled, the consequences for European peace and stability could be disastrous. This was not just a question of the Jews. A sovereign Poland, for instance, was likely to include, in addition to Jews, very substantial numbers of Germans, Ukrainians, Byelorussians, and Lithuanians.[22]

[18] Wolf to JFC presidents, 18 Jan. 1919, C11/2/14.

[19] Wolf to Dutasta, encl. JFC memorial, 21 Feb. 1919, *RDJBE* 77–8.

[20] Wolf to Mowschowitch, 29 Aug. 1918, MWS 10593–4.

[21] Wolf to Wake, 13 Aug. 1918, C11/4/1(3).

[22] Horak, *Poland*, 81, and Joseph Marcus, *Social and Political History of the Jews in Poland 1919–1939* (Berlin, 1983), 16–17, both refer to the 1926 census, which gives the ethnic mix in Poland as: Poles 69.2%, Ukrainians 14.3%, Jews 7.8%, Byelorussians and Germans, 3.9% each.

This situation would be replicated with different ethnic permutations in all the new or enlarged states of Eastern Europe. Britain was in a position to act as impartial mediator in these internal disputes. If they did not seize the initiative, Headlam-Morley grimly warned, others with a less disinterested policy, the Americans or even international labour, would do so.[23] The outcome of this internal debate did not favour the Political Intelligence Department approach. In November 1918, Lewis Namier, assisted by Arnold Toynbee, had presented his colleagues with a cogent if outspoken memorandum calling for a British declaration on Jewish National Rights.[24] This galvanized senior officials to convene to formulate their own peace conference guidelines on the Jewish question. Namier was not invited.

The meeting endorsed the Balfour Declaration, providing it in no way prejudiced the rights and political status of Jews outside Palestine. Similarly, it recognized the peacemakers' obligation to guarantee Jewish civil and political equality in the new states. Its response to the issue of national autonomy, however, was considerably more circumspect.

As regards the claim that the Jews where they form a considerable element in the population of a state should have special rights as a nationality, particularly rights of cultural or educational autonomy, it is clear that no British interests are at stake in this and that if any support or guarantee were given for such a claim it would be extremely difficult to enforce. His Majesty's Government should therefore not commit themselves to the recognition of any such claim either in principle or in particular cases.[25]

On this point the meeting agreed on a further proposal:

In all countries with Jewish inhabitants but especially in East and South East Europe where the Jews form a large and more separate element in the population than elsewhere, the spokesmen of this Jewish element, if they put forward demands for cultural autonomy as well as individual citizen rights, should be recommended in the first instance to discuss the question with the

[23] On FO deliberations on the Polish minorities subject see E. H. Carr memo, 14 Nov. 1918, FO 371/4353 (PID) PC 33/33, fos. 412–14 and J. Headlam-Morley memo, also 14 Nov. 1918, ibid., PC 23/23, fos. 1–4; also Alan Sharp, 'Britain and the Protection of Minorities at the Paris Peace Conference 1919', in A. C. Hepburn, ed., *Minorities in History* (London, 1978), 171–88.
[24] Namier–Toynbee memo on Jewish National Rights, 15 Nov. 1918, FO 371/3414/181911.
[25] Conference on the Jewish Question, 19 Nov. 1918, FO 371/3414/181911. Tyrrell, Howard, Crowe, Mallet, Paget, Ormsby-Gore, Carr, and Toynbee were present.

government or other representative parties of their respective countries. They should be discouraged from referring this question to outside Powers of the Peace Conference before they have done their utmost to arrive at a settlement with peoples among whom they respectively live.[26]

With national autonomy clearly beyond the scope of the government's brief, at least in so far as the recommendation of the Foreign Office was concerned, Wolf's chances of achieving even his limited 'cultural' programme looked remote. Indeed, the ministry response to his December proposals was not auspicious. Esmé Howard, who had been party to the guidelines, interpreted Wolf's proposal for educational autonomy as an invitation to develop revolutionary or anti-state propaganda. Neither Poland nor Romania should have to 'surrender any of their sovereign rights in the case of the Jews, even as far as education is concerned'. Though Eric Drummond disagreed and endorsed Wolf's programme to Balfour, Howard's position was bolstered by Wolf's old enemy, Crowe. 'All that we should demand', Crowe wrote, 'is that Jews should not be penalised *qua* Jews in the eyes of the law and for purposes of citizenship.'[27]

Nor from Wolf's point of view was the Foreign Office admonishment to negotiate with the respective parties in the new states likely to be much comfort. The same ministry had rejected his plan to work with the Zaleski people, and the hopelessness of attempting to come to an understanding with the alternative, the Polish National Committee, had precipitated his representatives to the government in the first place. However, knowing the government's predilection for a compromise settlement 'out of court', Wolf had continued to keep open his channels to the Poles. Swaythling and Henriques met again with Count Sobanski, the Polish National Committee delegate, in mid-November, this time accompanied by a non-committee man, Count Ostorog. Significantly, Tyrrell was also present for the Foreign Office. On this occasion, Sobanski was disposed to be more amenable on the question of Yiddish. After consideration, he agreed that 'it would be opportune to find the means of arriving at an *entente*'. Sobanski's offer had a sting in the tail, however. Reports of 'pogroms' in the English press were, on the eve of the peace conference, bringing the new Polish state into disrepute. This, said Sobanski, was a conscious effort;

---

[26] FO 371/3414/181911.
[27] Howard memo, 9 Dec., FO 371/3419/199696; Drummond to Balfour, 11 Dec. 1918, ibid.; Crowe minute, 11 Dec., ibid.

and though he did not mention Jews explicitly, the implication was clear. Jews were responsible for the reports, and Jews should and could stop them.[28]

The 'pogroms' were one symptom of what was happening all over Eastern Europe in October and November 1918. Austrian and German troops were pulling out. The fabric of the Austrian empire was in collapse, and this despite the last-ditch efforts of Emperor Karl to maintain unity by declaring it a federation of self-governing nations. The emerging states strove to impose their authority in the ensuing vacuum. The Romanians invaded Bessarabia and Transylvania, the Czechs Teschen, the Poles Silesia. The result was chaos and armed struggle.[29] This was particularly the case in Eastern Galicia, an area bitterly disputed between Poles and Ukrainians. The Jews, in the middle of it, declared themselves 'neutrals' with their own national council but the Poles entering Lemberg carried out pogroms all the same, claiming that the Jews had sided with the Ukrainians. The pattern of Jewish national councils developed everywhere where the Jews were caught out in this way, even in Transylvania, where the Jews were traditionally proud of their standing as *Israelitisch Magyars*.[30]

The dismantling of the Austro-Hungarian Empire and the superimposition, with or without international recognition, of new states as accomplished fact, ended Wolf's cherished ideal of an Eastern Europe arranged on Springer's principle. Paradoxically, however, the resulting turmoil served to strengthen Wolf's hand *vis-à-vis* the Foreign Office as they were now forced to recognize the risks inherent in letting the rampant nationalism of Poles, Czechs, or whoever, go unheeded by themselves.

This was in spite of the ministry's reading of the situation. Based on the reports of *The Times* correspondent and the Inter-Allied Military Mission which had made its way across war-torn Europe to Warsaw in December, the Foreign Office was inclined to minimize the extent of the outbreaks in either Eastern Galicia or Poland.[31] Sobanski's explanation, moreover, that the whole thing was a press plot fabricated by the enemies of Poland—Germans, Ukrainians, Bolsheviks, and

[28] JFC–PNC negotiations, 17 Nov. 1918, MWS 16267–8; Sobanski to Swaythling (copy), 30 Nov. 1918, FO 371/3281/101651.

[29] See *CHP* ii. 478; Seton-Watson, *Rumanians*, 528–9.

[30] Janowsky, *Jews and Minority Rights*, 275; Mendelsohn, *Zionism in Poland*, 95–7.

[31] *The Times* report, 4 Dec. 1918, and Col. Wake's report, 23 Jan. 1919, both enclosed in FO 371/3903/529.

Jews—for public consumption in the West,[32] was generally accepted as accurate. One official minuted, 'the Jews are determined to do everything in their power to prevent the foundation of a great and independent Poland'. Another eagerly pursued, 'there is I fear some justification for the suggestion that the Jews are the backbone of Bolshevism'.[33] Lewis Namier's counter-arguments, based on his own review of the foreign press and leading him to the consistent conclusion that the reports of anti-Jewish pogroms were indeed accurate, represented a strictly minority view.[34]

To this day, the extent or cause of the Polish pogroms has been a subject of heated controversy.[35] One thing though is certain; public opinion in the West was aroused to a pitch of moral indignation,[36] and the British government and its allies were unable to ignore it. Under this sort of pressure, Balfour on 14 November issued a statement to the press intended as a clear and unequivocal warning to the Poles and to the other new states to quell the disorders or suffer the consequences of Allied displeasure.

The Allies and the United States stand ready to lend their whole resources to the work of restoring the economic bases of orderly and civilised life to those countries, but to those countries alone which show by their acts that they desire order and civilisation. If any of the peoples of Central Europe give rein to the appetite for disorder, the Western democracies will be unable to do anything to promote their reconstruction.[37]

Balfour's rhetoric was, moreover, translated into more tangible action. A British military mission under Colonel H. H. Wade was already in Poland. Now the Foreign Office, albeit reluctantly, charged Esmé Howard with the task of leading a mission of enquiry to scrutin-

---

[32] Sobanski to Swaythling (copy), 30 Nov. 1918, FO 371/3281/101651; Sobanski to Gregory, 26 Jan. 1919, FO 371/3903/529.

[33] Kidston minute, 5 Dec. 1918, FO 371/3419/198168; unnamed official, 7 Jan. 1919, FO 371/3903/529.

[34] Namier's memo, 14 Mar. 1919, FO 371/3903/529, takes the Inter-Allied Mission to task for pro-Polish bias. It was not until later in the summer of 1919 that Namier's assertion that it was the Polish press that were involved in a 'conspiracy of silence' not to report the truth of the pogroms began to gain more credence in government circles. See Norman Davies, 'Great Britain and the Polish Jews, 1918–1920', *Journal of Contemporary History*, 8 (1973), 119–42.

[35] For a fuller discussion of the issue see Davies, 'Great Britain'.

[36] See Davies, 'Great Britain', 127, on Israel Cohen's reports in the *Manchester Guardian*, 30 Nov. and *JC* 6 Dec. 1918 claiming 1,100 Jewish dead in Lemberg.

[37] For JFC report at BD referring to Balfour's statement see *JC* 27 Nov. 1918.

ize and report on the causes of the Polish–Jewish dispute.[38] Despite the strictures of the Foreign Office's November guidelines, the government was thus being dragged into a re-examination of the national autonomy issue. Wolf found himself in a position where he could associate himself not only with this concern but also with the government's desire to find a settlement which would be equitable to all parties.

The Polish National Committee still represented an obstacle to this, Wolf feeling compelled in December to refuse Sobanski's proposal for a resumption of negotiations until it had publicly disavowed the boycott and the pogroms and taken public steps to counsel the Poles to friendly relations with the Jews.[39] But the situation was being made more flexible by dint of the fact that the committee, while recognized abroad, was not in control at home. The real power there was Josef Pilsudski, released by the Germans from the Magdeburg prison in November, and his government, though containing a few National Democrats, was overwhelmingly socialist.[40] True, Pilsudski had not been able to halt the disturbances, but he had explicitly stated his desire to dismantle restrictions based on origin or creed. Zaleski, meanwhile, now Pilsudski's agent as chairman of the Polish Representative Council in Berne, telegraphed to Wolf that the excesses in Galicia were caused by economic rather than political factors. Pilsudski, he added, would stop them.[41] Wolf, who implicitly trusted Zaleski, was reassured. He wrote to Marshall, 'the new government in Warsaw are, I believe, doing their best to help us.'[42] Though information Wolf later received suggested that Zaleski's complacency on the pogroms was misplaced, Wolf was cautious before joining the chorus of protests to the Foreign Office.[43] Moreover, the new government's apparent willingness to be helpful seemed to be confirmed when they invited the Joint Foreign Committee to send its own representative to assist them

[38] Gregory minute, 27 Nov. 1918, FO 371/3281/101651.
[39] Wolf to Marshall, 19 Dec. 1918, MWS 19891–2; JFC minutes, 3 Dec. 1918.
[40] MWS 24901–47, Mowschowitch, 'Notes on the Diplomatic History of the Jewish Question'; *CHP* ii. 478.
[41] Mowschowitch, 'Notes', MWS 24901–47; telegram from Zaleski encl. with Wolf to Carr, 27 Nov. 1918, FO 371/3281/101651 (also published in *JC* 29 Nov. 1918).
[42] Wolf to Marshall, 19 Dec. 1918, MWS 19891–2.
[43] See Wolf to FO, 6 Jan. 1919, FO 371/3903/529. This was despite the fact that Wolf continued to send the FO regular reports of pogrom-inciting material. I disagree, however, with Norman Davies, 'Great Britain', 139, which suggests the JFC competed with the EZF on this issue as part of their contest for leadership of the Anglo-Jewish community; Wolf's aim was to conciliate the Poles, not incite them.

in their pogrom investigations.[44] But the picture did not altogether change to Wolf's advantage. The Foreign Office were far from enthusiastic about the committee's choice of Joseph Prag to go to Poland, fearing, apparently on information received from Ignacy Paderewski, the new premier and minister of foreign affairs under Pilsudski, that Prag would spread Bolshevik propaganda. They refused to facilitate his journey.[45]

Nor was the danger *vis-à-vis* the Poles themselves yet passed. Paderewski had formerly been aligned to the Polish National Committee; indeed, back in 1917 he had, on their behalf, converted President Wilson to the Polish cause. Now, in January 1919, he was able to get Pilsudski and Dmowski to relent their mutual antagonism and pool resources for the peace conference. Thus the interlude in which Wolf hoped he would be able to dispense with the National Committee was a brief one. Instead, he was forced to take stock of the fact that with Dmowski now as number two to Paderewski in the Polish peace conference delegation, he and his acolytes would still be well placed to sabotage everything.[46]

This was of crucial significance to Wolf. He had in December 1918 received his mandate from the Joint Foreign Committee to act as their sole spokesman in Paris until such time as a full delegation could be mustered.[47] This meant that all negotiations would be dependent entirely on his acumen and judgement. Success or failure, in other words, would rest very much on his shoulders. The testing ground was clearly Poland. And Poland, given that Russia would not come within the scope of settlement, had the largest Jewish population of all the areas whose future was to be determined by the peacemakers. The terms of reference which the Poles accepted in relation to that population would hence be the model for the other new or transformed sovereign entities of Central–Eastern Europe represented in Paris.

Wolf, once in Paris in January 1919, was therefore fortunate inasmuch as the gap preventing his collaboration with the Foreign Office and accommodation with the Poles narrowed, if albeit imperceptibly.

---

[44] For Filipowicz (Polish under-secretary of state) invitation, 8 Dec. 1918, see JFC minutes, 17 Dec. 1918; see also Wolf to Mowschowitch, 20 Dec. 1918, MWS 10672.

[45] Memo of interview with Paderewski encl. with Wade to FO, 27 Jan. 1919, FO 371/3903/529; FO to Wolf, 26 Feb. 1919, ibid.

[46] See George J. Lerski, 'Dmowski, Paderewski and American Jews', *Polin*, 2 (1987), 95–116; J. Bradley, *Allied Intervention in Russia* (London, 1968), 186–8; *CHP* ii. 472.

[47] JFC presidents' instructions, 13 Dec. 1918, C11/4/2.

For instance, through Tyrrell, who had been placed in charge of the British delegation's arrangements, he was able to have Esmé Howard, at that time investigating the situation in Poland as part of an inter-Allied mission of enquiry, ascertain for the Joint Foreign Committee the views of representative Polish Jewish bodies. These, said Wolf, could then be placed before the peace conference.[48] The move was a shrewd one. The Foreign Office already knew what autonomy plans Wolf had proposed but he, in return, had no knowledge of their appreciation of them.

While Wolf waited for the replies, he attempted to probe the views of the delegation itself. William Ormsby-Gore was in Paris primarily to help expedite a smooth international recognition of the British–Zionist understanding over Palestine. He was believed to be sympathetic to Jewish aspirations, and Wolf seems to have used this opportunity to put forward to him a comprehensive case for autonomy as presented two years earlier in 'The Jewish National Movement'. The Jews, Wolf told him, in an interview on 12 February, would want full national and cultural rights on a par with other minorities.[49] Wolf himself strongly supported these demands, though he was aware that the problem before the peace conference was how to secure these 'without endangering the political solidarity of the Polish state'.[50] He proposed this could be done, not just in Poland, but throughout the new states, by adopting the Ukrainian constitution as model.

An enlightened Ormsby-Gore repeated to Mallet what he had been told.

It would seem that the Jews in Ukrainia are self-governing in all matters of education etc., and that there is a Jewish representative body which in fact administers all Jews. The connecting link between this body and the Ukrainian government is a Jewish Minister for Jewish Affairs appointed by the Ukrainian government and a member of its cabinet. The Jews have home-rule in Ukrainia not on a territorial but a personal basis.[51]

Gore continued:

I gathered that he contemplated no difficulty in extending very widely the powers granted to these bodies representative of National Minorities. These

---

[48] Wolf to Tyrrell, 21 Jan. 1919, FO 608/66/131/1/1.
[49] Ormsby-Gore to Mallet, 15 Feb. 1919, FO 608/151/493/1/1; Wolf put forward similar 'maximum' proposals to A. W. A. Leeper a few days later; see Wolf, Paris Diary, 18 Feb. 1918, fos 66–7.
[50] Wolf, Paris Diary, 18 Feb. 1918, fos 66–7.
[51] Ormsby-Gore to Mallet, 15 Feb. 1919, FO 608/151/493/1/1.

bodies would as it were administer their constituents on behalf of the central government of the state in which they dwell.[52]

Here was Wolf being much more forthright and specific about national autonomy than he had dared to be in his official representations. In turn, Ormsby-Gore not only grasped what national autonomy was, but in letters to his superiors heartily endorsed it as a model suitable for application.[53] However, with his task on Palestine completed in February, Ormsby-Gore returned to London. Concurrently, Mowschowitch, who was due to join Wolf's secretariat in Paris, ran into visa difficulties and postponed his voyage out. The two men who might well have kept Wolf on his autonomy tack were not there in the vital months to help him through.[54]

But this is to speculate unnecessarily. By March, Wolf was much clearer on what the British and indeed the Allied attitude in general was to national minority rights, and saw that this did not tally with Ormsby-Gore's positive approach. His new source of information was James Headlam-Morley, the official who more than any other was to guide him through the intricacies of the peacemaking process. In a later official history of the conference, Headlam-Morley delineated what the peacemakers' approach was to the issue:

The recognition of national rights of the Jews of Poland would have been completely inconsistent with the territorial sovereignty of the state, which is the basis of our whole political system. The view taken by the British delegation throughout and supported by the Plenipotentiaries was that if there was to be a Jewish Nationality it could only be by giving the Jews a local habitat and enabling them to found in Palestine a Jewish state. Any Jew who was however a national of the Jewish state would naturally *ipso facto* cease to be a Polish citizen.[55]

This refusal to deviate from the traditional conception of the nation-state seemed to make a mockery of Wolf's efforts to draw out the finer

[52] Ormsby-Gore to Mallet, 15 Feb. 1919, FO 608/151/493/1/1.
[53] Ormsby-Gore to Tyrrell, 13 Feb. 1919, FO 608/48/98/2/1.
[54] Mowschowitch to Wolf, 14 Dec. 1918, MWS 10700. Mowschowitch to Wolf, 20 Dec. 1918, MWS 10704. A third positive influence for national rights might have been Lewis Namier. It has been suggested by Julia Namier, however, that Dmowski's intrigues were responsible for his absence from Paris; see Namier, *Namier*, 141–2.
[55] H. W. V. Temperley, *A History of the Paris Peace Conference*, v (London, 1921), 137. The citation is from a chapter entitled 'Treaties for the Protection of Minorities' which was in fact written by Headlam-Morley.

distinctions between national–personal and national–political auto-nomy. Underlying this semantic inflexibility, however, there lay a more pragmatic reasoning.

In enlarging or creating altogether new states in Eastern Europe, the Western Allies hoped to produce strong, unified entities capable of resisting the twin threats of a revivified Germany and Bolshevik Russia. To encourage local 'minority' nationalism was, according to this logic, to undermine the cohesion of the state. As Lord Hardinge noted in June, 'the question of local autonomies is being overdone. The creation is only likely to make for trouble in the future. Freedom of language and religion is all that should be assured by treaty to minorities.'[56]

The peacemakers feared that to give substance to the national exist-ence of ethnic minorities—and they particularly had in mind German-speakers in Poland and Czechoslovakia—would provide sufficient grounds for Germany's post-war interference in and disaffection of those states. The threat of irredentism posed in this way could not of course be levelled against the Jews of Eastern Europe. Nevertheless, Jewish national demands were perceived as being equally menacing for quite different reasons. This lay in the popular equation of Jew and Bolshevik,[57] an equation which was endemic at the very juncture at which Bolshevism undoubtedly did present a serious political and military threat to Eastern and Central Europe. The equation, if Wolf himself is to be believed, was being given added credence by Weiz-mann. 'If the hopes of the Zionists were not realised,' he is reported to have warned, 'all the Jews in Poland would go over to Bolshevism and the result would be that the policies of the Allies in Eastern Europe would crumble to pieces.'[58]

Certainly from the British point of view, the possibility of a Bolshevik–Jewish nationalist conjunction, conscious or otherwise, seemed to be given substance by the behaviour of the Zionists themselves. In October 1918, their Copenhagen Bureau, in response to the creation of Jewish national councils all over Eastern Europe, used the occasion to issue a manifesto calling for Jewish 'national' representation at the League of Nations.[59] When in March the following year Zionists gathered for a

[56] Hardinge minute, n.d., c.5 June 1919, FO 608/151/493/1/1.
[57] See Poliakov, *History of Anti-Semitism*, iv. 180–6. Kadish, 'Bolsheviks', 7–20.
[58] Wolf, Paris Diary, 25 Mar. 1919, reporting a conversation between Weizmann and Wormser of the French Consistoire.
[59] Janowsky, *Jews and Minority Rights*, 273; Parkes, *Emergence*, 110–11.

congress in London, the manifesto received endorsement when Motz-kin proposed and had unanimously passed a resolution calling for Jews in new states to be recognized as a 'national' community with rights of a 'cultural, administrative and political nature', to be granted 'in such measure as these rights are demanded by the local Jewish National Council'. A further clause elucidated the Copenhagen manifesto: 'the Peace Conference shall recognise the Jewish Nation as a member of the League of Nations and admit to its councils such representatives as are appointed by the Jewish World Congress'.[60]

Such proposals were clearly far beyond anything the peace confer-ence would or could offer, and were received by the Foreign Office with a bewilderment which seemed to endorse Wolf's much earlier predictions that the proposals were a recipe for European Jewish disaster; as Toynbee remarked with understatement, recognition of 'a Jewish World Council' as a sovereign government 'would create con-siderable difficulties for all states with a Jewish element in their popula-tion and especially for the mandatory power in Palestine'. A. W. A. Leeper agreed. 'Are Polish, Rumanian and Salonika Jews to be allowed the rights of both local and foreign citizenship?'[61]

As for the obvious Zionist aspiration to increase Jewish national consciousness, for instance by giving Jews control of their own schools, even a sympathetic observer such as Headlam-Morley could not fail to conceal his fear that this would be to incite Jewish opposition to the state. 'There is a real danger', he argued in June, 'that if these schools are placed under Jewish management, the more extreme nationalist elements may use the schools . . . in such a way as to increase the separation which the use of their language produces between the Jew and other citizens of Poland.'[62]

On the other side of the coin, the Foreign Office recognized that to achieve internal peace and stability in Poland, a solution or at least diminution of the Jewish question would still have to be sought. Negotiations between the Poles and the Zionists were clearly a non-starter. Yet negotiations with a view to settlement had to be attained.

Again, Wolf's hand was strengthened. His scheme was non-

[60] Zionist Org. communiqué, 6 Mar. 1919, encl. with Ormsby-Gore to Toynbee, 14 Mar. 1919. FO 608/103/2/2.
[61] Toynbee minute, 17 Mar. 1919, FO 608/103/2/2; A. W. A. Leeper minute, 17 Mar. 1919, FO 608/103/2/3.
[62] Headlam-Morley to Hankey, 23 June 1919, in Headlam-Morley, *A Memoir*, 188–9.

political, moderate, and had the unique merit of being potentially acceptable to the Poles. Moreover, without prompting, Wolf had resumed negotiations with them. On 5 March he met again with Count Ostorog who was this time accompanied by Pilz and Kojicki, two high-ranking Polish delegates who were both associated with the Polish National Committee.[63] Exchanges at the meeting were initially icy. Neither Pilz nor Kojicki was a friend of the Jews.[64] Ostorog, moreover, raised objections to Wolf's cultural clause, which the latter smartly parried with the assurance that his committee would set itself against any Polish Jewish separatist tendencies. Indeed, said Wolf, they would advise their co-religionists 'to publicly identify themselves in all secular matters with their Polish fellow-citizens'. The Poles thus appeased, obstacles to a frank exchange of views began to evaporate. The Poles admitted that there was a Jewish problem in their country, Wolf proffering the suggestion that a compromise might be reached. This again raised the issue of the cultural scheme which, Wolf said, could be made acceptable by making the teaching of Polish language obligatory in the schools. No, said the Poles; the scheme would nevertheless retain its primary emphasis on Yiddish, which would simply lead to national–political separation.

Wolf was losing ground, even on the one essential point of his programme—the schools. In a desperate bid to accommodate the Polish diplomats Wolf pointed out that Jewish schools existed in Britain in the same form as non-conformist schools, subject to state supervision and curricula, and that the same formula could be applied in Poland. If the government in Britain were responsible for a Jewish community like that in Poland, the moderate concessions asked for in his scheme would, he said, be tolerated. Whether this in fact was likely is debatable. No Western state looked sympathetically on their own minorities' languages, and it is doubtful whether Britain could have accepted a system of Jewish schools with Yiddish as its language of instruction. Moreover, Wolf was engaging in double-think in knowing full well that one of the aims of the Jewish schools in Britain was to de-Yiddishize newly arrived Jewish immigrants as quickly as possible. Nevertheless, the Poles had shown interest in what Wolf had told

[63] Wolf, Paris Diary, 5 Mar. 1919, fos 105–12.
[64] On Kojicki, secretary-general to the Polish delegation at the peace conference, see Davies, 'Poles', 73. For further references to the 5 Mar. meeting see also Black, 'Lucien Wolf', 18–19.

them, and he promised to have Henriques draw up a memorandum delineating what exactly the situation was in Britain.[65] Communication between the two parties continued. Wolf thus gained a breathing space in which to take stock. It was self-evident that the Poles were not going to accept anything like the maximum Zionist–nationalist demands;[66] it was just possible, however, that they might acquiesce in school 'privileges', and that some sort of *modus vivendi* might be hammered out on this basis. This complemented exactly an evolving British view.

After some months of debate within the confines of the Foreign Office and British delegation, support for Jewish and other minorities' self-administration in schools and other cultural institutions, provided it was under the general aegis of the state, was the one aspect which most officials agreed ought to be applied to Poland.

The Jewish claim, when analysed, wrote Headlam-Morley in late March, 'comes down to this, they are for their own schools and full religious freedom, it is no more than the Roman Catholics ask for in England'.[67] A former school inspector, Headlam-Morley was confident that the arrangement by which non-conformist schools in Britain were tied to the general educational system could be applied in kind in Poland.

Esmé Howard, himself a Roman Catholic, spent some months collecting material on the subject in Poland and arrived at similar conclusions. The proposals he finally sent on, in April 1919, put special emphasis on the wishes of orthodox Jewry whom, he thought, 'it would not be difficult to satisfy . . . by adopting a system of confessional schools with state support and under state control, something like that which exists in England'. The Poles, he agreed, would be strongly opposed to separate curricula or the use of Yiddish, but this could be got round by granting its use in primary schools only and by assimilating the confessional schools curricula to those outside.[68]

The British, it seemed, were therefore willing to press for about as much on the question of Jewish cultural rights as they believed the

[65] This was the Henriques memo, 'Jews and Education in England', n.d., Mar. 1919, C11/2/14.
[66] The Polish rejection of Jewish 'maximalist' demands was reiterated by Ostorog in a further meeting with the JFC. See Wolf, Paris Diary, 17 Apr. 1919, fos. 197–200.
[67] Headlam-Morley minute, 22 Mar. 1919, FO 608/66/131/1/1.
[68] Esmé Howard report on the Polish Jewish question, 2 Apr. 1919, FO 371/3903/529.

Poles would grudgingly accept. If this included hedging on the use of Yiddish in schools (and Headlam-Morley, whose idiosyncratic view of the language as too inferior to warrant its use in higher institutions led him to be intractable on this score)[69] Wolf would simply have to comply.

But Wolf by now had his own reasons for siding quite openly with the British delegates' overview. He had come to Paris on the assumption that it would be he and the other traditional Western Jewish organizations who would be negotiating on behalf of their Eastern co-religionists. The arrival of Eastern delegates put into question his right to do this, especially as he had no direct mandate from the Eastern Jews themselves. Even then, an arrangement between himself and these delegations might still have been possible if he could have been satisfied that they were in fact the elected representatives of Eastern Jewry. But the organization that came to coalesce at the end of March as the Comité des Delegations Juives, contained neither Bundists, nor Folkists, nor orthodox Jews, nor any of the other groups Wolf would have expected to find represented in it.[70] It was overwhelmingly a contingent of Zionists.

Given that the Jewish elections in Russia prior to and just after the Bolshevik takeover had returned a majority of Zionists, Wolf might well have felt precariously placed to challenge their supremacy within the Comité. His communication, in November 1918, with Rosov, the Zionist representing the Russian Jewish National Council, seemed to be an acknowledgement of this reality. Certainly it seemed to deprioritize his relationship to Reuben Blank—much to the latter's mortification—on behalf of the alternative though considerably weakened Folksgruppe.[71]

Wolf quickly came to the conclusion that the Zionist delegates, far from representing Eastern Jewry, represented nobody but themselves. His doubts received endorsement from elsewhere. A committee

---

[69] Headlam-Morley memo, 11 Mar. 1919, FO 608/151/493/1/1. Cf. E. H. Carr memo, 14 Mar. 1919, FO 608/12/9/4/5, which pointed out that whether Yiddish was a debased form of German was totally irrelevant to the question at hand. It was Headlam-Morley's view, however, which prevailed in the actual Minority Treaty.

[70] The Comité des Délégations officially came into existence on 25 Mar. 1919; see Janowsky, *Jews and Minority Rights*, 309. Israel Cohen, *My Mission to Poland, 1918–1939* (New York, 1951), 18 Jan. 1919, notes Folkist complaints that the Polish Jewish National Council only represented the Zionists. In this regard see Mendelsohn, *Zionism in Poland*, 91–5, on the failure to set up an All-Polish Jewish Conference.

[71] Blank to Wolf, 30 Nov. 1918, MWS 1998–9.

representing Eastern Jewry domiciled in Paris, including the bacteri-
ologist Vladimir Haffkine, the lawyer Tchernov, and Baron Vladimir
Gunzburg, complained in early April to the American Jewish delegation
that all the Russian Jews on the Comité were Zionists.[72] This was not,
they said, to suppose there were no alternative non-Zionist delegates,
simply that these had as yet not been able to reach Paris. Certainly, the
fact that a three-man orthodox delegation from Poland did not arrive till
May 1919 lent plausibility to this argument. As for the Haffkine group,
it persistently refused to be fully absorbed into the Comité des Délégations, remaining in close touch with Wolf and the Alliance and producing
its own memorial which, despite the inclusion of the word 'national',
was moderate enough for Wolf to consider as an acceptable alternative
to his own peace conference submission.[73]

Meanwhile the Haffkine group's allegations as to the Comité's
unrepresentativeness seemed to be reinforced by the orthodox Jewish
delegation's claim to have been elected by six hundred delegates,
themselves appointed from four hundred individual congregations. By
contrast, the Polish Jewish National Council, they assured Wolf, had
been self-elected. More importantly, the autonomy proposals which
the orthodox delegates put forward to him, Wolf accurately characterized as 'the same as our own', neither asking for nor objecting to
national rights.[74]

The problem, however, even laying aside the question of represen-
tativeness (which as we shall see later became a dispute in itself), was
that the arrival of the orthodox delegates came too late to challenge the
primacy of the Zionists of the Comité des Délégations. Wolf recognized the need to come to some sort of *modus vivendi* with the Comité,
but also knew that the chances of achieving this were slim so long as
they stuck to their ideological demands for national–political autonomy. In other words, he recognized that the only way they might be

[72] Adler–Haffkine interview, 3 Apr. 1919, fo. 13, Adler Peace Diary, AJC.

[73] For a memo by the Comité des Juifs de Paris Descendants de l'Europe Orientale
see ibid., fos. 306–11. The autonomy proposal ran: 'Que des diverses minorités ethniques
ou religeuses jouissant de l'autonomie dans l'organisation et l'administration de leurs
institutions communales, regionales ou nationales . . .' For how Wolf presented the
proposal to the American Jews and Herbert Bentwich as a compromise with the Zionists
see Wolf, Paris Diary, 30 Mar. 1919, fo. 148.

[74] On Wolf's interview with the three Szlome Emoune Israel delegates (Avrach,
Rosenfeld, and Kaminer) see Wolf, Paris Diary, 11 May 1919, fos. 41–2. Their peace
conference submission (see AIU/France ii d 10, 12 May 1919) shows their proposals in
all major respects identical with Wolf's.

able to accommodate themselves to the requirements of the peacemakers was to relinquish the Copenhagen programme.

Nahum Sokolow, who was in charge of the Zionist caucus in Paris
prior to the Comité's formation and had a major hand in its creation,
seems, with his wide diplomatic experience, particularly in the negotiations leading to the Balfour Declaration, to have had some inkling
of this. At the conference of all the Jewish delegations including the
Comité, the Joint Foreign Committee, and the Alliance at the Consistoire (the representative body of French Jewry) on 5 and 6 April, he
was initially inclined to emphasize the cultural rather than political
aspects of nationality. Claude Montefiore, speaking soon after, commented that his speech was a staging post to consensus.[75] The
speeches which followed, however, completely unbalanced this impression of moderation. Rabbi Thon of Cracow, Menachem Ussishkin,
Leo Motzkin, and others were all uncompromising in their demands,
which together amounted to a national Jewish parliament elected by
the Jewish communities of each state, representation of each in a
World Jewish Congress, and admission of the Jewish nation to the
League of Nations.[76] Moreover, if Wolf and his associates hoped
Sokolow might still be able to steer his colleagues towards a more
sober approach, this was rudely shattered on the second day when
Sokolow recanted on his earlier conciliatory stance and endorsed
Ussishkin. The conference came to an abrupt close.[77]

Wolf's main contribution to these proceedings had been to attempt
to inject a note of realism. It was all very well, he noted on the second
day, for 14 per cent of the new Polish state to say 'divorçons' (Sokolow
in his later rejectionist speech seems to have consciously used the
French word for effect), but it was neither fair nor prudent, especially
as the peace conference had espoused the Polish cause as a great one.
If the Comité's proposals for special privileges in excess of those
granted to other minorities were pursued—and by this Wolf included
Sokolow's suggestions for electoral *curiae*—he categorically warned
that the Western Jews could not and would not remain silent.[78]

[75] 'Abstract of Report', see Adler Peace Diary: Sokolow, fos. 92–3; Montefiore, fos.
96–7. For a full discussion of the conference see Janowsky, *Jews and Minority Rights*,
299–308.
[76] 'Abstract of Report', Adler Peace Diary, fos. 94–5, 109–10.
[77] Ibid. 114–15. Sokolow claimed that the Thon–Ussishkin approach was not
'hidden' in his first address, in which he had avoided use of the term 'national', but
implicit in it. In his second address he explicitly used the word 'national'.
[78] Ibid. 111–12.

Wolf's warning seemed to be provoking a split between the Zionists and non-Zionists on 1917 lines. But while in 1917 Wolf had felt compelled to do this as a defensive measure, which was to his own immediate disadvantage, the situation in 1918 was reversed. Daily, he was becoming more and more confident that the intransigence of the Zionists would induce the British to adopt his own more moderate proposals. Interviewed on 18 March by H. J. Paton, one of their experts on Polish affairs, Wolf took the occasion to impress upon him 'that the success of our negotiations [with the Poles] depends upon the degree of support we might get from the Allied governments against the extreme demands of the Zionists'.[79]

What Wolf seems to have had in mind was an unwritten alliance in which he would square the Poles, and the British delegation would order the Zionists into line. E. H. Carr noted, the day after the Wolf–Pilz–Kojicki interview, that Wolf feared that any arrangement between them 'would be too much of a compromise to be acceptable to the Zionists and that our good offices with the Zionists would be necessary to prevent them opposing it'. Carr by way of commentary added, 'Mr. Wolf and his friends are evidently using the extreme claims of the Zionists to induce the Poles to accept his own comparatively moderate proposals but I doubt how far such arguments will carry weight with the Poles.'[80]

The British delegation clearly did not want to become involved in another internecine Jewish dispute. On the other hand, they clearly understood that a settlement enabling the Jews to become dutiful and contented citizens of the new states was imperative. The conundrum was how to avoid the national–political status demanded by the Zionists. Wolf was willing to be the British delegation's tool. Noted one official:

The widespread movement among Jewish extremists to secure from the Peace Conference a recognition of special national privileged status is being combatted, apparently successfully, by Dr. Lucien Wolff [sic] and the organisations which he represents who only wish for equal civil, educational and religious rights with other minorities religious or racial.[81]

British and 'liberal' Jewish interests as represented by Wolf were in fact converging. On 14 April he was interviewed by Headlam-Morley,

[79] Wolf, Paris Diary, 19 May 1919, fo. 122.
[80] E. H. Carr minute, 6 Mar. 1919, FO 608/151/493/1/1.
[81] E. G. F. Adam minute, 5 Apr. 1919, FO 608/48/98/2/1.

who offered to assist in overcoming the Polish *impasse*. Dmowski and
the Polish National Committee were, he told Wolf, in decline. By contrast, Paderewski was in the ascendant and moving more and more
towards moderation. Wolf should, said Headlam-Morley, meet him.
Wolf agreed, on the stipulation that Paderewski should know that it
was at the British behest. Headlam-Morley concurred.[82]

The meeting with Paderewski a week later on 23 April marked the
zenith of Wolf's Polish negotiations. Both men agreed on the advantages
of reconciliation and assimilation; the problem was whether equal
rights in the new state would be enough to achieve this. Paderewski
insisted that no more could be offered, to which Wolf interjected that
such a regime could only work if it were administered with scrupulous
firmness, protecting Jewish interests as a religious and cultural minority
and preventing the power of the majority from limiting 'their rightful
share in the political work of the country'.[83]

Wolf set down concessions to the Jews which he said would help
achieve this goal. Firstly, a Conspiracy Act in the Polish diet which
would outlaw the economic boycott. Next, a further act which would
favour religious and cultural institutions with 'the educational question
being treated on the same lines as in England'. Thirdly, Sunday trading
should be dealt with in the spirit of British legislation and practice.
Finally, the electoral and municipal laws should be framed to give the
Jews 'as near as possible' proportional representation. Wolf stressed
to Paderewski that these concessions would meet all the legitimate
aspirations of the Jews, though they did not constitute privileges and
they 'would have the great advantage of bringing Poland nearer the
liberal tradition of English governance'. In conclusion, Wolf offered
Paderewski the opportunity to lead Poland in a truly liberal direction.

Were these concessions offered by the Chief of the Polish state, in a spirit of
generous spontaneity, they would be recognised throughout the world as an act
of high reconstructive statesmanship and would enlist every effort Jewish and
Christian alike, to consolidate the work of reconstruction and to assure the
stable evolution of a regenerated Poland.[84]

Paderewski responded in kind to this liberal sentiment, and Wolf
euphorically noted in his diary that not only was he much nearer to his

[82] Wolf, Paris Diary, 14 Apr. 1919, fo. 189.
[83] Ibid., 23 Apr. 1919, fo. 211; Wolf, 'Note Verbale' on interview with Paderewski, 23
Apr. 1919, MWS 16403-4.
[84] Wolf, Paris Diary, 23 Apr. 1919, fo. 211.

own view of the question 'than any other Pole I have come across', but also was proving his sincerity by associating the liberal-minded August Zaleski in his most confidential political work.[85]

The situation was delicately poised. Wolf had found his Polish statesman; the problem was to keep him there. The Zionists, he reasoned, still had the capability to undermine his position by continuing to present extreme claims; 'should we render his tenure of office impossible the result would only be that we should open the door for anti-semitic extremists like Dmowski to seize power.'[86]

The next day, 23 April, a conference of Jewish moderates—Wolf, Bigart, and the Americans Henry Morgenthau and Isaac Landman— met and endorsed this view. Wolf had already frankly stated to Paderewski that his proposals were intended to deprive the 'Jewish national movement' of its *raison d'être*. Now Wolf flatly expounded that, given the Zionist terms of reference, electoral *curiae*, legislative councils, League of Nations membership, and the rest, his delegation could no longer give support to any minority clause which referred to the Jews as a 'nationality'. Wolf's only proviso was that he would not actively oppose any Zionist *démarche*.[87]

Wolf had come full circle in the quest for national minority rights. Galvanized by Mowschowitch in the heady days of the Russian Revolution to see the advantages of a Jewish nationality in a network of large federal units, the realities of the peace now forced him into a different mould, to take a more sober, calculating view of the issue. Zionist intransigence had helped this dissolution on its way. More significantly, Wolf's cognizance of the fact that the peace conference would not allow Jewish national autonomy *per se* quickly forced him to adapt, to flow with the tide of 'official' thinking. Whether this ultimately would be good for the Jews of Eastern Europe is a debatable point. It did, however, offer one clear bonus for Wolf in his capacity as director of the Joint Foreign Committee of British Jews. If he had been out of favour, an unwanted partner in winning the war for the British, he was not going to let this opportunity slip in helping them to win the peace.

---

[85] Ibid.   [86] Ibid.

[87] Record of conversations at the Hotel Chatham, 24 Apr. 1919, with Bigart and Henry Morgenthau (US peace delegation) and Isaac Landman (*American Hebrew*), MWS 8312–17.

PART IV

THE PEACE

East Central Europe between the wars

12

Problems

With the splitting up of the great corporate monarchies like Austria-Hungary and Russia, the unity of the various Jewish communities has been destroyed. Moreover, the intensified nationalist feeling of new and enlarged states on the one hand and the rancorous passions of many discontented and dissatisfied persons, in the various and more especially in the diminished nationalities, on the other, have given rise to a serious recrudescence of anti-semitism. Thus the Jewish communities have found themselves exposed to new external dangers at the very time that their internal organisation and powers of resistance have been gravely impaired.[1]

The ending of hostilities brought about by the Allied defeat of Germany and the ensuing armistice of November 1918 led, paradoxically, to a period of heightened tension and insecurity for Eastern Jewry. Since the collapse of Russia and the protrusion of German influence far into Russia's western provinces as a result of the Brest-Litovsk settlement in early 1918, their safety had ultimately been assured by the presence of German troops. The armistice required the removal of those troops, and the Jews would be at the mercy of whoever replaced them.

Not all the short-lived regimes which either survived or emerged on Russia's western hinterland in late 1918 were necessarily hostile to the Jews. In principle, the Ukrainian Directory, for instance, had good intentions. The problem was how to translate them into practice in a situation which was not simply unstable but deteriorating fast. The Directory was at that moment engaged in a life-and-death struggle with the Bolsheviks and hence entirely dependent on the armed forces and guerrilla bands at its disposal. Nominally, Symon Petliura, the Directory strongman, guaranteed Jewish safety; in practice the equation of Bolshevik and Jew combined with deeper-seated antipathies to turn the Ukrainian forces into veritable powder-kegs of antisemitism.

The outcome was inevitable. A rising crescendo of pogroms beginning in 1918 reached a peak late in the summer of 1919. By this time, however, those perpetrated by Petliura's bands had been superseded by the more systematic mass murders of Denikin's volunteer 'White'

[1] *AJA Report*, 49 (1919–20), 4–5.

army as it itself advanced from the south into the Ukraine.[2] One region after another was ravaged. The contagion spread to embrace a vast chunk of western Russia. Estimates of pogrom victims ranged from thirty-five thousand to over a hundred thousand dead. As many as a quarter of a million more are thought to have died as a result of ensuing disease, dislocation, lack of medical treatment, or malnutrition.[3] It all made the pogroms under the last tsars seem rather mild. Indeed, there had been nothing like it since the Chmielnicki massacres of 1648.

Russia, of course, was in the midst of a two-, three-, and sometimes four-cornered civil war, and as such Jews had to be grateful for protection from wherever it came. Sometimes the Jews were even able to organize to protect themselves. In Odessa, disbanded Jewish soldiers formed a self-defence militia along the 1905 Bundist pattern and thus saved the city's Jewry from abuse. Elsewhere this model either did not arise or was disallowed by the higher authorities.[4] The only other alternative was the Bolsheviks.

As already noted, the majority of Russian Jews in 1917 were not sympathetic to Bolshevism. Paradoxically, this was often particularly true of Jewish socialists; they objected both to its anti-democratic party structure and to its ideological refusal to countenance Jewish national autonomy rights. Later on, Bolshevik policy on this score was made manifest when, under the guise of the Yevsektsia, the party-controlled Jewish 'national' commissariat, all forms of independent Jewish community life and self-expression were extinguished. In the immediate aftermath of the Bolshevik takeover, however, this intention was obscured by a Declaration of Nationalities which, at least on paper, gave all 'national' communities, the Jews included, control over their own religious, cultural, and educational affairs. Much more important, the Bolsheviks, in contrast to their opponents, strove both rhetorically and physically to combat antisemitism. Indeed, an official declaration in August 1918 outlawing antisemitism in all its forms was repeated the following March, at a time when the pogrom movement was rapidly

---

[2] See Peter Kenez, *Civil War in South Russia, 1919–20* (Stanford, 1977), 166–77; W. Bruce Lincoln, *Red Victory, A History of the Russian Civil War* (New York, 1989), 319–24; E. Heifetz, *The Slaughter of the Jews in the Ukraine in 1919* (New York, 1921). For views on Petliura's culpability, or otherwise, in the first phase of these massacres see Taras Hunczak, 'A Reappraisal of Symon Petliura and Ukrainian–Jewish Relations 1917–21', *JSS* 31 (1969), 163–83, and Zosa Szajkowski, 'A Rebuttal', ibid. 184–213.
[3] Baron, *Russian Jews*, 179–84; Kenez, *Civil War*, 170.
[4] Baron, *Russian Jews*, 182–3.

escalating, by Lenin in person. On the ground, it meant that an increasingly victorious Red Army came in practice to replace the Germans as the protectors of Eastern Jewry.[5]

Looked at from another standpoint, the long-term safety and prosperity of Eastern Jewry depended not on the Germans, who were a defeated nation, nor on the Bolsheviks, who were legally recognized by no one, but on the ability of the wartime victors to impose a settlement which would promote peace and stability in the area.[6] Though this was a tall order it was, in November 1918, not entirely impossible.

The Allies, after all, had a liberal programme of their own, or rather one that had been dictated to them through America's entry into the war. President Wilson's fourteen points of January 1918 had proclaimed a new world order to replace the old alliances, one in which peace and justice would be preserved through democracy, national self-determination, and a League of Nations. The removal of an embarrassing and reactionary tsarist ally and the complete defeat of the Central Powers, in addition to the huge mass following for the Wilsonian ideal gave the Allies, in theory at least, an opportunity and impetus to put this programme into practice. 'The great task of reconstruction on which the Powers will embark', Wolf optimistically wrote to the Foreign Office in December 1918, 'will find all their liberal impulses unfettered.'[7]

In reality, the Allied peace conference deliberations beginning in Paris in January 1918 followed an entirely different course. French intentions were from the first dictated by their fundamental precondition for any settlement, viz., the paralysis and permanent debilitation of Germany. The creation of new states in Eastern Europe on the Wilsonian model, with its avowed emphasis on ethnographic boundaries, was therefore only valuable to the Quai d'Orsay in the degree to which it would cement this purpose. The British and Americans, by contrast, did attempt to adhere to the ethnographic principle. Even they, however, found this increasingly difficult as they succumbed to the ethnic,

[5] Gitelman, *Jewish Nationality*, 233–318, examines the Bolshevik's Jewish policy and the *Yevsektsia* in depth.

[6] The Allies at the 1919 peace conference had no direct jurisdiction over the territories of their former Russian ally, save for Poland and Finland. Conversely, due to the Russian civil war, there was no one, officially recognized Russian delegation in Paris. The Allies did however have some leverage through their prerogative to recognize one or more post-tsarist regime. See Arno J. Mayer, *Politics and Diplomacy of Peacemaking: Containment and Counterrevolution at Versailles 1918–1919* (London, 1968), 285–9.

[7] Wolf to FO, encl. JFC memo, 2 Dec. 1918, FO 371/3419/199696.

political, or economic complexities of Eastern Europe, or to their own particular prejudices.[8]

In the meantime, until the new states of Eastern Europe were ratified, the Western Allies had the very real problem of how to maintain order in the area. But how were they to do this? With the exception of a small holding force on the Salonika front and scattered military missions elsewhere, they had no troops in Eastern Europe.[9] They were, in other words, entirely dependent and reliant on the forces of the Associated States, notably Poland and Romania. From the Jewish point of view, these were the very elements considered least likely to guarantee their protection. Over and beyond this, the fact that both were at this very time involved in an enormous territorial free for all—the Romanians in Hungary, the Poles in Eastern Galicia—made a mockery of the peacemakers' commitment to self-determinatory principles.

In early 1919, however, the rights and wrongs of this situation were overshadowed in the minds of the peacemakers by a spectre from the East. Bolshevism, either in the form of the Red Army smashing through the Carpathians and into Central Europe, perhaps creating a bridgehead to the Germans, or as a contagion of ideas moving inexorably westwards, haunted their deliberations; so much so that the armistice clauses were surreptitiously whittled away in order that German troops on the point of evacuation westwards from the Russian hinterland could stay put to act as a counter-revolutionary force in Europe's defence.[10]

Indirectly, this situation had a crucial bearing on the success of Jewish diplomacy in Paris. Wolf and his Western associates were clearly dependent on the Allies formulating a 'liberal' settlement, coming to Paris piled high with documentation intended to remind them of their obligations to Jews and other minorities as set down in previous international protocol.[11] Yet if the Allies decided to promote a war of extermination against the Bolsheviks, it would not only in the long term

[8] On the latter point see F. R. Bryant, 'Britain and the Polish Settlement of 1919', D.Phil. thesis (Oxford, 1968), 520.

[9] Mayer, *Politics*, 296–8.

[10] Lionel Kochan, *The Struggle for Germany 1914–1945* (Edinburgh, 1963), 10–11.

[11] See esp. Wolf *Notes* and JFC, *Correspondence with His Majesty's Government relative to Treaty Rights of the Jews of Rumania* (London, 1919). These and other documents were intended for circulation among Peace Conference diplomats and Jewish delegations. For parallel American Jewish materials see Max Kohler, 'The Origin of the Minority Provisions of the Paris Treaty of 1919', in Luzzatti, *God in Freedom*, 755–6.

require their recognizing the reactionary 'White' Russian regimes of Koltchak or perhaps Denikin, but also, at least in the first instance, enlisting the aid of their Eastern associates. If they did that, however, liberal intentions, indeed Wilsonian terms of reference, would simply have to be thrown to the winds; the price the Allies would have to pay Poland or Romania for committing themselves to the crusade would be non-interference in their internal affairs and the recognition of territorial encroachments already made or likely to be made in the process. It was obvious that the Jewish diplomats' interest lay in the conclusion of a speedy and satisfactory understanding with the Bolsheviks; this, they hoped, would enable the Allies to turn their attention to curbing their Eastern friends' illiberal behaviour at home and insatiable appetites abroad. In fact, the Allied deliberations oscillated wildly between these two extremes, the French in particular favouring full-scale intervention with emphasis on a French-led Eastern force, the British and Americans being more inclined towards a conciliatory and circumspect approach.

From the Jewish standpoint, it was fortunate that the French plan, as proposed by Marshal Foch to the Supreme Council in February, was killed off by its prohibitively high cost and the vigorous opposition of Wilson and Lloyd George. On the other hand, the failure of Lloyd George's initiative to have all the warring Russian factions meet with Allied delegates at a conference at Prinkipo on the Sea of Marmara, followed by that of other peace initiatives proposed by the American president, meant that the Allies remained committed to a policy if not of direct coercion then of containment of Bolshevism in the form of a *cordon sanitaire*. This in turn led to a continuing supply throughout the period of the peace conference of vast quantities of military aid and *matériel*—especially from the French—to both the 'Whites' and the associated powers.[12]

The chances of a truly liberal peace continued to hang precariously in the balance. Polish or Romanian intolerance or misconduct towards the Jews or the overstepping of boundaries prescribed by Allied military

---

[12] Mayer, *Politics*, 296–303, 338–43; John M. Thompson, *Russia, Bolshevism and the Versailles Peace* (Princeton, 1966), 188–200. On the Foch plan and the key role assigned to Polish and Romanian troops in the French Armée d'Orient, see Bradley, *Allied Intervention*, 144. On French military aid to Romania see Sherman S. Spector, *Rumania at the Paris Peace Conference: A Study in the Diplomacy of Ioan I. C. Bratianu* (New York, 1962), 102–3, 106. It has been suggested that while Foch continued to exploit the threat of a Red Army breakthrough in the Carpathians to advance his case, few British diplomats believed in the threat by early 1919; see Bryant, 'Britain', 159.

missions might lead to reprimands, but the Allies dared not go so far as to alienate them altogether.

This did not mean that the Allies were unsympathetic to a settlement of the Jewish question. Both the French and the British had already responded positively the previous summer to representations by Wolf and the Alliance calling for Allied declarations favouring Jewish emancipation. The French had even proffered a special commission to scrutinize the Jewish question at the conference.[13] Both, however, had been careful to delimit their statements so as not to implicate themselves further. The complications arising from their relations with the Poles and the Romanians suggested that what they wanted more than anything was a settlement 'out of court'.

This requirement was strikingly brought to Wolf's attention by Headlam-Morley in March, ironically enough in relation to the League of Nations. It had always been possible in past treaties, Headlam-Morley told him, to insert stipulations protecting Jewish and other minorities rights, because, 'as everybody knew there were no means of enforcing them . . . if they were violated, as in the case of Rumania in 1878, nothing would or could be done'. With the creation of the League of Nations, however, and the judicial machinery set up by it, every stipulation in the Treaty of Peace would have to be observed.

> The Powers would have to scrutinise very closely the responsibilities they assume and they will certainly not care to bind themselves to intervene on questions of internal politics. Moreover, such intervention will only jeopardise the general peace which it is the first duty of the League of Nations to safeguard. The League will in short look after the relations of these states between themselves but will probably abstain from interference in the relations of these states with their own subjects.[14]

Headlam-Morley, in encouraging Wolf to see Paderewski in April, was consciously or unconsciously pursuing these guidelines, an attempt in fact to achieve Polish–Jewish reconciliation on the strength of a gentlemen's agreement. While the interview between Wolf and the Polish leader was certainly a success and augured well for the future, it was no guarantee, in the way that an international protocol was

[13] Wolf to Oliphant, 18 June 1918, FO 371/3386/856; Graham to JFC, 28 July 1918, ibid.; Alliance, *La Question Juive*, Bigart to MAE, 16 July 1918, 6. Feinberg, *La Question*, 40–1.

[14] Wolf, Paris Diary, 1 Mar. 1919, fo. 97.

intended to be, that Polish Jewry would be protected. With Wilson's efforts in February to include a clause in the covenant of the League of Nations protecting the rights of racial and national minorities in all states wrecked on the rocks of racial dispute between Japan and the white nations,[15] Wolf was faced with the bizarre paradox of a supposedly liberal peace possibly giving the Jews even less than they had received on previous occasions, and the guardian League, as he put it, 'destined to become our worst enemy'.[16]

More than ever, Wolf needed the goodwill of the Foreign Office to see him over these difficulties. Yet even at the opening of the peace conference, his position remained weak despite the moderation of his proposals. The wartime hostility of the senior cadres of the ministry had by no means abated, while his persistent efforts to restore relations on a personal basis, such as he had enjoyed prior to the hardening of the Anglo-Russian *entente*, continued to be rebuffed.[17] In November 1918, Eyre Crowe drily commented, 'Mr. Lucien Wolf's advocacy is not generally accepted to promote anybody's interests.'[18]

With Crowe destined to play an important role in the East European settlement,[19] Wolf's chances of closing the gap between himself and the delegation seemed remote. Moreover, the Foreign Office was still in informal alliance with the Zionists, and this again told against the Joint Foreign Committee. Thus, when Wolf sought Foreign Office assistance in getting Mowschowitch facilities to leave Stockholm (where he had been most of the war), and come and help him in London and Paris, the matter was held up for a month, while the Foreign Office sought the advice of Weizmann.[20] As a result, Mowschowitch did not attend the peace conference.

[15] Kohler, 'Origin', 764–9; Jacob Robinson, *Were the Minorities Treaties a Failure?* (New York, 1943), 8–15.
[16] Wolf, Paris Diary, 1 Mar. 1919, fo. 97.
[17] See Wolf to Oliphant, 21 Aug. and 3 Sept. 1919, FO 371/3396/13513; Oliphant reply, 9 Sept. 1919, ibid. Clerk commented: 'What Mr. Wolf really wants is an excuse to come and talk which is the greatest waste of time of all'; Clerk minute, 6 Sept. 1919, ibid.
[18] Crowe minute, 23 Nov. 1918, FO 371/3417/189591.
[19] Crowe was assistant under-secretary of state in Paris, British representative on the Greek and Albanian Commission, and following the return of Lloyd George and Balfour to London also British representative on the Council of Heads of Delegation; see Headlam-Morley, *A Memoir*, 186–7.
[20] Wolf to FO, 15 Nov. 1918, FO 371/3417/189591; Ormsby-Gore minute, 20 Nov. 1918, ibid.; Thwaites (Director, Military Intelligence) report on Mowschowitch, following consultation with Weizmann, 14 Dec. 1918, ibid. Final clearance was given on 27 Dec. 1918.

An analogous case, as we have seen, was Prag's intended visit to Poland. In the winter of 1918/19, travel across Europe was impossible without official warrant. Prag's visit was at the invitation of the Poles themselves, but whereas Israel Cohen on behalf of the Zionist Organization was given Foreign Office leave and facilities, following an approach by Weizmann to Cecil and Clerk, Prag received none. The result was that while Cohen reached Poland and filed numerous atrocity reports for English newspapers which helped inflame Polish–Jewish relations, the Joint Foreign Committee mission, whose aim was to diplomatically heal the breach, never left England.[21]

These setbacks were overshadowed by a much greater Zionist threat implicit in the acknowledgement the peace conference gave to them. On 27 February they were due to present their Palestine programme before the Council of Ten, an event acclaimed throughout the Jewish world but unfortunately coinciding with insistent Polish and Romanian claims, for the benefit of the Great Powers, that outstanding Jewish problems within their boundaries had already been satisfactorily settled.[22] The fragility of the situation in the East convinced Edmond de Rothschild (who had resumed friendly contact with Wolf at the beginning of the conference) that this gave the Great Powers an opportunity to grant Zionist Palestine aspirations while conveniently dispensing with the Jewish problem elsewhere.[23]

Fortunately for Wolf, de Rothschild's fears failed to materialize. The Council of Ten did give its blessing to the British–Zionist conjunction in Palestine, but not on the latter's reading of the Balfour Declaration as the basis for an immediate sovereign Jewish state. The British by this time had become more circumspect about the Palestine project. The immediate wartime relevance for supporting Zionism had become blunted, and London became wary after repeated warnings from their people in Cairo that full support of Zionism would lead to a collision with the Arabs unacceptable in terms of Britain's wider Near Eastern horizons.[24] Weizmann's efforts to revivify the threat of a

<hr>

[21] Wolf to FO, 17, 18, and 30 Dec. 1918, FO 371/3281/189591; Weizmann–Cecil interview, 29 Nov. 1918, ibid. See also Israel Cohen, *My Mission*, 149; Cohen was sent specifically to report on the Lemberg pogrom and was in Poland from December 1918 to February 1919.

[22] Wolf, Paris Diary, 21 and 28 Feb. 1919, fos. 75, 89. Weizmann, Sokolow, Ussishkin, and nominally Sylvain Lévi spoke on behalf of Zionist interests at the session; see Vital, *Zionism: The Crucial Phase*, 350–7.

[23] Wolf, Paris Diary, 28 Feb. 1919, fo. 89.

[24] Stein, *Balfour Declaration*, 628–30, 645–6.

Jewish–Bolshevik nexus unless 'destructive' (Bolshevik) tendencies were redirected into 'constructive' (Zionist) ones failed to rouse the British sufficiently in the required direction. Weizmann attenuated his Palestine objectives accordingly.[25]
Growing fractures in the British–Zionist accord were to Wolf's advantage in Paris. They facilitated his conversations with Ormsby-Gore and hence the opportunity to discuss the Joint Foreign Committee's own moderate Palestine programme. As noted above, they also, almost immediately made Wolf a useful British prop against the extreme national political demands of the Zionists in Eastern Europe.[26]
Similarly, though Eyre Crowe attempted to disrupt Wolf's growing access to developments and information emanating from the British delegation and peace conference secretariat,[27] any ill-effects were offset by the re-establishment of Wolf's pre-war Foreign Office ties. An old friend, George Prothero of the Historical Section, was on hand to assist, as was Sir William Tyrrell, who as head of the Political Intelligence Department promised to keep Wolf abreast of conference developments. Equally important were the new ties Wolf was able to forge with such members of the Political Intelligence Department as James Headlam-Morley, A. W. A. Leeper, and E. H. Carr, who shared not only his academic and informed approach to post-war problems but also his desire for a liberal peace.
Linked by mutual interests and by the common denominator of being a fellow Briton in a foreign capital, Wolf was drawn into closer social contact with these and other officials; often, for instance, he dined with them. In consequence, the high barriers both of formality and distrust which prevented his access to, and information from, Whitehall practically vanished in Paris. Indeed, nearly daily meetings with members of the British delegation, especially Headlam-Morley,

[25] On FO unwillingness to respond to Weizmann's efforts see Wolf, Paris Diary, 28 Jan. 1919, fo. 18. On the modifying of the Zionists' post-declaration objectives see Stein, *Balfour Declaration*, 600–17; Friedman, *Question of Palestine*, 319–20.
[26] On Wolf–Ormsby–Gore meeting see Wolf, Paris Diary, 12 Feb. 1919, fos 51–4. See also S. Ettinger, 'Jews and Non-Jews in Eastern and Central Europe between the Wars: An Outline', in Bela Vago and George L. Mosse, eds., *Jews and Non-Jews in Eastern Europe* (Jerusalem, 1974), 8.
[27] Crowe consistently attempted to sabotage Wolf's access to the British delegation at the peace conference; see e.g. his minute of 19 Apr. 1919, FO 608/48/114/1/3, where he objects to the 'betrayal of confidence' which had allowed Wolf access to information on the Romanian Commission.

ensured that Wolf was kept informed not only of developments on the Jewish question but with wider aspects of the settlement.

While there were obvious advantages in these close contacts, there were also major pitfalls. One false move and his access to the delegation might be irrevocably blocked. Caution thus became the watchword of Wolf's diplomacy in Paris.

The necessity for this was highlighted by his relationship with the emissaries of the already recognized or would-be states of Eastern Europe. If Wolf's role *vis-à-vis* the British was one of suppliant, with these Eastern plenipotentiaries he found the roles very often reversed; they petitioned him rather than *vice versa*. There were two basic reasons for this. Firstly, it soon became apparent that Wolf's proximity to the British delegation meant that he might be utilized as a channel of approach where it was otherwise blocked or limited. Secondly, the Joint Foreign Committee, along with other organizations present at the peace conference, merged in the minds of these suitors as part of an international Jewish body considered in its own right 'to be a weighty factor in international relations'.[28]

The conspicuousness in Paris of Jews in positions of seemingly great authority and influence lent credence to this belief. In the Italian delegation there was Baron Sonnino; in the French, Louis Klotz, the minister of finance; in the British, Edwin Montagu. The interpreter to the Big Four was another Jew, Professor Paul Mantoux.[29] At the top of the list, however, were the American Jews.

It will be remembered how during the war, the British considered the Zionist sympathies of leading Jewish Americans such as Judge Brandeis, Felix Frankfurter, and Louis Epstein to be of such considerable importance as to merit the formulation of a pro-Zionist declaration. The French belatedly jumped on to the Balfour Declaration bandwagon in 1918 for similar reasons, fearing that to ignore them would be to throw overboard 'la politique moderatrice . . . des juifs qui ont l'influence . . . sur les affaires de la guerre et de la paix', and in the process lose their support for French aspirations in the Levant.[30] Now in Paris there were not only Wolf's American opposite numbers, Marshall, Mack, and Cyrus Adler, but also Jews actually in the

---

[28] Ettinger, 'Jews and Non-Jews', 9–10.

[29] Wolf, 'The Jew in Diplomacy', in Roth, ed., *Essays*, 407–9.

[30] Wolf, Paris Diary, 28 Jan. 1919, fo. 251. On Jewish influence in the USA see also 'Notes de Eduard Brilly', 10 Feb. 1918, MAE, Guerre 1914–18, file 1200, fos. 148–50.

American delegation—including Henry Morgenthau, the financier, and Oscar Straus, the chairman of the US Commission 'for the Enforcement of Peace'.[31] It was surely no accident that many of the new states seeking recognition, notably weaker ones, like Lithuania and the Ukraine, sought to maximize their appeal and accessibility to these people and hence to the conference itself by including Jews in their own delegations' ranks. It explains moreover, suggests Shmuel Ettinger, why they went to such lengths to give constitutional and administrative expression to the Jewish national councils which had developed spontaneously within their boundaries.[32]

The various Jewish delegates thus found themselves, even before the peace conference had begun, in a position to bargain with the respective Eastern states. They could threaten and in turn be threatened. For instance, in April, Oscar Straus warned that if Czech pogroms did not stop, the supply of American food shipments to the country—a very weighty factor indeed with Europe on the brink of starvation—would be discontinued.[33] By contrast, the Austrians, via their Jewish national council, put pressure on Israel Cohen, on his way through Vienna to Warsaw, to have the Zionists persuade the Allies to send food to Vienna or risk the possibility of riots 'in which the Jews would be the chief victims'.[34]

Short-term food shipments, like long-term financial aid towards national construction and reconstruction, became for Wolf political bargaining-counters when it came to discussing the settlement of the Jewish question in the various East European countries.

But was it wise to bargain at all? To make such deals with the Eastern delegates was to lay them open to misinterpretations which might have fearful consequences for the lives of the millions of Jews whom Wolf and his colleagues were supposed to be protecting. Moreover, they threatened to implicate the Jews both nationally and internationally in disputes that they had little or nothing to do with, disputes which in fact only the peacemakers themselves could solve.

In particular, the Poles were prepared to concede Jewish aspirations only in return for compensation elsewhere. In conversation with Straus, Marshall, and Mack in November 1918, Dmowski had insisted that the economic boycott could only be terminated if American Jewry issued a statement urging their Polish brethren to support aspirations

[31] Wolf, 'The Jews in Diplomacy', 408.   [32] Ettinger, 'Jews and Non-Jews', 9.
[33] Naomi Cohen, *Dual Heritage*, 265.   [34] Israel Cohen, *My Mission*, 153.

for a free and enlarged Poland.[35] When Wolf saw Count Skrzynski, the Polish deputy foreign minister, in Paris the following April, he was presented with a similar quid pro quo: special concessions for the Jews, that is, a degree of local educational autonomy in return for internal Jewish support of a conservative settlement of the agrarian question—something Wolf obviously could not answer for—and Western Jewish endorsement of Polish claims to Danzig, Lemberg, and Teschen.[36]

Wolf was being made to walk a political tightrope. Only a week before, the whole Joint Foreign Committee delegation had seen the Czech plenipotentiary, Dr Edvard Beňes, who had asked them to give their support at the peace conference to Czech claims to Teschen. The situation was doubly embarrassing as the original Czech approach had come via a Czech Jewish delegation sent from Prague with the full blessing of Tomas Masaryk, the new president. The Czechs were known to have a liberal political orientation which was reflected in their attitude to their minorities. The Czech Jews, moreover, had informed Wolf that Prague was pre-empting the peace conference by accepting, in principle, Jewish national rights.

It was hardly surprising if Joint Foreign Delegation sympathies should be biased towards the Czechs. Indeed, Sir Stuart Samuel took the opportunity in the interview with Benes to let it be known that as a partner in the banking firm of Samuel, Montagu, and Co., he would be happy to facilitate Czech requests for the floating of loans through the opening up of credits entrusted to it by the British government. The territorial dispute with the Poles was a different matter. 'We cannot take sides,' Wolf bluntly told the Czech Jews; he and his committee would have to support whatever decision was reached by the British government.[37]

Wolf's counsel was wise. Within weeks a 'patriotic' Polish Jewish delegation had arrived in Paris.[38] If Wolf had supported one government against the other, he would have alienated not only his own government but also the Jews of both Czechoslovakia and Poland.

The necessity to maintain a diplomatic silence was stretched even

[35] Grabski had made a similar proposal to Cohen on 15 Jan. 1919 (ibid. 163–4). See also Naomi Cohen, *Dual Heritage*, 268–9.
[36] On Wolf interview with Skrzynski see Wolf, Paris Diary, 17 Apr. 1919, fos. 197–200.
[37] Ibid., 7 and 10 Apr. 1919, fos. 174, 177.
[38] This was the Natanson mission; see ibid., 27 June 1919, fo. 400.

more when it came to questions involving the Jews further East. The Ukraine was a very particular headache. Wolf was emotionally torn on the issue of an independent Ukraine. On the one hand, the Ukrainians had given the Jews the most far-reaching measure of autonomy and self-administration yet. Wolf had extolled its virtues in February to both Ormsby-Gore and Headlam-Morley. He hoped, too, that the Ukrainian delegation would support his own more watered down proposals as a leverage on the less compromising Poles. Good relations with the Ukrainian delegation were further assured by Wolf's acquaintanceship with two of its prominent—and Jewish—members, Dr Samuel Zarchi and Arnold Margolin, the latter a former associate in ITO.[39]

On the other hand, there was no certainty that the Ukraine as a viable entity would survive. Under threat of extinction from the Poles in the west, the Bolsheviks in the north, and Denikin's White Russian forces in the south and south-east, the final dissolution of the state seemed imminent. Internal chaos brought with it reports of wide-spread pogroms—their exact extent at this stage remained unknown—and though Wolf was able to prevail on Nikolai Vasilko, the head of the Ukrainian delegation, to make an official statement which promised that the Ukrainian government would 'erase this ignominy and execrable heritage of the Russian *ancien régime*',[40] it was becoming apparent that in reality they had no control over the situation.

Moreover, in Paris, Wolf was being pressurized by equally if not more distinguished Jews to support the incorporation of the Ukraine into an undivided Russia. Alexandre de Gunzburg, who was associated with Admiral Koltchak's Russian delegation, desired this, as did Maxim Vinaver, the veteran Cadet leader, who eventually arrived in Paris in the summer as foreign affairs minister representing Denikin's administration in south Russia.[41] The dilemma for Wolf was an acute one. In principle, he agreed with Vinaver that the best interests of the Jews were served by an undivided Russia. On the other hand, he felt none of Vinaver's optimism that the preponderantly reactionary and antisemitic elements in Koltchak's and Denikin's entourage would somehow be displaced in favour of a liberal regime if and when the Bolsheviks were

[39] Ibid., 19 Mar. and 20 Apr. 1919, fos. 125–6, 206; id., 'The Jews in Diplomacy', 409.
[40] Id., Paris Diary, 6 Aug. 1919, fos. 510–11. For Zarchi–Vasilko correspondence see ibid., 7 Aug. 1919, fos. 517, 521–3.
[41] Ibid., 6 June and 13 Aug. 1919, fos. 341–2, 534.

defeated. The situation was further complicated by Wolf's knowledge of an official declaration made in February 1919 and signed by Margolin for the Ukraine and representatives of four other semi-official South Russian entities. The declaration, which called on the *entente* to recognize a federation of independent Russian nationalities created from below rather than imposed from above,[42] was akin to Wolf's own preference for a federal solution.

These factors tended to make Wolf lean towards support of the Ukraine. When in June through the good offices of Gunzburg he saw Boris Bakhmetev, one of Koltchak's delegation, he put the point to him plainly. It was not, he said to the advantage of Ukrainian Jews to declare themselves opposed to their country's independence any more than for the Jews of any other state. Rather, the duty of Jews was 'to identify themselves with the national cause and to subordinate Jewish interests to it'.[43]

Plain speaking, however, could not resolve Wolf's Ukrainian dilemma. His own country, as a member of the *entente*, was, for reasons of *realpolitik*, intent on supporting Koltchak and Denikin's undivided Russia, and conversely ignoring, despite the existence of a Ukrainian nationality, the pleas of the Ukrainian republic for peace conference legitimization. Margolin and Zarchi persistently appealed to Wolf to get the British to change their minds, but this was a course he felt unable to pursue. Thus, though he did gain access for Margolin to the British delegation in April, when asked by Zarchi in August to find out what the Inter-Allied Commission in the Ukraine was doing in relation to the provisional demarcation of the Polish–Ukrainian frontier, he instantly retorted that this did not relate to his Jewish work. Zarchi courageously disagreed, pointing out that it was not in the interests of the Jewish population thus affected to find themselves under Polish sovereignty. Wolf refused to budge.[44]

[42] For memo to Supreme Commanders of the *entente* Powers, 5 Jan. 1919, see Marshall Papers, Paris Peace Conference, Box 2 (Treaties, Memoranda, Petitions), 1918–1919 file, repr. in Arnold D. Margolin, *From a Political Diary, Russia, the Ukraine and America 1905–1945* (New York, 1946), 46–7.
[43] Wolf, Paris Diary, 11 June 1919, fo. 364.
[44] Ibid., 20 Apr. and 6 Aug. 1919, fos. 206, 510–11. The British were not consistently hostile to the Ukrainians. When Denikin's power disintegrated in 1920, they leaned towards the possibility of a Ukraine in alliance with the Poles and Romanians. Michel Tydzkiewicz, Vasilko's aristocratic successor as leader of the Ukrainian delegation in Paris, proposed just this: but his background and the anti-semitic implications of his proposal led Wolf to change tack and declare it inimical to both Jewish and European interests; see Wolf, Paris Diary, 31 Sept. 1919, fo. 581.

The case illustrates Wolf's unwillingness to do anything which might have put his relationship with his own delegation in jeopardy, a constraint of which he was fully aware. After the final refusal of the peace conference to recognize the Ukrainian republic, he privately lamented the situation in the following terms:

For us to give any advice to the Jews of the Ukraine is impossible, we cannot advise them to be good Ukrainians without the risk that we are setting them against the *Entente* and asking them to be traitors to Russia. We cannot ask them to support the cause of an undivided Russia without pillorying them as enemies of their country's national cause. We cannot recognise them to be neutral without recognising a Jewish nationality and setting both Russians and Ukrainians and probably also Bolshevists, Poles and Rumanians against them ... the problem is an extremely difficult one. It shows how dangerous it is to mix up *raison d'état* with a *politique des principes*.[45]

British support of the White reactionary Russian forces in the fight against Bolshevism compounded Wolf's dilemma by threatening to involve him in a slanging match with the Foreign Office delegation such as had occurred in 1915. Whereas in the former case, however, Wolf had found himself contradicting the assertions of Britain's tsarist ally that the Russian Jews were responsible for pro-German activities including espionage, he now was faced with whether or not to accuse the British themselves of fabricating material blaming Bolshevism on the Jews.

The British interventionary presence in Russia was not large, consisting of small though influential military missions attached to Denikin and Koltchak's forces, and isolated British-led commands under generals Maynard and Ironside in and around Murmansk and Archangel. At the beginning of August 1919, Captain Jacob Harzfeld, an American Jewish officer who had been seconded for some time to the American military attaché in Archangel, arrived in Paris with disturbing news. He claimed that colonels Thornhill and Lindsay, the officers in charge of British intelligence and propaganda departments in the two northern ports, had been producing blatantly antisemitic pamphlets for distribution among American and British troops and for propaganda among the Red Army. Harzfeld furnished Wolf with two of these pamphlets. The first, ostensibly under the signature of General Ironside, called on the Red Guards to throw off the Jewish yoke and unite with the Whites; the second, directed primarily at Allied troops, blamed the

[45] Ibid., 13 Aug. 1919, fos. 537–8.

exploitation of Russia on the Jews and Germans. The second was in fact a lot less insidious than the first; nevertheless, Harzfeld told Wolf that he intended to gain the assistance of Felix Warburg and Louis Marshall 'to kick up a U.S. public agitation' against the British misdemeanour.[46]

In one sense, Harzfeld's report was simply an addition to Wolf's growing dossier on the subject. He already had information from the Jewish national council in the Ukraine that the army of Denikin was publishing antisemitic conspiracy material in an attempt to incite popular wrath against Russian Jewry. Wolf had in fact taken these allegations to Sazonov, now Denikin's representative in Paris.[47] Sazonov, however, in reply, pointed out that the material in question, and in particular a textual reproduction of a report stating that the execution of the former tsar had been conceived and carried out by Jews, had simply been borrowed from one sent by General Knox to the British government.[48] The implication was clear: the information was not propaganda at all, but authentic material from a thoroughly reliable source.

It was Knox who as British military attaché to the British embassy in Petrograd had caused so much trouble for Wolf over the espionage allegations back in 1915. Now, as chief adviser to Koltchak in Siberia, he hoped to inveigle Britain into a full-scale crusade against 'the blood-stained Jew-led Bolsheviks'.[49] 'So long as Knox is in the country,' wrote Claude Montefiore's son Leonard, 'British policy will be thoroughly anti-semitic.'[50] All this Wolf already knew. The problem, however, was how to tackle it, and the rumpus Harzfeld threatened to cause, in such a way that it would not upset his peace conference work. When at the end of 1919 the Knox allegation regarding Jewish involvement in the murder of the tsar was included in a published parliamen-

---

[46] On the Maynard and Ironside commands and the role of Thornhill and his 'Russifying' interests see Ullman, *Britain*, 21–3; Wolf, Paris Diary, 2 Aug. 1919, fos. 500–6. The offending pamphlets were distributed in Dec. 1918 and Mar. 1919; for copies see C11/3/1/3.

[47] Ukraine Jewish National Council, 'The Danger of anti-Jewish Excesses in the Army of Denikin', n.d., submitted by Wolf to Sazonov, 14 July 1919, C11/3/1/3.

[48] Wolf, Paris Diary, 26 June 1919, fos. 484–5; Knox to director of Military Intelligence (War Office), 5 Feb. 1919, FO 371/3977/983. Knox's message was passed on, without comment, by Rex Leeper of the PID to King George, and eventually to the press.

[49] For Knox and his attitude to the Jews see Ullman, *Britain*, 30.

[50] Leonard Montefiore to Wolf, 19 Dec. 1919, C11/3/1/4.

tary paper, Wolf felt compelled to challenge the Foreign Office on it; he consequently involved himself in a renewed bout of bitter feuding.[51]

While the peace conference lasted, and so long as the incriminating material remained outside the purview of the press, Wolf abstained from public controversy. Harzfeld was prevailed upon to refrain from his proposed course of action, Wolf promising confidentially to deal with the matter himself. In fact, E. H. Carr confirmed a few days later than Harzfeld's evidence on Thornhill and Lindsay was correct; the Ironside signature was a forgery, but technically responsibility did lay nevertheless with Ironside and Maynard as commanding officers.[52] Wolf elicited government admittance and apology. What might otherwise have blown up into a major scandal had, by backstairs diplomacy, been contained, perhaps at the relatively insignificant cost of a somewhat embarrassing interview with Carr.

The Thornhill–Lindsay affair highlighted the extremely precarious nature of Wolf's understanding with the British delegation. Many of their number, such as for instance, E. H. Carr, shared Wolf's distaste for the reactionary nature of the 'White' regimes and were themselves embarrassed by the way in which officers like Knox and Thornhill so willingly lent themselves to their antisemitic politics. The ultimate collapse of both Koltchak and Denikin was therefore fortunate inasmuch as it avoided the complications Britain would undoubtedly have found itself in had it been required to officially recognize either regime.[53] It was doubly fortunate for Wolf and his committee, who were thus spared a return to the stultified relations between themselves and the Foreign Office which had so determined their inability to act on behalf of Russian Jewry, before, and during, the early stages of the war.

Had Wolf opted to make an issue of the matter at the peace conference or had let Harzfeld do so, he would undoubtedly have aroused British public opinion against 'an attack by foreigners on British officers who are fighting the battles of their country—however

---

[51] *Russia No. 1: A Collection of Reports on Bolshevism in Russia*. Abridged Edition, Parliamentary Paper (London, 1919), nos 38, 45; JFC, *The Assassination of the Czar: Correspondence with His Majesty's Government* (London, 1920). On the ramifications of the murder allegation in Britain see Kadish, 'Bolsheviks', 25–6, 160–2; also Gisela C. Lebzelter, *Political Anti-Semitism in England, 1918–1939* (London, 1978), 18–19.

[52] Wolf, Paris Diary, 12 Aug. 1919, fo. 530.

[53] Ullman, *Britain*, 246–7; E. H. Carr report on Denikin, 7 Nov. 1919, FO 608/ 196/603/1/4.

badly they may have acted'.[54] Similarly, those members of the delegation who were otherwise sympathetic would most probably have rallied
to Thornhill's defence against an unwarranted interference.

Moreover, as Wolf himself astutely noted, to bring the issue into the
open would have been to allow 'all the unhappy facts about Jewish
participation in Bolshevism to be raked over afresh and exaggerated'.[55]
Since before the Bolshevik seizure of power in November 1917, right-
wing papers in Britain, including the *Morning Post* and *The Times*, had
been eager to note the prominence of Jews both in leading Bolshevik
positions in Russia and in the abortive revolutions in Central Europe at
the end of the war. The message was clear; the attack on 'Western
civilization' was Jewish-led, and synonymous with Jews generally.[56]
Elements within the Foreign Office were certainly infected with these
views. The situation may well have been exacerbated at the Paris peace
conference by a further, avowedly incriminating, piece of evidence.
The Protocols of the Elders of Zion, the classic work purporting to demonstrate how international Jewry was conspiring to enslave the world, had
come into the hands of the Foreign Office via American Naval Intelligence. It was soon proved to be a turn-of-the-century Russian forgery,
but not before one diplomat had urged, 'in view of recent developments', that Mr Balfour should see it.[57]

Assuming that Jews were Bolsheviks and Bolsheviks Jews, the conspiracy theory must have seemed quite logical to those already mentally
predisposed in this direction. Wickham Steed, foreign editor of *The
Times*, was certainly one who from Paris lent his efforts to proving that
there was an American finance–German military–Russian Bolshevik
axis in which the connecting link was 'international Jewry'. At home,

[54] Wolf, Paris Diary, 2 Aug. 1919, fo. 504.

[55] Ibid.

[56] Kadish, 'Bolsheviks', 7–20, 32–9; Lebzelter, *Political Anti-Semitism*, 14; Holmes,
Anti-Semitism, 141–2.

[57] For a blow-by-blow account on the development of the *Protocols* see Norman
Cohn, *Warrant for Genocide* (London, 1967). On the American Naval Intelligence
Connection see Naomi Cohen, *Not Free*, 128; Morton Rosenstock, *Louis Marshall,
Defender of Jewish Rights* (Detroit, 1965), 120–1; Bagley (consul-general, New York) to
Drummond, 19 Oct. 1918, FO 371/3414/183583. On the Bolshevik–Jewish link, in
some FO minds, see e.g. Crowe's comment on the Ukrainian pogroms: 'It is to be
remembered that what may be to Mr. Weizmann to be outrages against Jews, may in the
eyes of the Ukrainians be retaliation against the horrors committed by the bolshevists
who are all organised and directed by the Jews', FO 608/196/603/2/1. See likewise
Tyrrell's response to a report sent by Eliot from Ekaterinburg on Bolshevik doings:
'Jewish influence at work'; Tyrrell minute 18 Mar. 1919, FO 608/181/593/1/2.

ten leading Anglo-Jews, including Wolf's close friends Claude Montefiore, Isidore Spielman, and Leonard Cohen, were so intimidated by the *Morning Post*'s insinuations that they publicly disassociated themselves from foreign Jews in England who had adopted or might in the future adopt 'the theocratic principles of Russian Bolshevism'.[58]

In Paris, there were those in the Jewish camp, notably Gunzburg and Vinaver, who wanted to produce a similar manifesto against Bolshevism, one which would disassociate Jews *qua* Jews from the revolutionary leaders. Wolf did not like the idea:

If we were to publish a Manifesto in the sense proposed we should only provoke a counter manifesto from Jews in favour of Bolshevism or any rate some form of revolutionary socialism. We should then have it on permanent record that there was a strong tendency in this direction in the Jewish community. Hitherto we have been able, to some extent, to obscure the fact.[59]

In other words, Wolf was admitting what many of the other Jewish delegates at Paris preferred to ignore; that there were by this time many Russian Jews who were Bolsheviks. This did not mean, in Wolf's understanding, that they were naturally inclined in that direction, and he later forcefully argued that as an essentially bourgeois people they had nothing to gain from it. However, by the summer of 1919 he had accumulated enough evidence to surmise that 'the terrible pogroms carried out by the Polish and Ukrainian anti-Bolshevists and the increasing evidence of anti-semitism in all the other anti-Bolshevist armies are driving the Jews more and more into the Bolshevik camp'.[60] This, he submitted to Carr when they discussed the Thornhill pamphlets, was the truth of the matter.

But to have done anything but conceal these conclusions would, in the climate of 1919, have led to a gross misrepresentation. He could not deny that there were Jews who, perhaps as their best bet for survival, were Bolsheviks; nor could he condone, as Vinaver and Gunzburg seemed eager to do in the interests of their future relations with Koltchak and Denikin, those anti-Bolshevik regimes intent on

[58] Steed, *Through Thirty Years*, ii. 302–5; 'Letter of the Ten', *Morning Post*, 23 Apr. 1919; Sharman Kadish, ' "The Letter of the Ten": Bolsheviks and British Jews', *Studies in Contemporary Jewry*, 4 (1988), 96–112.

[59] Wolf, Paris Diary, 26 June 1919, fo. 408. See also Wolf to Montefiore, 29 June 1919, MWS file 210, expressing concern on the Gunzburg–Vinaver proposal.

[60] Wolf, Paris Diary, 12 Aug. 1919, fos. 532–3; Wolf to Montefiore, 11 Aug. 1919, MWS file 210. For a historian's confirmation of this analysis see Gitelman, *Jewish Nationality*, 164–7.

conducting pogroms against their Jewish populations. When the peace conference had ended, Wolf would direct his attention and energies towards combatting the more vicious calumnies and attempting to elucidate the true nature of the Jewish problem.[61]

In the meantime, what mattered was the consolidation of his work for the protection of Jews and other minorities in the new Eastern European states—work which, unlike the problems in Russia, fell under the direct jurisdiction of the peace conference, and which, from Wolf's point of view, needed the cooperation of the British delegation to carry it through. To have drawn these delegates into a confrontation on the conduct of British officers in Russia would not only have been beside the point but simply undiplomatic.

[61] See e.g. Wolf, 'Jews and Bolshevism', *Daily Telegraph*, 6 Nov. 1919, or id., *The Jewish Bogey and the Forged Protocols of the Learned Elders of Zion* (London, 1920).

13

A Case in Point: Romania

THERE were limits to how much Wolf was prepared to say 'yes' to his British patrons, however. Certainly to flow with the tide was to gain something; on the other hand, to do nothing was to gain nothing. The Romanian Jewish question, in particular, was one issue which forced Wolf from passive acquiescence into a more forceful presentation of his case.

Wolf's non-activity on the question in the first three years of the war had been necessitated by the exigencies of the *entente*'s efforts to cajole Romania into the alliance, and by the need for Wolf, as a good patriot, to subordinate Jewish interests to British ones. From a moral point of view, this was inexcusable. On the other hand, his possession of written assurances from 1913 and 1914 promising the government's intervention to reaffirm the Treaty of Berlin provisions 'when appropriate' gave him considerable leverage with which to remind the Foreign Office of its obligations.[1] In the wake of the March revolution in Russia, Wolf had considered seriously whether or not to reactivate them.

The revolution was of crucial significance for Romania, inasmuch as its plutocratic landowning regime was dependent on the existence of an equally entrenched order across the border. When this collapsed in March 1917, the Romanians were thus desperate to show signs of reforming from within for fear of themselves being swept up in the tide of revolution or falling foul of the new radicalizing forces in Russia.

At first, their schedule for reform focused on appeasing peasant land demands and did not include Jewish grievances. Pressure from outside —from Russia and possibly indirectly from Wolf himself—[2] seems however to have forced its hand. In June, a government declaration in

[1] Crowe to CJC, 29 Oct. 1913, FO 371/1742/1532; Crowe to CJC, 28 July 1914, FO 371/2089/11207. For the 'reminder' see (Balfour papers), Wolf to Balfour, 30 Jan. 1917, FO 800/210.

[2] Wolf to Edward Madge (British Intelligence), 9 May 1917, MWS 59010; Wolf to Madge, 17 May 1917, MWS 59015; Note on Wolf's interview with Misu (the Romanian ambassador, London), 14 July 1917, MWS 6133–5.

250 *The Peace*

parliament promised a complete solution to the Jewish problem 'sans réservations, sans compartiments, sans réserves'.[3]

This did not mean that the future of Romanian Jewry was secure. No timetable had been set for emancipation, only that it would be after Romania had been totally freed from occupation. Thus, changes in the international political climate—perhaps even a counter-revolution in Russia, might give the government of Ioan Bratianu the opportunity to renege on its promises, as on so many occasions in the past. To observers like Wolf, the complexity of Romania's legal machinery and the ability of successive governments to adapt it to suit their purposes made this outcome seem only too plausible.

In particular, if Romania continued to insist that emancipation be performed not automatically, as in the recent case of Russia 'without the necessity of any parliamentary or administrative machinery', but on the basis of documentary evidence to prove that each and every individual naturalized was in fact a Romanian subject, anything up to 80 per cent of Romanian Jewry—an estimated 100,000 Jews—could be excluded. This, noted the judicial expert Labin, owed nothing to the Jews being ineligible for citizenship, but was simply due to the fact that the official registers of births, marriages, and deaths had only been in good order since 1863. A loophole thus existed for the Romanian government to pick and choose who would, or would not, be naturalized, on the basis of the date and type of evidence that would be required in any future emancipation bill.[4]

Worse, this situation was fully legitimized by the revised Constitution of 1879, Article vii of which classed the Jews as a group as 'aliens' from the Romanian body-politic, a framework itself constructed upon a rigid adhesion to the *jus sanguinis* definition of nationality as dependent upon parentage, not place of birth. As most Romanian Jews, particularly from the northern province of Moldavia, were immigrants of one, two, or three generations, their exclusion from the benefits of citizenship thus seemed to be indefinite. Certainly, some three hundred wealthy Jews had been able to 'procure' naturalization in the period 1878–1912 by means of individual bills passed through parliament. Others had taken the opposite course by seeking foreign protection, notably from Austria-Hungary. The vast majority, however, remained stateless and, as a consequence, continued to suffer in the

[3] Report of Bratianu and Jonescu speeches (n.d.), 14 June 1917, MWS 6139–44.
[4] Labin memo, 'On Solving the Jewish Question in Rumania', n.d., spring 1918, MWS 20333–52.

shadow of an evolving grille of anti-alien laws.[5] What was needed was a drastic overhaul of Romania's constitutional laws.

Interestingly, in the summer of 1917 Wolf had the opportunity to construct a real alliance with which to exert pressure on this score. He knew that Russian Jewry were flexing their muscles over the issue and that they had called on the Alliance to assist them. More significantly, the Russian provisional government had stated that it would not condone any future annexation of Transylvania, a key Romanian war aim, until Romanian Jewry had been liberated.[6] Other considerations would also have impelled him in this direction. Accumulated evidence from Russian and Swedish sources suggested that there had been widespread antisemitic incidents in Romania during the course of the war, especially during its army's retreat into Moldavia in late 1917.[7] Labin, moreover, had warned that the country had no reserve of political leaders to replace the present governing class and thereby accomplish a liberal solution of the Jewish question of its own volition.[8] Romania in late 1917 was weakened by the war effort, partially overrun by the Germans, and isolated from the *entente*. A failure to make restitution on the Jewish question, Wolf might have argued, would lead to Western interference in its internal affairs and a possible embargo on economic aid, especially American loans, so vital for her reconstruction at the end of the war.[9]

Wolf was for once well positioned to press for concerted and public action. In 1916 he had warned the Western Allies of the embarrassing consequences which would accrue if they did not bring their reactionary associates to account. Given Romania's very particular history of side-

[5] Ibid. See also Joshua Starr, 'Jewish Citizenship in Rumania 1878–1940', *JSS* 3 (1941), 63–4, which puts the figure of naturalized Jews at 361, in addition to the 883 war veterans naturalized *en bloc* in 1879. Spulber, *State*, 109, notes the classification of Jews as *hzisovelti*, born in Romania, and *suditi*, under foreign protection.

[6] Mitrany memo, 'On Various Aspects of the Jewish Question in Relation to the War', 12 May 1917, MWS 6144–5; Mowschowitch to Wolf, 21 Oct. 1917, C11/2/12. See also Golder, *Documents*, 646–8, for *Izvestia* report (20 Oct. 1917) on Petrograd Soviet's instructions to its delegation to the Inter-Allied Conference in Paris to insist on immediate binding of Romania to Article 48 of the Treaty of Berlin.

[7] Jewish Press Bureau (Stockholm) reports of anti-Jewish excesses encl. with Wolf to Oliphant, 9 Oct. 1917, FO 371/2884/72706. One spoke of the hanging of 34 Jewish soldiers at Botescu on trumped-up charges.

[8] Labin, 'On Solving the Jewish question', MWS 20333–52, gives a minimalist view of the power of the Social Democrats in Romania. Cf. Mitrany, 'On Various Aspects', MWS 6144–5, which foresees 'democratic forces' emerging to supplant the old aristocratic order.   [9] Mitrany, 'On Various Aspects', MWS 6144–5.

stepping on the Jewish question and the Conjoint's equally tenacious, though frustrated, attempts to do something about it, one might have been surprised if he had not done so with a vengeance. However, while not abandoning his potential trump cards, Wolf chose to steer a much more diplomatic course. Neither Whitehall nor the Quai d'Orsay would be required participants; the onus and responsibility for reform would be squarely placed on the Romanians themselves.

The way to do this, he told Dimitrie Draghicesu, a senator sent by Ioan Bratianu on a mission to the West in October 1917, was through 'a private understanding with the great Jewish organisations of western Europe'.[10] This, said Wolf, would lead to a settlement of the issue immediately, or failing that, on the basis of solid guarantees, at the end of the war. In return, Wolf offered that he might be able to prevail on the Russian Jews from interfering further.[11]

To Draghicesu's objections that reform could not be carried out at once, Wolf pointed out the speed at which the Romanian constitution had been revised to deal with the franchise and agrarian questions. To fail to do something similar on the Jewish score, he warned darkly, was to risk putting Romania's good faith to the test at the peace conference, something the *entente* powers would not like, as it would place a weapon in the hands of the enemy and make difficulties for Romania's position there. Nothing, concluded Wolf, 'would please the Allies of Rumania more than to know they could go into the Peace Conference without risking any reproach on the score of Article 44 of the Treaty of Berlin and the treatment of the Jews during the last 40 years'.[12]

By a deliberate and delicate balance of threat and cajolery, Wolf hoped to achieve Romanian Jewish emancipation without upsetting the fabric of *entente* relations. We thus find him, for instance, in December 1917, demanding from Nicolae Misu, the Romanian ambassador to London, an explanation for the alleged anti-Jewish excesses, and yet in the same breath reassuring him that 'I am not making these representations to you in any spirit hostile to Rumania. My Committee are

[10] Note of interview with Draghicesu, 5 Oct. 1917, encl. with Wolf to Oliphant, 9 Oct. 1917, FO 371/2884/72706. The AIU, on Wolf's advice, made similar demands; see Bigart to Wolf, 16 Oct. 1917, C11/2/12.

[11] Note of additional Draghicesu interview, 8 Oct. 1917, encl. with Wolf to Oliphant, 9 Oct. 1917, FO 371/2884/72706. Wolf wrote to Mitrany: 'At Draghicesu's request I wrote to our friends in Petrograd suggesting a more indulgent attitude towards the Rumanians'; Wolf to Mitrany, 9 Nov. 1917, C11/2/12.

[12] Wolf–Draghicesu interview, 8 Oct. 1917, FO 371/2884/72706.

only anxious to clear up any misunderstanding which might render relations between the Allies difficult and our first desire is to act in complete harmony with you.'[13]

For a short while, Wolf was master of this situation. Through Mitrany's contacts, Wolf was cognizant of government support for his project; and though the Foreign Office was unable to comment to Wolf on the Draghicesu interview, Harold Nicolson acknowledged in private that he had been justified in submitting to the Romanian senator 'some home truths'.[14] On the Romanian side, Misu, perhaps through pressure from Mitrany, was keen to further the emancipation project, and Draghicesu returned home to prepare the ground for formal negotiations between his government and Wolf's committee.[15] Wolf himself set to work, in collaboration with Herbert Lousada and Elkan Adler, on the actual details of the projected revision of the constitution. According to this plan, Romanian law was either to be assimilated to the English *jus soli*, thereby giving all those born on Romanian soil automatic Romanian citizenship, or liberalized in such a way as to prevent the *jus sanguinis* code being used as an anti-emancipatory loophole.[16]

The essence of this exercise was speed. In early 1918, the Romanians were on the brink of defeat, the Russians already plunged into internal chaos. If, against all odds, Wolf had at this stage been able to keep the Romanians on course, he would have certainly won a prestigious threefold victory: the Romanian Jews would have achieved emancipation; his committee would have been applauded as the prime movers, and indeed Romanians' mentors in the process; and for the Allies, he would have snatched a solution to the problem from the encroaching Central Powers. But in March 1918, Romania sued for peace with the Central Powers. The provision of Jewish clauses in the ensuing Treaty of Bucharest thus found Wolf in the somewhat embarrassing position of being neither able to preside over an internal settlement nor support the German-imposed one.

There were in fact many technical weaknesses and complications in

[13] Wolf to Misu, 4 Dec. 1917, C11/2/12.

[14] Wolf to FO, 16 Oct. 1917, FO 371/2884/72706. H. G. Nicolson minute, 16 Oct. 1917, ibid.

[15] Wolf–Draghicesu interview, 8 Oct. 1917, ibid. Wolf to Mitrany, 9 Nov. 1917, C11/2/12, implies that Mitrany had some influence at the Romanian embassy. Misu returned to Bucharest as foreign minister in March 1918.

[16] AJA sub-committee report, 28 Oct. 1917, C11/2/12. The AIU also accepted these proposals; see Bigart to Wolf, 16 Oct. 1917, ibid.

the naturalization article of the treaty. These manifested themselves when Alexander Marghiloman, the new prime minister, presented an emancipation bill to both chambers. The bill, in effect, divided Jews into two distinct categories: those who had fought in the war were theoretically naturalized immediately; the rest had to furnish special tribunals with documentary evidence of their birth. However, as Article vii of the constitution had not been altered to legitimize the bill by the time some months later that Jews began appearing before the tribunals, the Romanian judiciary simply declared it null and void.[17]

Certainly, neither the German Jews in the VJOD, which had been instrumental in achieving the naturalization article for the treaty, nor the Labin people in Switzerland showed many signs of satisfaction at this state of affairs.[18] Indeed, Labin resorted to bombarding Wolf with appeals for *his* direct diplomatic intervention. If the law was not changed, Labin wrote, financial assistance would be needed to 'facilitate procuring of those documents required by the Act and to supervise and assist applications made to the proper officials'. Otherwise, he claimed, fifty or sixty thousand Romanian Jews would still remain unnaturalized.[19]

What could Wolf now do on Labin's behalf? Romania was no longer at war, nor indeed in the *entente*. Moreover, the war itself was again at a critical stage. Wolf's 1915 Romanian predicament was being replayed all over again. Labin's pleas stood to be ignored—or put another way, Jewish interests would, at least superficially, have to be sacrificed for the sake of *entente* ones.

Wolf's difficulty was amply demonstrated in an ensuing letter to the Foreign Office. His objections to the Bucharest Treaty, he stated, had nothing to do with the technical deficiencies of the German decree-law. On the contrary, these could be obviated 'by a precautionary enactment substituting a declaration on oath for certificate of origin', similar to those proposed by his own subcommittee. His objections were wholly political. British Jews and patriotic Romanian ones could have no truck with either a German-imposed peace or with a decree-

[17] For details of developments leading to the naturalization clause in the Treaty of Bucharest see M. Gelber, 'Rumanian Jews'; report on treaty of 13 May 1918 encl. with Wolf to Cecil, 3 June 1918, FO 371/3155/54323.

[18] Labin to AIU/JFC, 30 Apr. 1918, encl. with Wolf to Cecil, 3 June 1918, FO 371/3155/54323; on Hantke and Nathan's anxieties, see Mowschowitch to Wolf, 27 July 1918, MWS 10582-5, Gelber, 'Rumanian Jews', 242; Zechlin, *Deutsche Politik*, 245-50.

[19] Labin to Wolf, 6 July, 12 and 16 Aug., 9 Sept. 1918, C11/4/1(6); Labin to Wolf, 28 July 1918, MWS 8178-80.

law which would single them out as German or Austrian protégés.[20] Instead, Wolf insisted, the way forward was an internal liberalization of Romania's fundamental laws, along the lines he himself had previously proposed.

At least Wolf could now have the satisfaction that this line was consistent with that adopted by the *entente* governments. Their publication of the Romanian government statement of June 1917 was now propagandized as a full programme of Jewish enfranchisement, as opposed to the limited German-imposed one.[21] The problem was how was this going to be achieved, by whom, and when? If the issue was left in abeyance until the end of the war, the likelihood of it being dealt with adequately by the Romanians themselves diminished considerably. Wolf attempted to circumvent this possibility by discreetly communicating his own recommendations, via Mitrany, to the German-oriented government in Bucharest.[22] But Marghiloman did nothing. That left Ioan Bratianu, the veteran ultra-nationalist leader, who remained in opposition to the peace with the Central Powers.[23] His past ministerial record of broken promises on Jewish and other questions was notorious. If he returned as leader of a post-war successor government, Wolf and his associates might have no choice but to turn to the peace conference.

Mitrany, Wolf's long-time adviser on Romanian affairs, felt Wolf had made a major tactical error, and took him to task for rebuffing Labin's solicitations:

While you are constantly holding forth that you cannot offer anything less than first class carriages of which unfortunately you have none to spare at the moment, the Germans are supplying third class carriages which will take the Jews to their destination . . . I should like to suggest that you have submitted too readily to their [Foreign Office] decision. As the German government has a free hand in Rumania, everybody is becoming anti-German, but if you leave

[20] Report of 13 May 1918 encl. with Wolf to Cecil, 3 June 1918, FO 371/3155/54323.
[21] Ibid. Cecil replied to a House of Commons question on the subject on 30 May 1918: 'His Majesty's Government have the fullest sympathy with the cause of Jewish enfranchisement in Rumania and elsewhere, but it is to the full programme of liberation which the Rumanian government have themselves adopted prior to the Treaty and not this restricted scheme that His Majesty's Government will adhere'; see encl. in Graham to Wolf, 18 June 1918, FO 371/3155/54323, repr. in *JC* 6 July 1918. See also Marshall papers, Paris Peace Conference box 2, Rumania, for the complementary letter from Pichon to AIU, 24 July 1918.
[22] Wolf, note on interview with Mitrany, 15 May 1918, C11/3/1/3.
[23] On Bratianu see Spector, *Rumania*, 228.

it to the Foreign Office to deal with Rumania, they will as surely turn everybody into pro-Germans. These people [the Rumanian Jews] after all do not intend to help you in your quarrel with Germany, but they want you or for that matter Germany to help them in their troubles and the one sensible policy is to respond to an appeal which will gain for you their gratitude and then as a consequence and for the future also their support.[24]

Wolf still believed that he might be able to clinch victory by quiet diplomacy. Back in 1917, Mitrany had pointed to Take Jonescu, the new Romanian foreign minister in the wake of the first Russian revolution, as the man most likely to carry through the proposed agrarian and franchise reforms and solve the Jewish question. Jonescu was a curious phenomenon in Romanian politics, a cosmopolitan with liberal tendencies and an interest in the Western-style development of the country; he was an opportunist, and as such was prepared to work both with his xenophobic antithesis, Bratianu, and with the conservative Carp–Marghiloman group. An outsider, he walked the corridors of power but was never able to take full control.[25]

In the autumn of 1918, visiting Western Europe, he saw both Wolf and the Alliance chiefs and assured them that though he believed that the Bucharest Treaty would in fact emancipate the great bulk of Romanian Jews, he intended to broaden its base 'by proposing a revision of the Constitution which would liberalise the Rumanian theory of nationality', hence giving Jews their rights automatically.[26]

In practice, the project was not quite as simple. For instance, Wolf discovered that special tribunals would still be needed to grant the emancipated Jews the new certificates of nationality, and this raised again the complicated question of documentary evidence to prove whether a Jew was a Romanian subject or under foreign protection. Nevertheless, following the close scrutiny of the Joint Foreign Committee legal experts and a rigorous cross-examination of Jonescu by Wolf himself, the committee endorsed the project.[27] Wolf would get his revision of the constitution.

But supposing this plan, which depended on the ascendancy of

---

[24] CII/4/I(6), Mitrany to Wolf, n.d., July or Aug. 1918.

[25] MWS 6136–7, Mitrany to Wolf, 14 June 1917; Seton-Watson, *Rumanians*, 368, 448.

[26] On Wolf–Jonescu interview, 9 Aug. 1918, see *RDJBE* 63–4. On AIU–Jonescu interview, 10 Oct. 1918, see AIU/Rumanie vii C52, memo. On Labin's fears that the proposals were too 'vague' see Labin to Wolf, 14 Sept. 1918, CII/4/I(6).

[27] Jonescu to Wolf and vice versa, 10 Aug. and 18 Sept. 1918, *RDJBE* 63–4, 65.

Jonescu in the Romanian parliament, should be blocked? The only alternative, as Wolf admitted to Sieglestein, of an American-based Romanian Jewish committee was an appeal to the peace conference.[28] As the war drew to a close it became apparent that there was no other option.

On 6 November 1918, Marghiloman resigned, being replaced first by the reactionary General Coanda and then, a month later, by Bratianu.[29] Concurrently, the withdrawal of German troops from Romania gave the opportunity for reactionary organizations to incite antisemitic feeling. A wave of pogroms seemed daily imminent. The seriousness of the situation was such that appeals by Wolf and Bigart to their respective governments to make representations to Bucharest were acted upon immediately.[30]

Far more disturbing were the long-term implications of Romania's last-minute redeclaration of war on the Central Powers. Romania had come into the war in the first place purely for large-scale territorial gains. Already the diet of an autonomous Bessarabia (separated from Russia since the revolution) had voted, in April 1918, for union with the Danubian kingdom. Once Austria-Hungary had collapsed, the Romanian-speakers in Transylvania voted in like fashion. But by the terms of the secret treaty made between Bratianu and the *entente* in 1916, Romania stood to gain much vaster territories than these—in Bukovina, in the Banat, and in Dobrudja, territories which, unlike Transylvania where Romanians were balanced out by Hungarians, were overwhelmingly made up of non-Romanian nationalities. By redeclaring war Bratianu sought to reassert the legitimacy of his 1916 claims while in hastily occupying Transylvania he attempted to present the peacemakers with a *fait accompli*.[31]

From the Jewish point of view, this territorial issue served to throw into shadow the almost incidental cancellation of the Treaty of Bucharest, and hence of the Jewish articles, in consequence of the renewed state of belligerency. Romania's appalling record on the

[28] Wolf to Sieglestein, 21 Aug. 1918, C11/4/1(6).

[29] Seton-Watson, *Rumanians*, 535.

[30] Bigart to Wolf, 13 Nov. 1918, encl. with Wolf to FO, 27 Nov. 1918, FO 371/3160/196427.

[31] On terms of the 'secret' treaty see V. Vodosev in *Djen*, 24 May 1917, MWS 80201–2. On the Bessarabian Stat and Alba Julia National Assembly decisions see Seton-Watson, *Rumanians*, 535. On Bratianu's aims see Spector, *Rumania*, esp. 228–336. Romania's final aggrandizement was from 53,000 to 113,000 square miles, and from a population of 7.5 million to 16 million.

258 *The Peace*

maintenance of Jewish citizen rights in territories acquired or seized since the creation of the original Romanian entity, so much of a headache for Wolf in the pre-1914 period,[32] suggested that unless Romania now came clean, a great number of people in south-eastern Europe—and not only Jews—would become stateless. Wolf had already attempted to make provisions guarding against such an eventuality. Thus, when Finland had seceded from Russia in late 1917 but in its constitution had differentiated between Lutherans— the dominant religious group—and non-Lutherans, Wolf had intervened with the British government, not especially because of any injustice being done to the Jews in Finland (their numbers were negligible) but in order to establish a precedent: 'that no new state or transfer of territory which may emerge from the present war, shall be recognised by His Majesty's Government unless full guarantees for religious liberty and the civil and political equality of all religious denominations are given'.[33] The Foreign Office reply had been non-committal, though Oliphant privately assured Wolf that they would not lose sight of the question.[34] With Russia in late 1918 in the throes of civil war (leaving Bratianu to pursue his 'greater Romania' designs with impunity), Wolf found it more necessary than ever to invoke this principle. His pre-peace December programme thus called on the British government to guarantee that 'no enlargement of the present frontiers of Rumania shall be sanctioned until all laws . . . relative to Jewish emancipation have been enacted'.[35]

But neither Wolf nor the British government, regardless of the latter's sympathies or otherwise for the Jews of Romania,[36] were able to guarantee anything. The Western Allies, given their small Salonika-based force, were not physically capable of policing the Romanians; nor, given Bratianu's justification for invading Hungary as a counter to the Bolshevik threat, were they particularly willing to bludgeon him into submission. In the face of Bratianu's *fait accompli* in invading Transylvania, Wolf's demand for a guarantee was thus a dead letter before the peace conference had started. Moreover, Romania's accept-

[32] See Wolf, *Notes*, 36–54.
[33] Wolf to FO, 17 Jan. 1918, C11/2/12.
[34] Oliphant to Wolf, 21 Feb. 1918, ibid.
[35] Wolf to Balfour, 2 Dec. 1918, *RDJBE*, 75.
[36] Barclay, HMG ambassador in Bucharest, continued to insist that the Romanian Jews were thoroughly pro-German; see Barclay to FO, 12 Dec. 1918, FO 371/3160/196427.

ance in early 1919 (and hence in advance of the peace conference settlement itself) as a full-fledged member of the League of Nations alongside the other new European states seemed only to reinforce this fact.[37]

With the situation fast slipping out of his control, Wolf might still have taken cheer if Jonescu had been in a position to carry through his proposed decree-law. But he was not. With all the power passing into the hands of Coanda and Bratianu, and without any power base with which to challenge the traditional political system, Jonescu's chances of being able to carry through a reform programme single-handed proved to be illusory. Moreover, since Jonescu was under a cloud for having had conversations with Nikola Pasic, the Serb leader, on the Banat question, and since Jonescu was also an adherent of a Wilsonian-type peace, Bratianu was well positioned to exclude him from his obvious position as number two plenipotentiary in the Romanian peace delegation. In November 1918, Wolf learnt that Jonescu had given up his internal Jewish emancipation programme and was now putting his faith in an international solution, proposing that a clause be inserted in the peace treaty giving all inhabitants born in the old kingdom or in territories annexed to it, with the exception of those claiming foreign nationality, citizens' rights.[38]

Wolf's scope for manœuvre outside the confines of the peace conference was thus narrowing. True, information from Romania itself still hinted at the possibility of an internal settlement. Certainly, Astruc, the Alliance delegate in Bucharest, was exerting pressure in that direction via St Aulaire, the French ambassador,[39] and an 'embarrassingly friendly' Misu, who returned to Western Europe as Bratianu's second, assured Wolf persistently in December and January that this would indeed follow.[40] So it did. A decree-law passed in January purported to solve the Jewish question. A. W. A. Leeper, the Foreign

---

[37] Spector, *Rumania*, 237. On the entry of Romania, Poland, and Czechoslovakia into the League see Wolf, Paris Diary, 26 Feb. 1919, fo. 84.

[38] Seton-Watson, *Rumanians*, 538–9; Bigart to Wolf, 13 Nov. 1918, encl. with Wolf to FO, 27 Nov. 1918, FO 371/3160/196427; Mitrany had warned that Jonescu was dependent on his landed followers, and aired his doubts about whether the latter would be able to unite a new democratic front; see Mitrany to Wolf, 14 June 1917, MWS 1636–7. Labin believed that Jonescu had no basis for support within the actual political system; see Labin, 'Upon the Necessity of a Solution of the Question by an International Peace Conference', n.d., late 1918, MWS 20266–81.

[39] Astruc–St Aulaire conversation, 28 Dec. 1918, AIU/Rumanie vii C52.

[40] Wolf memo on meeting with Misu and Rosenthal, 24 Dec. 1918, MWS 19887–90; Wolf, Paris Diary, 19 Jan. 1919, fo. 24.

Office official who had held out for a 'spontaneous' settlement, was delighted, only to be shocked when Wolf sprung on him in mid-January his
committee's decision to insist on a decision from the conference.[41]
Wolf had quickly found out via his French colleagues that the
decree-law had been rejected out of hand by the Union des Juifs
Indigènes as a valueless sham, a complicated mass of stipulations
inoperable without a change in the actual form of the constitution.[42]
Labin, moreover, was insisting on an immediate prosecution of the
Jewish case at the conference, and the Alliance, the traditional protectors of Romanian Jewry, especially after the failure of conversations
between Edmond de Rothschild and Bratianu in early February, felt
duty bound to comply.[43] They drew up a draft memorial for the peace
conference secretariat which, using the precedent of a specific proposal for Romanian Jewish emancipation made by Count de Launay,
the Italian delegate at the Congress of Berlin, urged the inclusion of a
like article in the forthcoming peace treaty. For this purpose a special
'watertight' article specifically naming the Jews was formulated by the
Labin people.[44] Wolf agreed to support the proposal, the intention
being that it should complement and supplement a memorial prepared
by himself and Bigart a few days earlier which repeated the call for the
main lines of Wolf's December desiderata on Poland to be the basis
for a general solution of the Jewish question in each new state. This
time, however, it contained a significant addition suggested by the
Alliance: 'any persons or communities who may suffer from the non-
observance of any provisions of the Article shall have the right to
submit their complaints to the Executive Committee of the League of
Nations and to seek the protection of that body'.[45]
These draft memorials were tantamount to an admission by the two

[41] Text of Romanian decree-law, AIU/Rumanie vii C52; A. W. A. Leeper minute,
23 Jan. 1919, FO 371/3586/6132; Wolf, Paris Diary, 26 Jan. 1919, fo. 25, on Wolf–
Leeper interview.
[42] *RDJBE*, memorial 21 Feb. 1919, 77–80; A. W. A. Leeper minute, 23 Jan. 1919,
FO 371/3586/6132 recognizing that the Bucharest tribunal's refusal to accept Jewish
applications on the basis of the new decree-law made for a new difficulty.
[43] Labin, 'Upon the Necessity', MWS 20266–81; vii C52, Astruc note on Edmond
de Rothschild–Bratianu interview, 6 Feb. 1919, AIU/Rumanie vii C52.
[44] Wolf, Paris Diary, 10 Feb. 1919, fo. 37. The article ran, 'Sont declarés de plein
droit citoyens roumains tous les juifs nés ou habitant sur le territoire de la Roumanie à
l'exception de ceux qui inscrits sur les registres des Consulats étrangers appartient à une
nationalité étrangère la preuve à faire de leur naissance domicile ou nationalité étrangère
incombe au gouvernement roumain.'
[45] *RDJBE*, memorial 21 Feb. 1919, 77–80. See also Parkes, *Emergence*, 118.

Western Jewish organizations that they could not solve the Jewish questions in Poland, Romania, and elsewhere unaided but would require the active participation of the peacemakers themselves, if necessary to impose a settlement. Indeed, the 'Polish' memorial specifically called upon the Council of the Great Powers or a special commission set up by it to review the Jewish question with a view to submitting additional articles in special cases which could not be covered by any general formula on political and civil rights.

Wolf may still have been unhappy in shifting the onus in this way on to the peacemakers, perhaps in deference to his British patrons who continued to urge him to be satisfied with the Romanian decree-law.[46] Circumstances, however, were forcing his hand. Wilson's efforts to get an all-embracing civil and religious article into the League covenant which would have bound all states taking allegiance to it had recently failed; the Alliance proposal for a right of appeal to the League in case of treaty infractions being a direct consequence of it. Rumours were rife that Clemenceau had entered into a compact with Bratianu agreeing to abandon the Romanian Jews in return for a Romanian invasion, in the Allied interest, of the Ukraine.[47] More concretely, the Great Powers' decision in February to examine the actual claims of the small states led to the creation of territorial commissions, the first being for Romania; yet as far as A. W. A. Leeper, its British representative, was concerned, the Jewish question did not merit a special guarantee. Leeper reported his attitude to Wolf, who in turn wrote,

This conversation confirms me in my belief that action on the Rumanian question is urgent and that the Memorial . . . should be sent into the Conference immediately . . . at any moment the Committee may report in favour of Rumanian territorial claims and without stipulating any condition in favour of the Jews. It would be criminal in these circumstances to postpone action. The fact that we have done nothing so far is alone enough to make the Peace Conference think that the Jewish question is no longer of urgent importance.[48]

On 21 February, the Joint and Alliance submitted their parallel memorials to the peace conference secretariat.[49]

---

[46] See A. W. A. Leeper interview, Wolf, Paris Diary, 18 Feb. 1919, fos. 66–7.

[47] Ibid., 11 Feb. 1919, fos. 45–6.

[48] Ibid., 18 Feb., 1919, fos. 66–7. On claims of new states and Romanian territorial commission see F. S. Marston, *The Peace Conference of 1919: Organisation and Procedure* (Oxford, 1944), 102, 115.

[49] *RDJBE*, JFC memorial 21 Feb. 1919, 77–80; Alliance, *La Question juive*, AIU memorial, 21 Feb. 1919, 44.

14

French, American, and Other Jewish Delegations

WOLF'S diplomacy at Paris was governed in organizational terms by two important factors: when, or rather how, the peace settlement was to be achieved, and who was going to do it. Tyrrell had informed Wolf at the beginning of January that a preliminary inter-Allied conference would lay down general principles almost immediately, and more complex issues would be referred to special commissions 'whose labours would be of a protracted nature'.[1] This plan suited Wolf well. If the work load was, so to speak, spread out from the top downwards, Wolf's access to the commissions, perhaps through Tyrrell, who seemed in January to be his surest line of communication and information with what was going on on the 'inside', would be increased. A time lapse, moreover, increased the feasibility of a 'holding action' until reinforcements from his own committee and from other Jewish organizations arrived to press home the Jewish case.

Wolf was fully aware that what had to be achieved at Paris could only be done by co-ordinated action with other delegations. Even at the Congress of Berlin in 1878, where the magnitude of the problem had been far smaller and the Jews themselves much less organized, the nascent Jewish committees, alongside the surviving great *shtadlanim* (intercessionaries) like Bleichröder, had agreed to co-ordinate their actions even though working independently of one another.[2]

In 1919, the necessity to pool Jewish resources was much greater. Even if the peace was ultimately drawn in a Wilsonian sense, it could not be taken for granted that without concerted and competent guidance, it would, from the Jewish point of view, be just. Nor could

[1] Wolf to Marshall, 2 Jan. 1919, C11/3/2/4. It was the British intention that the Jewish and other minority questions should be dealt with alongside the various territorial settlements; see Percy memo cited in Kohler, 'Origin', 765–6.

[2] Mowschowitch, 'The Board', MWS 23534–42; Mowschowitch, 'Board Foreign Affairs', MWS 23512–28. For material relating to these events see also BDAI Papers, esp. Corr. box 5.

Wilson's principles of 'open diplomacy' be relied upon; as things turned out, with the centralizing of decision-making in the hands of 'the Big Three'—Wilson, Lloyd George, and Clemenceau—open diplomacy was, at the behest of Wilson, replaced by the utmost secrecy.[3] As a result, after March, when the Council of Four replaced the unwieldy Council of Ten,[4] the only sure way for Wolf and his associates to gauge what was really going on, and in turn to bring effective pressure to bear at the right time and place, was not by discreet conversations in the *coulisses* and corridors of power but by access to the inner sanctum itself. To achieve this required considerable influence in high places, something Wolf personally did not have. It also required an organizing apparatus capable of carrying it through.

What was needed, argued Mowschowitch in November 1918, expounding one of his favourite themes to Wolf, was a 'Conjoint' committee of the most influential Jewish delegations.[5] Federally organized, the corpus of this committee would be the English, French, Italian, and American Jewish delegations. This not only would reflect the key roles their respective countries were likely to play in the forthcoming peace, it was also a recognition that real influence on the peace conference could only be brought to bear by Jewish committees closest to the centres of power. What, perhaps, is most striking about Mowschowitch's proposal is the parties which were to be left out of this 'Conjoint' Jewish federation, a reflection of the deep wounds caused by the war and its aftermath.

Germany and Austria, as defeated nations, were denied a negotiated peace. Russia, being in the midst of civil war, had no peace conference status, and remained outside the scope of the settlement. In other words, three important Jewish communities that stood to be affected by the changes determined by the peace conference had no say in it, and their expert delegates on the Jewish question in Eastern Europe would be officially excluded from any access to the peacemakers. Their involvement in the projected federation was therefore quite pointless. This did not mean that they were not in Paris. Vinaver, Blank, and

[3] Marston, *Peace Conference*, 104: 'Never in all history has there been such complete centralisation of power in the hands of a few men.'
[4] Ibid. 98–9. The Council of Four originally included Orlando, the Italian premier, until dissensions over Italian territorial demands intervened. The involvement of the Japanese premier, for a time, created a Council of Five. The real kernel of power however, was the 'Big Three'.
[5] Mowschowitch to Wolf, 11 Nov. 1918, MWS 10634–40.

Gunzburg, on behalf of Russian Jews, lurked in the background, and there was also a German Jewish delegation, moulded out of VJOD, which presented its own memorials.[6] A renewed axis with Nathan[7] and Kaminka, such as Wolf had enjoyed prior to the war, was clearly unthinkable, however. So, too, was the opportunity which had looked so promising in 1917,[8] via the now non-existent Jewish Political Bureau in Petrograd, of cementing an alliance with Russian Jewry.

Wolf thus departed in January 1919 for Paris with instructions to work with the Alliance, the American Jewish Committee, and the Rome Committee for the implementation of the December desiderata[9] and with the personal intention of creating a secretariat which would consolidate the Jewish position there pending the others' arrival.[10] His own delegation, officially comprising presidents Montefiore and Samuel and vice-presidents Lords Swaythling and Rothschild (neither in fact were able to attend and were replaced by Henriques and Prag)[11] was not due to appear until negotiations on the Jewish question were well under way; it did not in fact do so until late March, the same time as the American and Italian Jews began arriving in force.

This two-month gap was of critical import. What Wolf, in conjunction with the Alliance, did or did not do in this period would to some extent determine the way the Jewish question would shape itself at the conference; more importantly, his handling of it would determine the degree to which it would be possible for the fully complemented secretariat to work in harmony. There was, after all, no surety that all the delegations would wish to work as a unit, despite the exigencies of

[6] No Russian–Jewish memorials representing the delegates associated with Koltchak or Denikin were presented to the peace conference. For Wolf's views on Vinaver and Gunzburg in Paris see Wolf, Paris Diary, 6 June 1917, fos. 341–2; 13 Aug. 1919, fo. 534. French Foreign Ministry, Receuil de Documents Etrangères, no. 46, for the German Jewish memo, 31 July 1919, MWS 8364–9.

[7] Ibid., encl., letter from Nathan to the *Vossische Zeitung*, 19 Nov. 1918, expressing doubts on national autonomy and suggesting that he might have been a useful ally to Wolf in Paris. On renewed post-settlement contact between the two men see Zosa Szajkowski, 'Nathan, Wolf and the Versailles Treaty', *PAAJR* 38–9 (1971), 179–201.

[8] See Wolf memo on the Russian revolution, 23 Mar. 1917, MWS 5782–7: 'We ought to make use of the new situation to enter at once, officially and openly, into the same relations with the Jewish community of Petrograd, for the purpose of dealing with the Jewish questions arising out of the war, as those in which we stand with the French and Italian communities.'

[9] JFC presidents' instructions, 13 Dec. 1918, C11/4/2; appointment of Delegation, 14 Nov. 1918, see *RDJBE* 71.

[10] Wolf, Paris Diary, 14 and 15 Jan. 1919, fos. 2, 7. [11] *RDJBE* 9.

the situation, nor that they would be willing to work under Wolf's nominal tutelage. The French and Italian organizations had long traditions of their own and were sensitive to *diktats* from outside. Wolf's 'considered views' *démarche* in 1916 had been prematurely wrecked for this very reason.[12]

Close association with the Alliance in January and February 1919 showed Wolf how carefully he had to tread if he wished to maintain their support. He wrote to Montefiore soon after his arrival:

I find that the Joint Foreign Committee wields very considerable authority and enjoys complete confidence here and there is a general disposition to follow its lead, although the Alliance is jealous of its formal primacy and every attention has to be paid to its natural susceptibilities in this respect. The centre of gravity however has passed to London.[13]

Wolf's analysis was correct. The Alliance, with a tradition of involvement on behalf of Jewish civil and religious rights far outstripping that of all other participants, and finding themselves in the fortunate role of host to the other Jewish organizations in their own city, were willing not only to provide the facilities for action but the leadership commensurate with their role.

However, the complacency and near-sluggishness which Wolf encountered in January suggested that the Alliance were, paradoxically, not well suited to their self-appointed commission. 'A vague impression seems to prevail', he noted, 'that a short formula asking for equal rights is all that is necessary.'[14] At a time when all other Jewish delegations were pressing for some form of national or cultural autonomy, the Alliance's stance seemed distinctly out of key, and Wolf had considerable difficulty bringing it into line with his own very toned-down proposals.

But there was more to the Alliance's posture than obdurate conservatism. The Alliance leaders saw themselves, first and foremost, as Frenchmen, just as Wolf saw himself primarily as an Englishman. In fact, there was between the Joint and Alliance a tension that reflected the tensions of spring 1919 between Britain and France. For instance, the Alliance had legitimized their February *revendications* to the French government on Salonika by arguing that unless it intervened against

[12] See Wolf to Sereni, 17 Aug., AIU 1J 8; Sereni to Wolf, 30 Aug., 25 Dec. 1916, ibid.; Wolf to Bigart, 27 Nov. 1916, 3 Jan. 1917, ibid.
[13] Wolf to Montefiore, 18 Jan. 1919, MWS file 210.
[14] Wolf, Paris Diary, 16 Jan. 1919, fo. 7.

266 *The Peace*

the Hellenizing efforts of the Greek government in the Alliance schools, the chances of maintaining, or continuing in the future, to promote French influence and interests in the Levant would be seriously jeopardized. Wolf had written many similar politico-economic epistles to his own Foreign Office arguing the case from the British standpoint, but he now noted that it was 'no part of our business to support French political aims'. The Alliance memorandum consequently gained no support from its English sister organization.[15]

The relationship between the Alliance and the Joint Foreign Committee was put under even greater strain by developments relating to the Anglo-French quarrel in the Levant proper. The usurpation, from the French point of view, of Palestine by the British, and the continued presence of their troops in Damascus—a wilful obstruction of the Sykes-Picot agreement to which the French, unlike the British, faithfully adhered—brought the two allies close to military confrontation in Syria in 1919.[16] The French were concerned to regain their lost position in the area, and when Sylvain Lévi, the Alliance president, spoke at the Council of Ten session on Palestine in February, he did so at least as much with French as with Jewish interests at heart. Wolf, of course, despite his irreconcilable opposition to Zionists and Zionism, wholeheartedly supported the proposed British mandate for the area and saw in the Alliance attitude to this question 'a clear undercurrent of Anglo-phobia . . . which is a reflection of the attitude of the Quai d'Orsay'.[17]

This 'reflection' of the Quai d'Orsay explains the Alliance's obduracy on national rights and other issues. France wanted, as we have seen, not a Wilsonian peace but a peace of security; and in the conditions of 1919, this entailed enlarged Polish and Romanian states. The Alliance could not challenge these French goals: 'The business of the Conference', Eugene Sée told a meeting of Western Jewish delegates on 31 March, 'is to create a sovereign state for Poland not for the Jews.'[18]

As a result, Alliance diplomacy at the peace had to be contained within narrowly defined boundaries; they might hammer away at the Quai d'Orsay for assurances on religious, civil, and political rights for

[15] Sée and Bigart to Quai d'Orsay, 12 Feb. 1919, AIU/France ii D 7; Wolf, Paris Diary, 14 Feb. 1919, fo. 58.
[16] Elie Kedourie, *England and the Middle East: The Destruction of the Ottoman Empire 1914–1921* (Hassocks, Sussex, 1968), 132–7.
[17] Wolf, Paris Diary, 1 Mar. 1919, fos. 93–5.
[18] Adler papers, Adler MS, Abstract of Report, 31 Mar. 1919, fo. 84.

Jews in Poland and elsewhere, but could not commit themselves on the more salient points in Wolf's programme. By comparison, Britain's primary interest in a durable peace at Paris, reflected most cogently in Lloyd George's March Fontainebleau memorandum,[19] gave Wolf greater scope for manœuvre. Logically, therefore, if the lines of the Wolf–Alliance cleavage followed that between the Quai d'Orsay and the British delegation, or between Clemenceau and Lloyd George, Wolf ought to have followed the pattern of the Anglo-American Lloyd George–Wilson compact[20] in focusing his attention on the American Jews in Paris.

The tilt from the Alliance and towards Louis Marshall and his associates, however, never materialized. The reason was an acute complication. When Wolf arrived in Paris, neither Marshall nor any of the important American Jews had yet arrived. As we have seen, however, there was already a strong presence of a group Wolf had not bargained for: the Zionists.

In 1917, Weizmann had insisted that what he wanted from Wolf and his committee was non-interference in Zionist matters. Wolf had interfered and suffered the consequences. Now the roles, and to some extent the consequences, were reversed. Wolf considered the Zionists unacceptable candidates for dealing with European matters and likely to compromise his carefully prepared peace conference diplomacy.[21] He was not alone in his view. Mowschowitch agreed that they were untutored on European questions; Herbert Samuel, Weizmann's loyal ally, went one step further in April when he insisted to Marshall and Cyrus Adler that the two Jewish issues at the conference, Palestine and Europe, should be kept quite distinct, and that spokesmen for one should not cross over and speak for the other.[22]

Wolf had been pre-empted on this score long before the peace conference began, however. With confidence gained through the Balfour Declaration and the association with the British government and by the very nature of an ideology which strove to safeguard and succour the Jewish people worldwide, the Zionists began probing into areas which Wolf and the Alliance would have considered strictly their own domain. Thus, when Sokolow, in June 1918, petitioned the

[19] Thompson, *Russia*, 196; Mayer, *Politics*, 578–81.
[20] For a general study of this issue see Tillman, *Anglo-American Relations*.
[21] Wolf, Paris Diary, 18 Feb. 1919, fos. 70–1.
[22] Mowschowitch to Wolf, 11 Oct. 1918, MWS 10634–40; Cyrus Adler, *I Have Considered the Days* (Philadelphia, 1941), 308–9.

Foreign Office on the question of Romanian Jewish emancipation at a
juncture almost identical to Wolf's own initiative on the question, the
danger of renewed competition and conflict between the two opposing
groups resurfaced.[23] When Wolf arrived in Paris to find Sokolow well
ensconced and with every intention of involving himself fully in non-
Palestine affairs, it seemed unavoidable.

In the event, Sokolow showed no desire to precipitate a controversy,
and readily agreed to co-operate in Wolf's proposed bureau.[24] 'We are
working in agreement with the Zionists', Wolf wrote in early February
to Eric Drummond, asking that this important information be passed
on to Balfour.[25] Sokolow alone represented no great threat to Wolf's
diplomacy; he was well experienced in the field on behalf of the Zionist
cause and fully recognized, with the odds heavily weighted against a
comprehensive Jewish settlement, the need to work tactfully and cautiously with the most influential and experienced of the Jewish delegations in Paris. Even after the split amongst the Jewish groups, he made
several private efforts to enlist both Joint Foreign Committee and
Alliance aid for his representations.[26]

But Sokolow was not to be left alone in Paris. In dribs and drabs,
other delegates began arriving from Eastern Europe: Podlichewski,
Farbstein, and Lewite from Poland; Albala and Stern from Yugoslavia;
Rosov from Russia. These delegates certainly had a strong and immediate awareness of the problems at home. As Zionists, they had, too,
an ideology which could provide guidelines for an affirmative response
to those problems. However, their knowledge or grasp of international
Jewish affairs was, according to the judgement of Wolf and his American counterparts, 'singularly inadequate and ineffective'.[27]

[23] Sokolow to FO, 3 June 1918, FO 371/3155/54323; Wolf to Cecil, 3 June 1918,
ibid. FO to Sokolow, 15 and 18 June 1918, ibid. See also Zionist Org. to FO, 30 Jan.
1919, FO 371/3686/6132, for a later Zionist appeal against the Romanian decree-law
which prompted Sir Ronald Graham to minute: 'This is only an attempt to go one better
than Mr. Lucien Wolff [sic] and his Committee, who have been agitating on the subject.'
[24] Wolf, Paris Diary, 15 Jan. 1919, fo. 3.
[25] Wolf to Drummond, 12 Feb. 1919, CI1/2/14.
[26] For Sokolow appeals to the JFC and AIU about Ukrainian pogroms, see Joint Foreign
Committee, *The League of Nations, Geneva... 1920* (London, 1921), 13–14. See also letter
from Sokolow, Wolf, and Zangwill to the League Assembly, 8 Dec. 1920, ibid. 43–4.
[27] Wolf to A. Abrahams, 15 Aug. 1918, MWS 1702; see also Adler papers, Adler
Diary, 10 Apr. 1919, fo. 19. For an opposing view putting great emphasis on the
importance of the work of the Eastern European Comité des Délégations see Feinberg,
La Question, 9.

The new arrivals were less interested in the executive action which
the Alliance and Joint were proposing and more in the actual nature of
the bureau which was to accomplish it. Up to this point, the functions
of the bureau had been ill defined. The Alliance, in a letter to the
Zionist Organizations on 25 February, argued that they had envisaged
it purely as a means of facilitating an exchange of information and a
way of giving 'exactitude' and 'precision' to the representations of the
various Jewish delegations.[28] Neither they nor the Joint Foreign Committee had any intention of it becoming a more formalized permanent
organization, and certainly not one where their own independence or
freedom of action was threatened. Besides, to do so would be to lay
Wolf's December proposals, already agreed to by his committee and
with amendments by the Alliance, open to rewriting. Such a development would contravene his instructions in Paris not to agree 'to any
essential modification of those proposals from whatever source (they)
may be proposed', without reference to his committee in London.[29]

Much more important, the failure of the peace conference to organize
itself on the basis Tyrrell had assured Wolf it would in January—the
sudden creation of territorial committees and the possibility of a greatly
expedited settlement of East European matters without regard to the
Jewish question—drove Wolf and his French colleagues into hasty
unilateral representations to the conference. To temporize, to wait
until all the other delegates had arrived and 'discussed matters of
principle and details of application', as Sokolow insisted they must,
struck Wolf as criminally negligent. 'The important thing was to act in
unison and to that (end) we ought to subordinate all questions of *amour
propre* and all abstract confessions of faith.'[30]

It was particularly unfortunate that the Zionist mid-February proposals for union, proposals which from the start were totally unacceptable to the older organizations, should be made at this crucial juncture.
They not only cut across Wolf's urgent appeals for action but left him
to suspect that their whole purpose amounted to 'delaying tactics'
aimed at creating paralysis until such time as the Zionists' own plans
were ready.[31] What the Zionists proposed was a complete merger.
Sokolow, seemingly throwing caution to the winds, led the attack. The

[28] Bigart to Zionist Org., 25 Feb. 1919, AIU/France ii D 8.
[29] JFC presidents to Wolf, 13 Dec. 1918, C11/4/2.
[30] Sokolow to Wolf, 14 Feb. 1919, AIU/France ii D 6 *bis*. Wolf, Paris Diary, 16 Feb.
1919, fo. 62.
[31] Wolf, Paris Diary, 16 Feb. 1919, fo. 62.

days of the 'grand dukes',[32] he told the assembled delegations at the Alliance headquarters on 18 February, were over. Moreover, 'their charitable traditions were no longer applicable', as the Jewish masses were now 'in the saddle'. Only a democratic organization could act on their behalf.[33]

The barely concealed ill feeling which underlay this speech, and the feelings of the East Europeans in general towards the Alliance, were not altogether unjustified. The latter had from the first caused acute and unnecessary rancour by demanding that the credentials of all delegates must be approved by themselves. As Sokolow noted to Wolf, 'their credentials consist of their election by the Jewries to which they belong'.[34] Certainly the Alliance consistently failed to disguise their peculiar understanding of the situation, that is, that the East Europeans were there to make representations to themselves who would in turn present their case, as they saw fit, to the peace conference.[35]

But if the Alliance's behaviour was tactless and ungracious, Sokolow's interpretation of 'democratic' was disingenuous. All the delegates present in February, outside the Alliance and the Joint (that is, Wolf himself) were elected by Zionist bodies. (This Zionist allegiance was made clear for all to see when, after the meeting at the Alliance, they transferred themselves *en masse* for a two week Zionist Congress in London.)[36] Sokolow's proposal for union was democratic in that it gave voting rights proportional to the number of Jews each organization was supposed to represent. On this basis the Alliance, Joint Foreign Committee, and Zionist Organization were to receive two votes each, while national delegations like the Ukrainians received three, the Americans four, and so on. But given the Zionist monopoly of these delegations, Wolf reckoned it would be tantamount to a 20–8 advantage to the Zionists. 'We are to give up our independence', he acerbically

---

[32] Wolf, Paris Diary, 11 Feb. 1919, fo. 44. Wolf suggested Sokolow's first tirade against what he called the 'Grand Dukes', a reference to the plutocratic leadership of Western Jewry, 'was chiefly intended as a vindication of Sokolow himself in the eyes of Rosov', who was also present at the meeting.

[33] Ibid., 18 Feb. 1919, fo. 69; Abstract of Meeting, 18 Feb. 1919, AIU/France ii D 6 *bis*.

[34] Sokolow to Wolf, 14 Feb. 1919, AIU/France ii D 6 *bis*. See also Bigart to Eastern European delegations, 18 Feb. 1919, ibid. D 7, asking for letters of mandate; Janowsky, *Jews and Minority Rights*, 285.

[35] .Abstract of Meeting, 18 Feb. 1919, AIU/France ii D 6 *bis*, comments of Eugene Sée. Janowsky, *Jews and Minority Rights*, 298.

[36] Wolf, Paris Diary, 20 Feb. 1919, fo. 73.

wrote, and to enter a hostile Confederation bound hand and foot.'[37] The effect was to bind Wolf more closely to the Alliance. Under these circumstances, with no decision reached at the 18 February meeting and the Alliance set against union, Wolf took the occasion of the Zionists' absence from Paris to promote 'a definite rupture'. On 20 February, he wrote to Sokolow, 'I am not authorised to postpone any longer the mission which has been confided to me. I am compelled to resume my liberty of action.' The letter attempted to finish on a conciliatory note, expressing the hope that this would 'in no way prejudice the eventual cooperation we all have in view';[38] but in fact Wolf's purpose—to sever relations with the Zionists—was barely disguised. The next day the Alliance–Joint Foreign Committee memorials were consigned to the peace conference secretariat.

That ought to have been the end of the matter, but it still left one important question unresolved: how would the American Jewish delegation react to the split when they arrived? Would they accept Wolf and the Alliance's behaviour as reasonable in the circumstances, or would they choose to make an issue of their failure to come to an understanding with the Zionists?

Wolf would have been able to justify his position more easily could he have shown something substantial had been achieved through the submission of the memorials. True, Headlam-Morley later assured him that they had come at a good time and had given the British delegation 'something solid to work upon'. Indeed, members of the delegation did as a result draw up their own clauses which Headlam-Morley suggested be inserted as special provisions for the new states as required, even going so far as to endorse Wolf's proposal that a special commission be appointed to deal with the problem.[39]

The nature of the conference, however, and in particular its weak organizational structure, militated against these proposals ever getting through to the Big Three so that they could act upon their recommendations. Headlam-Morley, with evident frustration, later noted that the minutes were 'never sent to the Heads of Office and week after week

---

[37] Marks (sec.-general, Zionist Org.) to Bigart, 19 Feb. 1919, AIU/France ii D 8 *bis*; Wolf, Paris Diary, 20 Feb. 1919, fo. 73.

[38] Wolf to Sokolow, 20 Feb. 1919, AIU/France ii D 8; Wolf, Paris Diary, 16 Feb. 1919, fo. 62.

[39] Wolf, Paris Diary, 3 Apr. 1919, fo. 161; Malkin memo, 21 Feb. 1919, FO 608/151/493/1/1; Headlam-Morley and E. H. Carr minutes, 18 and 24 Apr. 1919, FO 61/129/4/1; A. W. A. Leeper, 1 Mar. 1919, FO 151/493/1/1: 'Perhaps the whole question might be examined by a special Commission as Mr. Wolf suggests.'

went by without the matter progressing further. So far as the higher authorities went the question remained absolutely undecided until less than a week before the time when the Germans were to receive the copy of the Treaty'.[40]

This ever-narrowing time-gap was not the only problem. An increasingly tense international situation in the spring of 1919—the dangers of a German non-acceptance of the proposed treaty, Soviets in Bavaria and then in Hungary, even a possible Bolshevik breakthrough in the Carpathians—all seemed to conspire against the Jewish question being properly dealt with at the conference. More than ever, if it was not to be relegated into insignificance or entirely overlooked, the good offices of the American Jews, known to have access to and influence with President Wilson, seemed to be of the essence.

Wolf not unnaturally assumed that the American Jews would fall in with the line he had taken. Though the American Jewish Committee was of more recent lineage than either the Alliance or the Joint Foreign Committee (taking into account its former existence as the Conjoint), it maintained similar traditions and methods of approach, was oligarchic in form, neutral in its politics, and extremely venerable in its select list of key executive members. These included Jacob Schiff the financier, Oscar Straus the politician, and Judge Mayer Sulzberger.[41]

This did not mean that its relations with the old Conjoint Committee had been entirely free of friction. There was indeed an awareness that as the American Jewish Committee began to flex its muscles, it would implicitly represent a challenge to the supremacy of its English cousin, mirroring that posed by the United States to the British Empire. In 1912, for instance, the American Jewish Committee gained what appeared to be an outstanding success in getting the American Senate to revoke its commercial treaty with Russia, following the latter's discrimination against American Jewish traders. It had on this occasion mounted a very public campaign, which the Conjoint in its own unsuccessful efforts on the issue of British Jewish traders had chosen to eschew.[42] The Anglo-Russian *entente* of course loomed large as a major reason for their more softly-softly approach. Nevertheless, Louis Marshall, the American Committee's leading exponent and

---

[40] Headlam-Morley, *A Memoir*, n.d., c.18 May 1919, 113. Temperley, *Peace Conference*, v. 123.

[41] For formation and form of AJC, 1906, see Naomi Cohen, *Not Free*, 12–30.

[42] Ibid., chapter on 'Abrogation Campaign', 54–80. For the CJC's campaign see memo 'On the Grievances of British Subjects' encl. with Wolf to Norman, 23 Mar. 1912, FO 372/381/338.

prime mover, seems to have evinced some considerable annoyance at the Conjoint's failure to follow the American Committee's approach.[43]

With the coming of war and with the Conjoint Committee paralysed by inaction, the shift to the West was accentuated,[44] a situation which brought with it further complications and tensions. Thus, when the American Committee seemed on the verge of breaking with its proclaimed neutrality to make an arrangement with the papacy on the Polish–Jewish question, the so-called Pact of Lugano, Wolf felt compelled to warn them against involving themselves 'in certain highly controversial questions of international politics with which as Jews we have no concern'.[45] In fact, the American Committee had already wisely declined the proffered pact; but they felt that Conjoint interference reeked of high-handedness, and relations between the two organizations for some time remained cool.[46]

Once America was in the war on the side of the Allies, the tensions dissipated, communication increased, and co-operation became the order of the day, Wolf indeed following Marshall's lead *vis-à-vis* the Polish National Committee in 1918 in refusing to renegotiate with it until its anti-Jewish boycott had been withdrawn.[47] All the signs boded well for a promising co-operation at the peace conference, with Wolf sending his programme to Marshall and vice versa. Wolf certainly expected no discord, as is made evident by the tenor of his telegram to Marshall at the beginning of January: 'Ascertained best course for you to come as soon as possible . . . suffice for you to cooperate general principles. We watching special commissions.'[48]

[43] Marshall to Straus, 26 Dec. 1912, Marshall Papers (Wolf file 1912–16): 'Apparently these gentlemen [the CJC] gave little consideration to what had been done in this country or to the methods which were successfully pursued here. It would at least have been proper if they had conferred with us before taking the action that they did.' Cf. AJC Executive Committee minutes, 27 Jan. 1907, on AJC readiness to leave Russian questions to the CJC and to follow their lead, quoted in Bayme, 'Jewish Leadership', 272.
[44] Wolf to Montefiore, 15 Nov. 1914, C11/2/5. Combined Jewish action was impossible 'but we can all help and stimulate the neutral American community to take up the common cause'.
[45] Draft letter to Marshall, 23 Apr. 1916, encl. with Wolf to Drummond, FO 371/2817/78203. For more on the Deloncle affair see Szajkowski, *Jews, Wars*, i. 47–8; Black, *Social Politics*, 340–1.
[46] Wolf to Marshall, 29 June, Marshall to Wolf, 2 Aug. 1916, Marshall papers (Wolf file, 1912–16).
[47] JFC minutes, 3 Dec. 1918; Reznikoff, *Louis Marshall*, ii. 585, on interview with Dmowski, 6 Oct. 1918.
[48] Wolf to Marshall, 1 Jan. 1919, C11/3/2/4. Wolf's assumption that the AJC would work in tandem with himself is also made clear in Wolf to Marshall, 19 Dec. 1918,

Wolf, wilfully or otherwise, misread the situation. Though the American Jewish Committee had formulated its peace conference desiderata back in 1917 and had been holding these in readiness ever since, it was no longer in the driving seat. Despite a long rearguard action, it had finally given ground to the clamour for a popularly elected body. An American Jewish Congress had duly met in Philadelphia in December 1918, and it was its delegates, and, ostensibly, its programme, which would be going to Paris.[49]

Five years later, Marshall, writing to Cyrus Adler, inveighed against the inability or ineptitude of the Congress to decide on anything, the result being that Marshall's own programme was, with one major amendment, unanimously adopted. By the same token, though Marshall was *persona non grata* at the congress and not intended for candidature to go to Paris, his experience, contrasting with the complete lack of it on the part of the majority of other delegates, made him an essential ingredient to the delegation's success.[50] With Cyrus Adler, an old friend and associate of Wolf's,[51] being sent to Paris as separate delegate for the American Jewish Committee, the likelihood of its viewpoint and methods resurfacing as the dominant element in the American Jewish approach seemed assured. So too, therefore, should have been the conjunction with Wolf and the Joint Foreign Committee.

However, this was to ignore two very salient points. Firstly, Marshall had been selected not as leader of the American Jewish Committee delegation, accountable to no one save it, but as a member of a strongly Zionist-oriented one led, significantly, by Judge Julian Mack, a leading American Zionist, accountable to the American Jewish public at large. Marshall was highly conscious of this mandate, one which though it seriously hampered his scope for successful diplomatic manœuvre he

---

MWS 119891–2: 'I will not fail to advise you from Paris of all the decisions we may wish to recommend to your committee and other allied bodies.'

[49] Frankel, *Prophecy and Politics*, 451; Janowsky, *Jews and Minority Rights*, 298.

[50] Marshall to Adler, 6 June 1923, Marshall papers, Peace Conference Corr., box 1, 1919–23. The delegation consisted of Judge Mack (chairman), Louis Marshall, Stephen Wise, Henry Cutler, Revd B. L. Levinthal, Joseph Barondess, J. de Haas, Nachman Syrkin, Morris Winchevsky, and B. G. Richards (secretary). On the delegation's ideological composition see Frankel, *Prophecy and Politics*, 541–6. While some of the delegation were involved in Palestine affairs in Paris, only Marshall and Mack played any significant role in obtaining the Minorities Treaties; see Adler to Marshall, 20 June 1919, Marshall papers.

[51] The friendship went back to 1890, when Adler first visited England; Adler, *I Have Considered*, 78.

loyally and dispassionately observed.[52] To this extent, Headlam-
Morley's later remark that what the American delegates were thinking
of in Paris was the vote of New York Jews rather than the advantages to
be won for the Jews in Poland was equally applicable to Marshall and
his colleagues.[53] Secondly, and following on from this, was the nature
of Marshall's mandate. The 'Bill of Rights'[54] which the Congress had
adopted in Philadelphia was substantially in agreement with Wolf's
own agenda, the clause which had been amended in Marshall's programme being the main point of difference. Its reference to national
autonomy and to the principle of minority representation being 'provided for by the law' in fact represented only a difference of degree in
relation to Wolf's more subdued cultural formula. The problem was
that whereas Wolf, once he had recognized that there was no chance of
the peace conference accepting national minority rights, was able to
break away from these demands, and thus from the Eastern Jews in
Paris who persisted in demanding them, Marshall's mandate required
him to back these up to the hilt.

Interestingly, this dilemma applied equally to Adler, whose instructions were to 'support the petitions of the East European Jews for such
safeguards as they deemed necessary for themselves'. Unaware that
the East Europeans in Paris were not truly representative of the
communities from which they hailed—a situation rectified only in
May, on the arrival of the orthodox Polish Jewish delegation—Adler
initially felt impelled, though against his better judgement, to support
the request for full national rights.[55] The result was that the American
Jews, faithful to their pledge, fought for the recognition of Jewish, and
particularly the Polish Jewish right to organize themselves as a 'legal
entity', long after Wolf had abandoned the project. They did so in
complete contradistinction to the will of the conference, and despite
repeated warnings to this effect from leading Americans present at it,
including David Hunter Miller the legal expert, Herbert Hoover,
the all-important head of American relief to Europe, and finally
Wilson himself.[56] Even before their arrival, therefore, the leading

[52] Marshall to Adler, 6 June 1923, Marshall papers, Peace Conference Corr., box 1,
1919–23.
[53] Headlam-Morley to Namier, 30 June 1919, in Headlam-Morley, *A Memoir*, 176.
[54] For full text see Parkes, *Emergence*, 110–11.
[55] Adler to Marshall, 20 June 1919, Marshall papers, Peace Conference Corr., box 1,
1919–23. Adler was not involved in the Comité des Délégations, however.
[56] Adler Diary, Adler papers, on meeting with Hoover, 18 Apr. 1919, fos. 182–5; with

American Jewish diplomats had restrictions upon them strongly weighting them towards the Eastern Jews and away from the Joint and Alliance. The few American Jews in Paris, notably Oscar Straus and Henry Morgenthau,[57] who were strongly inclined to agree with Wolf's approach, though wielding considerable influence as members of the American peace delegation had no mandate *qua* Jews.

Wolf may not have known or not wished to have known the full details of these changed circumstances. Certainly he continued to lean heavily on the assumption that Marshall was leading the delegation and hence would carry it in his direction.[58] But Marshall's arrival in Paris anyway was preceded by that of Mack, an event which as far as Wolf was concerned had two important repercussions.

In the first place, Mack, whose sympathies were much more demonstrably in the direction of the Eastern Jews, almost immediately aligned his delegation to the Zionist bureau, resulting in a Comité des Délégations Juives with Mack himself acting as chairman. Wolf was astonished by this seemingly inexplicable *volte face* on the part of the Americans, but also equally concerned by the spectre it raised of a resuscitation of the Sokolow proposals for union which he thought he had successfully evaded the previous month.[59] A new arrangement was indeed quickly proposed but its framework—delegation by proportional representation with the minority acquiescing to the majority view—made it immediately unacceptable to the Joint Foreign Committee and Alliance. We have, wrote Wolf, 'the choice between ostracism and helpless association with an organisation in the making of which we had not even been consulted'.[60]

While the Alliance raged against the effrontery of the Comité's

Wilson, 26 May 1919, fos. 206–9. On Miller's efforts to moderate the national minority aspects of the Mack–Marshall proposals see David Hunter Miller, *My Diary at the Conference of Paris* (New York, 1924) i. 281, entry for 2 Apr. 1919. In retrospect, Marshall wrote that he fought for minority rights 'long after everybody else in the [Congress] delegation recognised the fact that it would be impossible to secure them'; Marshall to Adler, 6 June 1923, Marshall papers.

[57] On Morgenthau's opposition to national rights, see Wolf, Paris Diary, 24 Apr. 1919, fo. 212. On the willingness of Straus to help Wolf find a settlement with the Poles, see ibid., 5 Mar. 1919, fo. 105.

[58] On Wolf's avoidance of any reference to the American Jewish Congress or to Mack's leadership of its delegation see Janowsky, *Jews and Minority Rights*, 285 n. 29.

[59] Wolf, Paris Diary, 24 Mar. 1919, fos. 130–7.

[60] Bigart to Mack, 26 Mar. 1919, AIU/France ii D 6 *bis*; Wolf, Paris Diary, 24 Mar. 1919, fos. 130–7.

indelicate approach, and Wolf strongly sympathized with their hurt pride, he himself affected to be responsive to union. But this was purely a front, a camouflage for what he was really intending, which was a separate union of all those 'diplomatic' elements he had originally desired to work within his secretariat. 'What we are suffering from', he wrote in his diary, 'is a war of the extremists and the only antidote is a concentration of the moderates.'[61]

Wolf believed he had the means to effect such a 'moderate' union. Vladimir Haffkine had approached him on 25 March proposing that Baron Edmond de Rothschild might well act as a rallying focus for all the disparate elements in Paris.[62] The proposal was seriously worth considering, especially as de Rothschild, prior to Wolf's appearance in Paris, had successfully chaired a preliminary committee, both independent of the Alliance and inclusive of Sokolow, to prepare the Jewish question at the conference. Baron Edmond's standing as a Jewish leader and his ability to bridge wide ideological differences in the Jewish camp were well attested.[63] With the imminent arrival of Marshall and of Professor Colombo for the Italian Jews, Wolf may have reasoned that under his leadership the time was propitious for a shift in favour of the moderates.

To this end, while officially acknowledging Mack's unionization proposals, Wolf wrote to him privately on 26 March suggesting that they and Marshall put their heads together and devise a scheme— Wolf did not mention Haffkine's proposal by name—to smooth things over.[64] The complexion of things was completely altered, however, by the arrival of Marshall the following day. Though Marshall derided Mack's association with the Comité des Délégations without previously consulting the Joint Foreign Committee and Alliance, he immediately pressed for a union, a genuine broadly-based union[65] (unlike the limited one Wolf had in mind) of all parties. This cut across Wolf's intention to siphon off the Americans, so to speak, in a Haffkine-oriented direction, a plan now made doubly difficult by the fact that all access to and conversation with Marshall to explain his plans had now

[61] Wolf, Paris Diary, 24 and 26 Mar. 1919, fos. 137, 144.

[62] Ibid., 25 Mar. 1919, fos. 137–8.

[63] Ibid., 15 Jan. 1919, fo. 3. This of course begs the question whether Baron Edmond was in a position to unite all parties. Other information Wolf received in Paris suggested that both the Alliance and Zionists had by this time serious objections to him; on Wormser's pessimism see entry for 25 Mar. 1919, fo. 144.

[64] Janowsky, *Jews and Minority Rights*, 290.

[65] Ibid.; Wolf, Paris Diary, 30 Mar. 1919, fo. 145.

by the very nature of things to include Mack. Yet here followed another consequence of Mack's earlier arrival at the conference. All Mack's information of what had happened in the previous two months came from the Zionists, and they, by withholding Wolf's February letter to Sokolow reserving his right to liberty of action in Sokolow's absence, had convinced him that the Joint Foreign Committee and Alliance in submitting their February memorials had perpetrated a 'definite and outrageous act of bad faith'.[66] Mack in turn had passed this information on to Adler and Marshall. In fact, Wolf had already taken the precaution of ensuring that the Joint Foreign Committee presidents show Adler and Marshall the relevant passages in his diary, when they arrived in London, *en route* to Paris. However, this does not seem to have pre-empted the accusations and insinuations which undoubtedly clouded his initial Paris meeting with them and Mack on 29 March.[67]

After hearing Wolf's explanation of events in February, Marshall, eager to conciliate everybody, was prepared to condone the presentation of the memorials[68]—a brave approach unlikely to endear him to the stalwarts in the Comité des Délégations. But in so doing, he was himself misinterpreting the situation.

Marshall held out for union, a prospect which in the long term required the Alliance and Joint Foreign Committee to withdraw their original February submissions and unite with both the Americans and the Easterners on the basis of a completely new memorial. But Wolf could no more entertain this prospect than the Mack proposals for union. Besides, he was at this point in receipt of oral assurances both that the British delegation would support him against the Zionists on the autonomy issue and, via Baron Edmond, that the Romanian Commission would accept their joint formula for insertion in the Romanian Treaty of Peace.[69] To now abandon their submissions and instead associate with the Comité des Délégations even on the basis of a compromise national autonomy formula seemed to be courting disaster.

[66] Wolf, Paris Diary, 30 Mar. 1919, fos. 146–7.

[67] Janowsky, *Jews and Minority Rights*, 291; Wolf to Montefiore, 12 Mar. 1919, MWS file 210; 29 Mar. 1919, fos. 8–9; Adler Diary, AIU/France ii D 6 *bis*, abstract of meeting 29 Mar. 1919. Marshall first accused the JFC and AIU of profiting from their earlier memorials and then relented.

[68] Janowsky, *Jews and Minority Rights*, fo. 293.

[69] Wolf, Paris Diary, 30 Mar. 1919, fo. 148; ibid., 3 Apr. 1919, fo. 162. The 'autonomy' assurance came from the British delegate, Bourdillon, acting for Tyrell. Baron Edmond's assurance was repeated by Forbes Adams to Wolf in person.

Yet Marshall had exactly such a compromise formula in mind, and presented it in the committee stage of the discussions between the Western and Eastern delegations in mid-April. It was attached 'virtually to the original American text'. Wolf promptly rejoindered that there could be no substitution of the original Joint Foreign Committee–Alliance memorials. 'All we could do would be to notify the Peace Conference of such amendments of our formula as might be rendered necessary by our agreement with the East European delegations.'[70]

Marshall's hope of working a union which included the Alliance and Joint Foreign Committee was clearly a non-starter, and had been, from Wolf's standpoint, ever since Mack had quashed the Haffkine plan at their first meeting. This did not prevent Marshall from persisting with his project, from his arrival in late March until mid-April, through meeting after interminable meeting of all sections of the Jewish camp.[71] Nor did it prevent Wolf, whose primary aim now was to prevent a breach with Marshall, from concealing his real opinions and supporting the American's desire for unification.[72]

Perhaps Wolf hoped that Marshall could somehow be dislodged from the Comité des Délégations. An opportunity certainly seemed to present itself in the aftermath of the full conference of Jewish delegations, held on 5 and 6 April.[73] Failure to reach agreement on the question of national rights had led to it setting up a Committee of Seven, which it charged with producing a formula acceptable to all parties. For once, the Zionists were in a minority, the conciliatory Sokolow and the intractable Thon and Ussishkin ranged against four non-nationalists, Bigart, Wolf, Adler, and Marshall. The two Americans, however, refused to be deflected from their support of the Easterners' demands; though the resulting compromise formula was considerably toned down to meet the susceptibilities of the Alliance,

[70] Ibid., 10 Apr. 1919, fo. 179.
[71] For a full examination of these events focusing primarily on Marshall himself see Janowsky, 'Attempts to Unify the Jewish Delegations', *Jews and Minority Rights*, 283–308.
[72] Wolf, Paris Diary, 30 Mar. 1919, fo. 148. The nearest Wolf came to agreeing to amalgamation was when Cyrus Adler proposed a permanent conference in place of union, 'in which questions of voting would not arise and in which each delegation should reserve its independence should an agreement on any particular point of the programme prove impossible'. Both the JFC and the AIU favoured this scheme, but it got lost in the early meetings of the full delegations. Haffkine's scheme also seems to have failed to get off the ground. See Wolf, Paris Diary, 31 Mar. 1919, fos. 154–5; Janowsky, *Jews and Minority Rights*, 297. [73] Janowsky, *Jews and Minority Rights*, 305–7.

Wolf knew full well that its reference to national rights was incompatible with the framework of the peace.

The failure to reach a full accord with Marshall, the time spent in conferences and committees while the all-important diplomatic work was allowed to stagnate, forced him to break out of this *impasse*. The Alliance resolution on 16 April repudiating the compromise formula gave him his opportunity. The nationality issue had made the chances of compromise impossible, and the Joint Foreign Committee would therefore stand by the Alliance. 'I had consequently devoted myself', he told Marshall, 'to rendering the inevitable rupture as innocuous as possible.'[74]

Despite these tortuous efforts to reach agreement, it seemed that the Americans, the Alliance, and the Joint Foreign Committee were bound to present separate memorials and go their separate ways, the former in league with the weaker Eastern Jews, the latter two failing to make the necessary impact on the conference which they might have achieved in conjunction with the American Jews.

The Americans, and not only Marshall, quickly discovered, however, as Wolf had perceived much earlier, that the Comité des Délégations, far from promoting their work, were an encumbrance to it. The Comité was large, unwieldy, 'had no idea of anything', 'could not agree among themselves on any subject'; so Marshall insisted.[75] Not surprisingly, his relations with the Comité were not particularly harmonious. They—the East Europeans—were acutely suspicious of a non-nationalist in their midst, Mack's insistence being the sole basis upon which Marshall succeeded him as president of the Comité when Mack returned to America in May.[76]

But Mack, too, found it a near-impossible body with which to work. On more than one occasion he threatened to resign, for instance when a corpus of delegates demanded that their brief should be for Jewish equality of political status in multinational states.[77] This outlandish proposal, acceptable perhaps in 1917 but not given the international climate of 1919, illustrates the one outstanding weakness of the Comité:

[74] Wolf, Paris Diary, 10 Apr. 1919, fo. 177, and 16 Apr., fo. 195.
[75] Marshall to Adler, 6 June 1923, Marshall papers; Janowsky, *Jews and Minority Rights*, 310. For Wolf's views on the Comité see 'Notes on the Comité des Delegations Juives', n.d., 1920, MWS 11525–7.
[76] Janowsky, *Jews and Minority Rights*, 310.
[77] Parkes, *Emergence*, 118. In response to a Comité demand for recognition of the Jews as a 'world' nation, Mack threatened to leave and take the whole American delegation with him; see Adler Diary, 4 Apr. 1919, fo. 16.

lacking any diplomatic experience, it failed to recognize that the Jewish question would be dealt with at the conference not on the merits of the proposals the Jews themselves put forward but by the exigencies of the international situation. Failing to grasp this or to arm themselves accordingly, the Comité became totally bogged down in 'academic discussion', so much so that no Comité desiderata were submitted to the peace conference until June 10. This was long after the essential details of the Polish Minority Treaty had been formulated and concluded. Indeed, backdating their memorial one month, to 10 May, was only of assistance, in Marshall's words, 'in order to make the petitioners less ridiculous in the eyes of the world than they in fact were'.[78]

The inability of the Comité des Délégations to provide a framework for diplomatic action forced the Americans within it to take matters into their own hands, pursuing them in much the same way as Wolf had done two months earlier.[79]

There was one important difference, however. Wolf's representations had all been made through the official channels, to Dutasta, at the peace secretariat. He was not to know otherwise, as in response to his repeated request as made on 16 April, that 'the whole question of cultural and religious minorities in Eastern Europe . . . may yet be dealt with by a special commission', he received the constructive reply from Dutasta that this would be forwarded to the Supreme Council.[80] So probably it was—but without any tangible result. In other words, the incoherent organization of the conference meant that communication between the secretariat, the delegations, and the Big Four continued to be non-functioning. Noted E. H. Carr, 'Everyone is working in the dark and no one knows how far the Americans who are having strong Jewish influences brought to bear on them may press the question of Jewish rights.'[81]

The Americans were indeed pressing hard, but in doing so had been able to avoid Wolf's mistake. Through contact with the American delegation, they learnt that the correct method of approach was not via

[78] Adler to Marshall, 20 June and Marshall to Adler, 22 June 1923, Marshall papers; Marshall's letter was quoted in Reznikoff, *Louis Marshall*, ii. 568. Cf. Wolf, Paris Diary, 12 May 1919, fo. 251, where Wolf comments to Haffkine that the Mack memorial was 'so much eyewash'. For text of Comité memorial see Miller, *My Diary*, xiii. 192–5.

[79] Janowsky, *Jews and Minority Rights*, 312.

[80] Wolf to Dutasta, 16 Apr., and vice versa, 27 Apr. 1919, *RDJBE* 101–2.

[81] E. H. Carr, 24 Apr. 1919, FO 608/61/129/4/1.

the secretariat at all but directly to the Big Four.[82] Their efforts thus focused on getting personal access to Wilson.

In attempting to do so, they had yet another advantage over Wolf. The latter was many steps removed from Lloyd George. He might, if pushed, have been able to work up indirect pressure through Herbert Samuel, for instance, but he lacked personal knowledge of, or influence with, the premier. Not so Marshall and Mack *vis-à-vis* the president. In November 1918, Marshall had been in direct consultation with him in relation to the Polish situation and had presented the American Jewish Committee's proposals on the problem, to which Wilson had replied. Five months later, Wilson's interview with the leaders of the American Jewish delegation was the reason for Mack and Marshall's delayed arrival in Paris.[83]

In fact, on this occasion, in late April, Mack and Marshall failed to see Wilson, but they achieved the next best thing. By contact first with Robert Lansing, Secretary of State, then with Colonel House, the president's close adviser, and finally with David Hunter Miller and Manley Hudson, the two leading American legal experts, Marshall and Mack were able to make their case known and prepare a draft, based roughly on the December 'Bill of Rights' which, modified, by Miller, was presented to the president at the end of April.[84] In turn, Wilson drew up his own short formula for minority protection, and this and the Miller–Mack–Marshall draft appeared on the agenda of the Supreme Council on 1 May.[85]

Partially in consequence of this, a new committee, the New States Committee, was created, its mandate including the preparation of clauses for the protection of minorities (in the first instance, for Poland), which would thereby represent the international obligations owed by the new states to the Allies.[86]

Wolf received news of this committee on 3 May, the next day a

[82] Adler Diary, 11 Apr. 1919, fo. 20.

[83] Marshall to Wilson, 7, 14, and 16 Nov., and Wilson to Marshall, 13 Nov. 1918; encl. with Marshall to Wolf, 16 Nov. 1918, MWS 8099. On Wilson's contacts with the American Jewish Congress through rabbi Stephen Wise see Janowsky, *Jews and Minority Rights*, 283.

[84] These developments are fully documented in Kohler, 'Origin', 755, 775–80. For Marshall–Mack and Miller drafts see Miller, *My Diary*, ix. 182–5, docs. 886–7.

[85] Maurice Hankey, *procès-verbaux*, 1 May 1919, in *Papers relating to the Foreign Relations of the United States, vol. v, Paris Peace Conference 1919* (henceforth *FRUS*), (Washington, 1946), 393–4.

[86] Sharp, *Britain*, 173; Parkes, *Emergence*, 118–19.

request from Marshall to renew their co-operation.[87] The need for strong Jewish representation at the peace conference, it seemed, overrode both Wolf's loyalty to the Alliance and Marshall's to the Comité des Délégations.

[87] Wolf, Paris Diary, 3 and 4 May 1919, fos. 223–4.

15

The New States Committee and the Peace Settlement

It will probably postpone a settlement of the Jewish question beyond the signature of the Peace Treaty but it will be all the safer and solid for that. Instead of more or less banal clauses in the Peace Treaty, we shall now have a detailed Statute of Minorities which will probably be the subject of special Treaties with the states concerned.[1]

With these words, Wolf greeted the news of the creation of the New States Committee. He had reason to be optimistic. Its formation marked a major turning-point in the cause of the Jews at the Paris peace conference. Up to this point it had drifted almost aimlessly, dealt with here and there by several territorial committees, none of which had much inkling of what the others were doing; it was a side issue cursorily noted when 'extra-time' permitted. Now it was to be firmly anchored in a special compartment: a tightly knit committee of experts 'shielded from the political and ideological pressures that swirled around the Big Four'.[2] More important from the standpoint of Wolf's liberal politics, it was to be handled as a general minorities problem, not simply a Jewish one; and while the committee's mandate originally was to deal only with this issue as it impinged upon Poland, its scope was quickly widened to include not only the new states of Eastern Europe, but also the enlarged ones of Romania and Greece.[3] If sufficiently stringent clauses could be adopted in the Polish case it would most likely follow that these would serve as a model for the other states.

Wolf claimed this development as a major coup for his delegation. In one obvious way this was not so, for if it had been it would have been Lloyd George who had instigated it and not Wilson. In fact, despite the insistence of the British prime minister on 1 May that he was going to 'propose some sort of provisions',[4] the direct initiative came from

[1] Wolf, Paris Diary, 6 May 1919, fo. 228. [2] Mayer, *Politics*, vii.
[3] Committee of Four, 6 May 1919, *FRUS*, v. 483.
[4] Ibid., 1 May 1919, p. 393.

Wilson at the behest of the American Jews, an initiative in which Wolf played no part and of which, perhaps because of the recent schism, he was only dimly aware.

However, in other respects Wolf had advantages which did make this a coup for the Joint Foreign Committee, advantages which gave him the edge over his American colleagues and which became a factor in a growing rivalry between them.

One was the actual composition of the new committee. At the Big Four meeting on 1 May, David Hunter Miller and James Headlam-Morley were the only two appointees, and it was they who laid the foundations of the Minorities Treaties by writing in a clause into the German treaty, otherwise by then completed, which allowed for extra provisions to be incorporated at a later date.[5] Though they were joined by Berthelot, the distinguished French diplomatist (who became the Committee's chairman), an Italian, and occasionally a Japanese, it was the Americans and the British—E. H. Carr joined Headlam-Morley as secretary—who formed its nucleus. It was from them that the majority of clauses came, very often at the instigation of their respective Jewish delegations.[6]

The British, represented by Headlam-Morley and more briefly Lord Robert Cecil, did not always get their way in this process, and on one or two occasions suffered major reversals. There is nevertheless a good case for arguing that they represented the dominant element. For one thing, while delegates from the other countries were always chopping and changing—Miller, for instance, being replaced by Manley Hudson midway through the passage of the Polish Treaty—Headlam-Morley and Carr remained very nearly a consistent presence until the committee finally wound up its work, after sixty-four meetings, in December 1919.[7]

There was also the question of knowledge and experience. It has been noted on several occasions how the American team of experts, who collectively were known as the Inquiry, though academically high-powered, lacked the diplomatic skills of their European counterparts. One, Charles Seymour, who sat on the Czech territorial committee, frankly recalled, 'it seemed rather ridiculous for amateurs like

---

[5] Macartney, *National States*, 225; extract from Headlam-Morley diary, n.d., *c.*18 May 1919, in Headlam-Morley, *A Memoir*, 114–15.

[6] Headlam-Morley to Hankey, 2 May 1919, in Headlam-Morley, *A Memoir*, 91–2. For *procès-verbaux* of New States Committee meetings see Miller, *My Diary*, xiii.

[7] Miller, *My Diary*, xiii. Headlam-Morley left in mid-October.

ourselves to sit with these professionals but we seem to be the best the U.S. has been able to produce'.[8] Miller and Hudson were not professional diplomats, but lawyers; they had no previous experience of the minorities question, so when Mack and Marshall made their representations in mid-April, they were thrown into the deep end, so to speak. By contrast, Headlam-Morley and Carr had been examining the question since the armistice; they had had time to formulate their agenda and to evaluate this in the light of what they learnt from, among other people, Lucien Wolf.[9]

In this sense, Wolf had a head start over the American Jewish delegates. Months of careful diplomacy had already prepared him for the way the minority clauses were likely to shape up. He believed he knew what would and would not be acceptable; for instance, it was no surprise to him when the early drafts produced by the New States Committee definitively rejected national rights.[10]

The rapport which he was able to build up with Headlam-Morley was particularly important in this context. From their earliest meetings, the two men recognized each other's diplomatic skills and, more important, found they saw eye to eye on most essentials. Headlam-Morley, unlike many of his colleagues, shared Wolf's enthusiasm for the Minorities Treaties and his faith in the role the League would play in seeing that they worked. He agreed that the vital clauses, the ones it was most necessary to make watertight, were those relating to citizenship, the failure of which in the Berlin Treaty had had such dire consequences for Romanian Jewry. He shared too (it might be suggested, he acquired from Wolf), his distrust and dislike of Jewish nationalism and countered it whenever it resurfaced, through the medium of Hudson the American delegate, in Committee discussions.[11]

The understanding arrived at led Wolf to assume confidently that so long as Headlam-Morley was there, the New States Committee would and could be steered in the right direction. 'If the Treaties are carried out as Headlam-Morley proposes', he wrote in May, we shall have a

---

[8] Bryant, 'Britain', 176, quoting Seymour, *Letters from the Peace Conference*.

[9] E.g. Headlam-Morley minute, 22 Mar. 1919, FO 608/66/131/1/1. Namier was another important influence on Headlam-Morley; see Headlam-Morley to Namier, 24 Mar. 1919, Headlam-Morley, *A Memoir*, 54–5.

[10] Wolf, Paris Diary, 8 May 1919, fo. 233.

[11] Headlam-Morley minute, 31 May 1919, Fo 608/51/114/1/20. For Headlam-Morley's views on Jewish nationalists see his letter to Zimmern, 26 May 1919, in his *Memoir*, 124–6. Sharp, 'Britain', 176, notes the divergence between Headlam-Morley and other British diplomats on the importance of the Minorities Treaties.

great victory. They are based entirely on plans which we have initiated and worked out and for which we have consistently agitated both as to substance and method during the last three months. Crowe despairingly agreed, writing to Hardinge later that month that Headlam-Morley had swallowed Wolf's bait 'hook, line and sinker'.[12]

This is not to suggest that Marshall, Mack, and Adler did not have influence in the New States Committee. Indeed, along with Wolf and Filderman, the Romanian Jewish representative, they were among the very few people outside the Big Four who actually knew of its existence at all.[13] They saw much of Headlam-Morley and in the early stages of Miller too, one incident being used by a previous chronicler of these events to suggest that Mack and Marshall's understanding with Miller was in fact stronger than that of their English counterparts.[14] According to his version, when the New States Committee had finished its first draft of the Polish Treaty, around 12 May, Miller gave a copy to Marshall and Mack, but when Wolf, learning of this from Marshall, applied to Headlam-Morley for a copy, he was refused.[15] This is the barest outline of what did happen, an outline which omits to state why Headlam-Morley would have wished to deny a copy to Wolf, his Anglo-Jewish *confidante*. Wolf's Diary makes it clear that it was certainly not Headlam-Morley's intention to keep him in the dark—on the contrary, Wolf was able to go immediately through the clauses with him, finding them with one exception to be satisfactory. Rather, according to Wolf, Headlam-Morley was 'very upset' by Miller's action, since making confidential material not yet received by the Polish and Romanian governments available to all and sundry jeopardized the Committee's whole operation.[16]

[12] Wolf, Paris Diary, 8 May 1919, fo. 236; Crowe minute, 30 May 1919, FO 608/51/114/1/20.
[13] Headlam-Morley, *A Memoir*, diary extract, n.d., c. 18 May 1919, p. 117. Headlam claimed that not even the Allied foreign secretaries knew of the Committee's existence.
[14] Janowsky, *Jews and Minority Rights*, 333–4, 338–9, 349. Janowsky did note that Wolf had contact with Headlam-Morley, but cautiously added that 'no evidence is at hand to corroborate the conjecture' that he had any influence on him. Later on, Sherman Spector, then writing a Ph.D. thesis on the Allies and Romania in 1919, wrote to Mowschowitch suggesting that Janowsky had underestimated Wolf's role at Paris and saying that he hoped Mowschowitch would provide evidence which might 'serve to strengthen my opinion that Mr. Wolf influenced Mr. Headlam-Morley much more than Mr. Janowsky thinks'; see Spector to Mowschowitch, 19 Nov. 1956, MWS 24579.
[15] Janowsky, *Jews and Minority Rights*, 347; Macartney, *National States*, 226; Headlam-Morley to Namier, 17 May 1919, Headlam-Morley, *A Memoir*, 111.
[16] Wolf, Paris Diary, 16 May 1919, fos 255–7.

The incident in fact helped cement the Headlam-Morley–Wolf alliance, Headlam-Morley now putting his trust in Wolf to contact Marshall immediately 'and impress upon him the vital necessity of keeping the whole thing a dead secret'.[17] By contrast, Marshall and Mack's apparent 'victory' in receiving the document served only to draw attention to the underlying tensions existing between them and the American delegation.

The American Jews had broken off negotiations with the Poles in November 1918 and, unlike Wolf, had not resumed them. They had similarly stuck to their guns, despite their own ill ease on the subject, in partially supporting the demand of the Easterners for national rights, and had seemingly had some of these points endorsed for inclusion in the treaty, including national minority status and proportional representation, when they had first seen Miller in late April.[18]

These propitious signs, however, failed to take into account the strongly pro-Polish approach of Wilson and the American delegation as a whole—an approach totally inconsistent with their supposed resolve to produce a settlement on ethnographic lines. It similarly cut across the Jewish interest, which favoured solid guarantees on minority rights.[19]

Miller's espousal of the American Jewish case began to waver. Minority status, first as a 'legal entity', then as a 'public corporation', was dropped. Indeed, when Marshall and Mack saw the draft on 15 May they found themselves not endorsing it but railing against its injustice and ineffectiveness.[20]

This did not instantly make the British into Jewish patrons. Though they were, of all the Allies, the most unreservedly critical of Polish actions, particularly as they infringed upon a fair ethnographic settlement, this did not translate itself into partiality for the Jews. Far from it; Lloyd George took Paderewski's word at the Supreme Council that they had only themselves to blame for the misfortunes that had befallen them, and later matched Wilson blow for blow in whittling away

[17] Wolf, Paris Diary, 16 May 1919, fo. 257.

[18] Miller, *My Diary*, 19 and 21 Apr. 1919, vol. i, pp. 259, 262, 264.

[19] Bryant, 'Britain', 520; Tillman, *Anglo-American Relations*, 203–4; R. H. Lord, the Harvard academic who sat on the Polish Commission, was especially pro-Polish.

[20] Miller, *My Diary*, 5 May 1919, i. 289–90. Significantly, 'public corporation' status was deleted after Miller's conversations with Lord. See also ibid. ix. 387–9, for Mack and Marshall's suggestions, 15 May 1919, on New States Committee draft.

at some of the more crucial guarantees in the Minorities Treaty.[21] Nor did Miller's defection mean that Mack and Marshall lost all American advocacy; his successor, Hudson, returned in June to a more solid and obdurate defence of Jewish rights.[22] However, by this stage the framework of the treaty had already been decided and could not be gone back on; if anything, the Jewish minority clauses, in these final days before the signing on 25 June, were weakened still further.

The discrepancy between Miller and Hudson, between American policy towards Poles and that towards Jews (it is to be remembered the American delegates were under pressure from American Poles as well as Jews), tended to cast Headlam-Morley as the Jews' most reliable friend on the Committee. Indeed, Miller accused him in mid-May of having changed allegiance 'to the extent of being willing to go further in favour of the Jews than . . . reasonable'.[23]

Miller was referring in particular to Headlam-Morley's defence of the Sabbath clause, a point which paradoxically aligned Wolf and Marshall behind Headlam-Morley against the opposition of the American and other delegates. What concerned the Jewish diplomats was not the reference in the clause to the right of freedom of worship on the Sabbath; this had not in the past and was not likely in the future to be contested by the Poles. Rather what they feared—the delegation of orthodox Polish Jews claimed it was already on the cards—was the enactment of a Dmowskite-type law making Sunday a *repos dominical*. This would in effect extend the pre-war boycott of Jewish traders and particularly affect the Jewish *luftmensch* class, possibly curtailing their already precarious means of livelihood altogether.[24] Such a direct economic threat could be entertained by neither Wolf nor Marshall, who thus joined in pressing Headlam-Morley to outlaw it by international protocol.[25]

Headlam-Morley took their advice, but in so doing found himself more and more at odds with fellow Committee members—especially Miller, who saw the clause as a constraint on Polish sovereignty. Thus

[21] Tillman, *Anglo-American Relations*, 204; Bryant, 'Britain', 524; Mayer, *Politics*, 805. *FRUS*, vol. v, 1 May 1919, pp. 393–4; vol. vi, 5 and 23 June 1919, pp. 147–60, 624–8.
[22] *FRUS*, vol. vi, 23 June 1919, pp. 624–8; Headlam-Morley to Namier, 30 June 1919, Headlam-Morley, *A Memoir*, 176.
[23] Miller, *My Diary*, 13 May 1919, i. 306.
[24] Wolf, Paris Diary, 18 May 1919, fos. 260–1; Wolf to Lloyd George, 20 May 1919, *RDJBE* 82–3.
[25] Wolf to Lloyd George as in n. 24; Marshall to Tardieu, 14 May 1919, Marshall papers, Peace Conference Corr., Poland, 1919–20, box 1.

isolated, all Headlam-Morley was able to carry was a rump clause protecting the Sabbath against judicial and electoral violation but otherwise deprived of any value by the omission of any reference to Sunday trading. Even then he was forced to justify his case before the Council of Four, by among other things citing Wolf's 'most moderate' representations.[26]

Headlam-Morley's contention that he was fighting 'the battle of the Jews almost alone'[27] obscures the fact that his support for a wholeheartedly pro-Jewish treaty was constrained by political factors. True, the settlement had to safeguard as far as possible Jewish rights; hence his support of the 'cultural' and Sabbath clauses.[28] At the same time, however, it had to be seen as in no way infringing or insulting Polish sovereignty.

Such an approach suffered the obvious defect of being unlikely to satisfy either party; specific 'protective' clauses were unlikely to please the Poles, the barest framework was unlikely to meet the 'maximum' Jewish demands. The way round the problem was to revert to getting as much as possible of a settlement out of court, a sort of two-tier structure, one tier endorsed by international guarantee, the other dependent on the goodwill of the Polish and Jewish negotiators.

This tendency towards a compromise settlement, one which would create an understanding and reconciliation between Pole and Jew as much through private arrangement as publicly acclaimed treaty, finally stamped the minorities settlement as in the main a product of a Wolf–Headlam-Morley, rather than a Marshall–Miller, or Marshall–Hudson, accord.

Wolf consistently recognized the need to placate the Poles, Czechs, and even Romanians as a precondition for future Jewish well-being in these countries. Retrospectively, he argued that in framing the February formula

the Joint [Foreign Committee] realised from the beginning the importance of avoiding proposals which by their exacting tendencies might be calculated to abridge sovereign rights as understood by the public law of Europe and thus to stir up controversies and antagonisms which would have seriously jeopardised

---

[26] Miller, *My Diary*, 12 May 1919, i. 300; ibid., Polish Report no. 2, xiii. 57–8; *FRUS*, vol. v, 17 May 1919, pp. 678–81. Headlam-Morley to Namier, 17 May 1919, Headlam-Morley, *A Memoir*, 111.

[27] Headlam-Morley to Namier, as in n. 26.

[28] Ibid. Headlam-Morley also supported Wolf's argument for Jewish administration of public funds to be applied to hospitals as well as schools.

the end they had in view. Accordingly they limited themselves to recommending only such amendments and amplifications of the similar formula inserted under similar conditions in the great European Treaties from 1815 to 1878 as experience has shown to be absolutely necessary in order to give effect to these formulae.[29]

Such a rationale enabled Wolf, unlike Marshall, to reconcile himself to concessions Headlam-Morley felt it necessary to propose in order to save the Polish Treaty and later the Romanian Treaty, and to agree to Headlam-Morley's device—an exchange of notes with the plenipotentiaries concerned—for dealing with problems which would otherwise have been dropped from the treaties altogether.

Already in April, Wolf showed that he himself was thinking on these lines when he proposed that one such problem ought to be tackled outside the framework of the actual treaty. This related to the potential exclusion of Jews from an equitable participation in Polish parliamentary and municipal life through gerrymandering. A peace settlement solution would have required a clause specifying proportional representation or Jewish electoral *curiae*. What the New States Committee in fact opted for, whether or not on Wolf's direct instigation, was an exchange of notes containing assurances that constituencies would not be gerrymandered.[30]

Later on, in August, the threat by Eleftherios Venizelos, the Greek premier, to obstruct the Greek Treaty unless it was toned down, was similarly avoided by the omission of its Sabbath clause, its place being taken by a personal guarantee from Venizelos to Wolf assuring Salonika Jewry's right to trade on Sundays. Again, this arrangement was realized by prior consultation between Wolf and Headlam-Morley, though on this occasion with the former as an active participant.[31]

Wolf's skill in practising the craft of diplomacy, his optimism, foresight, and self-restraint were surely of some consequence in these developments. His optimism was of consequence because the arrangements arrived at were designed to make Polish and other Eastern European politicians amenable and hence more likely to keep their word. His foresight, because they were intended as not short-term but

[29] Wolf, 'Interim Report of the British Jewish Delegation', 20 July 1919, MWS 8345-59.
[30] Wolf, Paris Diary, 19 Apr. 1919, fos. 212-13. Wolf to Carr, 14 May, *RDJBE*, 81-2. Miller, *My Diary*, 9 May 1919, xiii. 76.
[31] Wolf to Venizelos and vice versa, 23 and 27 Aug. 1919, Wolf, Paris Diary, fos. 565-7; Miller, *My Diary*, 28 Aug. 1919, xiii. 408.

long-term goals which would heal the rift between Jew and non-Jew and make for a durable peace. Finally his self-restraint, in declining to demand the more onerous terms which seemed to his American colleagues so vitally relevant in the immediate conditions of 1919. Not that in the early summer of 1919 it was easy for Wolf to maintain an even, conciliatory keel. Just as the New States Committee was finishing its first Polish draft, a new stage began in Pilsudski's offensive against the Ukrainians and Lithuanians, an offensive which brought in its wake reports of serious and cold-blooded pogroms, especially in Pinsk, Lida, and Vilna.[32]

As in November and December 1918, the British Foreign Office was slow to endorse the atrocity stories. Their observers on the scene usually either denied that they had occurred or otherwise justified them, as the Poles did, as necessary military actions against the Bolsheviks.[33] However, English and American Jewry were in no doubt about the veracity of the reports or who was to blame. A popular grass-roots clamour quickly swelled, a clamour which expressed itself in preparations for mass demonstrations of indignation, and demands that the Allies should at once take action against the Poles.[34]

Once again, the British and American governments were acutely embarrassed, being forced first into admitting that antisemitic disturbances had taken place, then into sending urgent appeals and warnings to the Polish government to halt them. Finally, both governments were so overwhelmed by the need to pacify the protesters that they despatched Jewish-led commissions of investigation to Poland. The American Morgenthau Commission left almost immediately, the British Commission, under Sir Stuart Samuel, later that autumn.[35]

[32] FO 371/3903/529, Jan.–June 1919, is entirely devoted to pogrom 'reports'.
[33] E.g. Capt. Crewsdon (HMG Military Mission, Warsaw) report no. 14286, 11–13 June 1919, FO 608/67/131/1/1, justifying the execution of 34 Jews in Pinsk by firing squad on grounds that they were Bolsheviks. In fact they were members of a Jewish food distribution committee. For an attempt to unravel the truth of the Pinsk affair see Jozef Lewandowski, 'History and Myth: Pinsk, April 1919', *Polin*, 2 (1987), 50–72.
[34] See 'Jewish Protest Committee against the Pogroms'; Director of Intelligence, Special Branch report, 11 June 1919, FO 371/3903/529; Davies, 'Great Britain', 132, 139.
[35] FO to Wyndham (Warsaw), 12 June 1919, FO 608/67/131/1/1, no. 12554, Balfour to Paderewski, 25 June 1919, ibid. no. 12781; Curzon to Wyndham, 4 Sept. 1919, *Documents on British Foreign Policy 1919–1939*, ed. E. L. Woodward and Rohan Butler, 1st ser. (London, et seq. 1947), Davies, 'Great Britain', 132, 139. On Morgenthau Commission see Adler and Margalith, *With Firmness in the Right*, 150–61.

It was not only governments who were caught out in this way. Wolf learnt of plans for a mass rally at the Albert Hall in protest against the Pinsk massacre on the same day—6 May—as of the creation of the New States Committee. Rabbi Samuel Daiches, a long-term Zionist 'rebel' on the Board and a recently elected member of the Joint Foreign Committee, was one of its organizers. Just as the Anglo-Jewish establishment was thus being pushed to participate in and somehow canalize the protests for fear of being engulfed by them, Wolf too was himself under heavy pressure to adopt this line *vis-à-vis* the Poles in Paris.[36]

This he did not want to do. An indignation meeting, he told E. H. Carr, 'would only embitter Polish-Jewish relations and jeopardise my negotiations with Paderewski'. The way round the dilemma—the way, too, to appease the protesters, he hoped—would be to get the elder Polish statesman to send him a letter deploring the massacre and promising 'a vigorous investigation and stern punishment of the guilty'.[37]

Through the good offices of Zaleski in Berne, Wolf was able to communicate this appeal to Paderewski who had returned to Warsaw. The reply, however, though going some way to meet Wolf's requests, obfuscated the issue by implying that those killed at Pinsk were Bolsheviks. Wolf thus could neither print the Paderewski reply in its entirety nor, for fear of causing a rupture, openly censor it.[38] When, soon after, 'intelligence' from Felix Frankfurter confirmed that the Poles were indeed intent on exterminating the Jews, news which just happened to coincide with a Copenhagen Zionist report that more than two thousand Jews had been massacred in Vilna, Wolf's resolve to pursue a dispassionate diplomatic course began to crack.[39]

A comparison between Wolf's official correspondence and his private attitude at this juncture makes interesting reading. To Mowschowitch he wrote on 21 May: 'It is our opinion in which we are supported by our government and best friends that any ill-considered action in London in regard to the pogroms may easily jeopardise the triumph of our work—I say this most earnestly and with a full sense of responsibility.'[40] His diary entry for the following day, however,

[36] Wolf, Paris Diary, 6 May 1919, fo. 227. A Rothschild-led delegation to Harmsworth, 12 June 1919, aimed to counteract the effects of the 'less desirable' East End 'Protest Committee'; see FO 371/3903/529.

[37] Wolf, Paris Diary, 6 May 1919, fo. 227.   [38] Ibid., 8 May 1919, fo. 238.

[39] Ibid., 19 and 23 May 1919, fos 263, 272.

[40] Wolf to Mowschowitch, 21 May 1919, MWS 10705-6.

pursued a rather different tack. Here the Poles are portrayed as having set out on 'a deliberate attempt to thin out the Jewish population . . . by massacre'; Wolf resolved that they 'must be made an example of', especially given what appeared to be the impending victory of Koltchak and Denikin's forces in Russia. Thus, while urging his fellow American and French colleagues to have their respective governments make representations to Warsaw, a new contigency plan began to emerge. Wolf met with Marshall to prepare an anti-Polish publicity campaign.[41]

In fact, the fall in the reported incidence of pogroms in the following days and the exposure of the Copenhagen Bureau report as a gross exaggeration[42] caused Wolf's agitation to subside, and the return to calm reinforced his desire to work for a durable settlement. He explained, in what amounted to a personal testimony to Marshall, on 1 June:

In everything I have done here since the Peace Congress has been sitting I have endeavoured to bear steadily in mind the permanent interests of our brethren in Eastern Europe and not to allow myself to be deflected from that duty by the conflicts and bitterness of the moment. I look beyond the pogrom-stricken fields and the passions and recriminations in which ephemeral political conditions have given rise to a time when on the basis of equal rights the Jews of Poland will be full partners in a State in which they will be legitimately proud. But if the prospect is to be realised we must see that we do not poison the new relations of Poles and Jews at their source. And this we shall assuredly do, if, for the benefit of Jews alone, we abridge in any way the sovereign rights of Poland and humiliate her before the world.[43]

Ironically, on this occasion Wolf was justifying himself to Marshall for suggestions which though in specifics were a concession to the Poles, were overall intended to strengthen the framework of the Minorities Treaties. These were key stipulations which would place the rights and security of Jews and other minorities under the protection of the League of Nations, and in particular guarantee their right of direct appeal in case of treaty infractions. Without them, wrote Wolf to Headlam-Morley, the rest of the Polish Treaty would be 'mere waste paper'.[44] It was doubly ironic, therefore, that these clauses should have been the basis for a cleavage between Wolf and Marshall which had little to do with the defence of Jewish interests but a great deal to

[41] Wolf, Paris Diary, 21 May 1919, fo. 271; JFC minutes, 28 May 1919.
[42] Wolf, Paris Diary, 23 May 1919, fo. 272.
[43] Wolf to Marshall, 1 June 1919, MWS file 209; also in Wolf, Paris Diary, fo. 320.
[44] Wolf, Paris Diary, 8 May 1919, fo. 233.

do with divisions at the peace conference between their respective countries.

There was little Marshall could object to in Wolf's plan. The February formula specifically referred to the right of a Jewish minority in any of the new states to organize itself 'for the management of its internal affairs' and for the purposes of appeal to the League.[45] This statement could be taken to embrace national minority status, and more important still, was a clear indication of Wolf's conviction that Eastern Jewry should not as in the past be beholden to their Western co-religionists but sufficient unto themselves.[46] Moreover, Wolf's favoured mechanism for achieving this was technically sound, envisaging that the guardianship of the treaties should be removed in entirety from the political field (that is, the Council of the League), and placed squarely in the hands of a judicial body, the International Court of Justice.

Wolf's reasoning was logical. Forty years of pressure from the Western Jewish organizations had failed to get the Powers to budge either unilaterally or as a group on the question of Romanian Jewish rights, thus leaving Article 44 of the Berlin Treaty a hollow sham. He therefore shrewdly argued that control of the guarantees must rest not with those governed by political prejudices and exigencies but with a body of a purely legal nature. In this way, the political overtones of any dispute brought before it would be sidestepped. Minorities would no longer be in the invidious position of appealing to a foreign state against their own, nor would they in turn consider this an affront to their sovereignty as the matter was purely legal, being adjudged by a tribunal which was political only in so far as it represented the totality of states in the League.[47]

In the light of the peacemakers' failure in February to provide the Covenant of the League with the infrastructure necessary to make proposals such as Wolf's work, Headlam-Morley and Carr, his British

---

[45] Wolf to Dutasta, 21 Feb. 1919, *RDJBE* 77–8. The point about the need for a right of appeal was reiterated and expanded in a letter to E. H. Carr, 14 May 1919, ibid. 81–2.

[46] Cf. Elizabeth E. Eppler, 'Lucien Wolf and the Minorities Treaties', JHSE lecture Apr. 1962 (kindly lent by the author). Eppler misconstrues Wolf's continuing diplomatic role on behalf of Eastern European Jewish rights in the 1920s as proof of his opposition to any independent action by the communities concerned.

[47] Wolf, Paris Diary, 7 June 1919, fo. 348. Cf. Georg Gothein, 'The Protection of National Minorities', *Berliner Tagblatt*, 27 Sept. 1917, C11/2/11, where similar views were expressed.

advisers, were sceptical of its likely endorsement in the Minorities Treaties. Moreover, Headlam-Morley, desiring that the scope of the settlement should be limited to Eastern Europe, was disinclined to favour any inducement to minorities outside that area to appeal to it.[48] Eventually, after much sympathetic consideration of Wolf's scheme, he came in June to the firm conclusion that the League was a compact between states, and hence only they should have immediate access to its court or council.

This did not signify Wolf's isolation from his British patrons. They were not hostile to infractions being dealt with, nor to the proposal that the body for doing this should be a judicial tribunal. Moreover, in the persons of Lord Cecil and his aide Philip Baker, whom both Carr and Headlam-Morley urged Wolf to see, the British had an alternative scheme which, Wolf was quick to decide, it would be 'dangerous and ungracious to oppose'.[49]

The scheme, essentially Baker's, was that instead of having direct appeal to the International Court of Justice, Jews and other minorities would go in the first instance to the Polish courts, taking the matter to international adjudication only if it was not resolved. This was essentially Wolf's idea much diluted, but it had the advantage of also containing other stipulations, for example giving the League the right to act on its own initiative in emergencies such as pogroms.[50]

However, these proposals were likely to come in for a rough passage when Cecil presented them to the New States Committee on 29 May. What was needed was some sort of pressure on the more conservative elements in the New States Committee, notably Berthelot, to bring them round; Wolf readily agreed with Cecil on 28 May that this could be achieved if his American and French Jewish friends discreetly prompted Clemenceau and Klotz.[51]

What Wolf did not bargain for was the opposition of Marshall. Co-operation between them since the beginning of May had been tenuous. Both men, according to Cyrus Adler, were 'strong-willed' and had little liking for one another, Adler having to act as a go-between.[52] They were moreover of quite different political tendencies, which

[48] Wolf, Paris Diary, 8 May and 7 June 1919, fos. 233, 348; for Headlam-Morley memo on right of appeal to League of Nations, 16 May, 1919 see his *Memoir*, 108–110; see also Headlam-Morley to Namier, 11 June 1919, ibid. 141–2.

[49] Wolf, Paris Diary, 23 May 1919, fo. 273.

[50] Ibid., 23 May 1919, fos. 274–9.   [51] Ibid., 28 May 1919, fo. 291.

[52] Adler, *I Have Considered*, 326.

inevitably affected their understanding of and response to the Jewish question.

Marshall, for instance, as a staunch Republican, had little interest in the League but much in the rights of property; this led him to argue that those who lost it in pogroms should be indemnified. Wolf, by contrast, was a lifelong Liberal and, like Cecil, a League enthusiast. In his mind, property clauses were of little importance compared with the necessity for overall guarantees to make the treaties operable.[53] These differences need not have upset their working relationship. They had for instance a common interest in the question of right of appeal, and put in almost identical claims to the New States Committee on this score in mid-May.[54] This consensus was completely shattered, however, as a result of the interview Marshall—and Adler—had with Wilson on 26 May—three days, it may be noted, before Cecil's appointment to the New States Committee. Wilson had already expressed his opposition to a Jewish right of appeal at a Council of Four meeting earlier in the month.[55] Now he restated his case to the American Jews; he assured them that the Great Powers would deal with treaty infractions, and suggested further that the Western Jewish organizations ought to continue their traditional role of bringing such infractions to their notice.[56]

Whatever Marshall's feelings about Wilson's proposals—and the evidence does not necessarily point to his wholehearted support[57]—he nevertheless loyally presented them to Wolf. He did so on the very same day that Wolf had intended to win him for the Baker formula.[58] This juxtaposition was unfortunate in the extreme.

Wilson's suggestions seemed to Wolf not a progression but regression

---

[53] Ibid. 316; Adler to Wolf, 26 May 1919, Marshall papers, Paris Peace Conference, Corr. box 1; Marshall to Wolf, 24 May, and letters to Wilson and Hudson, 26 May 1919, ibid.; Wolf, Paris Diary, 16 May 1919, fo. 257.

[54] Marshall to Tardieu, 14 May 1919, Marshall papers, Paris Peace Conference, Poland, box 1, Wolf to Lloyd George, 20 May 1919, *RDJBE* 82–3.

[55] *FRUS*, vol. v, 17 May 1919, p. 680.

[56] Adler Papers, Diary, interview with Wilson, 26 May 1919, fos. 206–9.

[57] Marshall's alternative formula referred only to the signatories of the Covenant, i.e. the Great Powers, having the right to take up infractions. However, Wolf does seem to have misconstrued a further reference in Marshall's formula to 'authorised representatives' as meaning foreign representatives, i.e. the JFC, AJC, etc. Marshall denied this interpretation; see Wolf, Paris Diary, for Marshall to Wolf and vice versa, 29 May and 1 June 1919, fos. 309–24. Wolf added: 'unfortunately Marshall always thinks in the end as the President thinks'; ibid., 3 June 1919, fo. 337.

[58] Ibid., 27 and 28 May 1919, fos. 283–4, 289.

to 'the ineffective Berlin model'.[59] To add insult to injury, Marshall not only seemed to be supporting them, but further objected to Baker's Polish court procedure, which he considered an inadmissible breach of obligations of international concern.[60] The effect of his subsequent refusal to assist in backing the Baker formula was to bring into the open all the simmering antagonisms not only between Marshall and Wolf but between the British and American delegates involved in the issue.

The curtailment and eventual rejection of Baker's clauses in the committee at the beginning of June were blamed squarely and bitterly by Baker and his chief on the lack of American support, a desertion compounded in Wolf's eyes by the knowledge that Marshall, who according to Baker had great influence with Hudson, had failed to bring pressure to bear.[61] Headlam-Morley agreed, complaining to Wolf that Marshall 'would do nothing unless you persuaded him that what you wanted him to do was his own handiwork'. Later, again undoubtedly echoing Wolf, he claimed that Marshall and the other American Jews were more interested in the New York vote rather than in the real gains to be had for Eastern Jewry.[62]

In turn, Headlam-Morley's own bitterness over the way he had been opposed by Miller over the Sabbath clause spilled over into a burst of unadulterated Americaphobia on Wolf's part. 'Owing to difficulties with the Japanese', he wrote at the end of May, 'they had to withdraw the Civil and Religious clause in the League of Nations Covenant. Then they opposed and defeated the Sunday Trading clause. Now they threaten to deprive the Polish and similar Treaties of all the guarantees which will make of any practical use.'[63]

At the same time the clash over the right of appeal highlighted the quite profound differences between Marshall and Wolf's respective methods of approach. The American throughout was hawkish, intransigent, and obdurately anti-Polish. While Marshall put his trust in the

---

[59] Wolf, Paris Diary, 27 May 1919, fo. 284. It might be noted, in fairness to Marshall, that he had much less experience of the 'Berlin model' than had Wolf in the previous 20-odd years.

[60] Ibid., Marshall to Wolf, 29 May 1919, fos. 309–17.

[61] Miller, *My Diary*, 29 and 31 May 1919, xiii. 96, 105, 109; BM Add. MS 51131 (Cecil papers), Paris Peace Conference Diary, 4 June 1919, 93–4; Wolf, Paris Diary, 3 June 1919, fo. 337.

[62] Wolf, Paris Diary, 28 May 1919, fo. 290; Headlam-Morley to Namier, 30 June 1919, *A Memoir*, 176. Headlam added, 'The whole thing has ended with a definite difference between Marshall and the American Jews on the one hand and Lucien Wolf and his Committee on the other.'   [63] Wolf, Paris Diary, 28 May 1919, fo. 290.

political muscle of the Great Powers as guardians of Jewish rights, Wolf's approach was always more flexible—more willing, indeed, to see the issue from the Polish side and therefore to concede where sense and practicality dictated.[64] It was these differences which ultimately determined why the end product of the Minorities Treaties was more acceptable to Wolf and in conformity with his guidelines.

When, at the end of June, just prior to the signature of the treaty, Polish objections threatened its survival, Headlam-Morley consulted Wolf, not Marshall, with a view to further concessions to the Poles: that Polish be made the medium of instruction in Jewish higher schools, that the sanctity of the Sabbath might not exempt Jews from occasions of 'military necessity', and finally that only the articles concerning rights of citizenship, liberty, and equality be embodied as fundamental laws. Examining these, Wolf found them not liable to 'alter the substance of the Treaty', and readily acquiesced.[65]

The effect was to make Wolf a protagonist of the treaty and Marshall its unhappy—though temporary—opponent.[66] Unconsulted on the concessions though aware that they had been made, Marshall appealed to Wilson, only to find himself at odds with, and hence isolated from, the final orientation of the treaty makers, save for the unrepentant Hudson.[67]

Marshall had similarly become isolated from the two main streams of Jewish strategy at Paris. His alliance with the Comité des Délégations could not survive the unauthorized inclusion of his name in their published appraisal of the treaty as a victory for national rights,[68]

[64] Ibid. See Marshall to Wolf and vice versa, 29 May and 1 June 1919, fos. 309–24.

[65] Wolf, Paris Diary, 19 and 21 June 1919, fos. 381–3, 397; Miller, *My Diary*, 19–23 June 1919, xiii. 189–201. On New States Com. modifications endorsed or changed by the Council of Four see *FRUS*, vol. v, 27 June 1919, pp. 624–8.

[66] Soon after, the American Jews and Sokolow officially acclaimed the treaty as an act of the first magnitude, the basis upon which they urged their Polish co-religionists to co-operate in the new state; see Marshall, Adler, Sokolow to Bogen, 11 July 1919, Adler Papers, Diary, fos. 393–5. Kohler, 'Origin', lays special emphasis on Marshall's role in the formulation of its provisions though latter admitted 'perhaps my American citizenship induces me to emphasise Louis Marshall's services in this connection rather than Mr. Wolf's'. See Kohler to Mowschowitch, 19 Nov. 1932, MWS 24528.

[67] Marshall to Wilson, 2 June 1919, Marshall papers, Paris Peace Conference, Corr. box 2, Wilson file; Headlam-Morley to Namier, 30 June 1919, *A Memoir*, 176; *FRUS*, vol. v, 27 June 1919, pp. 624–8.

[68] Marshall to Motzkin, 23 June 1919, Adler Papers, Diary, fos. 369–72; Feinberg, *La Question*, 135, argues that the Minorities Treaties were implicitly a victory for national rights. Cf. Clemenceau to Paderewski, 24 June 1919, *RDJBE* 86, explaining that they were not intended to foster Jewish national separation from the Polish state.

which it was not. His co-operation with Wolf could likewise not continue. There had, it is true, been some attempt to patch things up after the right of appeal dispute, but the private arrangement between Headlam-Morley and Wolf seems to have put paid to that. The *coup de grâce*, from Marshall's point of view, came when Morgenthau solicited Wolf's advice as to whether he should lead the American mission to Poland to investigate the pogrom charges. Wolf's sin, on this occasion, was not only that he did not consult Marshall on the matter, but that he offered advice diametrically opposed to Marshall's own; Wolf thought Morgenthau should go (which he did), Marshall strongly deprecated.[69] In early July Marshall returned to America, the relationship having been reduced to bitter character assassination on both sides.[70]

The ill feeling left its mark in more important ways. Marshall and Wolf were the two outstanding Jewish diplomats at Paris, and their failure to work together properly in the weeks before the completion of the Polish Treaty was of some consequence. Although Wolf professed that the outcome was 'on paper the best solution that has been dreamt of',[71] in reality it was marred by discrepancies.

Thus, while the first seven clauses of the treaty did provide Jews and other minorities with watertight clauses which fixed them 'more firmly and explicitly in the nationality of the lands of their birth than they had ever been before'—a signal defeat for the Zionists—these clauses might have been strengthened still further if Wolf had heeded that section of the American Jewish Bill of Rights which proposed provisions for Jews expelled, or Jews who had fled, to return and claim their citizenship rights. No such stipulation appeared in the Joint Foreign Committee formula or final text of the treaty, and in consequence Wolf was faced with thousands of Jewish stateless refugees in post-war Eastern Europe quite unprotected by the Minorities settlement.[72]

These discrepancies showed up even more clearly in specific

[69] Marshall to Wolf and vice versa, 26 June 1919, MWS file 209.
[70] Marshall to Zangwill, 10 Nov. 1919, in Reznikoff, *Marshall*, ii. 640; Wolf to Montefiore, 17 July 1919, MWS file 210. Adler was also involved in the dispute; see Wolf to Adler and vice versa, 6 July 1919, Marshall papers, Paris Peace Conference, Corr. 1919–23, box 1.
[71] Wolf, Paris Diary, 16 Sept. 1919, fo. 623.
[72] Wolf to George Wolf, 9 Apr. 1920, MWS 1603–4; Wolf public reply to Dubnow, 26 Oct. 1928, *Jewish Guardian*. On *Staatenlosigkeit* see Wischnitzer, *To Dwell*, 150–3. See further JFC report, *The League of Nations, 1926* (London, 1927), 10–11.

clauses. Certainly, Wolf had triumphed in that the clauses in Article 9 were 'cultural', providing for 'educational and charitable' autonomy only. However, Article 10 provided specifically for Jewish educational committees, a point which Wolf soon admitted 'formed no part of the proposals of our Committee', adding, 'we should have preferred that the privilege granted in it had been extended equally to all religious minorities'.[73] This specific reference to Jews, which Wolf consistently (with the exception of the Sabbath issue and Romanian citizenship) opposed because it singled them out for privilege rather than subsuming them in a movement for 'general freedom and general political progress',[74] thus represented an out of place rump concession to Marshall and Hudson's obstinate defence of national rights.

Finally, the Sabbath clauses and League guarantees, both of which Wolf battled to strengthen right up to the treaty's signing,[75] represented further disappointments to Wolf's ideal. Though the problem of right of appeal was partially rectified following Wolf's energetic representations to the newly established League in Geneva in 1920,[76] the failure to carry it in the first instance in 1919 again reflected on the inability of Marshall and Wolf to work harmoniously in the Jewish interest.

If the treaty was not the unqualified success Wolf suggested it was, and if its wording, as James Parkes suggests, represented a 'compromise between the wishes of the four parties concerned—the Great Powers, British and French Jews, American-Eastern Jewish groups and the Poles'[77]—Wolf nevertheless still remained clear victor on one point. In agreement in principle with the guidelines pursued by him, the treaty assured his accord with its makers,[78] especially of course the British. His work in Paris was thus extended into many more years of strenuous diplomatic activity. He was in future to represent at the League of Nations in Geneva not only the Joint Foreign Committee

[73] Wolf, Paris Diary, 19 and 24 Aug. 1919, fos. 547, 560. Wolf had in mind in particular the Protestants and Unitarians of Transylvania and the Muslims of Thrace.

[74] *JC* 19 Dec. 1919, reporting Wolf at AGM of AJA, 14 Dec. 1919.

[75] Wolf to Dutasta, 16 June 1919, FO 608/67/131/1/1. Esmé Howard minuted, n.d., 'I fear it is too late to do anything now.'

[76] JFC interim report, 13 Dec. 1920, C11/2/15. AJA *Report*, no. 49, 1919–21 (London, 1922), 6. Wolf's action contributed towards getting the Permanent Court of Justice to deal with infractions though still failed to get minorities the direct right of appeal.

[77] Parkes, *Emergence*, 123.

[78] Macartney, *National States*, 280, agrees.

but also on many occasions the Alliance and the Jewish Colonization Association. It was in this role as spokesman, indeed 'minister pleni-potentiary' of the Western Jewish organizations, that the new states of Eastern Europe sometimes themselves turned to him for the arbitra-tion and resolution of outstanding internal disputes with their own Jewish communities.[79]

Wolf's work in the post-war years was extended in other directions too. A founder of the Advisory Committee to the League's High Commission for Refugees, of which he became president in succession to Fridjhof Nansen in 1930, Wolf was recognized as an expert witness and delegate to countless committees and conferences on both Jewish and non-Jewish *staatenlos*. He became, too, the foremost authority on procedures for bringing minority rights infractions to the International Court of Appeal.[80] These new involvements underscored the fact that a comprehensive settlement of the Jewish question had been far from realized at the Paris Peace Conference. However, the Minorities Treaties did confer on Wolf the prestige to continue the struggle for Jewish rights in the international arena, and a framework within which to pursue it. Confident that in the end the liberal principles which had been responsible for the treaties would win through, Wolf remained a key player, at Geneva and elsewhere, right up to his death in August 1930.

[79] See JFC reports, *The League of Nations* (London, 1921–30) for details of Wolf's Geneva work. 'A Memoir: The Man' in Roth, ed., *Essays*, 10–12, gives a brief descrip-tion of this period in Wolf's work. For an example of Wolf's interventionary diplomacy at the request of the Polish state in 1925 see JFC, *The Jews of Poland* (London, 1926). There has, to date, been no major study of Wolf's post-1919 diplomacy.

[80] 'A Memoir' in Roth, ed., *Essays*, 11. On refugees see JFC, *Report on the Conference on Russo-Jewish Refugees in Eastern Europe 1921–1924* (London, 1921 et seq.). On Treaty infractions see JFC, *The Procedure for Giving Effect to the League of Nations Guarantee of the Minorities Treaties and the Proposals Thereon Submitted to the 54th Session of the Council of the League* (London, 1929).

Conclusion: In Alliance with the British?

The Jewish delegates were not the final and decisive forces that were at work. These they had to seek in the high statesmanship and unwearying goodwill of the Conference itself, of the Allied and Associated Powers and more particularly of the Commission [*sic*] of New States ... in which the great altruistic traditions of British policy were so worthily and admirably represented ... by Mr. Headlam-Morley ... It is true that the first detailed plan was the Joint Committee's and that they were privileged to have frequent opportunities of discussing its application and redaction with members of the New States Committee but if they had been successful in carrying these points it had been because the ... governing principles of these Treaties had already been accepted by the leading statesmen of the Conference.[1]

The summer and autumn of 1919 marked the zenith of Wolf's diplomatic career. True, the situation was touch and go all the way. The new states, encouraged by Bratianu, had already, at the end of May, staged before the Supreme Council a 'revolt' against the whole conception of a minorities settlement. Time-wasting tactics and obstructionism attempted by the Poles in early June and then in the autumn by the Romanians also threatened to jeopardize the settlement,[2] especially once the 'Big Three' had departed for home, leaving the final solution of the issue in less authoritative hands. Moreover, Wolf had to deal with these crises practically single-handed. The American Jews had gone home. The Comité des Délégations had dwindled away. The Alliance refused to take the initiative. Labin and Wilhelm Filderman, meanwhile, for the Romanian Jews, insisted to Wolf that they were dependent on his resolve to stay put and finish the job.[3]

These setbacks served to reinforce Wolf's 'accord' with the British delegation and to enhance his prestige as co-author of the Minorities Treaties. Thus, when in mid-June Paderewski challenged the draft treaty as an unwarranted limitation on Polish sovereignty, it was Wolf who furnished Headlam-Morley with a chapter and verse response.

---

[1] *JC*, 11 July 1920, reporting Maccabeans dinner of 8 July.
[2] Parkes, *Emergence*, 126–7.
[3] Wolf, Paris Diary, 16 July 1919, fo. 461.

'Precise obligations' relating to civil and religious rights, Wolf reminded him, were required of new states by international convention, beginning with the United Netherlands in 1814. These guidelines were embodied in Clemenceau's reply to Paderewski, on 24 June, rejecting the Polish premier's complaint and confirming the treaty's 'irreducible minimum' of guarantees to Jews and other minorities in the new Poland.[4]

Aligned with the treaty-makers in this way, Wolf found himself in July being urged by Headlam-Morley and A. W. A. Leeper, and George Riddell of the British delegation's press section, to explain and defend the treaties. It was another moment of crisis. Public apathy and misunderstanding were playing into the hands of the Romanian government, abetted in France by a stridently pro-Romanian press.[5] Guarantees in the Romanian treaty, for the Jewish and many other minorities, were imperative. Wolf took up the journalistic cudgels. By contrast, when concessions in the Jewish case—the removal of Articles 10 and 11, which Wolf anyway considered irrelevant or useless—were advised by Headlam-Morley in order to ease Romania's path to signing, he readily acquiesced. Assured in October 1919 that in all other respects the treaty would remain unimpaired, indeed an extra article (Article 7) was added on the basis of the Labin–Filderman formula expressly obliging the Romanians to recognize the Jews *ipso facto* as nationals, Wolf felt sufficiently confident to return home to England.[6]

That it was only he who was privy to the secret of the concessions is in fact testified by the near-panic which swept the delegates of the alliance and the Romanian Union des Juifs when the Romanians finally did submit in December. Wolf wrote reassuringly to Bigart:

Mr. Headlam-Morley and I all along have had it in mind that if Rumania signs the Treaty we ought to assist her with such concessions as will enable the government to boast that they have obtained a victory. As a matter of fact they have obtained no victory at all. All the essential clauses of the Treaty remain intact.[7]

It might be tempting to view the problems which beset liberal Anglo-

---

[4] Wolf, Paris Diary, 20 and 25 June 1919, fos. 390, 404. Clemenceau to Paderewski, 24 June 1919, *RDJBE* 83–7; Parkes, *Emergence*, 124–5; Macartney, *National States*, 2379.

[5] Wolf, Paris Diary, 12 July 1919, fo. 416; Wolf, 'Rumania and the Minorities Treaties', *Westminster Gazette*, 12 Sept. 1919.

[6] Wolf, Paris Diary, 19 Aug. and 9 Sept. 1919, fos. 547, 606. For final Romanian treaty draft see *RDJBE* 106–8.

[7] Wolf to Bigart, 8 Dec. 1919, C11/2/14. On Romanian obstructions of autumn 1919, see Spector, *Rumania*, 180–217.

Jewish diplomacy in the period of the First World War as a microcosm of the wider British scene. Lucien Wolf and his committee, holding on to outworn ideological baggage and misinterpreting the realities of the Jewish situation, were bound to fail in much the same way, and for much the same reasons, as did the Liberal government of Herbert Asquith. In this view, the wartime replacement of Wolf, as of Asquith, by people with a more up-to-date and realistic approach to British and Jewish interests takes on an aspect of inevitability. If neither Asquith nor Wolf could muster an effective response to the crisis of war, Weizmann and Lloyd George not only could, but were able to use the crisis strategically to develop and achieve objectives commensurate with their wider aims. The Balfour Declaration in this interpretation becomes not only linked to, but subsumed within, the British pursuit of victory. A chapter of Whig history is thus neatly explored and explained, the dynamic personalities in the process having been contrasted with the static, the forward-looking makers of history compared with antediluvians clinging onto a useless past.

Except that it wasn't entirely like that. Far from being soundly routed by the Balfour Declaration in 1917, Wolf not only lived to fight another day but returned in 1919 as the key Jewish player in the European settlement. If ultimately his liberal Jewish diplomacy was eclipsed—and there seems little doubt about that—the process was certainly more gradual than has often been assumed in Zionist historiography. Moreover, it owed less to any special ability on the part of the Zionists (the Comité des Délégations continuing, in his words, to masquerade as an international diplomatic organization defending Jewish rights)[8] and much more to the near-impossible conditions prevailing in Eastern and Central Europe in the late 1920s and 1930s.

Be that as it may, it is more difficult to assess, or even to determine, what Wolf's wartime efforts on behalf of the Conjoint and Joint Foreign Committee's achieved, or even could have achieved. They were constructed, after all, on a tenuous mid-Victorian premiss that the interests of an Anglo-Jewish foreign office could be sponsored by and indeed subsumed within general British foreign policy. If this may have had some passing relationship to reality in the age of Cobden, all it managed to do in the epoch of the Anglo-Russian *entente* was trap the Conjoint in a grudging subservience to a foreign policy with which it was at total variance. Optimism gave way to despondency and

[8] Wolf to Sliosberg, 12 Dec. 1928, MWS 3758.

confusion, and confidence in its ability to influence international relations in favour of Jewish interests gave way to an almost complete sense of powerlessness.

This crisis in Anglo-Jewish foreign policy was underscored by a value system which denied the existence of any Jewish interest which could run counter to a national British one. Yet the outbreak of the First World War did just that. In geopolitical terms, Jewish interests *were* best served by alignment with the cause of Germany and the Central Powers; the Conjoint, and indeed the whole Anglo-Jewish community, finding itself stranded, so to speak, on the wrong side. This crisis, with the consequent psychological and actual paralysis which it engendered, should have spelt the end of the Conjoint. Terrified of antisemitic denunciation or worse, the Anglo-Jewish establishment could hardly have done a complete about-turn and stated, as leading Zionists might have proffered, that Jews did, after all, have their own sectarian interests.

Nor was sitting the war out and hoping for better times a realistic option. As the war passed its third full year in the summer of 1917, it became increasingly clear that Allied sponsorship of a territorially recast Eastern Europe in favour of the most dominant nationalities would not be to Eastern Jewry's benefit. By contrast, once Russia, after its brief liberal revolutionary phase, had unequivocally collapsed into Bolshevism and civil war, a victory for Germany and the Central Powers remained the best available option, not least because in ensuring the survival in some form of the old empires it would preserve Jewish economic and cultural integrity.

Wolf's achievement in this context was remarkable. Not only did he rescue the Conjoint Committee from complete oblivion, but with great dexterity kept its lines to the Foreign Office open by dissembling the real contradiction between the Conjoint's defence of Eastern Jewish interests and its patriotic duty to support the war effort of Britain and its Russian ally. The problem, of course, is that this was an achievement in negation. Wolf would certainly have had it otherwise. When, for instance, in 1915, the Progressive Bloc emerged in Russia, he seized on this as an opportunity to influence the Foreign Office towards an alternative Russian strategy which, as a by-product, would have reforged the traditional Conjoint–Foreign Office understanding.

The failure of this project serves to underline the inherent inability of a non-state Jewish body to determine the course of events, or indeed to achieve any of its goals, without recourse to, or the tangible assistance of, a sovereign power.[9] Yet if this statement defines the actual limitations on Wolf's Conjoint activities, there is a further crucial dimension which cannot be ignored. This dimension has less to do with reality than with perceptions of reality: the mental image of Jews prevalent in this period among the establishments of Europe. It is also, paradoxically, the dimension which translates Wolf's wartime actions into something that can genuinely be called diplomacy.

A number of historians in recent years have focused some attention on this area, namely, the psychological obsession that turned the Jew, the collective Jew, into a power which, through finance, or revolutionary activity, had the potential to manipulate and control the world.[10] This obsession was certainly not confined to a British Foreign Office responsible for the Balfour Declaration, but the fact that many key members of the British Foreign Office held to this fantastic and totally imaginary misconception is central to our understanding of Wolf's wartime response.

First of all, Wolf undoubtedly knew about it. 'It is a curious circumstance, which is not generally known,' he later wrote, with considerable understatement, 'that all the belligerents miscalculated the importance of securing Jewish support.'[11]

Secondly, it provided him with opportunity. Whereas in pre-war years the supposed power of the Jews had provided no scope for manœuvre in itself, the prolonged stalemate of war translated it into a highly valuable tool. The Allies wanted Jewish support. Their information was that the Germans had it. Wolf was on one level busily protesting otherwise. On another, he had nothing to gain by disinvesting them of their error. On the contrary, it provided him with the best, possibly the only, opening in the Conjoint's history with which to force the issue of Jewish rights, and in the place where it really mattered: Russia.

Thirdly, it created for Wolf's wartime diplomacy a real conundrum.

[9] For a wider discussion on the scope and limitations of Jewish action without sovereign power see Yehuda Bauer, *The Jewish Emergence from Powerlessness* (Toronto, 1979); for a fine corrective see David Biale, *Power and Powerlessness in Jewish History* (New York, 1986).
[10] See esp. the preface to Poliakov's *History of Anti-Semitism*, vol. 4. Also Bauer, *Jewish Emergence*, 53–8; Rogger, *Jewish Policies*, 101–10; Vital, *Zionism: Crucial Phase*, 375; Jonathan Frankel, 'An Introductory Essay—The Paradoxical Politics of Marginality: Thoughts on the Jewish Situation During the Years 1914–1921', *Studies in Contemporary Jewry*, 4 (1988), 13–18.
[11] Wolf, 'Jew in Diplomacy', in Roth, ed., *Essays*, 407.

The tool might be useful, but it was also highly fissile. To agree that the Jews were financially powerful was to promote the bogeyman image of the Jew, which was hardly in Anglo-Jewish interests. The same went for the 'revolutionary Jew' story. Wolf had to find a basis for playing upon the Foreign Office's psychosis but in such a coded form that it would not upset the Conjoint's long-term *raison d'être*. That Wolf plumped for the propaganda card and by extension, Palestine, a year before Weizmann had made a serious impact on the ministry, shows how keenly he recognized its potential.

But Palestine was for Wolf only a subterfuge, a prop to be jettisoned once his real goal of Russian Jewish emancipation had come within his sights. He was not interested in Palestine for its his own sake any more than he was willing ultimately to confirm the Foreign Office in its antisemitic obsessions in order to win it for Zionism. If the pseudo-Palestine project marks the zenith of Wolf's wartime diplomacy in early 1916, the nearest he came to getting within a whisker of success, it is also the point at which he was upstaged by Weizmann, who could not only play a more purposeful tune to the Foreign Office but play it without any discordant notes about Eastern European baggage. By the early summer of 1917, the practical and ideological limitations of Wolf's policy were only too obvious.

Yet that is not the end of the story. Certainly, a new Jewish–British understanding had been born out of Weizmann's successful diplomacy, one which superficially at least seemed to be based on a more solid footing than that which had governed the Conjoint–Foreign Office relationship. But this disguises the fact that it was itself based on a wholly suspect and misconceived notion: the idea of Jewish power. Once the wartime emergency and hence the supposed urgent need for Jewish support had ceased, its potency ebbed. The degree to which we can talk of an ongoing Zionist–British relationship in the 1920s and 1930s is debatable.

Nor did it resolve the problem of the millions of Jews who remained in Eastern Europe. The war had drastically altered their circumstances and threatened to place them, at its end, in new national state units which implicitly stood to jeopardize their cultural and socio-economic existence. Forewarned of the danger, Wolf, in 'The Jewish National Movement', had intellectually attempted to guard against it by advocating a system of 'cultural' autonomy rights for Jews and other nationalities incorporated *within* the existing imperial frameworks.

Wolf and his Conjoint associates have sometimes been characterized as a complacent, self-deluded assimilationist clique who were out of touch with the Jewish masses and essentially uninterested in their welfare. It may be that they misunderstood the intrinsic realities of the Jewish situation. It does appear, too, that at crisis moments such as at the outbreak of war and again in 1919, when the 'Jewish international conspiracy' press scare reached its peak, they were more interested in saving their own frightened skins than those of anybody else. Having said that, however, Wolf's new thinking, as expressed in his 'Jewish National Movement' and associated with the guidance of David Mowschowitch, displays an honest and singular determination not only to come to grips with Eastern Jewry's predicament but to find pragmatic ways of ensuring its survival and well-being. Indeed, Wolf's new emphasis on national–cultural and ethnic autonomy and the rights of Jews as Jews, rather than simply as prospective citizens of new states, would qualify him, according to Yehuda Bauer's criteria,[12] alongside the Agudas Yisroel, the Bundists, the Folkists, the Territorialists, and the Zionists, as a Jewish nationalist.

What Lucien Wolf would have made of that assessment is anybody's guess. The facts of the matter are, however, that his potentially radical realignment of Anglo-Jewish foreign policy, not only in the direction of minority rights but also, by extension, towards centre-left forces in East European political life, were forestalled by the British Foreign Office. At the end of the day, their interests, like Wolf's, were in the prevention of another European conflict, and hence in achieving a framework for a durable peace. That meant dealing with the minority question, including the Jewish question in Eastern Europe. However, the geopolitical realities of 1918–19 dictated that they would have to be dealt with within the context of new or enlarged nation states, such as Poland and Romania. Wolf could have chosen, like the Zionists, to stand out for full Jewish national demands, but this would have ensured the maximum rift between Jew and Gentile. Indeed, it may be that the Zionist-oriented Comité des Délégations consciously strove for this in order to accelerate the movement towards, and urgency for, an immediate sovereign Jewish state in Palestine. Alternatively, Wolf could moderate his minority rights stance and thereby bring himself into closer accord with the peacemakers. He chose the latter.

There were of course other factors involved in this process. One, for instance, was the fortunate appointment of individuals such as

---

[12] Bauer, *Jewish Emergence*, 46.

Headlam-Morley to the relevant peace conference committees; Eyre Crowe would never have partnered Wolf in seeking solutions to Eastern Jewish problems. Headlam-Morley not only could, but fully shared Wolf's liberal sentiments. Nevertheless, the fact remains that in order to shore up a fragile peace, the British in particular needed Jewish partners. Given the other options in Paris in 1919, that could only mean Lucien Wolf.

Given the discord which had characterized Conjoint–British relations for so long, it is another paradox that, in the aftermath of war, Wolf was able not only to find an echo of his own proposals in the desiderata of the Foreign Office but to come close to recreating that old, highly elusive Conjoint version of its relationship to British state and foreign policy. With Jewish movement eastwards blocked by the Russian chaos and westwards by increasingly restrictive immigration laws, Wolf had plumped for a solution which would anchor Eastern Jewry more firmly in the lands where they already were. That entailed minimizing the friction between Poles and Jews and finding a basis for reconciliation between them. In so doing, Wolf's main contribution to the settlement was less in the actual wording of the Minorities Treaties and more in reflecting its faith in a consensual, liberal, post-war politics.

This, then, nearly two years after the Balfour Declaration, was the high-water mark of liberal Jewish diplomacy, the momentary point at which British and British Jewish interests converged. It was the moment, indeed, at which Wolf would have been able genuinely and proudly to proclaim that he was acting not only on behalf of Jewish interests but also as an agent of His Majesty's Government.

Wolf was far too astute, however, to assume that a settlement on paper would itself solve the problem. That depended, he told an audience in 1920, less on parchment and sealing wax than on goodwill and understanding.[13] Even then, what Wolf wanted most from the settlement was an apparatus which would ensure the automatic guarantee for protection of minority groups vested in the League of Nations. That Wolf could look forward, after the Paris peace conference, to a relationship with the League and its International Court of Justice in Geneva, instead of having to take up infractions or violations of the Minorities Treaties with the British Foreign Office, seemed at the time a major step forward. It turned out to be a colossal error of judgement.

[13] *JC*, 11 July 1920, on Maccabeans dinner of 8 July.

Whereas in the past, according to the practice of the Berlin Treaty, the protection of minorities had been vested solely in the Great Powers, its transference to the League gave Britain, as the leading post-war power represented in it, a loophole with which to abdicate its responsibilities at least as fully as under the previous system, yet without giving the replacement League the necessary authority with which to enforce or have its mandate respected. If, as Headlam-Morley had hoped in 1919, Britain had taken the initiative in the League Council, things might well have turned out differently. Such a dilemma might not have arisen at all if, as Wolf had been confident in 1919, the Bratianus and Dmowskis had really been defeated and a new liberal era inaugurated in which the new Eastern regimes obligingly kept to the letter of the more than adequate treaty stipulations.[14]

Instead, abjuring the reconciliation which Wolf constantly sought of them, the regimes moved increasingly to the right, flouting Jewish and other minorities' rights, making a comprehensive mockery of the League safeguards. The ensuing polarization throughout the 1920s and 1930s—the Eastern European states moving towards Fascism or some sort of accommodation with it, a new generation of young Jews, increasingly excluded from the body-politic, moving towards more radical solutions—all seemed to suggest that the Jewish–Gentile split was, as the Zionists said, irreconcilable after all. Wolf fortunately did not live to see the *dénouement*. It was a paradox that in the Great War of 1914–18, psychological delusions about the Jews, rather than the economic and social realities of the Jewish question, gave an undeveloped Jewish diplomacy its great opportunity. In the next war, those same obsessive delusions would prove to be the block upon which the Jewish fate in Europe was sealed.

[14] Wolf, Paris Diary, 8 and 16 Sept. 1919, fos. 600, 622–3; Sharp, 'Britain', 183; Robinson, *Minorities Treaties*, 67–76, 240–1.

The Polish Minorities Treaty 1919

The text of the treaty signed at Versailles on 28 June 1919 became the model for subsequent treaties required by the Allies of either 'new' or defeated states in the 'New Europe'.

Article 1

Poland undertakes that the stipulations contained in Articles 2 to 8 of this Chapter shall be recognised as fundamental laws, and that no law, regulation or official action shall conflict or interfere with these stipulations, nor shall any law, regulation or official action prevail over them.

Article 2

Poland undertakes to assure full and complete protection of life and liberty to all inhabitants of Poland without distinction of birth, nationality, language, race or religion.

All inhabitants of Poland shall be entitled to the free exercise, whether public or private, of any creed, religion or belief, whose practices are not inconsistent with public order or public morals.

Article 3

Poland admits and declares to be Polish nationals *ipso facto* and without the requirement of any formality German, Austrian, Hungarian or Russian nationals habitually resident at the date of the coming into force of the present Treaty in territory which is or may be recognised as forming part of Poland, but subject to any provisions in the Treaties of Peace with Germany or Austria respectively relating to persons who became resident in such territory after a specified date.

Nevertheless, the persons referred to above who are over eighteen years of age will be entitled under the conditions contained in the said Treaties to opt for any other nationality which may be open to them. Option by a husband will cover his wife and option by parents will cover their children under eighteen years of age.

Persons who have exercised the above right to opt must, except where it is otherwise provided in the Treaty of Peace with Germany, transfer within the succeeding twelve months their place of residence to the State for which they have opted. They will be entitled to retain their immovable property in Polish territory. They may carry with them their movable property of every description. No export duties may be imposed upon them in connection with the removal of such property.

Article 4

Poland admits and declares to be Polish nationals *ipso facto* and without the requirement of any formality persons of German, Austrian, Hungarian or Russian nationality who were born in the said territory of parents habitually resident there, even if at the date of the coming into force of the present Treaty they are not themselves habitually resident there.

Nevertheless, within two years after the coming into force of the present Treaty, these persons may make a declaration before the competent Polish authorities in the country in which they are resident, stating that they abandon Polish nationality, and they will then cease to be considered as Polish nationals. In this connection a declaration by a husband will cover his wife, and a declaration by parents will cover their children under eighteen years of age.

Article 5

Poland undertakes to put no hindrance in the way of the exercise of the right which the persons concerned have, under the Treaties concluded or to be concluded by the Allied and Associated Powers with Germany, Austria, Hungary or Russia, to choose whether or not they will acquire Polish nationality.

Article 6

All persons born in Polish territory who are not born nationals of another State shall *ipso facto* become Polish nationals.

Article 7

All Polish nationals shall be equal before the law, and shall enjoy the same civil and political rights without distinction as to race, language or religion.

Differences of religion, creed or confession shall not prejudice any Polish national in matters relating to the enjoyment of civil or political rights, as for instance admission to public employments, functions and honours, or the exercise of professions and industries.

No restriction shall be imposed on the free use by any Polish national of any language in private intercourse, in commerce, in religion, in the press or in publications of any kind, or at public meetings.

Notwithstanding any establishment by the Polish Government of an official language, adequate facilities shall be given to Polish nationals of non-Polish speech for the use of their language, either orally or in writing, before the courts.

Article 8

Polish nationals who belong to racial, religious or linguistic minorities shall enjoy the same treatment and security in law and in fact as the other Polish nationals. In particular they shall have an equal right to establish, manage and control at their own expense charitable, religious and social institutions, schools and other educational establishments, with the right to use their own language and to exercise their religion freely therein.

Article 9

Poland will provide in the public educational system in towns and districts in which a considerable proportion of Polish nationals of other than Polish speech are residents adequate facilities for ensuring that in the primary schools the instruction shall be given to the children of such Polish nationals through the medium of their own language. This provision shall not prevent the Polish Government from making the teaching of the Polish language obligatory in the said schools.

In towns and districts where there is a considerable proportion of Polish nationals belonging to racial, religious or linguistic minorities, these minorities shall be assured an equitable share in the enjoyment and application of the sums which may be provided out of public funds under the State, municipal or other budget for educational, religious or charitable purposes.

The provisions of this Article shall apply to Polish citizens of German speech only in that part of Poland which was German territory on August 1, 1914.

Article 10

Educational Committees appointed locally by the Jewish communities of Poland will, subject to the general control of the State, provide for the distribution of the proportional share of public funds allocated to Jewish schools in accordance with Article 9, and for the organisation and management of these schools.

The provision of Article 9 concerning the use of language in schools shall apply to these schools.

Article 11

Jews shall not be compelled to perform any act which constitutes a violation of their Sabbath, nor shall they be placed under any disability by reason of their refusal to attend courts of law or to perform any legal business on their Sabbath. This provision, however, shall not exempt Jews from such obligations as shall be imposed upon all other Polish citizens for the necessary purposes of military service, national defence or the preservation of public order.

Poland declares her intention to refrain from ordering or permitting elections, whether general or local, to be held on a Saturday, nor will registration for electoral or other purposes be compelled to be performed on a Saturday.

Article 12

Poland agrees that the stipulations in the foregoing Articles, so far as they affect persons belonging to racial, religious or linguistic minorities, constitute obligations of international concern, and shall be placed under the guarantee of the League of Nations. They shall not be modified without the assent of a majority of the Council of the League of Nations. The United States, the British Empire, France, Italy and Japan hereby agree not to withhold their assent from any modification in these Articles which is in due form assented to by a majority of the Council of the League of Nations.

Poland agrees that any Member of the Council of the League of Nations shall have the right to bring to the attention of the Council any infraction, or any danger of infraction, of any of these obligations, and that the Council may thereupon take such action and give such direction as it may deem proper and effective in the circumstances.

Poland further agrees that any difference of opinion as to questions of law or fact arising out of these Articles between the Polish Government and any one of the Principal Allied and Associated Powers or any other Power, a Member of the Council of the League of Nations, shall be held to be a dispute of an international character under Article 14 of the Covenant of the League of Nations. The Polish Government hereby consents that any such dispute shall, if the other party thereto demands, be referred to the Permanent Court of International Justice. The decision of the Permanent Court shall be final and shall have the same force and effect as an award under Article 13 of the Covenant.

References

UNPUBLISHED SOURCES

ADLER PAPERS
Correspondence and Peace Conference files of Cyrus Adler, including Peace Conference Diary (1919). *American Jewish Committee, New York*

ALLIANCE ISRAÉLITE UNIVERSELLE PAPERS (AIU)
Files 'Angleterre', 'France', 'Rumanie', relating to Conjoint and Alliance diplomacy, propaganda, and Zionism. *Alliance Israélite Universelle, Paris*

BOARD OF DEPUTIES OF AMERICAN ISRAELITES COLLECTION
Correspondence with Alliance and Anglo-Jewish Association, 1872–80. *American Jewish Historical Society, Brandeis University, Boston, Mass.*

CABINET PAPERS
CAB 23–4: Zionism, Bolshevism, 1917–18. *Public Record Office, Kew*

CECIL PAPERS
Lord Robert Cecil's Foreign Office memoranda, 1915–18; Peace Conference diary (1919). *British Library, London* (Add. MSS 511505, 51131)

CONJOINT AND JOINT FOREIGN COMMITTEE PAPERS
Minutes, 1878–1921; C11 files (papers and Wolf correspondence, 1881–1921). *Board of Deputies of British Jews, Woburn House, London*

FOREIGN OFFICE PAPERS
FO 2: Miscellaneous, 1905. FO 104: Romania, 1901. FO 368: Commercial, 1916–17. FO 371: Political, 1908–21. FO 372: Treaty (Russia), 1912–13. FO 608: Peace Conference, Paris, 1919. FO 800: Private papers: Balfour, Bertie, A. Nicolson, 1916–17. *Public Record Office, Kew*

MOSES GASTER PAPERS
Correspondence, 1901–18; Conjoint–Zionist file, 1915–17. *Mocatta Library, University College London*

SIR JAMES HEADLAM-MORLEY PAPERS
Correspondence and letters relating to the Peace Conference and New States Committee. *Private Collection, Wimbledon, London*

HOME OFFICE PAPERS
HO 45: Registered Papers (Baghdad, conscription, Polish Jews), 1915–19. *Public Record Office, Kew*

JOINT FOREIGN COMMITTEE MINUTES
see Conjoint Foreign Committee minutes

LOUIS MARSHALL PAPERS
Correspondence Box 1: 1919–23 (relating to Wolf and Peace Conference). *American Jewish Committee, New York*

MINISTÈRE DES AFFAIRES ETRANGÈRES RECORDS
Series: Guerre 1915–18; Sionisme 1914–18; Turquie 1914–18; Anglo-French mission to USA 1915. *Ministère des Affaires Etrangères, Paris*

DAVID MOWSCHOWITCH COLLECTION
Wolf personal and public correspondence, 1870–1930. Conjoint and Joint Foreign Committee reports, 1902–30. Press cuttings and Mowschowitch correspondence and articles on Wolf. *Yivo Institute for Jewish Research, New York*

MISS RUTH PHILIPS'S DIARY 1906–12
Mocatta Library, University College London

DAVID SOSKICE PAPERS
Correspondence with Wolf on Russian Jewish situation and the Bund, 1905–6, 1916. *House of Lords Record Office, London*

LUCIEN WOLF:
DIARY OF THE PEACE CONFERENCE, PARIS, 1919
Mocatta Library, University College London

WOLF PAPERS
Correspondence relating to Zionism, 1903–22. *Central Zionist Archives (CZA), Jerusalem*

WOLFFSOHN PAPERS
Correspondence relating to Zionism, 1903–22. *Central Zionist Archives (CZA), Jerusalem*

ISRAEL ZANGWILL PAPERS
Correspondence relating to Zionism, 1903–22. *Central Zionist Archives (CZA), Jerusalem*

PUBLISHED SOURCES

Contemporary Newspapers and Periodicals

Daily Chronicle, Wolf articles (1915–16)
Daily Graphic, Wolf articles (1906–14)
Daily Telegraph, Wolf articles, letters (1913, 1917, 1919)
Darkest Russia (1912–14)
Fortnightly Review, Wolf article, 'What is Judaism?' (Sept. 1884); Wolf 'Diplomaticus' articles (1896–1902, 1911)
Graphic, Wolf 'FO Bag' articles (1907–14)
Jewish Chronicle (1882–1921)
Jewish Opinion (1919)

Jewish Quarterly Review, Wolf article, 'The Zionist Peril' (Oct. 1904)
Jewish World, Wolf leaders (1905–7), Greenberg leaders (1914–17)
Manchester Guardian, Wolf articles (1919)
Morning Leader, Wolf–Pares debate (1909)
Morning Post (1914, 1919–20)
National Review, Maxse articles (1914)
Pall Mall Gazette, Wolf articles (1885, 1905–6)
Russian Correspondence (1905–6)
The Times (1903–20)
Westminster Gazette, Wolf articles (1902, 1904, 1906, 1919)

Books and Articles

ABRAMSKY, CHIMEN, *War, Revolution and the Jewish Dilemma* (London, 1975).

ACTON, LORD, 'Nationality', *The History of Freedom and Other Essays* (London, 1907), 270–300.

ADELSON, ROGER, *Mark Sykes: Portrait of an Amateur* (London, 1975).

ADLER, CYRUS, *Jacob H. Schiff: His Life and Letters*, 2 vols. (London, 1929).

ADLER, CYRUS, *I Have Considered the Days* (Philadelphia, 1941).

ADLER, CYRUS, and MARGALITH, AARON A., *With Firmness in the Right: American Diplomatic Action Affecting Jews, 1840–1945* (New York, 1946).

ALDERMAN, GEOFFREY, *The Jewish Community in British Politics* (Oxford, 1983).

ALLIANCE ISRAÉLITE UNIVERSELLE, *La Question juive devant la conference de la paix* (Paris, 1919).

AMERICAN JEWISH COMMITTEE, *The Jews in the Eastern War Zone* (New York, 1916).

ANGLO-JEWISH ASSOCIATION, *Annual Reports, 1910/11–1920/1* (London, 1911–21).

ARONSFELD, C. C., 'Jewish Enemy Aliens in England during the First World War', *JSS* 18 (1956), 275–83.

—— 'Jewish Bankers and the Czar', *JSS* 35 (1973), 87–104.

ARONSON, GREGOR, 'Jews in Russian Literary and Political Life', in Jacob Frumkin, Gregor Aronson, and Alexis Goldenweiser, eds., *Russian Jewry, 1860–1917* (New York, 1966), 253–99.

BARON, SALO W., *The Russian Jews under Tsars and Soviets*, 2nd edn. (New York, 1976).

BAUER, YEHUDA, *The Jewish Emergence from Powerlessness* (Toronto, 1979).

BAYME, STEVEN, 'Jewish Leadership and Anti-Semitism in Britain 1898–1918', Ph.D. thesis (Columbia University, New York, 1977).

BEAUMONT, COMYNS, *A Rebel in Fleet Street* (London, 1944).

BEHR, ALEXANDER, 'Lucien Wolf: A Recollection', *The Jewish Monthly*, 4 (Aug. 1950), 260–1.

BELOFF, MAX, *Lucien Wolf and the Anglo-Russian Entente, 1907–1914* (London, 1951).

BERLIN, ISAIAH, 'The Biographical Facts', in Meyer W. Weisgal and Joel Carmichael, eds., in *Chaim Weizmann, A Biography by Several Hands* (London, 1962), 17–56.

BERMANT, CHAIM, *Troubled Eden: An Anatomy of British Jewry* (London, 1969).

—— *The Cousinhood* (London, 1971).

BERNSTORFF, COUNT, *The Memoirs of Count Bernstorff* (London, 1936).

BERTIE OF THAME, LORD, *The Diary of Lord Bertie of Thame 1914–1918*, 2 vols., ed. Lady Algernon Gordon Lennox (London, 1924).

BEST, GARY D., *To Free a People: American Jewish Leaders and the Jewish Problem in Eastern Europe, 1880–1914* (Westport, 1982).

BIALE, DAVID, *Power and Powerlessness in Jewish History* (New York, 1986).

BLACK, EUGENE C., 'Lucien Wolf and the Making of Poland, Paris 1919', *Polin*, 2 (1987), 5–36.

—— *The Social Politics of Anglo-Jewry, 1880–1920* (Oxford, 1988).

BODENHEIMER, M. I., *Prelude to Israel: The Memoirs of M. I. Bodenheimer*, ed. Henriette Hannah Bodenheimer (New York, 1963).

BRADLEY, JOHN, *Allied Intervention in Russia* (London, 1968).

British Documents on the Origins of the War, 1898–1914, vols. vii, x, xi, ed. G. P. Gooch and H. W. V. Temperley (London, 1932) et seq.

BROTZ, HOWARD, 'The Position of Jews in English Society', *JJS* 1 (1959), 94–113.

BRYANT, F. R., 'Britain and the Polish Settlement of 1919', D.Phil. thesis (Oxford, 1968).

BRYM, ROBERT J., *The Jewish Intelligentsia and Russian Marxism* (London, 1978).

BUSH, JULIA, *Behind the Lines: East London Labour, 1914–1919* (London, 1984).

CALDER, KENNETH J., *Britain and the Origins of the New Europe, 1914–1918* (Cambridge, 1976).

The Cambridge History of Poland, vol. ii: *1697–1935* (Cambridge, 1951).

CHOURAQUI, ANDRÉ, *Cent ans d'histoire: L'Alliance Israélite Universelle et la renaissance juive contemporaine* (Paris, 1965).

COHEN, ISRAEL, *My Mission to Poland, 1918–1939* (New York, 1951).

COHEN, NAOMI C., *A Dual Heritage: The Public Career of Oscar S. Straus* (Philadelphia, 1969).

—— *Not Free to Desist: The American Jewish Committee, 1906–1966* (Philadelphia, 1972).

COHEN, STUART A., 'The Conquest of a Community? The Zionists and the Board of Deputies in 1917', *JJS* 19 (1977), 157–84.

COHEN, STUART A., *English Zionists and British Jews: The Communal Politics of Anglo-Jewry, 1895–1920* (Princeton, 1982).

COHN, NORMAN, *Warrant for Genocide* (London, 1967).

Comité des Délégations Juives auprès de la Conference de la Paix (Paris, 1919).

CONJOINT FOREIGN COMMITTEE, *A Memorandum on the Grievances of British Subjects of the Jewish Faith in Regard to the Interpretation of Articles i and ix of the Anglo-Russian Treaty of Commerce and Navigation of 12 January 1859* (London, 1912).

DAVIES, NORMAN, 'The Poles in Great Britain 1914–1919', *Slavonic and East European Review*, 50 (1972), 63–82.

—— 'Great Britain and the Polish Jews, 1918–1920', *Journal of Contemporary History*, 8 (1973), 119–42.

D'AVIGDOR-GOLDSMID, HENRY, 'The Little Marconi Case', *History Today*, 14 (1964), 283–6.

Documents on British Foreign Policy 1919–39, 1st ser., vols. i, ii, iii, vi, ed. E. L. Woodward and R. Butler (London, 1947 et seq.).

Documents diplomatiques français, 1871–1914, 2nd ser. (1901–11), vols. vii, viii, xii (Paris, 1935 et seq.), 3rd ser. (1911–14), vols. ii, iii, iv (Paris, 1929 et seq.).

Documents of Russian History, 1914–1917, ed. Frank Alfred Golder (Gloucester, Mass., 1964).

DUKER, ABRAHAM G., 'Jews in the World War: A Brief Historical Sketch', *Contemporary Jewish Record*, 2 (1933), 6–29.

Encyclopaedia Judaica (Jerusalem, 1971), 16 vols.

ENDELMANN, TODD, 'Native Jews and Foreign Jews in London, 1870–1914', in David Berger, ed., *The Legacy of Jewish Migration: 1881 and its Impact* (New York, 1983), 109–30.

EPPLER, ELIZABETH E., 'Lucien Wolf and the Minorities Treaties', paper presented to the Jewish Historical Society of England, 1962.

ETTINGER, S., 'The Jews at the Outbreak of the Revolution' in Lionel Kochan, ed., *The Jews in Soviet Russia since 1917* (Oxford, 1970), 14–28.

—— 'Jews and Non-Jews in Eastern and Central Europe between the Wars: An Outline', in George L. Mosse and Bela Vago, eds., *Jews and Non-Jews in Eastern Europe* (Jerusalem, 1974), 1–19.

FARRER, DAVID, *The Warburgs* (London, 1975).

FEDER, ERNST, 'Paul Nathan: The Man and his Work', *Leo Baeck Year Book*, 4 (1958), 60–80.

FEINBERG, NATHAN, *La Question des minorités à la conference de la paix de 1919–1920 et l'action juive en faveur de la protection internationale des minorités* (Paris, 1929).

FINESTEIN, ISRAEL, 'Anglo-Jewish Opinion during the Struggle for Emancipation, 1828–1858', *TJHSE* 20 (1959–61), 113–43.

—— 'Arthur Cohen, QC', in James M. Shaftesley, ed., *Remember the Days* (London, 1966), 279–302.

—— 'The Uneasy Victorian: Montefiore as Communal Leader' in Sonia and V. D. Lipman, eds., *The Century of Moses Montefiore* (Oxford, 1985), 45–70.

FISCHER, FRITZ, *Germany's Aims in the First World War* (London, 1967).

FRAENKEL, JOSEF, 'Lucien Wolf and Theodor Herzl', *TJHSE* 20 (1959–61), 161–88.

FRANKEL, JONATHAN, *Prophecy and Politics: Socialism, Nationalism and the Russian Jews, 1862–1917* (Cambridge, 1981).

—— 'An Introductory Essay. The Paradoxical Politics of Marginality: Thoughts on the Jewish Situation During the Years 1914–1921', *Studies in Contemporary Jewry*, 4 (1988), 3–21.

FRIEDMAN, ISAIAH, *The Question of Palestine, 1914–1918* (London, 1973).

—— *Germany, Turkey, and Zionism, 1897–1918* (London, 1977).

FRUMKIN, JACOB, 'Pages from the History of the Russian Revolution', in Jacob Frumkin, Gregor Aronson, and Alexis Goldenweiser, eds., *Russian Jewry, 1860–1917* (New York, 1966), 18–84.

GAINER, BERNARD, *The Alien Invasion: The Origins of the Aliens Act of 1905* (London, 1972).

GARTNER, LLOYD P., *The Jewish Immigrant in England, 1870–1914* (London, 1960).

GELBER, N. M., 'The Problem of the Rumanian Jews at the Bucharest Peace Conference, 1918', *JSS* 12 (1950), 223–46.

—— 'An Attempt to Internationalise Salonika, 1912–1913', *JSS* 17 (1955), 105–20.

GITLEMAN, ZVI, *Jewish Nationality and Soviet Politics: The Jewish Sections of the CPSU, 1917–1930* (Princeton, 1972).

GOODMAN, PAUL, *Zionism in England, 1899–1929* (London, 1930).

GOTTLIEB, W. W., *Studies in Secret Diplomacy during the First World War* (London, 1957).

GREENBERG, L. S., *The Jews in Russia* (New Haven, 1965).

GUINN, PAUL, *British Strategy and Politics, 1914–1918* (Oxford, 1965).

HAMM, MICHAEL F., 'Liberalism and the Jewish Question: The Progressive Bloc', *Russian Review*, 31 (1972), 163–72.

HANAK, HARRY, *Great Britain and Austria-Hungary during the First World War: A Study in the Formation of Public Opinion* (Oxford, 1962).

HEADLAM-MORLEY, SIR JAMES, *A Memoir of the Paris Peace Conference 1919*, ed. Agnes Headlam-Morley, Russell Bryant, and Anna Cienciala (London, 1972).

HEIFETZ, E., *The Slaughter of the Jews in the Ukraine in 1919* (New York, 1921).

HENRIQUES, U. R. Q., 'The Jewish Emancipation Controversy in Nineteenth-Century Britain', *Past and Present*, 40 (1968), 126–46.

—— 'Journey to Romania', in Sonia and V. D. Lipman, eds., *The Century of Moses Montefiore* (Oxford, 1985), 230–53.

HERTZBERG, ARTHUR, *The Zionist Idea: A Historical Analysis and Reader* (New York, 1959).

HOLMES, COLIN, *Anti-Semitism in British Society, 1876–1939* (London, 1979).

HORAK, STEPHEN, *Poland and her National Minorities, 1919–1939* (New York, 1961).

HOWARD, MICHAEL, *War and the Liberal Conscience* (London, 1978).

HUNCZAK, TARAS, 'A Reappraisal of Symon Petliura and Ukrainian-Jewish Relations, 1917–1921', *JSS*, 31 (1969), 163–83.

HYAMSON, ALBERT M., 'Don Pacifico', *TJHSE* 18 (1953–5), 1–39.

HYMAN, PAULA, *From Dreyfus to Vichy: The Remaking of French Jewry, 1906–1939* (New York, 1979).

JANOWSKY, OSCAR I., *The Jews and Minority Rights (1898–1919)* (New York, 1933).

The Jewish Chronicle, 1841–1941 (London, 1949).

JEWISH TERRITORIAL ASSOCIATION, *Manifesto and Correspondence*, Pamphlet no. 1 (London, 1905).

JOHNPOLL, BERNARD K., *The Politics of Futility: The General Jewish Workers' Bund of Poland, 1917–1943* (New York, 1967).

JOINT FOREIGN COMMITTEE, *Constitution* (London, 1917).

—— *Correspondence with His Majesty's Government relative to Treaty Rights of the Jews of Rumania* (London, 1919)

—— *Palestine: Statement of Policy* (London, 1919).

—— *The Assassination of the Czar: Correspondence with His Majesty's Government* (London, 1920).

—— *The Peace Conference, Paris: Report of the Delegation of Jews of the British Empire on the Peace Conference 1919* (London, 1920).

—— *The League of Nations, Geneva: Report of the Secretary and Special Delegate of the Joint Foreign Committee on Jewish Questions dealt with by the League 1920–9* (annual), (London, 1921–9).

—— *Report on the Conference on Russo-Jewish Refugees in Eastern Europe, 1921–4* (annual), (London, 1921–4).

—— *The Jews of Poland* (London, 1926).

—— *The Procedure for Giving Effect to the League of Nations Guarantee of the Minorities Treaties and the Proposals thereon Submitted to the 54th Session of the Council of the League* (London, 1929).

KADISH, SHARMAN I., 'Bolsheviks and British Jews: The Anglo-Jewish Community, Britain and the Russian Revolution', D.Phil. thesis (Oxford, 1986).

—— ' "The Letter of the Ten": Bolsheviks and British Jews', *Studies in Contemporary Jewry*, 4 (1988), 96–112.

KATZ, JACOB, *Out of the Ghetto: The Social Background to Jewish Emancipation, 1770–1870* (New York, 1978).

References 323

KEDOURIE, ELIE, *England and the Middle East: The Destruction of the Ottoman Empire, 1914–1921* (Hassocks, Sussex, 1968).

—— 'Sir Mark Sykes and Palestine, 1915–1916', *Middle Eastern Studies*, 6 (1970), 340–5.

—— 'Young Turks, Freemasons, and Jews', *Middle Eastern Studies* 7 (1971), 89–104.

—— *In the Anglo-Arab Labyrinth: The MacMahon–Husayn Correspondence and its Interpretations, 1914–1939* (Cambridge, 1976).

KENEZ, PETER, *Civil War in South Russia, 1919–1920* (Stanford, 1977).

KLIEMAN, AARON S., 'Britain's War Aims in the Middle East in 1915', *Journal of Contemporary History*, 3 (1968), 237–51.

KOCHAN, LIONEL, *The Struggle for Germany, 1914–1945* (Edinburgh, 1963).

KOHLER, MAX, 'The Origin of the Minority Provisions of the Paris Treaty of 1919', in Luigi Luzzatti, ed., *God in Freedom* (New York, 1930), 751–94.

KUZNETS, SIMON, 'Immigration of Russian Jews to the United States: Background and Structure', *Perspectives in American History*, 9 (1975), 35–124.

LAQUEUR, WALTER, 'Zionism and its Liberal Critics, 1896–1948', *Journal of Contemporary History*, 6 (1971), 161–82.

LATAWSKI, PAUL, 'The Dmowski–Namier Feud, 1915–1918', *Polin*, 2 (1987) 37–49.

LEBZELTER, GISELA C., *Political Anti-Semitism in England, 1918–1939* (London, 1978).

LEFTWICH, JOSEPH, *Israel Zangwill* (London, 1957).

LEON, ABRAM, *The Jewish Question: A Marxist Interpretation*, 2nd edn. (New York, 1972).

LERSKI, GEORGE J., 'Dmowski, Paderewski, and American Jews', *Polin*, 2 (1987), 95–116.

LEVY, ELKAN D., 'Anti-Semitism in England at War, 1914–1916', *Patterns of Prejudice*, 4 (1970), 27–30.

LEWANDOSKI, JOZEF, 'History and Myth: Pinsk, April 1919', *Polin*, 2 (1987), 50–72.

LINCOLN, W. BRUCE, *Red Victory, A History of the Russian Civil War* (New York, 1989).

LIPMAN, SONIA, and LIPMAN, V. D., *The Century of Moses Montefiore* (Oxford, 1985).

LIPMAN, V. D., *Social History of the Jews in England, 1850–1950* (London, 1954).

—— 'The Age of Emancipation, 1815–1880', in V. D. Lipman, ed., *Three Centuries of Anglo-Jewish History* (London, 1961).

LLOYD GEORGE, DAVID, *The War Memoirs*, vol. ii (London, 1936).

LOWE, C. J. and DOCKRILL, M. L., *The Mirage of Power: British Foreign Policy, 1902–1922*, vol. ii, *1914–22* (London, 1972).

LUZZATTI, LUIGI, *God in Freedom* (New York, 1930).

MACARTNEY, C. A., *National States and National Minorities* (London, 1934).

McCAGG, WILLIAM O., *Jewish Nobles and Geniuses in Modern Hungary* (New York, 1972).

MAGNUS, LAURIE, *Aspects of the Jewish Question* (London, 1917).

MANDEL, NEVILLE J., *The Arabs and Zionism before World War I* (Berkeley, 1976).

MARCUS, JOSEPH, *Social and Political History of the Jews in Poland, 1919–1939* (Berlin, 1983).

MARGOLIN, ARNOLD D., *From a Political Diary: Russia, the Ukraine and America, 1905–1945* (New York, 1946).

MAROM, RAM, 'The Bolsheviks and the Balfour Declaration, 1917–1920', *Wiener Library Bulletin*, 29 (1976) 20–9.

MARRUS, MICHAEL R., *The Politics of Assimilation* (Oxford, 1971).

MARSHALL, LOUIS, *Louis Marshall, Champion of Liberty*, 2 vols., ed. Charles Reznikoff (Philadelphia, 1957).

MARSTON, F. S., *The Peace Conference of 1919: Organisation and Procedure* (Oxford, 1944).

MAYER, ARNO J., *Politics and Diplomacy of Peacemaking: Containment and Counterrevolution at Versailles, 1918–1919* (London, 1968).

MENDELSOHN, EZRA, *Class Struggle in the Pale* (Cambridge, 1970).

—— *Zionism in Poland: The Formative Years, 1915–1926* (New Haven, 1981).

MENDES-FLOHR, PAUL R., and REINHARZ, JEHUDA, eds., *The Jew in the Modern World* (New York, 1980).

MILLER, DAVID HUNTER, *My Diary at the Conference of Paris* (London, 1924), vols. i, ix, xiii.

MONTEFIORE, C. G., *Nation or Religious Community?* (London, 1917).

MONTEFIORE, C. G., and HENRIQUES, BASIL L., *The English Jew and his Religion* (Keighley, 1918).

MORRIS, A. J. ANTHONY, *Radicalism against War, 1906–1914* (London, 1972).

MOWSCHOWITCH, DAVID, 'Bibliography of the Jewish Historical Writings by Lucien Wolf, 1879–1929', in Cecil Roth, ed., *Essays in Jewish History* (London, 1934), 37–47.

MURRAY, JOHN A., 'Foreign Policy Debated: Sir Edward Grey and his Critics, 1911–1912', in L. P. Wallace and W. C. Askew, eds., *Power, Public Opinion and Diplomacy* (Durham, North Carolina, 1959), 140–71.

NAMIER, LADY JULIA, *Lewis Namier: A Biography* (London, 1971).

NEVAKIKI, JUKKA, *Britain, France and the Arab Middle East, 1914–1920* (London, 1969).

NICOLSON, HAROLD, *Diplomacy*, 3rd edn. (London, 1963).

NORMAN, THEODORE, *An Outstretched Arm: A History of the Jewish Colonisation Association* (London, 1985).

PANAYI, PANIKOS, 'The Bully Boys of Britain', *Weekend Guardian* (5 June 1989), 2–3.

PARKES, JAMES, *Emergence of the Jewish Problem, 1878–1939* (London, 1946).

PEARSON, RAYMOND, *The Russian Moderates and the Crisis of Czarism* (London, 1977).

PINSON, KOPPEL S., 'The National Theories of Simon Dubnow', *JSS* 7 (1948), 335–8.

POLIAKOV, LEON, *The History of Anti-Semitism*, vol. iv, 'Suicidal Europe, 1870–1933' (Oxford, 1985).

Prologue to Revolution: Notes of A. N. Iakhantov on Secret Meetings of the Council of Ministers 1915, ed. Michael Cherniavsky (Englewood Cliffs, New Jersey, 1967).

REINHARZ, JEHUDA, '*Deutschtum und Judentum* in the Ideology of the Centralverein Deutscher Staatsburger Judischen Glaubens', *JSS* 36 (1974), 19–39.

—— *Chaim Weizmann: The Making of a Zionist Leader* (New York, 1985).

RINOTT, MOSHE, 'The Zionist Organisation and the Hilfsverein: Cooperation and Conflict 1901–1914', *Leo Baeck Year Book*, 21 (1976), 261–78.

ROBBINS, KEITH, *Sir Edward Grey* (London, 1971).

ROBINSON, JACOB, *Were the Minorities Treaties a Failure?* (New York, 1943).

ROGGER, HANS, *Jewish Policies and Right-Wing Politics in Imperial Russia* (London, 1985).

ROSENSTOCK, MORTON, *Louis Marshall: Defender of Jewish Rights* (Detroit, 1965).

ROTH, CECIL, 'Lucien Wolf: A Memoir', in Cecil Roth, ed., *Essays in Jewish History* (London, 1934), 1–34.

—— 'The Court Jews of Edwardian England', *JSS* 6 (1943), 355–66.

ROTHWELL, V. H., *British War Aims and Peace Diplomacy 1914–1918* (Oxford, 1971).

Russia No. 1: A Collection of Reports on Bolshevism in Russia—Abridged Edition of Parliamentary Paper (London, 1919).

SACHER, HARRY, ed., *Zionism and the Jewish Future* (London, 1916).

SALBSTEIN, M. C. N., *The Emancipation of the Jews in Britain: The Question of the Admission of the Jews to Parliament, 1828–1860* (London, 1982).

SAMUEL, VISCOUNT HERBERT, *Memoirs* (London, 1945).

SANDERS, RONALD, *The High Walls of Jerusalem* (New York, 1983).

SCHAMA, SIMON, *Two Rothschilds and the Land of Israel* (London, 1978).

SCHAPIRO, LEONARD, 'The Role of the Jews in the Russian Revolutionary Movement', *East European and Slavic Review*, 40 (1961–2), 148–67.

SCHECHTMAN, JOSEPH B., *Rebel and Statesman*, vol. i (New York, 1956).

—— 'The USSR, Zionism, and Israel', in Lionel Kochan, ed., *The Jews in Soviet Russia since 1917* (Oxford, 1970), 99–124.

SCHOLEM, GERSHOM, 'The Crypto-Jewish Sect of the Dönmeh (Sabbatians)', *The Messianic Idea in Judaism* (New York, 1971), 142–66.

SCHWARZFUCHS, SIMON, *Napoleon, The Jews and the Sanhedrin* (London, 1977).

SCOTT, JAMES W. ROBERTSON, 'Who Secured the Suez Canal Shares?' *Quarterly Review* (July 1949), 341–2.

SEMENOFF, E., *The Russian Government and the Massacres: A Page of the Russian Counter-Revolution* (London, 1907).

SETON-WATSON, R. W., *A History of the Rumanians* (Boston, 1963).

SHARP, ALAN, 'Britain and the Protection of Minorities at the Paris Peace Conference 1919', in A. C. Hepburn, ed., *Minorities in History* (London, 1978), 171–88.

SHERMAN, A. J., 'German-Jewish Bankers in World Politics: The Financing of the Russo-Japanese War', *Leo Baeck Year Book*, 28 (1983), 59–73.

SPECTOR, SHERMAN D., *Rumania at the Paris Peace Conference: A Study of the Diplomacy of Ioan I. C. Bratianu* (New York, 1962).

SPRING-RICE, SIR CECIL, *The Letters and Friendships of Sir Cecil Spring-Rice*, 2 vols., ed. Stephen Gwynne (Boston, 1929).

SPULBER, NICHOLAS, *The State and Economic Development in Eastern Europe* (New York, 1966).

STARR, JOSHUA, 'Jewish Citizenship in Rumania, 1878–1940', *JSS* 3 (1941), 57–80.

STEED, HENRY WICKHAM, *Through Thirty Years: A Personal Narrative*, 2 vols. (London, 1924).

STEIN, LEONARD, *The Balfour Declaration* (London, 1961).

STEINER, ZARA, *The Foreign Office and Foreign Policy, 1898–1914* (Cambridge, 1969).

STERN, FRITZ, *Gold and Iron: Bismarck, Bleichröder, and the Building of the German Empire* (London, 1977).

STONE, NORMAN, *The Eastern Front, 1914–1917* (London, 1975).

—— *Europe Transformed, 1878–1919* (London, 1983).

SUMMERS, ANTHONY, and MANGOLD, TOM, *The File on the Tsar* (London, 1976).

SZAJKOWSKI, ZOSA, 'Conflicts in the Alliance Israelite and the Foundations of the Anglo-Jewish Association, the Vienna Allianz, and the Hilfsverein', *JSS* 19 (1957), 29–50.

—— 'Jewish Diplomacy', *JSS* 22 (1960), 131–58.

—— 'The Impact of the Beilis Case in Central and Western Europe', *PAAJR* 31 (1963), 197–218.

—— 'Nathan, Wolf, Schiff and the Jewish Revolutionary Movement in Eastern Europe, 1903–1917', *JSS* 29 (1967), 3–26, 75–91.

—— 'Symon Petliura and Ukrainian-Jewish Relations, 1917–21: A Rebuttal', *JSS* 31 (1969), 184–213.

—— 'Nathan, Wolf and the Versailles Treaty', *PAAJR* 38–9 (1971), 179–201.

—— *Jews, Wars and Communism*, vol. i (New York, 1972).

TAYLOR, A. J. P., *The Troublemakers: Dissent over Foreign Policy* (London, 1957).

—— 'Old Diplomacy and New', in id., ed., *Europe: Grandeur and Decline*, Pelican edn. (London, 1967), 364–71.

TEMPERLEY, H. W. V., *A History of the Paris Peace Conference*, vol. v (London, 1921).

THOMPSON, JOHN M., *Russia, Bolshevism and the Versailles Peace* (Princeton, 1966).

TILLMAN, SETH, *Anglo-American Relations at the Paris Peace Conference* (Princeton, 1961).

THE TIMES, *The History of the Times, 1912–1948*, vol. i. *1912–1920* (London, 1950).

ULLMAN, RICHARD M., *Britain and the Russian Civil War, November 1918–February 1920* (Princeton, 1968).

US, DEPARTMENT OF STATE, *Papers relating to the Foreign Relations of the United States*, vol. v. *Paris Peace Conference 1919* (Washington, 1946).

VAGTS, ALFRED, 'Die Juden im Englisch-Deutschen Imperialistischen Konflikt vor 1914', in Joachim Radkau and Immanuel Geiss, eds., *Imperialismus im 20. Jahrhundert: Gedenkschrift für George W. F. Hallgarten* (Munich, 1976), 113–44.

VERETÉ, MAYIR, 'The Balfour Declaration and its Makers', *Middle Eastern Studies*, 6 (1970), 48–76.

VITAL, DAVID, *The Origins of Zionism* (Oxford, 1975).

—— *Zionism: The Formative Years* (Oxford, 1982).

—— *Zionism: The Crucial Phase* (Oxford, 1987).

WARMAN, ROBERTA M., 'The Erosion of Foreign Office Influence in the Making of Foreign Policy, 1916–1918', *Historical Journal*, 15 (1972), 133–59.

WASSERSTEIN, BERNARD, 'Herbert Samuel and the Palestine Problem', *English Historical Review*, 91 (1976), 753–5.

WEISBORD, ROBERT E., 'Israel Zangwill's Jewish Territorial Organisation and the East African Zion', *JSS* 30 (1986), 89–108.

WEIZMANN, CHAIM, *Trial and Error* (London, 1950).

—— *The Letters and Papers of Chaim Weizmann*, ed. M. W. Weisgal, vol. vii, *August 1914–November 1917* (Oxford, 1975).

WISCHNITZER, MARK, *To Dwell in Safety: The Story of Jewish Migration since 1800* (Philadelphia, 1948).

WOLF, LUCIEN, *The Russian Conspiracy or Russian Monopoly in Opposition to British Interests in the East* (Birmingham, 1877).

—— 'Zionism', in *Encyclopaedia Britannica*, 11th edn. (London, 1901).

—— 'The Zionist Peril', *The Times*, 8 Sept. 1903.

—— 'The Zionist Peril', *Jewish Quarterly Review* 17 (Oct. 1904), 1–25.

—— 'Introduction', in E. Semenoff, *The Russian Government and the Massacres: A Page of the Russian Counter-Revolution* (London, 1907).

WOLF, LUCIEN, *The Legal Sufferings of the Jews of Russia* (London, 1912).
—— *Jewish Ideals and the War* (London, 1914).
—— 'The Jewish National Movement', *Edinburgh Review* (April, 1917), 303–18.
—— *Notes on the Diplomatic History of the Jewish Question* (London, 1919).
—— *The Jewish Bogey and the Forged Protocols of the Learned Elders of Zion* (London, 1920).
—— 'The "Grenzboten" Jubilee', 'The Romance of a Bohemian Village', 'The Queen's Jewry, 1837–1897', 'Anti-Semitism', 'The Jew in Diplomacy', in Cecil Roth, ed., *Essays in Jewish History* (London, 1934), 51–4, 55–9, 309–62, 383–410, 411–60.
YISRAELI, DAVID, 'The Struggle for Zionist Military Involvement in the First World War (1914–1917), *Bar-Ilan Studies in History* (Ramat Gan, 1978), 197–203.
ZEBEL, SYDNEY, H., *Balfour: A Political Biography* (London, 1971).
ZECHLIN, EGMONT, *Die Deutsche Politik und die Juden im Ersten Weltkreig* (Gottingen, 1969).
ZEMAN, Z. A. B., *A Diplomatic History of the First World War* (London, 1971).
ZIPPERSTEIN, S., 'The Politics of Relief: The Transformation of Russian Jewish Communal Life During the First World War', *Studies in Contemporary Jewry*, 4 (1988), 22–40.

Index

Index

333

79, 119
see also Joint Foreign Committee
(post-1918)
conscription, in Great Britain 30, 138,
145
see also enlistment
Consorzio delle Comunità Israelitiche
Italiane 37, 101–2, 105, 133
at Paris peace conference 264
Constantinople 52
Copenhagen 140
Courland 175, 196
Cousinhood, the 2, 158
and Anglo-Jewish foreign policy 6,
124
Cowen, Joseph 14, 86, 114–16, 118,
123, 130
Cremieux, Adolphe 101
Crewe, Lord 60, 95
Crowe, Sir Eyre 210, 235, 237, 287
curiae, Jewish electoral 166, 180, 223,
226, 291
Czechoslovakia 217, 240

Daiches, Samuel 151, 158, 293
Daily Chronicle 107
Daily Despatch 31
Daily Graphic 15, 31, 32, 34
Daily Review of the Foreign Press 208
Damascus 266
Dan, Fyodor 135
Danzig 240
Darkest Russia 25 n., 31–2, 36, 57, 65
Declaration of Nationalities 30
Denikin, General A. I. 229, 233,
241–5, 247, 294
Derby, Lord 6
Dernberg, Dr 62
Dickstein, Professor Samuel 182, 184,
188–9
diplomacy, definitions of 1
'Diplomaticus' see Wolf, journalistic
career
Directory, Ukrainian 329
Disraeli, Benjamin 7
Djemal Pasha 85

Dmowski, Roman 190–1, 195, 202,
214, 225
antisemitism of 182, 191–4, 198, 226
conversations with American Jewish
leaders 239
Don Pacifico affair 5
Dobrudja, Jews in 42, 257
Dorpat, disturbances in 133–5
Draghicesu, Dimitrie 252–3
Drogheda, Lord 149
Drummond, Sir Eric 152, 190, 210, 268
Dubnow, Simon 166–7
duma 65, 66, 67–8, 74, 181
debates on Jewish question in 48–9
Dutasta, M. P. 281
Dwa grosha 191
Dyelo naroda 135

East Africa 86, 109
East End (London) 28, 58
in Jewish politics 146
Eastern Galicia 48, 211, 232
see also Ukraine; Galicia, Jews in
East Prussia 49
Eastern Jewry 42, 181, 229, 231, 298
economic and cultural position of
164–5, 168
within Zionist movement 113, 221–2
delegates from, in Paris 221–2,
275–6, 279, 280; see also Comité
des Délégations Juives
Edinburgh Review 167
Edward VII 24
Ehrenpreis, Rabbi Dr Marcus 147,
170, 172
Eiger, A. 182
emancipation 10, 46, 119, 200
Act of Emancipation (Poland, 1862)
202–3
ideology of 3, 5–7, 163, 169
struggle for 17, 99, 106, 111, 234;
in Romania 17, 56, 250, 252–3,
258–60; in Russia 17, 38, 48, 68,
102–3, 132, 141
English Zionist Federation 86, 159
leadership of 29, 115, 117, 130
enlistment 29, 146, 148
see also conscription

342 *Index*

Russia (*cont.*)
civil war in 230, 249, 258, 263
commerce and finance in 58–9, 71
delegations from, in Paris 263, 268
Jewish political and social tendencies
in 60–4, 133–7, 140–1, 241–4
Jews in 35, 97–8, 181, 229; pursuit
of civil and political rights by 31,
37, 47–8, 67, 82, 89, 97–8; support
of, for Russia in the war 12, 48,
52–3, 169
Law on Primary Education (1914)
184
'liberal phase' in government 66, 72,
73
and Pale of Settlement 10, 50–1,
61, 64, 72, 141, 165, 167
under the provisional government
(1917) 132, 183
writers and the Jewish question in
70
Russian Council of Journalists 135
Russian Correspondence 139
Russian Government and the Massacres
50
Russian Jewish National Council 221
Russian Jewish Workers' Bund 14,
134, 136, 139, 141
and nationality issue 111, 165–6,
168, 199
and Yiddish 166, 221
Russian revolutions (1905) 13, 168
Russian Revolution (1917) 132, 139,
163, 183, 186, 190, 226
and Zionist movement 137–8
Russo-American trade relations 58–9
Russo-Japanese War 57
Russo-Jewish Congresses (1917–18)
137–8, 140–1
Russo-Turkish War 5

Sabbath clause *see under* Minorities
Treaties
Sacher, Harry 116–18, 125
St Aulaire, Comte de 259
St James Gazette 15
Salisbury, Lord 15, 18, 81
Salonika 171–2, 265, 291

alleged role of crypto-Jews in
52
Allied troops in 232, 258
autonomy proposals for 113, 169,
207, 218
Samuel, Herbert 24, 44–5, 60, 78,
96–7, 117, 282
and conscription 145
and Zionism 124, 267
Samuel, Sir Stuart 24, 157–8, 201,
240, 264
and Commission to Poland 292
Samuel, Montagu and Co. 24, 240
Sanhedrin (1807) 110
Sarajevo, assassinations at 179
Savenko, A. I. 66
Sazonov, Count D. S. 51, 69, 72, 97
issues denial of Russian government
anti-semitism 64
in Paris 244
Scherbatov, Prince N. B. 61
Schiff, Jacob 28, 57–9, 80, 82, 97, 132
Schiff, Mortimer 59
Scott, C. P. 131
See, Eugene 266
Segal, Revd. M. H. 130
Seidler, President (Austria) 196
self-determination, principles of 177
Semenoff, E. 50
Sephardic Jews 170
Serbia 7, 33, 37, 172, 179
Sereni, Angelo 102
Seton-Watson, R. W. 464, 176–8, 180
Seymour, Charles 285
shtadlanut 2, 262
see also Montefiore, Sir Moses
Silesia 211
Silistria, Jews in 42
silver bullion scandal 24
Simon, Sir John 88
Skryzinski, Count 240
Slousch, Dr Nahum 80–1, 92
Sliosberg, G. B. 73, 136, 183–4
Smuts, General Jan 176
Sobanski, Count Wladyslaw 201,
210–11, 213
Social Revolutionary Party (Russia)
183
Sokolow, Nahum 94, 99, 137, 140

Index compiled by Mark Levene and Penelope Johnstone

Printed and bound by CPI Group (UK) Ltd, Croydon, CR0 4YY

09/06/2025

14685820-0001